Virginia White Water

A CANOEING GUIDE
TO THE RIVERS
OF THE OLD DOMINION

H. ROGER CORBETT

SENECA PRESS
1977

Preface

This book, Virginia White Water, is a compilation of technical data, trip descriptions, maps, and historical facts for eighty-seven rivers, creeks, or runs in Virginia. It is the first volume of a two volume series; it covers the Potomac River, the Shenandoah River, the Rappahannock River, the York River, and the James River watersheds. The next volume will cover the Chowan, Roanoke, New, Tennessee, and Big Sandy River watersheds, plus some of the coastal rivers.

The author is basically an open-boat, white-water canoeist. Although he owns and has paddled decked boats (C-1's, C-2's), his descriptions and stream ratings are basically those of an open-boat paddler. His dislike for flat-water, however scenic it may be, is rather apparent, and the descriptions of rivers with rapids are always longer than those of rivers without rapids.

This book includes a wide variety of streams, big and small, flat and white-water, low-risk and dangerous, scenic and ugly. The difficulty and scenery ratings for these streams are solely those of the author and reflect his experiences and personal values. Every attempt has been made, however, to be consistent with the guidelines published by the American White-Water Affiliation.

There are numerous canoeing books that provide a great deal of information about river safety, canoe rescue, equipment selection, canoeing clubs, paddling techniques, reading water, racks for automobiles, check lists, and similar subjects. The author has not included this readily available information in this book, even though it is important to paddlers of all types and skill levels. He leaves these subjects to those writers who have the flair, the interest, and the experience necessary to do a good job. This book, Virginia White Water, is simply and basically a river guide book.

Acknowledgements

The author would like to acknowledge the many people who have made this book possible. It is not easy to give credit to all people, as there have been so many who have helped in so many ways.

First of all, Randy Carter and Louis Matacia introduced the author to white-water canoeing and led him on many Virginia rivers. Next, Chester Summit, Owen Cecil, John Corbett, Tex Nunnally, Art Glazier, and others paddled many of the streams with the author to collect information. Many trips tested their stamina, their sense of humor, and their patience.

Many canoeists contributed to the trip descriptions for the various streams, particularly in the James River watershed. Les Fry and Bob Whaley of the Coastal Canoeists made major contributions; without their assistance, it would have been much more difficult to produce this book. Sandy Williams and many other canoeists, too numerous to list, gave valuable information, provided technical data, and assisted in many other ways.

Then there are a lot of other canoeists, now best described as former friends, that paddled streams on the author's recommendation to collect data, expecting white-water and scenery and finding little more than pain. The author acknowledges their help on the flat-water trips that he preferred to avoid.

The author also wishes to acknowledge the contributions of some very special individuals who worked in the production phase of this book. The book format, the typography, and the general appearance of this book are the result of the imagination of Jayne Bierman and the staff of The Galley. The cover design was created by Clina Kostner of The Galley. The shuttle maps were drawn by Harriet Caffey and the manuscript was typed by Dot Tatum, both of whom worked from rough drafts of dubious legibility. The author's wife, Bobbie Corbett was invaluable in the preparation of the initial draft, the proofreading, and the liaison necessary to produce the final product. Linda Wright of the George Banta Company assisted in the actual printing tasks, and Jeff Wright provided the photographs for the cover. Art and graphics assistance was provided by Dave Badura and Elody Blomberg.

Finally, the book could not have been written without the support and assistance of the staff at the Geological Survey Office Library, Reston Virginia.

Contents

LIST OF MAPS

List of Tables

List of Figures

*To the many friends and good companions
that I have met while enjoying the greatest of
sports— white-water canoeing.*

HRC

Chapter 1

Introduction

Chapter I introduces the reader to the geology and hydrology of Virginia, describes the general characteristics of the various watersheds in Virginia, describes the river classification system used in the trip descriptions, and discusses the river gauging/marking systems used to determine water levels in the various streams. Chapters II to VI provide the detailed trips descriptions, the technical data, the stream/shuttle maps, the historical information, and other data/facts/information for eighty-seven streams in the Potomac, Shenandoah, Rappahannock, York, and James River watersheds. Chapter VII describes the canal systems and river navigation improvements that were developed in the 1700's and 1800's; this chapter was written by Dr. William E. Trout III, President of the American Canal Society, eminent Virginia historian, inquisitive outdoorsman, and most unique individual.

GEOLOGY/HYDROLOGY

The Commonwealth of Virginia has a diversity of rivers and streams that is matched by few other states. It is drained by rivers and streams that flow into nine major river basins, plus numerous small streams that drain into the Chesapeake Bay and the Atlantic Ocean. These rivers and streams flow through five major geological regions, changing their nature and size as they pass through.

The Potomac River borders Virginia on the north; its major tributary is the Shenandoah River. The James River is the longest river and drains the central part of the state. The York and Rappahannock Rivers lie between the James River and the Potomac River, draining into the Chesapeake Bay. The Roanoke River and the Chowan River drain the southern-central parts of Virginia, flowing into North Carolina. The far southwestern part of Virginia is drained by streams that flow into the Tennessee River in Tennessee and the Big Sandy River in Kentucky. The New River enters from North Carolina, crosses between the south central and southwestern streams, and enters West Virginia, becoming the major tributary of the Kanawha River. Figure 1 depicts watersheds for those rivers in Virginia.

The geology of Virginia is extremely diverse and includes the Coastal Plains, the Piedmont Province, the Blue Ridge Province, the Valley of Virginia, and the Appalachian Plateau. The Coastal Plain region is generally described as the tidewater area of the state, varying from 80 to 130 miles in width and stretching from the Potomac River to the North Carolina line. The Piedmont Province is that area between the Coastal Plains and the Blue Ridge Mountains, varying in width from 40 miles to 185 miles. The Blue Ridge Province stretches for about 350 miles from the Maryland border to the North Carolina border, varying from 10 to 60 miles in width. The Valley of Virginia stretches over 360 miles from the West Virginia border to the Tennessee border, varying in width from 20 miles to 100 miles; it includes the Shenandoah, Roanoke, Abingdon, Powell, Fincastle, and Dublin Valleys. The Appalachian Plateau extends only a short distance into Virginia and includes part of the Cumberland Plateau and the Kanawha Plateau; it is in the far western parts of the state. Figure 2 depicts these geologic regions.

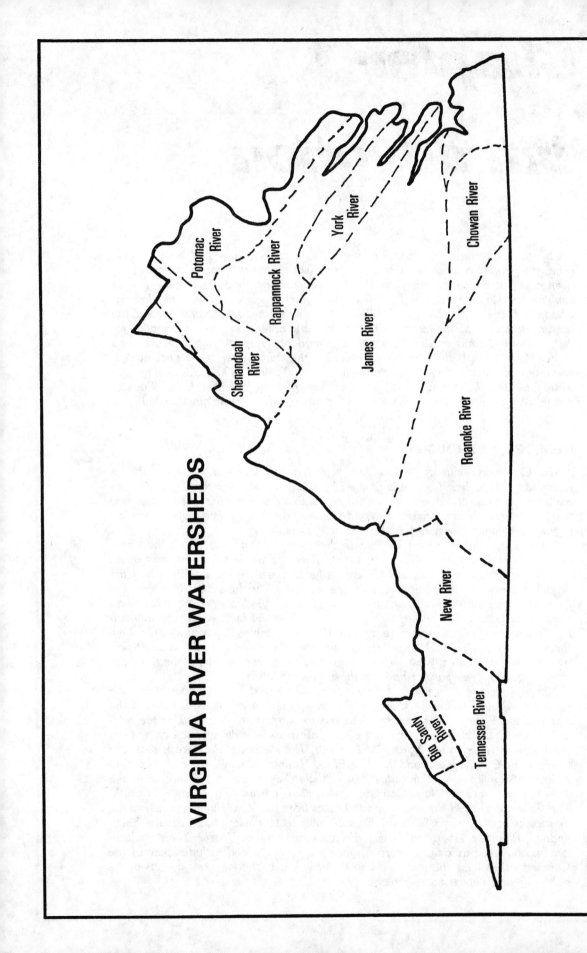

VIRGINIA RIVER WATERSHEDS

Potomac River

Rappannock River

York River

Chowan River

Shenandoah River

James River

Roanoke River

New River

Big Sandy River

Tennessee River

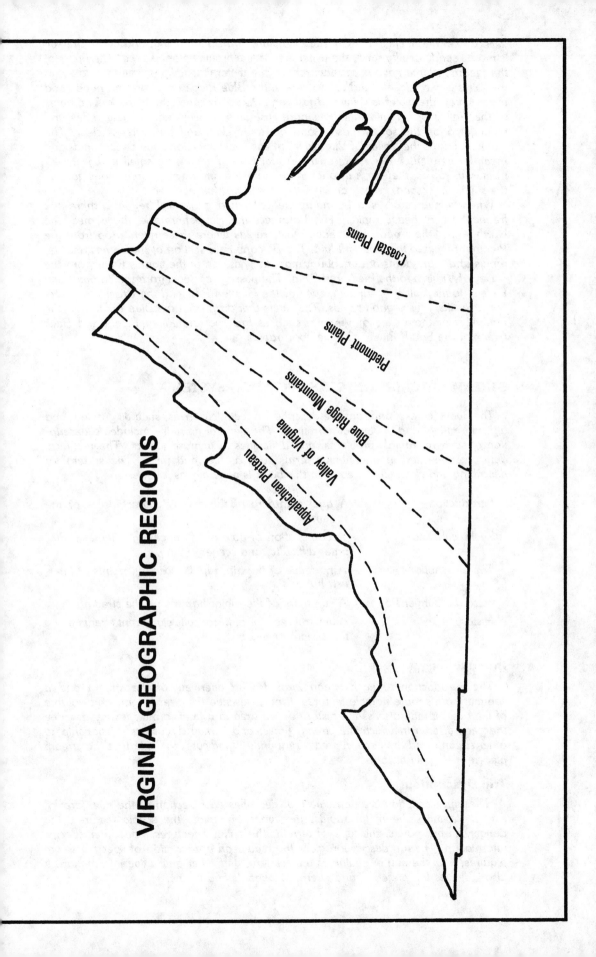

VIRGINIA GEOGRAPHIC REGIONS

Coastal Plains

Piedmont Plains

Blue Ridge Mountains

Valley of Virginia

Appalachian Plateau

As a rule, the rivers in the Coastal Plains are flat, slow-moving, and deep; the soil is mostly sandy or silty sand; the water is mostly a brown color, like tea. The rivers of the Piedmont area have occasional rapids, the water is usually yellow in color, and the soil is clay or clayey sand. The rivers in the Blue Ridge are short and have good white water, the water is clear and fast, and the soil is sand/gravel/rock. The rivers of the Valley of Virginia that flow northeast or southwest have a few riffles and meander a lot; the soil is mostly sand or sandy clay; and the water is clear. The rivers that cross the Valley of Virginia in an east-west direction have better rapids and meander very little. The rivers of the Appalachian Plateau are small and fast with numerous rapids; they dash through narrow valleys and through precipitous gorges; the soil is rock/sand/gravel, and the water is almost always clear.

When a river crosses a boundary between two geological regions, there are frequently very heavy rapids. The Potomac, the Rappahannock, the James, the North Anna, the Appomatox, have major rapids where these rivers drop from the Piedmont Plain to the Coastal Plain. The Balcony Falls section of the James and the rapids under the dams at Lynchburg mark the passage of the James River from the Valley of Virginia to the Piedmont Plain. The passage of rivers from the Appalachian Plateau to the Valley of Virginia, such as the Goshen Pass and the Brocks Gap sections, results in very good rapids. The rivers that drop from the Blue Ridge into the Piedmont or the Valley of Virginia, such as the Tye and Piney Rivers and Back Creek of the South River, all have good rapids.

STREAM DESCRIPTION/CLASSIFICATION SYSTEM

The rivers, creeks, and runs are described in technical terms, such as gradient and difficulty rating, and in general narratives. The general narrative includes a description of scenery, rapids, problems, and difficulties in a prose format. The technical data are presented in quantitative terms such as feet and miles. The system for describing and classifying streams in this book is generally as follows:

Introduction	- A brief summary of the overall characteristics of the stream
Technical Data	- A compilation of data on distances, gradients, width, time, difficulty, and scenery rating.
Trip Description	- A narrative of the trip; rapids, scenery, points of interest, hazards.
Hazards/Danger Points	- A summary of the major hazards on the stream.
History	- A general recount of historically significant events along the stream or nearby.

Introduction

The introduction to each stream provides an overview of the stream and a summary of its more notable features. It may describe the size, length, and volume of the river; it may discuss the history of the area in a brief format; it may describe the general area in which the stream flows; and it may discuss its relationship to other streams and the general area. Frequently, it indicates the role that the stream played in Virginia history.

Trip Description

The trip description is a narrative that describes each section of the river/creek/run. It describes the major rapids, the types of rapids, the scenic features, the danger/hazard points, the type of terrain, the cultural features, and other specific information. The trip description gives the reader an appreciation of specific stream features, how the author evaluates the scenery, and other qualitative information. It also indicates the preferred and alternate takeouts and putins.

Technical Data

The technical data includes the distance on each section, the average gradient, the gradient in areas with most drop, the difficulty of the rapids, the time required for the trip, the width of the stream, and the gauges for determining if the stream is canoeable.

- The distance is expressed in statute miles, expressed to the nearest one-half mile. (14.0, 12.5, 9.0 miles)
- The average gradient is expressed in feet per statute mile to the nearest half-foot. It is computed by dividing total drop from start to finish by the total distance. (5.0 ft/mile, 9.5 ft/mile).
- The gradient is also computed for short sections with biggest rapids. It is expressed in feet per mile for a specific distance. (*2 miles at 60 feet/mile).
- The time required is expressed in hours, to the nearest half-hour, excluding time required for lunch stops, swim calls, rescues, swampings, etc. (1 hour, 2.5 hours, etc.)
- The width of the stream is expressed in feet to the nearest five feet (40 feet, 15 feet, 20-30 feet, etc.).
- The gauge readings are expressed in feet to the nearest tenth of a foot for U.S. Geological Survey gauges and Randy Carter gauges. (2.1', 4.0', etc.).
- The river classification system is based on the international scale of 1 to 6 for rapids and A-B-C for flat water. See Table 1 for the rating system.

Table 1

SYSTEM FOR CLASSIFYING THE DIFFICULTY OF RIVERS

Rating	River or Rapids Characteristics
	SMOOTH WATER
A	Pools, lakes, rivers with water velocity less than 2 mph.
B	Rivers with water velocity of 2 to 4 mph.
C	Rivers with water velocity more than 4 mph, may have sharp bends and/or obstructions.
	WHITE WATER
1	**Easy.** Sand banks, bends without difficulty, occasional small rapids with waves regular and low. Correct course is easy to determine but care is needed to avoid minor obstacles. No rescue problems. Generally ledges less than one foot, waves less than one foot. No maneuvering required in riffles. River speed less than hard back paddling speed.
2	**Medium.** Fairly frequent but unobstructed rapids, usually with regular waves, easy eddies, and easy turns. Course generally easy to recognize. Only minor maneuvering required in rapids. Rescue spots are convenient. Waves and ledges are less than two feet. River speeds occasionally exceeding hard back paddling speed.
3	**Difficult.** Maneuvering, frequently extensive, required for rapids. Small falls, large irregular waves, numerous rapids. Course not always easily recognizable. Ledges and waves less than three feet. Main current may push boat under bushes, branches, or overhangs. Rescue becoming a bit more com-

5

plex. Rapids may be long and fairly continuous. Current speed usually less than fast forward paddling speed.

4   **Very difficult.** *Long extended stretches of rapids, high irregular waves with boulders directly in current. Difficult broken water, strong and complex cross-currents, abrupt and intricate turns. Course often difficult to recognize and scouting from the bank is frequently required. Rescue becoming a serious problem. Very swift current. Special precautions.*

5   **Exceedingly Difficult.** *Long rocky rapids with difficult and completely irregular waves, cross-currents, hydraulics that are unavoidable. Very fast eddies, abrupt turns, vigorous wave action, big drops. Rescue becomes very difficult, scouting becomes more necessary, overall difficulties tend to complicate all aspects of the trip.*

6   **Limit of Navigability.** *All previously mentioned difficulties increased to the limit. Only negotiable under favorable water conditions/levels. Cannot be attempted without risk of life. All possible precautions.*

Hazards/Danger Points

The descriptions of hazards and danger points are primarily concerned with risk-of life aspects of the streams. It includes dams, low-water bridges, trees across the stream, fences (of all types), weirs, waterfalls, impassable rapids, deadly obstacles in the stream, and major rapids. (Class 4 or higher).

Note: Rapids of Class 3 or less are not considered to be hazards; however, the trip description may discuss those rapids.

History/Background

The history of the stream is discussed for those rivers/creeks/runs that have interesting backgrounds. The early explorations, the colonial settlements, the Indian wars, the Revolutionary War events, the Civil War events, and normal (but interesting) developments are outlined for many streams.

RIVER GAUGES AND MARKINGS

There are two basic methods for determining if there is sufficient water in a stream for paddling and, if so, how much water there is above the minimum level. First of all, there are the gauges installed by the U.S. Geological Survey (USGS) for measuring water flows. Then there is the canoeing gauge system developed by Randy Carter.

USGS Gauges

The government gauges are placed along virtually all streams with a watershed greater than 15 to 20 square miles. The gauges are checked periodically, some daily by telephone, some daily by people who mail the reading to USGS, some weekly, some only when the water is high, and some only when performing measurements on water flow. These gauges are usually located near bridges and can be recognized by the metal silo (a drain culvert) that protrudes vertically from a spot near the stream. The USGS topographic maps indicate the locations of the government gauges.

The readings from the USGS gauges for the Potomac, Shenandoah, and Rappahannock Rivers can be obtained from River Services, Weather Bureau, Suitland, Maryland, by calling 301-889-3210 after 11:00 a.m. for a prerecorded message. Or the same information can be obtained from the NOAA weather broadcast from Manassas on 162.55 mc. A few of the James River gauges may be obtained from the Weather Service, Byrd Airport, Richmond, Virginia.

The USGS gauge readings must be interpolated/adjusted to determine the amount of water in the river -- i.e., if there is enough to canoe or if there is too much to canoe. This process is quite simple if you know how much to subtract from the USGS reading to determine the water level for canoeing. As a general rule, the USGS gauges are buried so that the river bottom is level with the 2.00' reading on the gauge; some USGS gauges read 3.00' at the river bottom; few read higher.

Randy Carter Gauges

Randy Carter, a pioneer white-water canoeist and the author of an early white-water river guide, devised a system of marking bridge abutments/piers/footings to indicate the amount of water available for paddling. Randy canoed the streams in his book and noted the depth of the water in the widest, shallowest parts of the stream. If there was barely enough water to get through without stepping out of the canoe, as a general rule, this was considered a "0" level for canoeing. And he marked the bridges accordingly.

The Randy Carter gauge may appeal confusing, but it must be remembered that his system indicates a zero level for canoeing -- not that there is no water in the river. If the river is widest at the bridge where there are markings, then the canoeist's zero (on the gauge) will mean that there is about 3" of water flowing at this point. If the river is narrow at the bridge and wide downstream, then there may be a foot of water flowing under the bridge where the RC gauge indicates a zero canoeing level.

Randy Carter set up a system in which paddlers could call people who lived near his gauge markings and would provide the readings for a fee. This system worked well while Randy was alive, but it is not always reliable/consistent at present. As a point to ponder, Randy was one of the best canoeists in the nation when it came to paddling in low water. So, canoeists must have a lot of experience in reading and paddling in low water to attempt a river at a Randy Carter "zero" without walking through a lot of shallow areas.

Figure 3 illustrates the Randy Carter gauge system and the USGS gauge system as they might appear at a river put in. This system has been adapted by the Coastal Canoeists, the Blue Ridge Voyageurs, and the North Carolina Canoe Club for marking rivers. The author uses the same system.

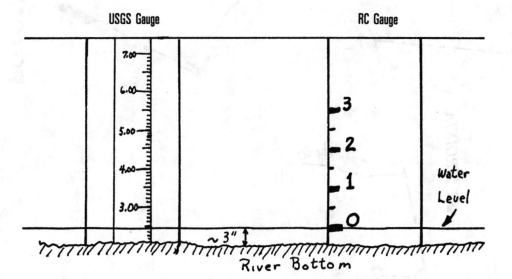

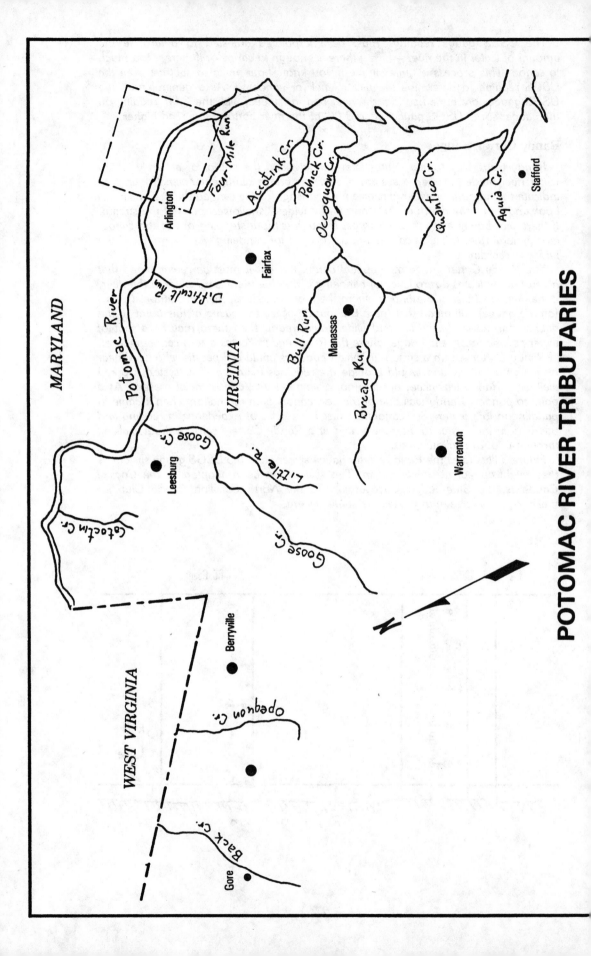

POTOMAC RIVER TRIBUTARIES

Chapter 2

The Potomac River Watershed

The Potomac River watershed includes portions of Virginia, Maryland, West Virginia, Pennsylvania, and the District of Columbia. Its watershed encompasses 14.670 square miles, 5705 square miles of which is in Virginia, if the Shenandoah River is included. The Potomac River watershed in Virginia, not including the Shenandoah River is about 2660 square miles; it drains 6.6% of the state, 14.1% including the Shenandoah. It forms the northern border of Virginia from near Harpers Ferry to the Chesapeake Bay. It has no major tributaries entering it from Virginia in that section and it is tidewater below Washington, D.C.

The following streams, whose locations are shown on Figure 4, are described in this chapter:

> Potomac River
>   Back Creek
>   Opequon Creek
>   Catoctin Creek
>   Goose Creek
>   Little River
>   Difficult Run
>   Four Mile Run
>   Accotink Creek
>   Pohick Creek
>   Occoquan Creek
>   Broad Run
>   Bull Run
>   Quantico Creek
>   Aquia Creek

The Shenandoah River and its tributaries are included in Chapter III.

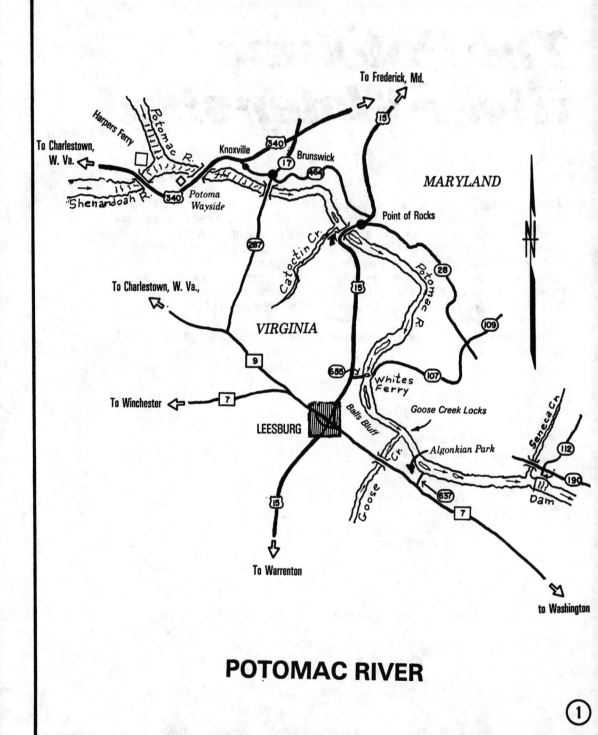

POTOMAC RIVER

①

Potomac River

INTRODUCTION

The Potomac River is the river of all Americans since it is the river of our national capitol, Washington, D.C. But it is a fact that it is not a Virginia river although it borders the state for over one hundred miles. The Potomac river belongs to the state of Maryland by virtue of a treaty between the two states covering the Potomac River and Chesapeake Bay. But to Virginians, it is also their river.

The Potomac River has its beginnings in the western part of Virginia, where the South Branch is a small rill west of Monterey, near Hightown. It enters West Virginia after a distance of about ten miles and remains in West Virginia until the North Branch and South Branch join. It then becomes the main Potomac River and it forms the border between West Virginia and Maryland until it reaches the Shenandoah at Harper's Ferry: then it forms the border between Maryland and Virginia until it joins the mighty Chesapeake Bay.

Section 1. Sandy Hook (Rte 340) to Point of Rocks (Rte 15)

Gradient	Difficulty	Distance	Time	Width	Scenery	Map
3	1-2	11.5	2	200-250	Good	1

Trip Description: Canoeing on the Potomac River should begin at the Potoma Wayside, on the south side of the Route 340 bridge across the Potomac River. Below Route 340, the river is wide and fairly shallow during the summer and there are only two Class 2 rapids (Short Hill Rapid, Knoxville Rapid) before arriving at the Brunswick bridge (Route 17 in Md., Route 267 in Va.) Below Brunswick, the river has no rapids for the next 5.5 miles to Point of Rocks and the take-out at the Virginia Game Commission landing at Route 15.

The river is very wide in this section, and it is no place to be when the river is high and the water/weather is cold. In the first part of the trip, the river flows past small islands; on the last part, past large islands. Just upstream from the takeout. Catoctin Creek, the Maryland version enters on the left with clear water. Then Catoctin Creek, the Virginia version, enters on the right with yellow, muddy water.

This is probably a great section for fishing during the summer when the water is low, but it is not really a white-water trip. The best rapids are in the first 3 miles, which can be paddled to a takeout just upstream of Knoxville on the Maryland side.
Hazards: None
Water Conditions: Canoeable all of the year, even following a long dry spell.

Section 2. Point of Rocks (Rte 15) to Whites Ferry (Rte 655)

Gradient	Difficulty	Distance	Time	Width	Scenery	Map
2	A	13	5	200-300	Good	1

Section 3. Whites Ferry (Rte 655) to Algonkian Park

Gradient	Difficulty	Distance	Time	Width	Scenery	Map
1	A	11	4	200-300	Good	1

Trip Description: The Potomac River from Point of Rocks to Whites Ferry and from Whites Ferry to Algonkian Park is the flattest section in Virginia. For over twenty-four miles, the Potomac passes through a beautiful valley, preparing for its final plunge from the Piedmont to the Coastal Plains. The current is still moderately strong because of the sheer volume of water in the river.

The river is big, wide, and strong, and it is no place to be during high water and cold weather. While there are no rapids in this section, a swamping could be a most hazardous event. So always wear a life jacket and do not canoe alone.

The scenery is quite good in these two sections as the Potomac valley has high hills to the north and high bluffs on the south bank (the Virgina side). The water varies from clear in low water to yellowish and muddy in high water. The C&O canal locks on the Maryland side, the entry of the Monocacy River and Goose Creek, the ferry "Jubal Early", the magnificant Algonkian Park, all combine to make the trip memorable.

Hazards: None

Water Conditions: Canoeable all of the year, even following a long dry spell.

Section 4. Algonkian Park to Great Falls Park

Gradient	Difficulty	Distance	Time	Width	Scenery	Map
2*	1-2	10	4.0	200-250	Good	1,2

*1 mile at 10 feet/mile

Trip Description: The trip from Algonkian Park to Great Falls Park is comprised of three different sections. The first two miles is the flatwater section behind the old C&O canal dam at the start of the Seneca rapids; this is called Seneca Lake and is a favorite spot for water skiers during warm weather. The next 1.5 miles is a white water section, the Seneca rapids; it is canoeable in the main river and in the bypass area where the old Potowmack Canal was built. Then there is a 6.5 mile section between Blockhouse Point and the Great Falls Dam that is seldom paddled.

The first section has no riffles or rapids, and there is very little current to help the paddler. The river is very wide and any wind is a problem. The scenery is only fair and there are many signs of litter and civilization. Motorboaters find it very challenging to see how close they can come to canoeists, so beware. For a trip on this backwater, the putin will be the Algonkian Park on the Virginia side and the takeout will be at Violets Lock on the Maryland side.

The Seneca rapids section is a good Class 2 white-water trip that is very popular with many canoeists. The putin is on the Maryland side at Violets Locks, west of the town of Potomac. The takeout is also at Violets Locks, since the trip is a round trip in which the paddler returns to the starting point by the C&O canal. This means no shuttle is necessary for this trip.

The Seneca section can be canoed by two different routes. The obvious route is across the remains of the old C&O canal dam, now a nice Class 2 rapid, and down the river. There are many small ledges, rock gardens, and narrow passages around islands for the next 1.5 miles, so many different routes are possible. At the end of the last rapid, paddle to the left (north) bank, portage 150 feet to the C&O canal, and then paddle back to the putin. Simple.

The other route for the Seneca rapids is through the remains of the old canal of the Potowmack Canal Company on the Virginia side. It is entered through a small inlet on the right bank; it looks like a southern bayou from a distance. If starting at Violets Lock, paddle directly across the river from the putin, just upstream from the old dam rapid. Then follow the current and enjoy the Class 1-2 ledges and rockgardens. About one mile downstream, return to the river below the last little ledge (there is a sign with an arrow) and continue down the Potomac about 400 yards. Portage to the C&O canal on the left bank just below the last riffle and paddle back to the parking lot.

Below the Seneca rapids, the Potomac is very scenic, with many islands, large and small. There are no rapids for the next five miles, but it is a rather disconcerting trip; the thought of being swept into Great Falls is always with the paddler. Most

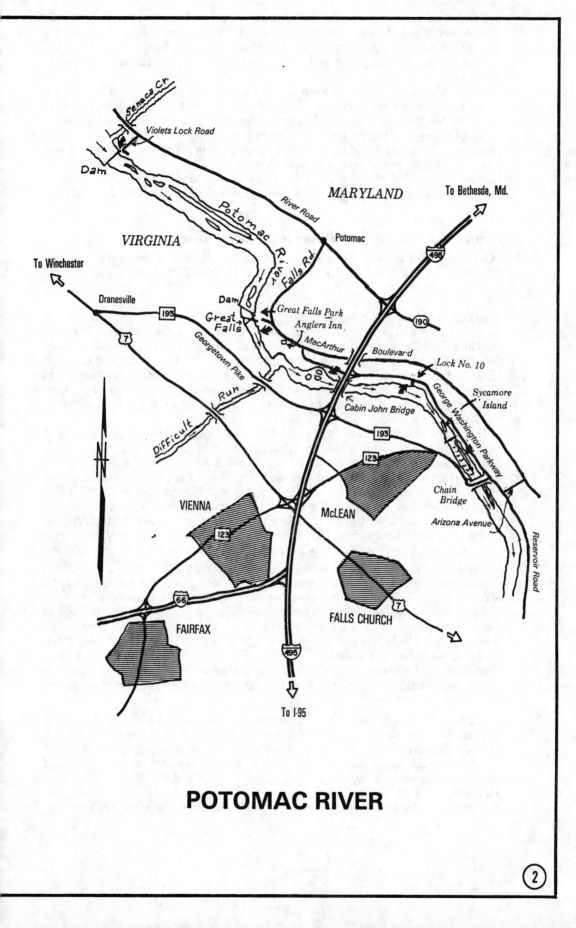

POTOMAC RIVER

paddlers tend to stay close to the left bank so as to make sure that they do not miss the takeout at the Maryland Great Falls Park. Do not try the Virginia side; do not attempt the low dam upstream of falls; watch for the warning buoys; stay alert or become a statistic. Takeout at the park and do not be lured by the fast water along the left shore.

Great Falls is a beautiful sight from the shore; there has never been an eyewitness report based on a river level view. On the Virginia side, it is a precipitous drop of about 80 feet into extreme turbulence; on the Maryland side, it cascades over a series of drops into turbulence, crosscurrents, hydraulics, and waves of awesome proportion. Close on the Maryland bank, there is a bypass to the fishladder that is just as dangerous as the main falls area. Beware.

Hazards: Great Falls Dam and Great Falls at the takeout.

Water Conditions: Canoeable all of the year, even following a long dry spell.

Section 5. Great Falls Fishladder to Sycamore Island.

Gradient	Difficulty	Distance	Time	Width	Scenery	Map
6	2-3	8	3	250-300	Very Good	2

Trip Description: The canoeist begins this trip *below* Great Falls and ends the trip *above* Little Falls. If paddling from upstream, the portage on the Maryland side from the Great Falls Dam to the Sandy Beach putin or the Rocky Cove putin below Great Falls is a damn long portage, but it is a most necessary portage. If starting from the Great Falls parking lot on the Maryland side, carry the canoe down the towpath to Billygoat Trail and then to the river. The putin on the Virginia side is longer, tougher, and misses Wet Bottom Chute; so don't portage on this side or putin on this side.

The rapids between Great Falls and I-495 bridge include Fishladder Rapid, Wet Bottom Chute, Difficult Run Rapids, Offut Island Chute, Yellow Falls, Calico Falls, and Stubblefield Falls. These are fairly honest Class 2-3 rapids. Fishladder Rapid can only be reached by lining the boat upstream from the put in below Great Falls — or by the lesser alternative of running Great Falls. Wet Bottom Chute (Class 2-3) is marked by a room size rock in the left center at the river and big waves for quite some distance. Difficult Run Rapid (Class 2) is comprised of three routes; Virginia Chute, Maryland Chute, and Center Section; none present any problem. Offut Island Chute (Class 2) is just below the Angler's Inn putin on the left; no problems.

Yellow Falls (Class 3) is a two step ledge rapid on the right side of the island; it has a famous rock in the middle at the bottom; the rapid is recognized by a house on the cliff above it. Calico Falls (Class 2) is the section around the other side of the island from Yellow Falls; an easy section worth running. Stubblefield Falls (Class 3) is the largest rapid and it is within sight of Cabin John Bridge (I-495); it gets meaner in low water. Below Stubblefield Falls, there are no more rapids until the Little Falls section. It is a wide river with small islands and rock gardens. Takeout at Lock 10, or line back up to Carderock, or continue to Sycamore Island for a takeout. Do not continue below Sycamore Island, easily recognized by the Clubhouse and boat storage shed; Brookmont Dam is just downstream.

This is the best section of the Potomac River, without a doubt. Rapids -- good competitive, low-risk ones. Scenery -- a magnificent gorge below Great Falls (Mather Gorge). Convenience -- near Washington with easy, closely-spaced access points (Anglers Inn, Carderock, Lock 10). Islands -- small and large ones for lunch stops and camping. Beaches -- sandy and rocky ones for sunning and picnicking.

Hazards: None

Water Conditions: Canoeable all of the year, even following a long dry spell.

14

Section 6. Sycamore Island to Chain Bridge (Rte 123)

Gradient	Difficulty	Distance	Time	Width	Scenery	Map
15	2-3-4-5	2.5	1	60-300	Good	2

Trip Description: Below Sycamore Island, the Potomac River changes its character before it makes its final plunge to Tidewater. No longer is it a forgiving, benevolent, relaxing trip; it is now a challenge to the best under ideal conditions and a deadly threat to the inexperienced, overconfident, or unwary under any conditions. This Little Falls section can be run only in periods of low water and then with the risk of swamping or loss of boat being rather high. It should not be undertaken by any one or any group that does not have a trip leader who has proven his abilities, who exercises good judgement, and who has run this section before. Remember when the gauge increases by 1", the water in the rapids increases by at least one foot, as the gauge is at the widest part of the river.

You can enter the Little Falls section by two routes. You can paddle down from the upper section, lining Brookmont Dam or running Brookmont Dam close to Snake Island, a long narrow island that divides the river. Running Brookmont Dam is a serious risk, as the hydraulic is river wide and may keep both canoe and canoeist below the dam until both are unrecognizable. Again, the trip leader must know the preferred procedure; if he doesn't, you are in serious trouble. The second route is to putin on the by-pass canal below Brookmont Dam, at the old lock house, and paddle upstream to the quiet section between the Brookmont Dam and the old C&O Canal Dam. Just don't drift up into the Brookmont Dam hydraulic.

The first rapid on the Little Falls section is the old C&O dam; it begins with a complex chute into a small pool, a 30 yard run through a downhill rock garden, climaxed with an intricate four foot drop. A definite Class 4 for complexity. Below the dam, you must work your way through a shallow rock garden to the right (Virginia) side of the river. Note: if it isn't shallow here, you have problems ahead. When the water funnels to the right under high bluffs, there is a series of four rapids with big waves. Nothing complicated, no intricate turns, no dodging rocks; the waves can be sneaked. The final rapid is the most serious rapid in the Potomac River watershed, and that includes a lot of white water. It merits a detailed discussion in itself.

Little Falls Rapid should be scouted from the Rocks on the left bank, where the view is good but the judgment is frequently bad.

The river funnels to the left a bit past a couple of mild drops to a point where it divides around a house-size rock in the middle. The left (Maryland) passage is almost a straight passage with a complex drop of 3 to 4 feet at the bottom. The right (Virginia) passage is an S-turn through very tight passages with a couple of sabertooth rocks just waiting for canoes. The S-turn is run principally by making an eddy turn behind the rock on the left side and ferrying across while paddling upstream -- by good paddlers at reasonable water levels. It has been run without an eddy turn, a straight shot from above, but this is very, very risky. The probability of wiping out, on the Virginia side, even at optimum water level with good paddlers, in the straight entry is about 90%; the probability of badly damaging or destroying the boat is about 50%. One canoeist who tried the Virginia chute and wiped out remarked that he knew that he was in trouble when he realized that while he was underwater he was standing on his bowman's shoulders.

The takeout is on the right bank at Chain Bridge. The carry to Glebe Road is tough and the traffic is merciless on Glebe Road. The trip is worth it in spite of its shortness, the tough takeout, and the upstream paddle at the putin.

For planning purposes, the following table can be used to correlate the USGS Little Falls gauge with the difficulty of the rapids in this section.

15

Table 2
Leiter Gauge Reading for Little Falls

U.S.G.S. Gauge	Difficulty	Minimum level
2.54	3	for open boats
2.85	3-4	Good level for open boats
3.0	3-4	Good level for open boats
3.25	3-45	Difficult level for open boats
3.50	4-5	Maximum level for open boats
4.0	4-5	Decked boats only
5.0	4-5	Maximum for decked boats

Hazards: Brookmont dam 1-1½ foot high. Big, strong rapids. In high water, risk-of-life rapids.

Water Conditions: Can be paddled only when the Potomac river is at minimum flow levels.

OTHER INFORMATION

The Potomac river has claimed a lot of lives in recent years and has been associated with a lot of horror stories. Fishermen have gone out in small prams with a lot of people just above Great Falls; canoeists have tried Little Falls in high water during cold weather; boaters have been marooned on islands after losing their boats; canoeists have been hanging from trees after trying to canoe the river during a flood caused by a hurricane; hikers and tourists have fallen into the river near Great Falls; people in small rafts have been trapped below Brookmont Dam and drowned. There are many horror stories associated with the overconfident, the unwary, the inexperienced, and the stupid -- more than you can believe. So do not treat this river with contempt or casually.

The scenery along the Potomac River from Sandy Hook to Chain Bridge has a lot of different things. There are mountain bluffs near Harper's Ferry, there is open farmland on the Maryland and Virginia shores, and there are sheer rock cliffs in Mather Gorge and at Little Falls. There are high sand bluffs, high mud banks and low sand-gravel beaches, islands in rapids and islands in flat water. You can see the viaducts where the Monocacy River and Seneca Creek pass under the C&O canal, the remains of dams that diverted water into the old C&O canal, the ruins of the C&O canal on the Maryland side and the remains of the Potowmack Canal Co. bypass canals on the Virginia side. There are small remote lakes/ponds high among the rocks along the river, numerous small streams cascade into the river from each bank, and birdlife/wildlife abound in the remote sections.

The historic sites include the locks and canals of the C&O canal on the Maryland side and the Potowmack Canal on the Virginia side, the Ball's Bluff section where a Union Force met disaster during the Civil War, the remains of Indian villages and settlements near Leesburg, and the crossing point for Confederate troops after the Battle of Antietam Creek. The bypass canal for Great Falls on the Virginia side can be seen easily from just below Wet Bottom Chute, looking upstream. The old locks, dams, tow paths, canals can be seen almost continuously along the Maryland side, but the canals on the Virginia side are more difficult to detect. The Big Bend area of the Potomac, just above Great Falls, was the location where Captain John Smith was held prisoner by the Onawoniente Indians. The wide part of the Potomac River just below the Little Falls takeout at Chain Bridge, near Fletcher's, is where the colonists anchored their ships and traded for furs with the Susquehannock Indians.

It is truly amazing that the beauties of the Potomac River have escaped the plans of the federal bureaucracies. The National Park Service considered a plan to build a roadway over the magnificent rock formations on the Maryland side of Great Falls so that drivers could see the falls from the comfort of their cars. There was a plan to fill in the C&O canal and build a road over the canal; this plan considered a two lane parkway to be more important than a national park. The Corps of Engineers has conducted numerous studies to determine optimum dam sites; a study completed in the late 1960's recommended construction of many (more than a dozen) new dams on the Potomac River and its tributaries. The Federal Power Commission has surveyed the watershed to determine sites for power dams; they consider an unharnessed river to be a waste of natural resources.

It is equally amazing that the Potomac River has been able to survive the industrial and municipal pollution that has been dumped into it and its tributaries. Many of the towns and small cities did not provide any treatment of sanitary wastes until the mid-1960's; raw sewage was dumped directly into the river and its tributaries. Mills, quarries, non-metallic mines, coal mines, chemical plants, paper mills, food canning/processing plants, tanning plants, and coke ovens drew water from the river and returned water laden with all types of pollutants. Farmers have been careless in preventing soil erosion, railroads have allowed overburden to spill over into the river during construction, and citizens have used its banks for trash disposal. But towns, industries, and people, somehow, have not ruined this river.

There are so many places to go and things to do along the Potomac River that it is difficult to describe them all. Waterford, near Leesburg, is a quaint, beautiful village that was settled by the Pennsylvania Dutch; there is a festival day in October and there is good sightseeing all year. The old railway station at Point of Rocks, Maryland, just across Route 15 bridge, has been designated a national monument; it is a classic building with architecture that will endure. The General Jubal Early is a ferry that crosses the river near Leesburg; the fare is $1.50 per car, a maximum of six cars per trip, but it is worth it for the experience. Balls Bluff National Cemetery, near Whites Ferry, is the smallest national cemetery in the nation; it is such a peaceful spot on high bluffs over the river that one tends to linger. Algonkian Park, River Bend Park, and Great Falls Park provide access to the river for hiking, canoeing, picnicing, sight-seeing, fishing, and just being there near the water.

Back Creek

INTRODUCTION

Back Creek, in its upper reaches, is one of the smallest and fastest streams in the Virginia watershed of the Potomac River. Its gradient is deceptive, as it seems to have a much steeper drop than 37 feet/mile. But that may be largely due to the suspense that one feels while being flushed down a stream that is barely wider than a canoe length for most of the trip. The suspense is largely associated with trees blocking the stream in fast water. Consequently, this is a stream for people who want to lick their weight in wildcats, who like to jump out of their boat into a torrent, and who think that pulling canoes off trees is great fun.

Section 1. Rte 704 Bridge to Gore (Rte 50)

Gradient	Difficulty	Distance	Time	Width	Scenery	Map
37	2-3	6	2.5	20-25	Good	3

Back Creek races across a rock bottom for most of the trip above Gore, through rock gardens and over small ledges. It picks up speed to the point that forward paddling is almost unnecessary and eddy turns are almost impossible. It pauses briefly in the backwater of a seven foot dam at the silica quarry, about 4 miles downstream from the putin. Then, when it resumes its mad dash, life becomes a bit complicated. First of all, there is an underwater bridge just upstream of the railroad bridge; the bridge should be portaged. Then the railroad bridge abutments present a hazard, not being parallel to the stream bed and usually jammed with trees or debris. It could spoil your whole day to tangle with the abutments, the underwater bridge, and the debris and not come out the winner.

The stream can be inspected for a large part of the trip while enroute to the Route 704 Bridge upstream (south) from Gore, Virginia. A claustrophobic type should not consider this stream, neither should the faint of heart. And decked boaters should view it with extreme caution unless highly experienced in jumping out of their canoes/kayaks in fast water on short notice. Below Rte 50, it cannot be inspected very easily, but there is little cause for concern in that section.

Hazards: Seven-foot dam. Trees blocking the stream. Underwater bridge followed by bridge abutments.

Water Conditions: Canoeable only in winter and spring following a prolonged wet period or very heavy rain.

Section 2. Gore (Rte 50) to Dehaven (Rte 671)

Gradient	Difficulty	Distance	Time	Width	Scenery	Map
11	1-2	12	4	25-40	Good	3

Trip Description: Below Route 50, Back Creek becomes a winding stream, characterized by a sandy bottom, quick turns, small passages, and trees blocking the view from the stream. It is joined by Hogue's Creek and Issacs Creek before reaching Rte 671, and, consequently, it picks up a good deal more water. It is pretty below Rte 50, but it is such a change from the upper section that one should not try both of them on the same day. If the lower section is canoed after the upper section, the second section will seem too flat; if the lower section is canoed first, one may be too tired for the strong water in the upper reaches.

18

The rapids on this section are mostly small ledges and gravel bars; the water is clear, fast, and clean; the terrain is rolling and wooded. It offers enough riffles/rapids to make it very enjoyable, and there are two bridges near the mid-point so that the trip can be shortened.

Hazards: Trees blocking the stream.

Water Conditions: Canoeable normally in winter and spring following a wet period or a moderate rain.

GAUGE

None. Three inches of water across the underwater bridge is zero for the trip.

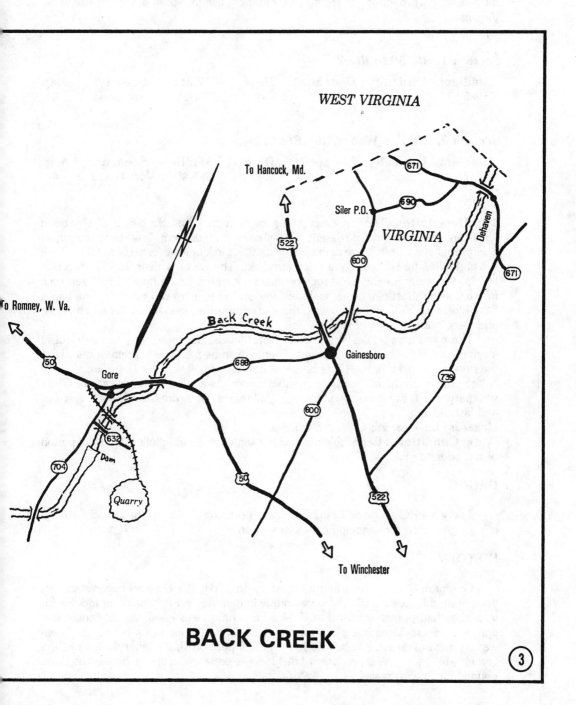

BACK CREEK

3

Opequon Creek

INTRODUCTION

Opequon Creek is a small fast-flowing stream that is one of the prettiest trips in Virginia. In the upper reaches, it is a very small stream with clear green water flowing over a solid rock bottom or a solid rock bottom with occasional coarse sand and broken rock. In the lower portions, it widens a little bit, but the water and the bottom are still beautiful. Throughout, there may be more big fish in it than any other stream in Virginia.

Section 1. Rte 50 to Rte 7

Gradient	Difficulty	Distance	Time	Width	Scenery	Map
6	1	9.5	4	25-30	Very Good	4

Section 2. Rte 7 to Wadesville (Rte 672)

Gradient	Difficulty	Distance	Time	Width	Scenery	Map
7	1	9	4	30-40	Very Good	4

Trip Description: The trip descriptions for Section 1 and Section 2 of Opequon Creek are so similar that one description will cover both of them. The stream begins as a very small run through one of the prettiest valleys in Virginia. As a rule the right bank is high bluffs, the left banks are open farmland. The water is clear, fast, and unpolluted; the bottom is either solid rock or solid rock with sand and gravel between rock formations; in most parts, the banks are low so the scenery can be seen. The banks have high rock bluffs in many areas, there are numerous gravel bars for lunch stops, and there are few signs of litter.

There are many riffles at the lower water levels, but these tend to wash out at levels above 6" on the Route 7 gauge. There are some particularly pretty spots where the stream wanders through little passages between small islands. There are no difficulties other than the low water bridge that is too low at all water levels above 0". In summary, this is not a white water stream, all rapids/riffles are Class I, but it is scenic and fast moving.

Hazards: Low water bridge on Section 2.

Water Conditions: Canoeable normally in winter and spring following a wet period or a moderate rain.

GAUGE

There is a RC gauge on Route 7 bridge. A reading of 4.8' on the USGS Remington gauge is zero for canoeing on either section.

HISTORY

Opequon Creek is not without its history. In 1731, the Quakers began their settlement on this creek, and they were unique in that they actually paid the Indians for what they had purchased. And in 1754 a Frenchman was killed with an Indian war party on this creek; he had plans for an attack on Fort Loudon (Winchester). There was an Indian massacre at Nealy's fort on the Opequon shortly after the end of the French and Indian War, at which time Indians were collecting a bounty of three pounds for English scalps.

In 1864, General Sheridan launched his famous raid through the Shenandoah Valley from Berryville. His main forces marched west from Berryville, crossing where Route 7 now crosses, and fought a major battle two miles west of Opequon Creek. His cavalry crossed to the north, where the Route 761 low water bridge is now, and fought another battle before moving west toward the Clearbrook area.

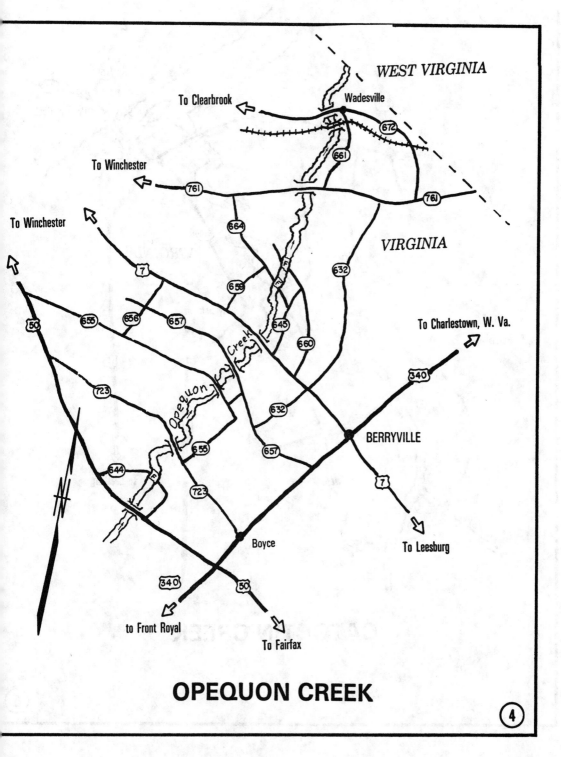

OPEQUON CREEK

④

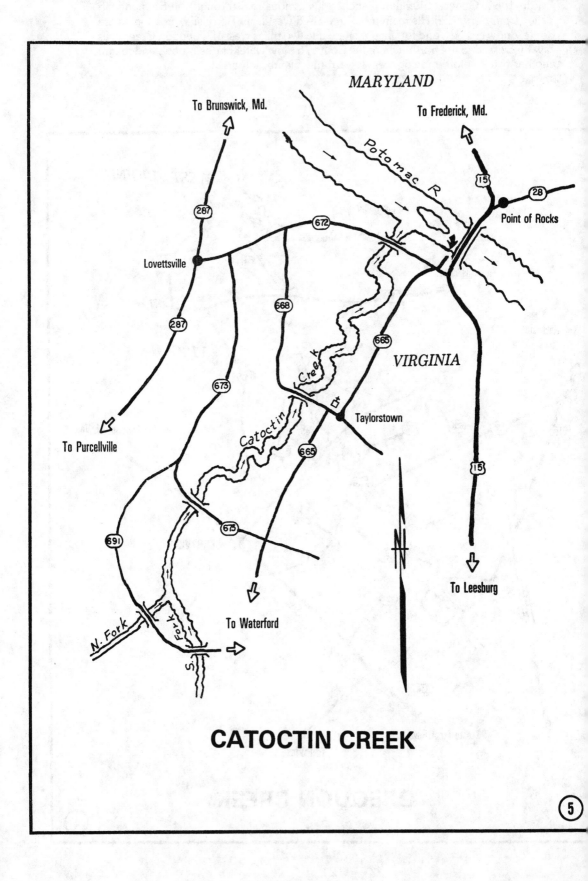

CATOCTIN CREEK

Catoctin Creek

INTRODUCTION

Catoctin Creek is a small stream that drains Loudoun Valley, beginning near Waterford and ending at the Potomac River near Point of Rocks bridge. This valley was settled by industrious Amish families and their influence is apparent in the well-tended farms and historic Waterford.

Section 1. Rte 673 to Point of Rocks (Rte 672)

Gradient	Difficulty	Distance	Time	Width	Scenery	Map
8	1-2	9.5	3.5	20-35	Good	5

Trip Description: Catoctin Creek begins at the confluence of its North Fork and South Fork just west of Waterford. The trip can begin at the Route 681 Bridge over the North Fork, if there is enough water; this extends the trip by about four miles. The normal putin, however, is Route 673 on Catoctin Creek. The takeout can be Route 672 bridge on Catoctin Creek, about 200 yards from the Potomac River, or at the Virginia Game Commission landing beneath Point of Rocks bridge (Route 15).

Catoctin Creek is a pretty stream in many respects. It has clean water flowing over a bed of solid rock, sand, and gravel. It has low banks so that the good scenery can be seen. The right side is mostly well-manicured farmlands, the left bank is mostly wooded. Both sides have high rock bluffs and ledges sloping into the stream. The rapids are mostly gravel bars and rock gardens, with occasional small ledges. Near the Potomac, there are two or three Class 2 ledges in a particularly scenic spot.

There is a beautiful old mill at the midpoint bridge at Taylorstown. It has been rehabilitated and is now a private residence. There are a number of magnificent estates along the right bank; the owners think they own the creek also, so be prepared for a hassle.

Hazards: One barbed/woven wire fence.

Water Conditions: Canoeable normally in winter and spring following a wet period or a moderate rain.

GAUGE

A reading of 5.0' on the USGS Remington gauge is probably zero for canoeing this stream. At the Route 673 bridge, if there is enough water across the ledge, there is enough water for the trip.

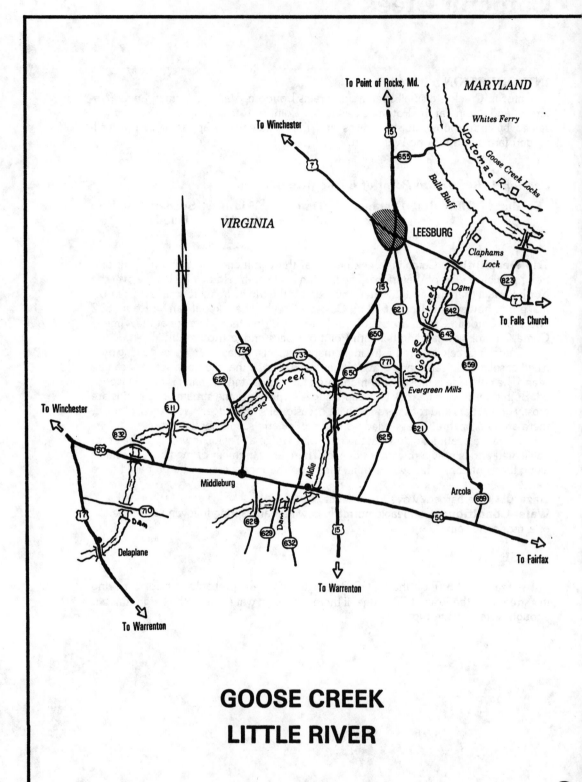

To Point of Rocks, Md.

MARYLAND

To Winchester

Whites Ferry

15

Potomac R.

355

Goose Creek Locks

VIRGINIA

Balls Bluff

LEESBURG

Claphams Lock

15

Goose Creek

Dam

621

642

823

650

643

7

To Falls Church

734

735

771

559

626

Goose Creek

650

Evergreen Mills

511

832

50

625

621

To Winchester

Middleburg

Aldie

Arcola

659

17

710

Dam

626

Dam

15

50

629

632

To Fairfax

Delaplane

To Warrenton

To Warrenton

GOOSE CREEK
LITTLE RIVER

6

Goose Creek

INTRODUCTION

Goose Creek begins as a very small stream meandering through a beautiful Virginia valley and ends as a small river where it joins the Potomac River near Leesburg. Beginning at the confluence of two little runs at Delaplane, it travels for about 45 miles through farmlands, past old mills, over old canal dams, and near remains of magnificent canal locks. It has numerous putin points, is crossed by many bridges, and has a major dam. Few streams offer such a diversity.

Section 1. Delaplane (Rte 17) to Middleburg (Rte 611)

Gradient	Difficulty	Distance	Time	Width	Scenery	Map
8	1	14	5	20-30	Good	6

Trip Description: At the Delaplane putin, Goose Creek is a tiny stream that is canoeable only because a number of small tributaries enter just above the bridge. It increases in width and volume as a number of small runs enter, but it remains a small creek. It has a moderate current, flowing over a sandy/clayey bottom, and it has 2' to 4' clay banks alongside. The rapids are all gravel bar riffles and the most competitive portions of the trip are the fast chutes and sharp turns. There is not much in the way of scenic vistas, but the open farmlands are quite pretty. There is a six foot, unrunnable mill dam near the midpoint of the trip, a good lunch stop. The old stone bridge just downstream from Route 50 is a magnificent structure with an arch that can only be admired.
Hazards: Six-foot mill dam. Trees may block passage.
Water Conditions: Canoeable normally in winter and spring following a wet period or a moderate rain.

Section 2. Middleburg (Rte 611) to Oatlands (Rte 15)

Gradient	Difficulty	Distance	Time	Width	Scenery	Map
6	1	14	5	30-45	Good	6

Trip Description: The trip from Route 611 to Oatlands is a fairly long trip, but it can be broken into shorter sections. There are two bridges crossing it and Route 733 is right beside the creek for many miles. That is good, for this is really a slow stream with few riffles to break the monotony and pain of paddling flat water. There is an increased volume of water as a number of small creeks enter from the north (left side) but it is also a wider stream. The terrain is closed, the area is wooded, and there are few farms. The riffles are of the gravel bar type although there is at least one Class 1 rock garden at the remains of an old dam. There is one very good swimming hole about a mile upstream from Route 15; you will recognize it when you get there.
Hazards: None
Water Conditions: Canoeable in winter and spring normally or during the early summer following an extended wet spell or very heavy rain.

Section 3. Oatlands (Rte 15) to Fairfax Dam (Rte 642)

Gradient	Difficulty	Distance	Time	Width	Scenery	Map
5	1-2	8.5	4	50-200	Fair	6

Trip Description: Oatlands was the point that the Goose Creek and Little River Navigation Company had designated as the upstream terminus of its canal system. The canal never reached this point, the last lock being near Evergreen Mills, but the remains of the mill/canal dams between Oatlands and the backwater of the Fairfax water supply dam are still there. These rock dams provide a bit of excitement in the form of Class 2 rapids. It must be remembered, however, that the mile of backwater paddling to reach the dams is the price that must be paid for 50 feet of excitement. Portage on the right around the high dam at the takeout.

Basically, this section of Goose Creek is a series of short (relatively) flat stretches between the remains of the dams, terminating in the backwater of a 22 foot dam that backs up water for at least three miles. It does not have any scenic areas, although the Murray Ford Bridge (Route 643) is a beautiful stone bridge. The current is quite slow for most of the trip, the banks are very high in the upper parts, the countryside is mostly farmland or dairies.

Hazards: Major dam (22') at takeout

Water Conditions: Canoeable in winter, spring, and early summer, except following periods of little precipitation. Canoeable after a heavy rain in the summer and fall.

Section 4. Fairfax Dam to Goose Creek Country Club (Rte 7)

Gradient	Difficulty	Distance	Time	Width	Scenery	Map
7	1-2₃	3.5	1	50-60	Good	6

Trip Description: The best rapids on Goose Creek are in the section below the Fairfax water supply dam. In this section, there are at least four Class 2 rapids and one Class 3 rapid, plus a number of Class 1 riffles. All rapids are the rock garden type at the sites of old mill/canal dams and all are interesting.

One rapid, located just before the golf course, is a reasonable Class 3; it is recognized by the broken abutments of a high dam (8'-10') on the right and left banks. It is the last rapid before Route 7. At the foot of this rapid (Golfcourse Rapid), on the left bank, there are the remains of an old mill that is still impressive although devastated and neglected. The scenery and the rapids more than compensate for the sand/mud bottom and the high clay banks, making this a very enjoyable, but all too short trip.

This section had a special hazard in the past. On weekdays, when the quarry on the right bank blasted, canoeists on Goose Creek were showered with rocks. It was a dangerous situation, but that quarry has been closed in recent years. Imagine, telling your insurance agent how the canoe (or canoeist) was damaged (or injured) by rocks not in the water.

Hazards: None.

Water Conditions: Canoeable in winter, spring, and early summer, except following periods of little precipitation. Canoeable after a heavy rain in the summer and fall.

Section 5: Country Club (Rte 7) to Potomac River

Gradient	Difficult	Distance	Time	Width	Scenery	Map
2	1₂	3.5*	1.5	60-80	Good	6

*plus travel on Potomac River

Trip Description: The main reason for paddling Goose Creek below Route 7 is "because it is there". The problems associated with the takeouts, the flat water near the Potomac River, and the trespassing signs along the banks outweigh the pleasures of the two good Class 2 rapids. They are the only rapids on this section, a long rock garden and a 2 foot ledge at the remains of an old concrete dam. Below the last rapid, the backwater from the Potomac River begins and the flat water paddling begins. The creek bottom is sand and mud, the banks are high at first but low at the end, and the banks are heavily wooded.

The first takeout for this trip is directly across the Potomac River at the Goose Creek Locks of the C&O Canal; it is reached by Edwards Ferry Road and a myriad of other Maryland secondary roads. The second takeout is 1.5 miles downstream on the right bank between an island and the mainland, just after passing under a private bridge to the island. Get permission to cross this property or face a hassle. Hobson's choice.

Hazards: None.

Water Conditions: Canoeable most of the year except following a long dry spell. Canoeable after a moderate rain in the summer.

GAUGE

A reading of 4.8' on the USGS Remington gauge or 3.8' on the USGS Frederick gauge is probably zero for canoeing on Section 1. Readings of 3.5' and 2.3' are zero for Section 5. Interpolate between these sections. There are RC gauges on the Route 15 and Route 7 bridges.

HISTORY

In 1832, the Goose Creek and Little River Navigation Company was chartered by the Commonwealth of Virginia to establish a navigation system twenty miles up Goose Creek and five miles up Little River. By 1839, enough shares had been subscribed to allow a meeting of stockholders and for election of officers. There was a great deal of enthusiasm, as the canal would provide a trade route from three counties (Loudoun, Fauqier, and Prince William) to the C&O Canal. The C&O Canal, which was on the north bank of the Potomac would carry the farm products to Washington and points east. The C&O Canal had its Goose Creek Locks (at Edwards Ferry) ready in 1833, but it was sixteen years later before the GC&LRNC actually contracted for construction to begin on the Goose Creek canal system. Most of the initial twelve miles were already navigable at that time, but not continuously so: there were five mill dams (Claphams, Cook's, Cockrans, Francis's, and Ball's) that had navigable stretches behind their dams, but each dam required a portage. The company had planned from the first to use these existing mill dams, constructing a lock and short canal about the dams to connect the ponds. Fortunately, the mill owners strongly supported this plan, as it provided an ideal route to the markets for their products. Without their cooperation, the project would have been impossible.

The canal company installed a number of money-saving plans during its construction phase. It built additional dams at good mill sites and leased the dams/mills to local people, and it made its locks only half as wide as the C&O locks, decreasing their costs significantly. It did not attempt to economize by using wood locks; instead it built stone locks that still stand. By the end of 1850, a number of the major projects were completed, including a one-mile canal and the magnificent two-stage lock at Claphums Mill (downstream of Route 7 on Xerox property on the right bank). By 1851, the first seven miles were open, up to Cochrans Mill (now at Murrays Ford Bridge); by 1854, twelve miles were open, up to Balls Mill, near the mouth of the Little River. In 1857, the navigation company was dissolved, a victim of the railroads. No construction was ever undertaken on the Little River. Just below the Evergreen Mills bridge, the outline of an old canal boat can be seen when the creek is at minimum flow.

The early name for Goose Creek was "Gohongrestan" — "River of Swans." How could such a beautiful name be changed to Goose Creek?

Little River

INTRODUCTION

Little River is the biggest tributary of Goose Creek, but it is still a very small stream. It starts out like it might be a white-water gem, but it quickly becomes a flat, meandering stream.

Section 1. Aldie (Rte 632) to Goose Creek

Gradient	Difficulty	Distance	Time	Width	Scenery	Map
10	1	5.5*	2	25-30	Fair	6

* plus 1.5 miles on Goose Creek to Rte 621.

Trip Description: The trip begins with riffles just below a beautiful stone dam that provided water to the old mill in Aldie. The riffles continue for about one mile to Route 50 and then become less frequent. The current moves fast to Route 15 bridge, the bottom is sandy, there are islands in the stream, banks are 4 to 6 feet high, and two trees block the stream.

Below Route 15, the current slows a bit, the terrain becomes open farmland, more trees block the stream, and the Little River joins Goose Creek. Goose Creek appears to be a major river after looking at the Little River, and the 1.5 mile section of Goose Creek is a short, fast run to a steep takeout on Route 621 at Evergreen Mills.

You can start upstream from the six foot dam just west of Aldie (it's worth the time to stop and look at it) where the Little River is small and fast. There are a number of bridges just west of Aldie for convenient putins, but no rapids. You can takeout at Route 15 (and not miss any rapids) where you will be in the biggest deepest pool on the stream; and you will meet a lot of fishermen at this pool which seems to be known throughout the area.

Hazards: Numerous trees across the stream. One six-foot dam at Aldie if the trip is started further upstream.

Water Conditions: Canoeable only in winter and spring following a prolonged wet period or very heavy rain.

GAUGE

About 1' of water of the Rte 7 bridge on Goose Creek is zero for canoeing on the Little River.

HISTORY

Aldie is a historic town that has an old mill that dates back to the colonial days. It was fed by water from the dam just west of town, a dam that is close to Route 50 but is not visible. It is worth a few minutes to stop and look at this dam and the canal that carried water to the mill. The canal bank looks like a levee passing through the town and is visible from Route 50.

Little River was going to be converted into a canal system, using dams and slack-water navigation, as part of the Goose Creek Canal system. A colonial road was built from Alexandria to Aldie; it was called the Little River Turnpike. Route 236 from Alexandria to Fairfax and Route 50 from Fairfax to Aldie trace the old road.

Difficult Run

INTRODUCTION

Difficult Run appears to be a meandering country stream between the Route 7 and Route 193 bridges and it can deceive the unsuspecting canoeists. For below Route 193, Difficult Run begins a final plunge into the Potomac River through a spectacular and dangerous gorge. This stream is a beauty to hike along and to admire from the shore, but one rapid is certainly in the risk-of-life category.

Section 1. Old Georgetown Pike (Rte 193) to Potomac River

Gradient	Difficulty	Distance	Time	Width	Scenery	Map
107	2-6	1	1	40-60	Excellent	7

Trip Description: Below the Route 193 bridge, Difficult Run enters a rock garden of jagged rocks, increasing from a mild Class 2 to a Class 4 drop with a hard turn. And this may be the easiest rapid on the trip. The second rapid is a big drop (Class 4) with two turns following a complex entry. The third rapid is just below an island; one side of the island has a tree limb at neck height. The rapid ends in a Class 3 or Class 4 drop at the end of the rock garden that complicates the entry.

Then the *big* rapid, recognized by a fifty foot sheer cliff on the left. The rapid begins with a 4' to 5' drop with a 75' pool below it, where the stream funnels to less than 15' in width. Then three chutes form a complex Z with less than 10 feet between each chute, making an almost impossible rapid. If the water level is high enough to run the upper rapids, then this rapid appears as a nightmare. About 50' below this big drop is a complex drop of 4' through a rat's nest of rocks. Luck, prayer, and skill (in descending order of importance) are necessary for this rapid. It can be portaged on the right bank with considerable difficulty and outstanding discretion.

The final rapid is around an island below Disaster Gorge; the left channel is a strong Class 3, the right a Class 4 rapid. Then you are on the Potomac River, glad to be alive.

There is a trail for hiking along the left bank of Difficult Run; every canoeist should make this .8 mile hike regardless of whether he/she intends to paddle it. You can see an honest-to-goodness Class VI rapid and you can see a lot of beautiful scenery. You can also see the jagged/broken rocks along the side of the stream; imagine the tremendous force necessary to rip whole rock formations away from the banks, as if blasted by man in recent days.

It is possible to start this trip at the Route 7 bridge at Colvin Run Mill. Between Route 7 and Route 193, a distance of 3.5 miles, Difficult Run drops at a rate of 5 feet-mile. It is a Class 1 trip that cannot begin to match the final drop into the Potomac River.

Hazards: Strong complex rapids. One risk-of-life rapid where a canoe and canoeists could be trapped.

Water Conditions: Canoeable normally in winter and spring following a wet period or a moderate rain.

OTHER INFORMATION

In the early 1970's, a small group of CCA paddlers attempted to run this stream; conditions: cold weather, high water. One of the kayakers had his boat pinned in one of the rapids and he had to sit in water up to his chest (in February) until a Rescue Squad with special equipment could get him out. The kayak, which was underwater beneath a chute, had collapsed on his legs; both legs were broken in extracting him.

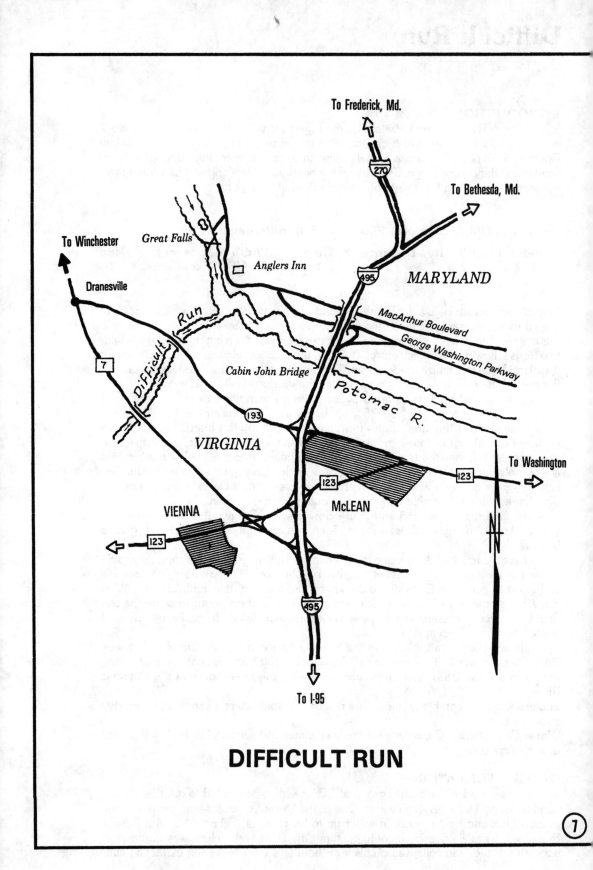

To Frederick, Md.

270

To Bethesda, Md.

To Winchester

Great Falls

☐ *Anglers Inn*

495

MARYLAND

Dranesville

Run

MacArthur Boulevard

George Washington Parkway

7

Difficult

Cabin John Bridge

193

Potomac R.

VIRGINIA

123

To Washington

McLEAN

VIENNA

123

N

495

To I-95

DIFFICULT RUN

⑦

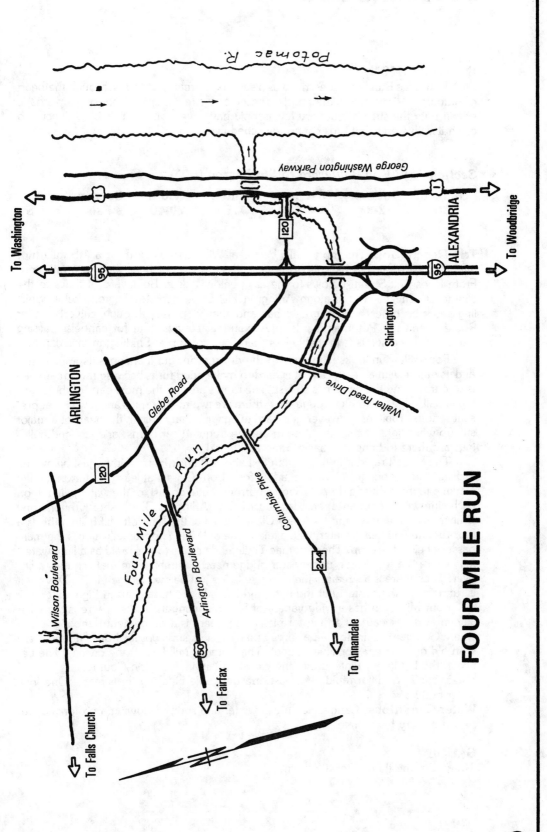

FOUR MILE RUN

Four Mile Run

INTRODUCTION

Four Mile Run is best described as a suburban stream, as it runs through the heart of Arlington, Virginia, and the shuttle is based on a street map. Millions of people have driven over the stream, but very few people have ever canoed it. It is so difficult to catch it with water that trips cannot be scheduled on it.

Section 1. Wilson Boulevard to Shirlington (I-95)

Gradient	Difficulty	Distance	Time	Width	Scenery	Map
36	2-34	4.5	1.5	20-40	Fair	8

Trip Description: The trip usually begins at Wilson Boulevard for a 4.5 mile trip, but it can be started as high as Roosevelt Street in very high water for a 6-mile trip. From Roosevelt Street, it flows to the east; below Wilson Boulevard, it flows to the southeast. The takeout is along Arlington Hill Drive near Shirlington; below Shirlington, it becomes a wide gravel bar and then it passes through culverts under Route 1 and the Potomac Yards in Alexandria; survival rate for canoeist passing through these culverts is probably less than 2%, so stop at Shirlington or Arlandria.

Four Mile Run looks fairly mild in the dry season, but it changes its appearance and its nature with a heavy rain. It is hard to make eddy turns because the stream bed is so narrow and the current is so fast. The rapids are, for the most part, of the gravel bar, small ledge and broken ledge type; there are two major rapids and a weir that present serious problems, however. It is hard to imagine that one is in the heart of a major suburb while fighting this little stream, but the frequent car horns, bridges, and buildings are there to bring one back to the real world.

The biggest rapid is in the section just above Patrick Henry Drive, just below the McKinley Street bridge; it is at least a five-foot drop (Class 4 at least). Enter on the left working to the right and drop through a narrow chute; go fast, or the water piling in on each side will swamp an open boat. Just below Arlington Blvd., shortly after Long Branch enters on the right, there is a Class 4 rapid at the Barcroft Mill Ruins; this is a four-foot drop in heavy water, with a telephone pole lying horizontally across the main passage below the drop. The Potomac Trail Guide refers to this rapid as a little waterfall. There is a low-water/underwater bridge near Columbia Pike that requires a liftover. Then there is a stream-wide concrete ledge just below George Mason Drive -- it is runnable in the center, but the right and left side are hazardous in high water.

Four Mile Run has a wide variety of features along its banks. There is the Glen Carlyn Park, a beautiful setting for picnicking; there is a monument denoting a tree where George Washington left a survey mark while a surveyor for Lord Fairfax; there is an old quarry near Roosevelt Street. The Barcroft Mill Falls is the dividing line between the Piedmont Plateau and the Coastal Plain in Arlington County.

Hazards: Two major rapids. At least one tree/pole blocking the stream. One low-water bridge.

Water Conditions: Canoeable only in winter and spring following a prolonged wet period or very heavy rain.

GAUGE

None. Just be there after a 2" rain.

Accotink Creek

INTRODUCTION

The Accotink Creek watershed drains a number of the major residential areas of Fairfax County, including Annandale, Springfield, and Fort Belvoir. It is a winding, fast little stream above Lake Accotink, but it is not recommended for canoeing in that section because of the many trees across the stream. Below the Lake Accotink dam, it is a very fast stream with an increased width and large volume of water. It is a short-lived stream, however, as it joins the Potomac about 10 miles downstream.

Section 1. Lake Accotink to Telegraph Road (Rte 611)

Gradient	Difficulty	Distance	Time	Width	Scenery	Map
15.5	1-2	7	1.5	30-40	Poor	9

Trip Description: The trip from Lake Accotink to Telegraph Road is not a continuous trip; it is a two-section trip that is broken in the middle by the Engineer Proving Ground. From Lake Accotink to Hooes Road is four miles. From below EPG fence to Telegraph Road is three miles. The EPG fence is a formidable barrier and permission to canoe on the base is not likely. This means two putins and two takeouts for one trip.

The four miles below Lake Accotink is an uncomplicated trip through Springfield, Va. It has a few riffles or mild rapids but not enough to really call it a white-water trip. The bottom is sand and clayey-sand. The banks are two to four feet high, and they are tree-lined. The trip is through a protected watershed so there are no houses/buildings beside the stream. That is a good thing in light of the floods that pass through fairly frequently.

The putin below the EPG fence is reached by a devious route from Alban Road through an industrial park; it involves a long carry to reach the first part of the rapids. Below the EPG fence there is a mile of Class 2 rapids, the best of Accotink Creek. Below the rapids, there is a low-water bridge that must be portaged. Then it becomes quite flat, flowing over a bed of sand and clayey sand, past banks that are 4' to 5' high. There are more signs of commercialization and residential areas in this area and more bridge crossings.

Below Rte I-95, the stream twists past gravel bars and narrow passages until it runs into the biggest mess of trees, timbers, and debris that one could ever imagine. The first batch of downed trees make you think things could not get worse, but then you arrive at a seven-foot jam that has dammed the creek and flooded the banks. A stick of dynamite would create a scene similar to the "breaking of the log jam" scene in the movies of the 1930's.

These logs, debris, timbers are there through the courtesy of the U.S. Army Engineer Center which dumped thousands of gallons of flammable liquid in Accotink Creek and then suffered it to be ignited. The fire killed all trees along the stream for two miles, blocked traffic on Shirley Highway, and damaged a number of bridges. No reparations, cleanup, or restoration, of course. Not by the Corps of Engineers.

Below the Telegraph Road bridge, the stream is very fast and very pretty, but it flows through another security area (a U.S. Army airfield) and is closed for canoeing. The gradient in this area is 22 fpm and there must be several good rapids, probably ledges like on Pohick Creek.

Hazards: Low water bridge on lower section. Trees across the stream. Major log jam just above Telegraph Road.

Water Conditions: Canoeable in winter and spring normally or during the early summer following an extended wet spell or very heavy rain.

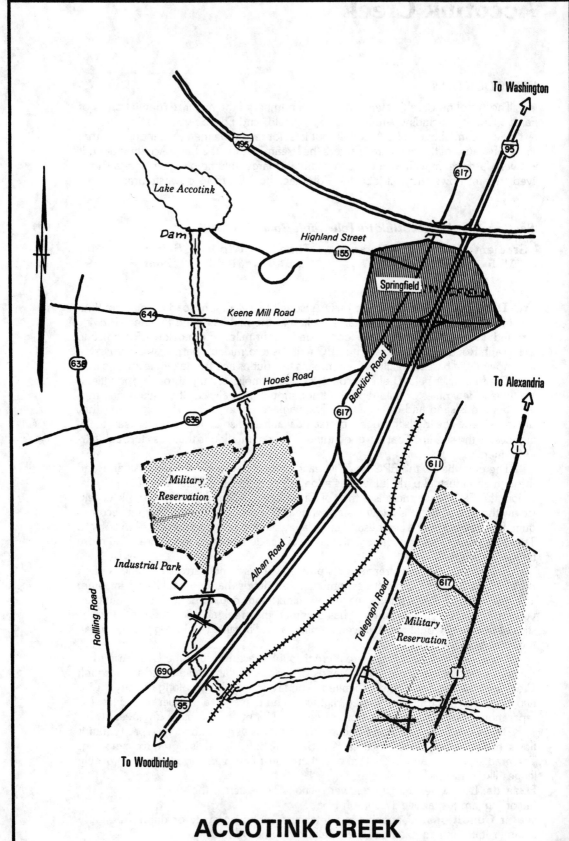

ACCOTINK CREEK

GAUGE

A reading of 3.3' on the USGS Culpeper gauge is probably zero for canoeing on Accotink. Enough water just below Lake Accotink is enough for all sections.

OTHER INFORMATION

Accotink Creek, Fort Belvoir, and the U.S. Army Corps of Engineers are so closely linked that it is difficult to discuss one without the others. Above I-95, there is the Engineer Proving Ground, where engineer equipment for the U.S. Army has been tested for many years. Below Telegraph Road, there is the U.S. Army Engineer Center, the Engineer School, The Mobility Equipment Research and Development Center, and the Davidson Airfield. Fort Belvoir is the home of the Army Engineers, mostly the combat engineer type— not the dam building types.

Lake Accotink is a tremendous recreation facility with picnic areas, boats for rent, and a concession stand; in the late 1940's and early 1950's, it was known as the Fort Belvoir Reservoir. Accotink Creek becomes Accotink Bay just below Route 1; Accotink Bay joins Pohick Bay to form Gunston Cove, which empties into the Potomac River. Gunston Hall, the colonial home of George Mason, is on Gunston Cove, directly across from Fort Belvoir. The town of Accotink is a small enclave at the junction of Accotink Road and Route 1, surrounded by Fort Belvoir; it and the creek was named after an Indian tribe.

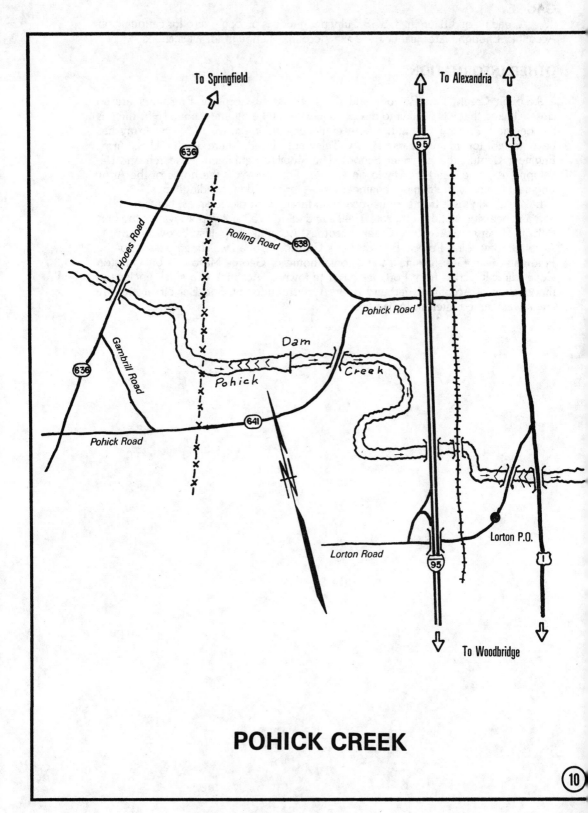

POHICK CREEK

Pohick Creek

INTRODUCTION

Pohick Creek is a very small stream that has a lot of everything for the advanced white water canoeist. It has gravel bar rapids, steep ledges, broken ledges, rock gardens, and a 5' dam that is runnable. It starts out as swift current over gravel bars but it changes to strong complex rapids in a very short distance, after lulling the paddler into a false sense of security. It is a stream to be respected but it is not a stream to be trusted.

Section 1. Hooes Road (Rte 636) to Lorton P.O. (Rte 1)

Gradient	Difficulty	Distance	Time	Width	Scenery	Map
21	1-4	5.5	2	20-35	Fair	10

Trip Description: Pohick Creek begins at Hooes Road as a meandering little stream with light riffles, gravel bars, swift runs, and mud banks. For three miles, it is a Class 1 stream where the principal hazards/difficulties are trees blocking the stream. Shortly after Middle Run joins from the right, the riffles become mild rapids. After passing under the power lines the rapids become Class 2,3, and 4. They are the boulder garden type in a very confined stream bed; they are not easy and some are fairly long. Each succeeding rapid becomes more complex, stronger, and longer than the previous rapid until Double Z is reached. It is difficult to recognize the most difficult rapid, Double Z, until you are in it; when you are in it, you recognize it easily. Don't foul up on Double Z; the legs of the Z are less than 15 feet and there are five turns in about 50 feet. After Double Z, the next action of note is the remains of a five foot dam which is runnable by open boats — in the middle with a lot of speed. (There is no hydraulic to worry about) After the dam, there are only light riffles until you pass under Pohick Road. When the stream moves away from I-95, there are four good rapids (Class 2,3) of the broken ledge type. Below the last rapid on this loop, the South Run enters Pohick Creek. From this point, which is about where Pohick goes under I-95 to Lorton Road Bridge, the stream has light riffles.

Immediately below the Lorton Road bridge, there are four good ledges. In high water, the hydraulics become a real threat to the open boats. The takeout is within sight of the last set of ledges. The grand finale.

Hazards: Two or three trees across the stream. Two or three Class 4 rapids, one of which is a runnable 5' dam.

Water Conditions: Canoeable only in winter and spring following a prolonged wet period or very heavy rain.

GAUGE

There is a RC gauge on the Pohick River Road bridge. It takes a lot of water to make this steam canoeable.

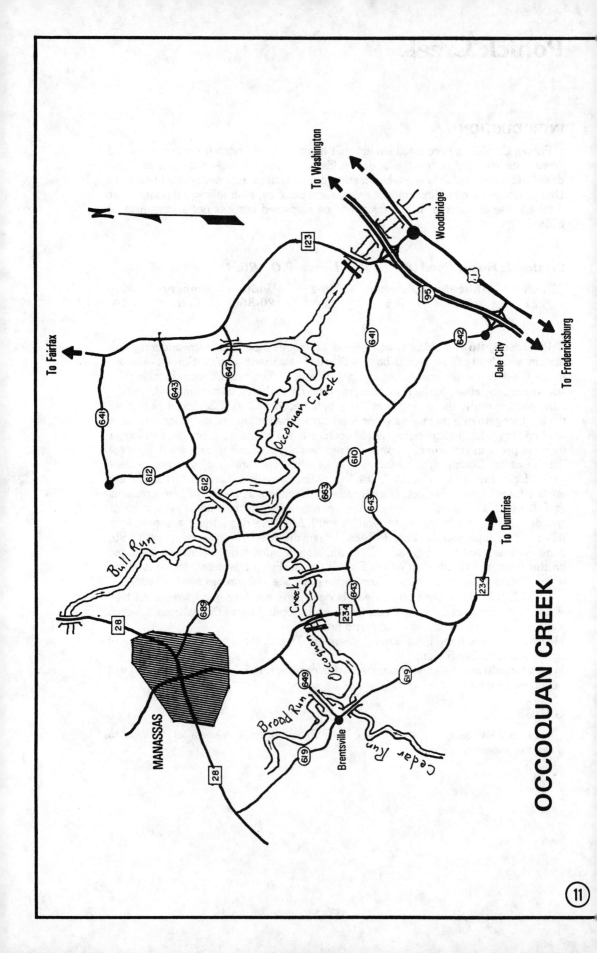

OCCOQUAN CREEK

Occoquan Creek

INTRODUCTION

Occoquan Creek is a stream that have been dammed extensively to provide a water supply for Northern Virginia and for recreational boating. It begins where Broad Run and Cedar Run join near Brentsville and ends in Belmont Bay; the total distance is only 23 miles, only one mile of which is free-flowing. It is a good lake system for fishing and flat water paddling, but it cannot be considered to be a free-flowing river.

Section 1. Brentsville to Occoquan (Rte 123)

Gradient	Difficulty	Distance	Time	Width	Scenery	Map
**	A	22	**	*	Good	11

*Over 200' wide in lake areas, 60-70' in short sections
**All gradient behind dams, except for two very short stretches.

Trip Description: The trip on the upper part of Occoquan Creek begins on Cedar Run, about 200 yards above the point where Broad Run joins Cedar Run to form Occoquan Creek. Shortly after joining Occoquan Creek, the backwater from Lake Jackson begins. Lake Jackson Dam is a high (40') concrete dam about 100 yards above Route 234; the dam is about 4.5 miles below the putin. Below Lake Jackson, the creek is free-flowing for about a mile over Class 1 ledges and riffles. Then the backwater behind the Occoquan Dam begins; this lake is big, wide, deep, and very long. Below the high (50') dam, there is another dam about 800 yards downstream; this lower dam is for the Lorton Prison system on the north bank.

Below the two dams at the town of Occoquan, there is a 600 yard stretch of rapids where the fallsline of the Occoquan Creek occurs; this is the transition from the piedmont plains to the coastal plains. This stretch, which is normally accessible to canoeists from downstream only, is Class 2 to Class 4; the last drop is a real boat-bender. These rapids could become a tremendous slalom course with a minimum of effort and it would provide very strong rapids convenient to the metropolitan Washington area.

There is one bridge that crosses Lake Occoquan about five miles below Route 234 and there are a number of landings on the lake on the Fairfax County side. There are two public landings near the point where Sandy Run enters the lake about 3 miles above the Occoquan Dam. This lake is for motorboaters and fishermen, not for canoeists. Below the Route 123 bridge, the river is strictly tidewater.

Hazards: Forty foot dam just above Route 234. Fifty foot dam followed by a twelve foot dam just above Occoquan. Heavy fallsline rapids for ½ mile below two dams near Occoquan.

Water Conditions: Backwater of dams can be canoed throughout the year Sections below dams for ½ mile are too low during the summer and fall.

GAUGE

None required for backwater from dams.

Broad Run

INTRODUCTION

Broad Run is one of the smaller canoeing streams in Northern Virginia, beginning near Markham, passing through Thoroughfare Gap, and joining Cedar Run near Brentsville to form Occoquan Creek. For most of its existence, it is either a small meandering stream or the backwater of the Manassas water supply dam. For one very short stretch, however, it has major rapids that will challenge the best of the canoeists.

Section 1. Beverly Mills (Rte 55) to Buckland (Rte 29-211)

Gradient	Difficulty	Distance	Time	Width	Scenery	Map
12	1-2	5.5	2	25-30	Fair	12

Trip Description: The trip from Route 55 Bridge to Buckland is a mild trip with about six Class 2 rapids in the first mile. One rapid is the remains of a low-water bridge that has a difficult turn on the left side. Careful on this one. There are a lot of riffles over gravel bars and at least four trees that complicate the passages below this low-water bridge. But no more white water until a Class 2 ledge just above the take-out. About 1.5 miles below Route 55, there are plenty of signs of beaver -- such as stripped limbs, tree stumps, and slides on the mud bank. For the next mile, virtually every side stream has a beaver dam within 50 feet of Broad Run. And beaver can be seen or heard if paddling very quietly.

This is not a very scenic stream. The banks are high, trees have been pushed over the banks during land clearing, the bottom has sand and mud in about equal proportions. There is only one rock formation along the stream that is significant enough to be remembered.

It is possible to putin about Route 55 bridge; the pool below the mill near the Post Office road is a good putin. There are a couple of Class 2 rapids and one Class 3 rapid before the bridge that one should not miss. It is also possible to putin at the low-water bridge above Thoroughfare Gap, just off Route 55 on a private road -- with permission and discretion. This section from the low water bridge above the gap to Route 55 bridge is for advanced paddlers — no beginners, no intermediates. It starts with a long Class 3 rock garden and then it drops over two honest Class 4 ledges in quick succession. The turbulence below the two big ledges has been known to mangle canoes and spit them out in a condition that brings tears to the eyes of the hard-hearted. Scout very carefully before deciding to try it. It drops at 120 feet/mile for 3/4 mile.

Hazards: Upper section above Route 55, two major ledges (Class 4). Below Route 55, trees blocking the stream.

Water Conditions: Canoeable normally in winter and spring following a wet period or a moderate rain.

Section 2. Manassas Dam (Rte 675) to Rte 28

Gradient	Difficulty	Distance	Time	Width	Scenery	Map
8	1₂	8.5	4	25-35	Fair	12

Trip Description: This trip begins below the Manassas Dam instead of starting at Buckland (Rte 29-211) for two reasons. One, there is a 3½ mile backwater behind

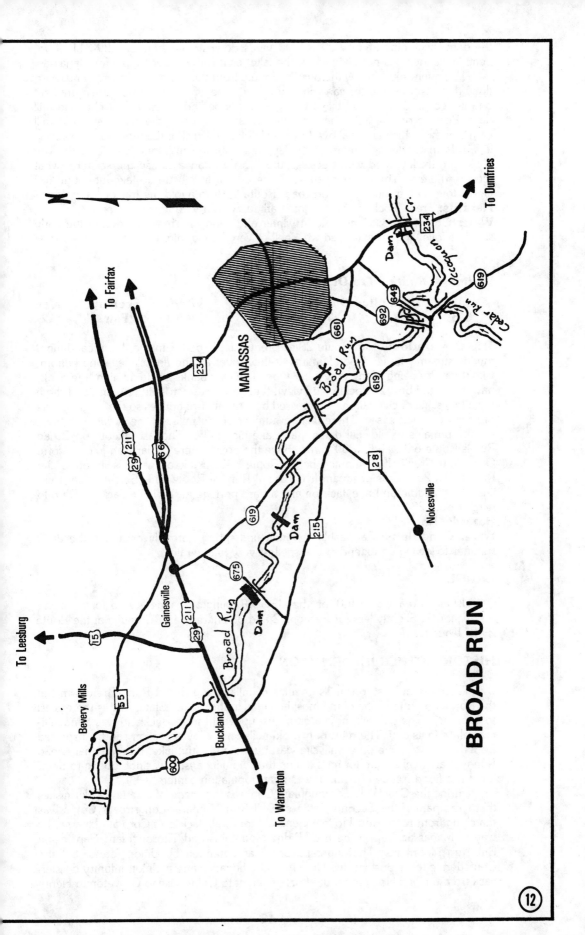

BROAD RUN

the dam, beginning about 600 to 800 yards downstream from Rte 29-211. Two, boating/canoeing is not allowed on the lake, as it is the water supply for Manassas.

The putin is just below the overflow chute from the 20' dam; if there is no overflow, there is no water for canoeing, none whatsoever. There is not much gradient on this section and a good bit of that gradient is behind an eight foot concrete mill dam. Portage on the left. There are two Class 2 rapids at the remains of old mill dams, one of which is just above Linden Hall (Rte 619). For the most part, however, it is a flat meandering stream, with clay banks and a sand/mud/clay bottom. The banks are thickly lined with trees, so there is no chance to see the scenery, what scenery there is. The takeout can be Route 28, but it is better to takeout about 400 yards downstream on the airport road (Route 660) to avoid the traffic.

Hazards: Trees blocking the stream. Barbed/woven wire fences.

Water Conditions: Canoeable in winter and spring normally or during the early summer following an extended wet spell or very heavy rain.

Section 3. Route 28 to Occoquan Creek

Gradient	Difficulty	Distance	Time	Width	Scenery	Map
5.5	A,1	7.5	3.5	30-50	Fair	12

Trip Description: From Route 28 to Brentsville, Broad Run is a flat, meandering, muddy stream with few good features. It flows over a sand and clayey-sand bottom, with the riffles being of the gravel bar type. The clay banks are fairly high, the banks have trees and bushes blocking the view, there are trees across the stream, and there are a few signs of civilization. It is crossed by a number of bridges so the length of the trip can be varied easily. There were a number of old mills on the stream, so there are the remains of old mill dams that make nice riffles. The last takeout on Broad Run is Route 649, about 800 yards above the point where Cedar Run joins to form Occoquan Creek. If continuing below Route 649, a takeout is possible on Cedar Run, about 200 yards upstream from Broad Run, at Route 619. Below Cedar Run, it is a long paddle on Lake Jackson and a hard portage at the Lake Jackson Dam to reach Route 234.

Hazards: None.

Water Conditions: Canoeable in winter and spring normally or during the early summer following an extended wet spell or very heavy rain.

GAUGE

Usually a reading of 5.0' on the USGS Remington gauge is zero for canoeing on Section 1. Slightly less for Sections 2 and 3. There is an RC gauge at the Route 29-211 bridge.

HISTORY/OTHER INFORMATION

There are at least four mills or ruins of mills along Broad Run. The old mill at the Route 55 putin is one of the most beautiful in the United States and is the easiest to approach. The old mill, now a barn, just upstream from Buckland was a magnificent place in its day. The ruins of two old mills on the lower section can be inspected from the stream. One other mill site was inundated by the lake. It seems that Broad Run was an ideal stream for mills during the colonial days; it was not too big to dam, it did not flood frequently, and it was near population centers.

During the Civil War, Thoroughfare Gap was the scene of a series of skirmishes that were part of the Second Battle of Bull Run. General Longstreet's Corps was marching from Front Royal to join General Stonewall Jackson's Corp at Manassas by way of Manassas Gap in the Blue Ridge Mountains and Thoroughfare Gap in the Bull Run Mountains. Thoroughfare Gap was defended by Union forces, but the Confederate force pushed two Union cavalry brigades and a Union infantry division back from the gap along the route to Haymarket to Gainesville to Groveton to Henry

House Hill. There Longstreet joined Jackson for a bloody two day battle that cost the Confederates 9,500 casualties, almost 20% of General Lee's force of 50,000; Union casualties totalled 14,500 in a force of 62,000, almost 25% of the troops commanded by General Pope. If Thoroughfare Gap and the nearby routes through the Bull Run mountains could have been held by the Union forces, then Lee's forces might have defeated in detail in 1862. And history would have been quite different.

It is quite difficult to remember the names and locations of all the many streams in Virginia, and when there are two or more streams with the same name, it becomes quite confusing and even more difficult. There are many Broad Runs in Virginia, two of which are in the Potomac watershed in close proximity. It seems that there is at least one very small stream with the name of Broad Run in every watershed. Most are too small to canoe, but when crossing the stream on a long drive, one must use total recall to determine if that Broad Run is the one that is in a canoeing guidebook.

There are even more problems with names other than Broad Run; names like Little River, Back Creek, Mill Creek, and South River are very common. There are at least five Little Rivers (Clinch, New, North Anna, Goose Creek, and North River tributaries); at least four Back Creeks that are canoeable (Jackson, Potomac, Shenandoah, and Middle River tributaries). There are an uncounted number of Mill Creeks, as every small stream that had a mill on it was a good candidate to be named Mill Creek.

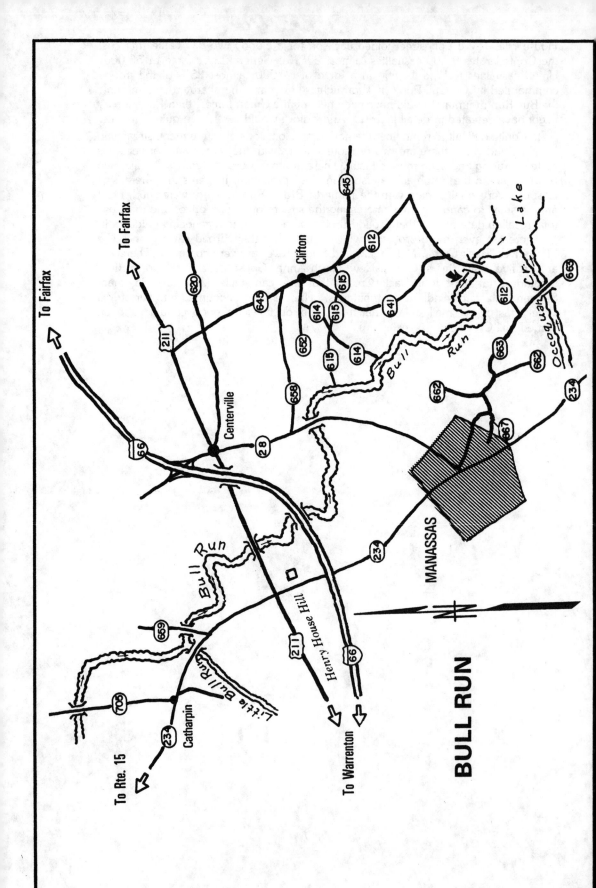

BULL RUN

Bull Run

INTRODUCTION

Bull Run is the biggest tributary of Occoquan Creek, but it is best known as the location of the first land battle of the Civil War and the location of one of the bloddiest battles later in the war; in 1861, there were over 4,000 casualties; in 1862, over 25,000 casualties. As you canoe on this stream, you wonder what prompted the commanders to return for a second time to this now historic site. And why so many men fought and died here.

Section 1. Catharpin (Rte 705) to Bull Run Park (Rte 29)

Gradient	Difficulty	Distance	Time	Width	Scenery	Map
7	12	9.5	4	25-35	Good	13

Trip Description: Bull Run at the Route 705 putin is just a very small run, barely wider than a canoe length. It has a fairly fast current over a sand and mud bottom, it has gravel bar riffles, and it flows through a wooded area with few signs of litter or civilization. There are a few trees blocking the stream, but these present no major problem. One small dam (2' to 2½' high) has been run, but with all precautions. About 7 miles downstream, Little Bull Run enters on the right and the water volume increases considerably. About 1½ miles further downstream, Bull Run passes under the old stone bridge that dates back to the 1700's, then Route 29-211 bridge comes into view.

Hazards: A couple of trees across the stream.

Water Conditions: Canoeable in winter, spring, and early summer, except following periods of little precipitation. Canoeable after a heavy rain in the summer and fall.

Section 2. Bull Run Park (Rte 29) to Manassas (Rte 28)

Gradient	Difficulty	Distance	Time	Width	Scenery	Map
5	1	6	3	30-40	Fair	13

Trip Description: From Bull Run Park to Route 28, Bull Run is a flat, meandering stream that is marred by civilization. There is a major trailer camp on the left bank and houses on many sections. The current is fairly slow, the water is acquiring a muddy color, the clay banks are high, and the scenery is not particularly interesting. The bottom is sand and mud, the riffles are just gravel bars, and trees block the best passages. There is rumored to be a Class 2 rapid in this section.

Hazards: None.

Water Conditions: Canoeable in winter, spring, and early summer, except following periods of little precipitation. Canoeable after a heavy rain in the summer and fall.

Section 3. Manassas (Rte 28) to Bull Run Marina

Gradient	Difficulty	Distance	Time	Width	Scenery	Map
5	12	7	4	50-70	Fair	13

Trip Description: The final section of Bull Run begins with a flat section with few riffles and ends in the backwater of a major dam on Occoquan Creek. It has a very slow current flowing over a bed of sand and mud through an area that is not too scenic. There is one rapid that appears to be a Class 2, but that classification is probably a bit high. The clay banks are high at the start but they are much lower in the backwater area, and the water goes from quite shallow to quite deep. It is about 1.5 miles from the Marina to Occoquan Creek, all of which is lake paddling.

Hazards: None.

Water Conditions: Canoeable in winter, spring, and early summer, except following periods of little precipitation. Canoeable after a heavy rain in the summer and fall.

GAUGE

A reading of 5.0' on the USGS Remington Gauge is probably zero for canoeing on Section 1; a reading of 4.5' is zero for Section 2; 4.0' for Section 3.

HISTORY

Bull Run was the scene of two major battles in the Civil War; the first in 1861, the second in 1862. These battles were fought for control of Manassas Junction, a railroad station where the railroad from Washington met the lines that went west to Fort Royal and southwest to Charlottesville.

In the first battle, Union columns advanced westward from Centerville, crossing Bull Run at two sites. The major attack column crossed at a ford near Little Bull Run and turned south toward the Confederate forces located near Henry House Hill. A second column attacked across the stone bridge just upstream from Route 29-211. It was in this battle that General Jackson received his nickname "Stonewall" while leading the 1st Brigade, Virginia Volunteers, later named the "Stonewall Brigade".

In the second battle, strangely enough, the Union forces were attacking from the south while the Confederates were defending behind the railroad tracks. Again, General Jackson played a major role in this battle, his First Corps bearing the brunt of the Union attack. This was one of the bloodiest battles in the war for both forces.

Quantico Creek

INTRODUCTION

Quantico Creek could be a very interesting white-water canoeing stream if: (1) there is sufficient water, (2) the park officials give permission for its use, and (3) the trees were cleared from the stream. After all, it is close to an Interstate highway (I-95), it flows through a beautiful forest with no signs of mankind, it has easy putins and takeouts, it has a good steady gradient, and it has numerous points that are scenic or interesting. It is truly unfortunate that the problems outweigh the good points.

Section 1. South Branch: Rte 619 to Dumfries (Rte 627)

Gradient	Difficulty	Distance	Time	Width	Scenery	Map
22	1-2-3	8.5	3	20-40	Very Good	14

Trip Description: The South Branch Quantico Creek is the principal tributary of Quantico Creek, draining a much larger area than the North Branch. At Route 619, the South Branch is a very small stream, but the North Branch is not even a small run at Route 619. The South Branch and North Branch join about a mile above the town of Dumfries to form Quantico Creek; about two miles below Dumfries, Quantico Creek enters the Potomac River.

The creek begins as a very small stream flowing swiftly over a sand and gravel bottom. The banks are low, the scenery is uncut woodlands, there are no signs of litter. There are many swift turns through narrow passages and a number of trees blocking the entire passage. About two miles downstream, there is the backwater from a 20 foot dam; it backs the water up less than a mile. Portage on the right.

Below the dam, the South Branch Quantico Creek is a little terror for about a mile. It flows at an incredible speed over a solid rock bottom at a horrid gradient, over small ledges, through rock garden rapids. There are few eddies in this section. Below this section, the stream becomes a meandering, mild run over gravel bars, sandy bottoms, and occasional rock gardens. It is crossed by three park bridges and blocked by a number of trees during the next three miles. Then there are some impressive rock formations along the banks and two Class 2 ledges, followed by a high footbridge across the stream.

The North Branch joins about 200 yards below the footbridge and Quantico Creek begins to descend to Tidewater. Between the confluence and the takeout just upstream from I-95, alongside Mine Road, Quantico Creek drops over three Class 3 rapids and a couple of Class 2 rapids in the short distance of ½ mile. The last rapid occurs after a long gravel bar that makes the paddler think the rapids are all upstream. This set of rapids is a most pleasant surprise.

Hazards: Numerous trees blocking the stream. Twenty foot dam.

Water Conditions: Canoeable only in winter and spring following a prolonged wet period or very heavy rain.

Section 2. North Branch: Trail 7 to Dumfries (Rte 627)

Gradient	Difficulty	Distance	Time	Width	Scenery	Map
30	2-34	4	2	15-25	Very Good	14

Trip Description: The North Branch of Quantico Creek is a very small stream that can be reached only by a long portage on Trail 7. It is not too pleasant to carry a

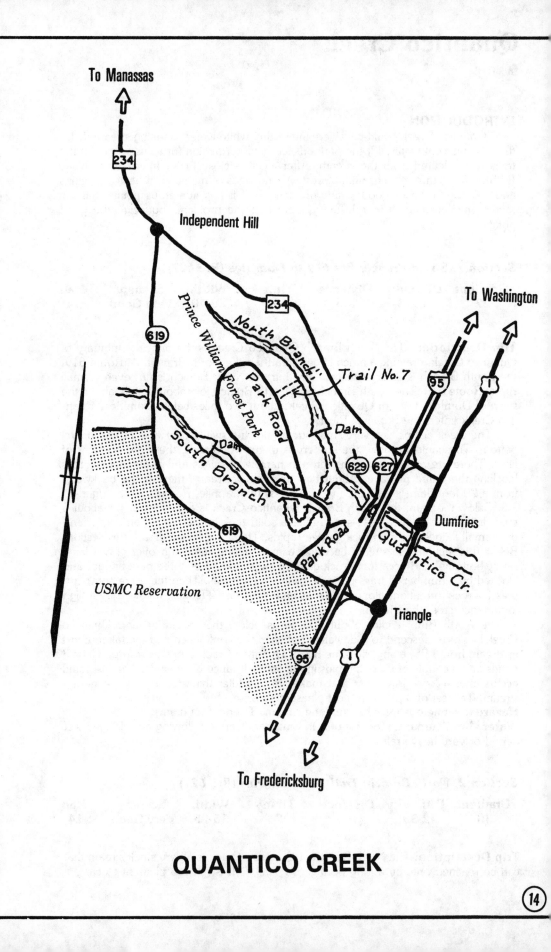

QUANTICO CREEK

boat one mile to canoe four miles, but that is the way it is. About a mile downstream from the putin, the backwater of the dam begins; the 20 foot dam backs the water for about ½ mile. Below the dam, there is a rather competitive stretch where the stream drops at the rate of 120 feet/mile. Hike it. Don't paddle it. Just before joining the South Branch, there are the remains of a pyrite mine beside the stream. The smell of sulfur is easily detected

Hazards: Numerous trees across stream (four above dam backwater). Twenty foot dam. Beaver dams (3' to 4' high). Very big rapid below dam Class 4-5.

Water Conditions: Canoeable only in winter and spring following a prolonged wet period or very heavy rain.

GAUGE

There is a USGS gauge on the South Branch at Route 619; a reading of 3.0' is about zero for Section 1. A reading of 3.5' on the USGS Culpeper gauge is probably zero for canoeing on Section 1. Section 2 requires 6" more water.

HISTORY/OTHER INFORMATION

The town of Dumfries is not much to look at now, but in the late 1600's and early 1700's, it was a seaport town. Ocean-going ships sailed into and anchored in Quantico Creek near the Potomac River to pick up tobacco hogsheads. The tobacco was brought to the piers over "rolling roads", where the hogsheads were rolled by oxen teams -- hence the name rolling road in many areas of tidewater Virginia. There is the trace of the Dumfries' rolling road through the Prince William Forest Park. Dumfries' role as a seaport ended when the port of Alexandria became a major shipping center. Just south of Prince William Forest Park is the Marine Corps Base, Quantico, one of the largest military bases in the country and the site of a new national military cemetery.

There was a pyrite mine on the North Branch that operated from 1898 to 1919. It closed when the giant sulfur deposits were discovered along the Gulf Coast. It had two vertical shafts and one inclined shaft, going to a depth of 1,000 feet; traces of the inclined shaft are still there. Pyrite is known as "fools gold" and the ground on the north bank has a golden glitter in the sunlight. Those nuggets are not for real, son. This mine site can be reached from park trails or by the old railroad bed from where Mine Road ends west of Dumfries.

Quantico Creek can be canoed only if advance permission is obtained from the Park Superintendent in writing; since the water levels are unpredictable and depend on heavy rains, it is difficult to schedule a trip on this stream. But if a trip is organized, if there is water, and if permission is secured, then it will be a beautiful trip. There are some of the most pleasant hiking trails through a natural forest and there are excellent facilities for camping and picnicking.

Aquia Creek

INTRODUCTION

Aquia Creek is a small stream that serves as the southern boundary for the vast Marine Corps Base, Quantico. It begins in rolling farmland, it travels through an area with few signs of civilization, it suddenly becomes a major lake (Stafford water supply), and then becomes a broad tidewater estuary below the takeout. It is the most southern stream in the Potomac watershed that is canoeable.

Section 1. Garrisonville (Rte 610) to Aquia (Rte 1)

Gradient	Difficulty	Distance	Time	Width	Scenery	Map
16	1-2	10.5	3.5	30-40	Good	15

Trip Description: The trip on Aquia Creek begins at the ford alongside Route 610 bridge. There is a nice riffle there, but there are few riffles for many miles after that point. About two miles downstream, there is a low water bridge over 4-foot culverts; it is runnable through the culverts at low water levels. This bridge was built to support tanks, so it is heavier and stronger than a masonry outhouse. There are a few trees across the stream and there are beaver dams and remains of beaver dams.

The water is usually muddy, the bottom is sand and mud, there are high clay banks (8' to 10'), and the banks are tree lined. On the right bank, there are farms and old farmhouses; on the left, beautiful woodlands. Just before Route 641, Aquia Creek enters a beautiful rocky gorge (one-half mile long); the trip is worth the chance to see the rapids, evergreens, and the limestone cliffs in this area. There is one strong Class 2 chute in this area.

There is consistently swift water above Route 641, but then there is a two mile backwater for a dam below Route 641; this backwater begins about one-half mile below Route 641. The area inundated by the Stafford water supply dam must have been very good white water, as it was the falls line area with the most gradient. A lower dam probably would have been adequate for this sparsely populated county, but it is too late to save Aquia Creek. Below the Stafford reservoir dam, Aquia Creek moves very fast over a sand and gravel bottom, and there are Class 1 riffles until it reaches Route 1. A short distance below Route 1, it becomes a flatwater tidal stream.

Hazards: Low water bridge. Twenty foot dam. Trees blocking the stream.

Water Conditions: Canoeable normally in winter and spring following a wet period or a moderate rain.

GAUGES

A reading of 5.0' on the USGS Remington gauge should be zero for canoeing this stream.

HISTORY

In 1675, the white settlers from Stafford County crossed the Potomac to attack a hostile Indian tribe, but they attacked the friendly Susquehannock tribe instead. The Indians then killed several settlers, provoking the Maryland and Virginia settlers to combine forces. The colonists surrounded the Susquehannock and, when the Indian chiefs came out under a flag of truce to negotiate, they were put to death. The outraged Indians then massacred 36 colonists in the Stafford County area, which brought anguished cries to the royal governor to crush the savages. Governor Barkeley had little sympathy for those that betrayed a trust such as they had, but he did order a series of forts to be built along Aquia Creek, which became the northern frontier for colonial Virginia.

In the early 1800's, a railroad from Richmond through Fredericksburg terminated at Aquia Landing, with ships and boats providing service between Washington and Aquia Landing. During the Civil War, the Union forces usually held the Northern bank across from Aquia Landing which was usually in Confederate hands. Lincoln met with General Burnside and General Hooker at Aquia Landing during the Fredericksburg-Chancellorsville campaign. This landing was not used after rail service was established between Fredericksburg and Washington after the Civil War and it is now hard to see signs of its earlier importance.

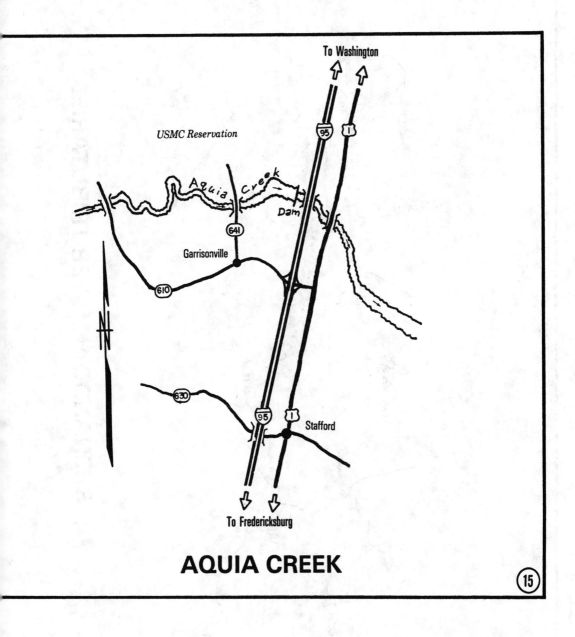

AQUIA CREEK

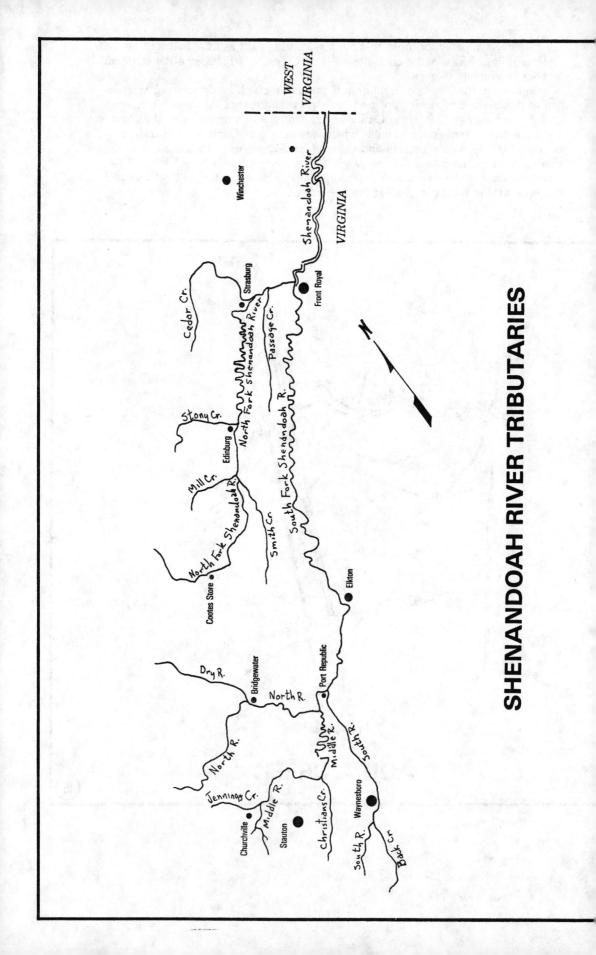

SHENANDOAH RIVER TRIBUTARIES

Chapter 3

The Shenandoah River Watershed

The Shenandoah River watershed is mostly in Virginia, with a very small portion in West Virginia where it joins the Potomac River at Harpers Ferry. It's total watershed is about 3040 square miles, most of which is in Virginia; only 1% lies in West Virginia. The Shenandoah drains about 7.6% of the state, all of which is in the in the northern part of the Valley of Virginia; its principal tributaries are the North Fork Shenandoah River and the South Fork Shenandoah River, each of which have many tributaries.

The following streams, whose locations are shown on Figure 5, are described in this chapter:

Shenandoah River
North Fork Shenandoah River
Smith Creek
Mill Creek
Stony Creek
Cedar Creek
Passage Creek
South Fork Shenandoah River
South River
Back Creek
North River
Dry River
Middle River
Christians Creek
Jennings Branch

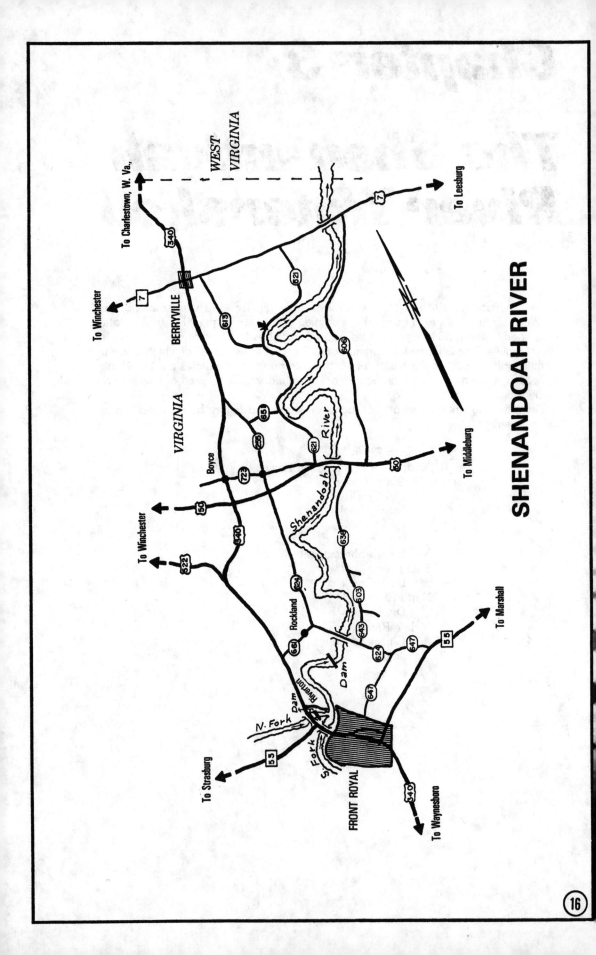

SHENANDOAH RIVER

16

Shenandoah River

INTRODUCTION

The Shenandoah River from Front Royal to the West Virginia line, just below Rte 7, is one of the most pleasant canoeing rivers in the nation. It has been canoed by more beginning canoeists than any stream in Virginia, without a doubt, and the advanced canoeists occasionally return to refresh old memories. It justly deserves its name, "Daughter of the Stars". And it deserves to have towns, songs, counties, ships, and dirigibles named after it.

Section 1. Confluence North Fork/South Fork to Morgan Ford Bridge (Rte 624)

Gradient	Difficulty	Distance	Time	Width	Scenery	Map
5	1	7.5	3.5	100-120	Poor	16

Trip Description: The trip from Front Royal to Morgan Ford Bridge is begun at the Riverton landing on the North Fork Shenandoah River, at the Virginia Game Commission landing. It is a short trip through a rather heavily populated area. There is a big limestone quarry on the right about a mile downstream with a conveyor over the river to a lime plant. There is a twelve-foot dam that backs up the water for at least two miles; the backwater has a lot of cabins along the bank and a lot of motorboats on the flatwater. The water is still polluted by the viscose plant at Front Royal, there is much litter along the banks, and the portage around the dam is tough. There are a few riffles where one-inch ledges rise in low water, but very little else in the way of white-water. There is a Virginia Game Commission landing at the takeout.
Hazards: One twelve-foot dam about 4 miles downstream.
Water Conditions: Canoeable most of the year except following a long dry spell. Canoeable after a moderate rain in the summer.

Section 2. Morgan Ford Bridge (Rte 624) to Route 50

Gradient	Difficulty	Distance	Time	Width	Scenery	Map
5	1-2	12.5	5	110-130	Fair	16

Trip Description: The section below Morgan Ford Bridge is an improvement over the previous section in that it does not have a dam, there is much less litter, the buildings are a distinct improvement, and the water pollution is almost gone. The valley is truly a beautiful sight. The well-tended farms and "second home" developments along the bank do not distract too much. There are more riffles and mild rapids on this section than any other part of the Shenandoah in Virginia. (Remember, the Staircase is in West Virginia). The rapids are mostly of the ledge type and present few problems; most of the riffles/rapids seem to be in the middle portion of the trip with flat stretches at the start and at the finish.
Hazards: None.
Water Conditions: Canoeable most of the year except following a long dry spell. Canoeable after a moderate rain in the summer.

Section 3. Rte 50 to Castleman's Ferry (Rte 7)

Gradient	Difficulty	Distance	Time	Width	Scenery	Map
3	12	15	6	120-140	Good	16

Trip Description: From Route 50 to Route 7 is a very long trip over a lot of flat water. There are a lot of small ledges, there is one good ledge that is usually by-passed to the left, and there are caves high above the bank. The water is clear and flows over a sandy bottom; the banks are fairly low so it is easy to see the farmlands that border the river. The valley is quite wide in many spots and the Blue Ridge Mountains can be seen for the entire trip. There is at least one location of an Indian fish dam that can only be seen in low water. The trip can be shortened by five miles by taking out at Lockes Landing, a Virginia Game Commission landing; this is recommended quite strongly. There is a VGC landing at the Rte 7 takeout.
Hazards: None.
Water Conditions: Canoeable most of the year except following a long dry spell. Canoeable after a moderate rain in the summer.

GAUGE

A reading of 1.0' at the USGS Front Royal Gauge is zero for canoeing the Shenandoah.

HISTORY

The tidewater area of Virginia had been settled for fifty years when John Lederer, a German immigrant, procured a license from the Virginia governor to trade furs across the Blue Mountain Wall to the west of the colony. Even though most reasonable people considered the mountains to be impassible, Lederer was given a license. In March 1669, he reached a crest on the Blue Ridge Mountains and first saw the Shenandoah valley and the Appalachian Mountains beyond; he returned with no further scouting to report his findings.

Lederer returned with a larger party in May 1669 and explored more of the valley. When the accompanying party returned to civilization, Lederer continued traveling south through the valley, staying with friendly Indians. He returned east, coming out near the Appomattox. He returned in August 1670, crossing at Manassas Gap (Route 55) and explored the northern reaches of the valley. He published his experiences in two very modest descriptions of his travels in the valley of Virginia.

Other explorations were conducted by a group from Annapolis, Maryland, which travelled from Harper's Ferry to Powell's Fort (Passage Creek area). Governor Spotswood led a group of Virginia gentlemen with guides, servants, and rangers to the Shenandoah in 1716.

The Shenandoah valley was not settled by the English Virginians from the Tidewater and Piedmont area of the Colony. These settlers had come to regard the Blue Ridge as a barrier to the Indians and the French and did not go beyond it. While a few explorers, John Lederer and Abraham Wood being the more important ones, crossed into the Shenandoah valley, the thought of populating the valley was not actively considered by the tidewater people. It was the German and Scotch-Irish immigrants from Pennsylvania who moved southwestward into the great valley, and within a generation, the valley was settled, forts and roads were built, and towns were started. The northern valley area was mostly settled by Virginians of English descent, the middle valley by Germans from Pennsylvania, the southern area by the Scotch-Irish.

The English settlers largely retained the customs and practices of the Tidewater. They were not very frugal, they did not practice good farming policies, and they tended to live in villages. The German Virginians stuck to their old world customs longer, lived in scattered farmhouses instead of villages, were frugal and worked hard, practiced crop rotation, raised wheat instead of tobacco, and built magnificent barns. Their legacy is still apparent in the middle valley area, as it sometimes reminds one of the Pennsylvania Dutch area. The Scotch-Irish Virginians lived in the less fertile, more mountainous, and isolated upper valley area. There were the frontiersmen, the Indian fighters, the explorers, the hunters; they were the independent, self-reliant, tough settlers that resented any interference by English kings or Tidewater Virginians.

The valley had been a major route for Indians travelling south from as far north as New York state and for Indians traveling north from the Carolinas to raid and loot. The early settlers fought many a fierce attack, particularly during the French and Indian War. The tales are not pleasant and the feelings were not conducive to peace talks as the roll of settlers killed lengthened. It was not until 1766 that the terror stopped, but the settlers gave no quarter to any Indian for at least the next ten years. By 1780, there were no Indians in the valley and only occasional excavations along the South Fork give an indication of their ever having lived there.

During the French and Indian War, Winchester was a major base for the British regulars and colonial militia. General Braddock marched from Winchester to Cumberland and thence to his defeat and death. During the Revolutionary War, the lower valley provided the Virginia Riflemen, commanded by Daniel Morgan, a resident of the Berryville area. No men were drafted to serve in this unit, as the quota had been filed by volunteers who fought from Quebec to Georgia against the British, the Tories, and the Indians. The men of the valley believed so strongly in independence, in freedom, in religious tolerance, that they fought willingly.

Between the Revolutionary War and the Civil War, the valley expanded and many famous Americans were born in the valley and lived in the valley. John Sevier, the founder of Tennessee, Sam Houston, founder of Texas, John Marshall of the Supreme Court, Daniel Boone, the explorer, Daniel Morgan, the hero of two wars, Cyrus McCormick, inventor of the reaper, as well as familiar names such as Lincoln, Bryan, and Bowman were from the valley. Iron furnaces were built from Harper's Ferry to Staunton, although it was never a major industry. The major occupation was farming, and the North Fork valley, the South Fork valley, and the main valley proved to be bountiful. Slavery was the exception rather than the rule.

During the Civil War, the Shenandoah valley was a constant battlefield. The battles at Harpers Ferry in 1861, the valley campaign of Jackson in 1862, the raid by Sheridan in 1864, and the frequent battles/marches of 1863 took their toll on the valley. Winchester, for example, changed hands between Union and Confederate forces about 70 times. The valley provided many brave men for the Confederacy, the most well-known of which was the 1st Brigade, Virginia Volunteers, the "Stonewall Brigade". The casualties suffered by this brigade were still almost unbelievable and the entire manhood of many towns/villages was lost in a series of bloody battles. Two regiments originated in the northern (lower) end of the valley; one regiment came from the Staunton/Augusta county area; one regiment from the southern (upper) end of the valley; and one regiment from the Lexington area. From its full strength of 3,000 men, it had dropped to 635 men at Second Manassas, to 200 men after Chancellorsville, and 210 men and officers at Appomatox, in spite of continued replacements of losses. The battles at Gettsburg, Spotsylvania, Chancellorsville, and Second Manassas, left many empty places at the tables and many aching hearts in the valley.

After the Civil War, the valley prospered, river navigation increased, mills returned to operations, industry recovered, towns expanded, resorts flourished, and railroads opened the area. Today, it is a major part of our American heritage, a showplace of our early history.

North Fork Shenandoah River

INTRODUCTION

The North Fork of the Shenandoah River is a river of many different moods. The upper reaches, the Brock's Gap section, is a challenging white-water trip; the section from Edinburg to Mount Jackson is a series of backwaters from three high dams; the other sections have light riffles, small ledges, good current and an occasional rapid. The section from Mount Jackson to Strasburg is the most meandering river in the United States, without a doubt.

Section 1. Riverside Church (Rte 921) to Cootes Store (Rte 259)

Gradient	Difficulty	Distance	Time	Width	Scenery	Map
19	2-3	9.5	3	30-40	Very Good	17

Trip Description: The Brock's Gap section from Riverside Church to Cootes Store is a white-water trip to delight the heart. It is such a pleasure that it is frequently extended by starting further upstream at Route 820, near Bergton. From Bergton to Riverside Church (Route 921), the North Fork is a fast mountain stream, dashing over a bed of rocks. It is very fast and presents no difficulties other than an occasional barbed wire or electric wire fence. It can be scouted from Route 259 for the entire distance.

Below Riverside Church, the North Fork offers a wide variety of challenges, varying from long cobble bars, to small ledges, to big chutes with heavy waves, to blind turns with ledges immediately below, to swift passages around small islands. It also offers a low-water bridge that has a taste for aluminum canoes (always there), a barbed wire fence (not always there), and a tree blocking the main passage (almost always there). It has a scenic rock formation, Chimney Rock; a large cross painted on a high rock bluff; and a rock cliff covered with sheets of ice and icicles in cold weather.

The trip is over all too fast, with a takeout at Route 259 or at Riverside Garage, just downstream from the bridge on the right.

Hazards: Low-water bridge. Tree blocking part of stream. Barbed/woven wire fences.

Water Conditions: Canoeable normally in winter and spring following a wet period or a moderate rain.

Section 2. Cootes Store (Rte 259) to Timberville (Rte 42)

Gradient	Difficulty	Distance	Time	Width	Scenery	Map
10	1-2	6	2	30-50	Good	17,18

Trip Description: The trip from Cootes Store to Timberville starts out with a low-water (or underwater) bridge about ½ mile downstream. It is a fast flowing stream with good current, occasional riffles, fast chutes, and gravel-bar rapids. There are a few small ledges and frequent rock gardens, but none are really difficult. The banks are lined with trees, the right bank is a rather high bluff, the bottom is sand and gravel, and the scenery is farmland and the backyards of a couple of small towns. At Timberville, there is an eight-foot dam for the local water works; portage, by all means.

Hazards: Eight-foot dam at Timberville. Underwater or low-water bridge, depending on water level.

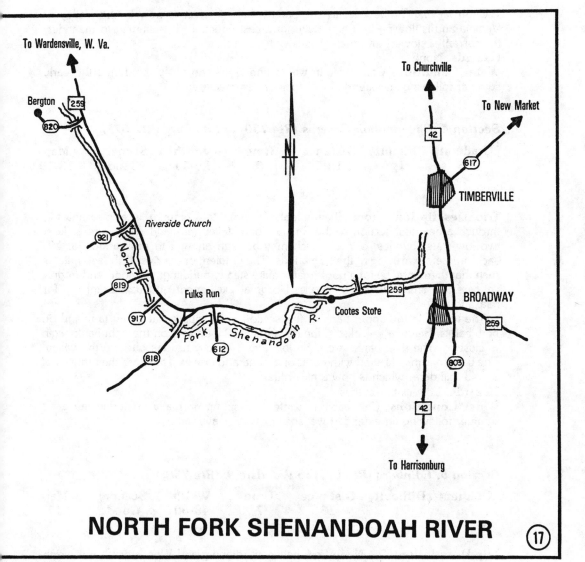

NORTH FORK SHENANDOAH RIVER

(17)

Water Conditions: Canoeable normally in winter and spring following a wet period or a moderate rain.

Section 3. Timberville (Rte 42) to Shenandoah Caverns (Rte 730)

Gradient	Difficulty	Distance	Time	Width	Scenery	Map
10	1-23	12	4	30-50	Good	18

Trip Description: From Timberville to Shenandoah Caverns, the river moves fast; there is, however, only one rapid of note, a Class 2-3 on a left turn about 3 to 4 miles below Timberville. The river flows steadily in a northeastern direction, although it has a slight tendency to meander; the scenery is mostly farmland and moderately high banks with rock bluffs on the left bank in many stretches; the bottom is cobble and sand for the most part although there are a few signs of ledges. The Route 720 bridge, which is about one mile below Route 730, is a covered wooden bridge that is a masterpiece of construction; the curved arches, the massive beams, the feeling of history, the timelessness of the design. Stop at this bridge even if you are not canoeing or even if it is not your takeout.

Upon leaving Timberville, it is apparent that the river is now in the Valley of Virginia and is flowing in a generally north-east direction. It is starting to meander, the current is slower, and the valley is wider and flatter.

Hazards: None

Water Conditions: Canoeable in winter and spring normally. or during the early summer following an extended wet spell or very heavy rain.

Section 4. Shenandoah Caverns (Rte 730) to Edinburg (Rte 675)

Gradient	Difficulty	Distance	Time	Width	Scenery	Map
7.5	12	13.5	6	35-50	Good	18,19

Trip Description: From Shenandoah Caverns to Edinburg is a pleasant trip through a beautiful section of the Shenandoah Valley farmland. There are at least two low-water bridges, one of which may be high enough to pass under (at Mt. Jackson) before arriving at the 675 bridge. The gradient of the river (7.5 feet/mile) is such that there may be long pools that require steady paddling; the pools end in gravel bars and small ledges, as a rule. No great excitement, just a pleasant trip for relaxation.

The terrain in the upper parts of this section is principally flat valley farmland on both banks. Below Mt. Jackson, the Massanutten Mountains on the right bank begin to close in. The river banks are fairly low and it is easy to look out into the valley. The bottom is mostly sand with occasional sand and gravel. There are the remains of an old mill dam, which is now a nice riffle.

Hazards: Low-water bridges.

Water Conditions: Canoeable in winter and spring normally or during the early summer following an extended wet spell or very heavy rain.

Section 5. Edinburg (Rte 675) to Woodstock (Rte 758)

Gradient	Difficulty	Distance	Time	Width	Scenery	Map
7.5	1	16	7	40-60	Good	19

Trip Description: The North Fork between Edinburg and Woodstock is not worth canoeing. It may be excellent for fishing, it may be good exercise, and it may build character. But it is not white-water. It has three high dams that make for three long paddles in flat water with little or no current. In high water, these dams present a major hazard to the canoeist, and the portages are complicated by "No Trespassing" signs.

The area from Edinburg to Woodstock is known as the Seven Bends of the North Fork Shenandoah. There are seven major loops (bends) in which the river reverses direction while still flowing to the northeast. It is possible to paddle in every direction of the compass (even southwest) in this stretch. One part of the trip that will always be remembered is how the river has a big mountain to the east to which it always returns. Also the clear, clean water over a sandy bottom with nice sandbars and gravel bars for lunch stops.

The sixteen-foot dam at the takeout has a 15' wide section broken out on the right with a drop of 10' remaining. It would be wise to resist any temptation.

Hazards: Three high dams, ten feet to sixteen feet high. Low water bridges.

Water Conditions: Canoeable in winter, spring, and early summer, except following periods of little precipitation. Canoeable after a heavy rain in the summer and fall.

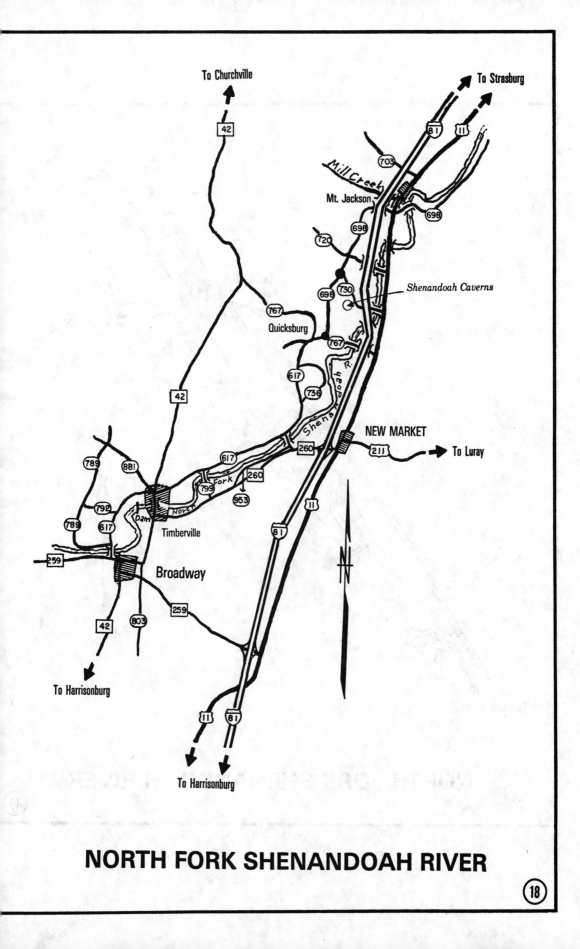

To Churchville

To Strasburg

42

81   11

703

Mill Creek

698

Mt. Jackson

698

720

698   730   Shenandoah Caverns

Quicksburg

767

617

736

Shenandoah R.

42

617   New Market

789   881   260

Fork   211   To Luray

617

799   260

792   953

Dam   North   11

789   617

Timberville   81

259

Broadway

259

N

42   803

To Harrisonburg

11   81

To Harrisonburg

NORTH FORK SHENANDOAH RIVER

18

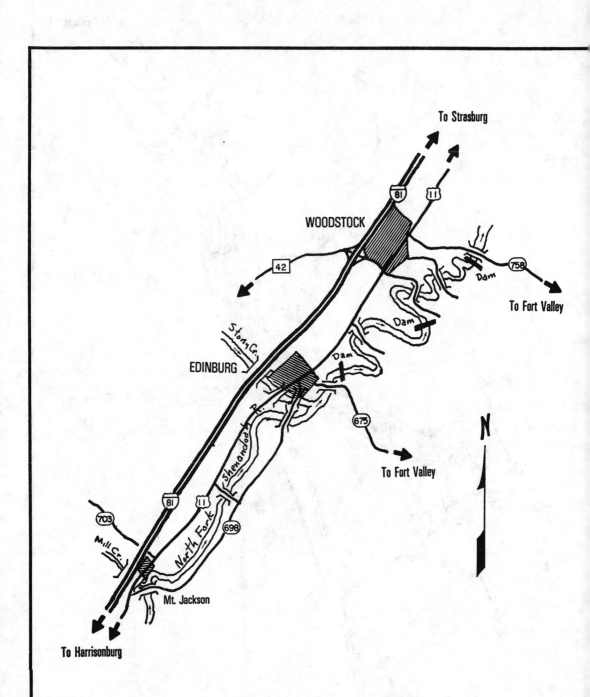

To Strasburg

WOODSTOCK

81 11

42

Dam 758

To Fort Valley

Stony Cr.

EDINBURG

Dam

Dam

675

To Fort Valley

N

81 11

Shenandoah R.

703

698

Mill Cr.

North Fork

Mt. Jackson

To Harrisonburg

NORTH FORK SHENANDOAH RIVER

19

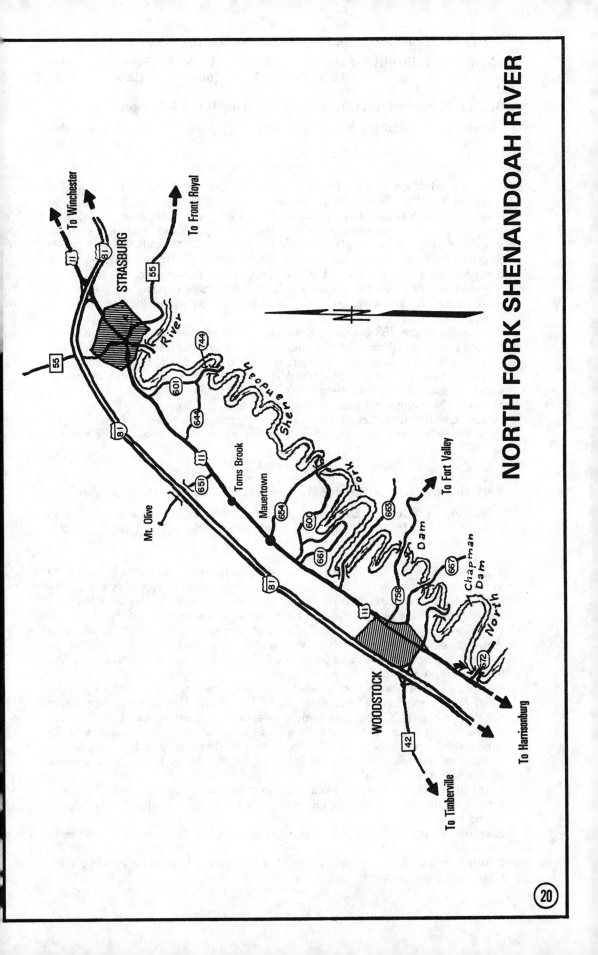

NORTH FORK SHENANDOAH RIVER

20

Section 6. Woodstock (Rte 758) to Maurertown (Rte 654)

Gradient	Difficulty	Distance	Time	Width	Scenery	Map
3.5	1₂	13.5	5.5	50-60	Good	20

Section 7. Maurertown (Rte 654) to Strasburg (Rte 648)

Gradient	Difficulty	Distance	Time	Width	Scenery	Map
4.5	1	15.5	6	60-70	Good	20

Trip Description: From Woodstock to Maurertown and from Maurertown to Strasburg, the North Fork is really a pretty stream. It meanders in all directions, or so it seems, through beautiful farmlands, and there are no commercial or industrial or second-home developments to blight the scenery. About two miles below Woodstock, there is the remains of an old 4-foot dam, just above Route 663, where Stonewall Mill once stood; these remains can be run on the left side or portaged on the right. Other than this rapid, the only dangers on this section of the North Fork Shenandoah are the frequent low-water bridges and cattle standing in the shallows. It seems that the low-water bridges were built in the middle of the best riffles, by design, not chance.

From the Route 758 bridge to Strasburg, the North Fork has at least six loops moving from the high mountains to the east to the high bluffs to the west. It would seem that it should have more riffles/rapids, but there are only Class 1 gravel bars and small rock gardens in this section. Very few signs of ledges. The gradient is so slight that there is very little current flowing over a sandy bottom.

Hazards: Numerous low-water bridges. Cows in the stream.

Water Conditions: Canoeable in winter, spring, and early summer, except following periods of little precipitation. Canoeable after a heavy rain in the summer and fall.

Section 8. Strasburg (Rte 648) to South Fork Shenandoah (Riverton)

Gradient	Difficulty	Distance	Time	Width	Scenery	Map
5	1₂	13	5	80	Fair	21

Trip Description: The Section from Strasburg to Riverton Landing is much similar to the other sections of the North Fork Shenandoah except that the rapids are the small ledge type. There must be two hundred ledges, all about one inch high; no higher. The river no longer meanders as it moves slowly eastward to join the South Fork Shenandoah near Front Royal. There are two dangers on this trip, a four foot dam just below where Cedar Creek joins on the left and a ten foot dam at Riverton Landing. Portage both of these dams, the first on the right, the second on the left; they are both dangerous.

This area of the North Fork is where the river leaves its main valley to join the South Fork. It moves in a fairly direct line to Riverton, picking up water from Cedar Creek and Passage Creek. The scenery deteriorates a great deal here as there are several homes, litter, and camping grounds along the bank. It is still a fairly flat stream with a very slow current flowing over a sand bottom past high clay banks. The two shallow areas (riffles) below the Cedar Creek dam are fords used in colonial times and in the Civil War.

The Shenandoah River, the North Fork, and the South Fork join about 300 yards below the Riverton takeout. The next takeout below Riverton is Morgan Ford Bridge on the Shenandoah.

Hazards: Four foot dam about seven miles below putin. Ten foot dam at Riverton takeout.

Water Conditions: Canoeable most of the year except following a long dry spell. Canoeable after a moderate rain in the summer.

64

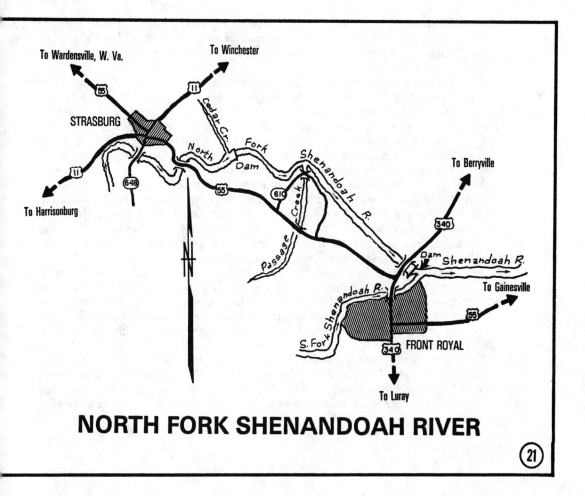

NORTH FORK SHENANDOAH RIVER

(21)

GAUGE

A reading of 3.5' on the USGS Cootes Store gauge is zero for canoeing on Section 1; 3.0' for Section 2 and 3; 2.5' for Sections 4,5,6. A reading of 1.5' on the USGS Front Royal gauge is zero for canoeing on Section 6,7,8. There is an RC gauge on the Riverside Church bridge on Section 1.

HISTORY/OTHER INFORMATION

The North Fork Shenandoah Valley was the main valley for settlement in the colonial days. It is a wider valley than the South Fork Shenandoah Valley, it was more removed from the claims of Lord Fairfax, and it was less likely to flood. It was also the valley that had the most Indian massacres and produced the more famous people in American history. Strangely enough,, Stonewall Jackson's campaigns were in the South Fork Valley in 1862, but Sheridan's campaign was in the North Fork Valley in 1864.

After the battle at Winchester in 1864, the Confederate forces fell back to Strasburg and prepared strong defensive positions on Fishers Hill. These forces were deployed with their right flank on the North Fork where Tumbling Run enters and their left flank near North Mountain. Union forces circled Fishers Hill to the west by what is now Route 623 and the Confederates were attacked from the North and West. In this battle, General Crook, who was later known for his Indian campaigns in the Southwest, distinguished himself, as did one of his division commanders,

Colonel Rutherford B. Hayes. Union casualties were only 528, compared to the Confederate losses of 1,235. The Confederate forces fell back along the Valley Pike (now Route 11), fighting half-hearted delaying actions near Woodstock, Mount Jackson, and Edinburg.

After the Battle of Fishers Hill, Sheridan began the burning of crops, homes, and barns; the driving off of horses, cattle, sheep; the killing of hogs and chickens. The valley was filled with smoke, and it was said that "a crow would have to pack his lunch while travelling the valley". After burning the upper valley, Sheridan withdrew north to the Cedar Creek area, being harrassed by Confederate cavalry. At Toms Brook, Custer's force turned on the Confederates, virtually destroying the Southern cavalry and capturing its guns, wagons, and supplies.

In 1864, New Market was the scene of a well known battle in which 247 cadets, mostly teenagers, from the Virginia Military Institute fought with Confederate regulars to stop a superior Union force under General Segal. Ten cadets were killed, 47 were wounded, and their professor-leader was mortally wounded. Later, the New Market area was overrun by Sheridan's troops, preparatory to their attack on the James River and Kanawha Canal near Lynchburg.

Strasburg was originally known as "Pot Town". A Pennsylvanian named Samuel Bell set up a pottery in Strasburg in 1833 and founded an industry. There were soon six potteries in operation, the last of which ended operations in 1908. Front Royal was known as "Hell Town". Its reputation was one of fighting, drinking, and wenching and the frugal, religious Pennsylvania Dutch settlers of the North Fork Valley avoided it.

The North Fork Shenandoah has a number of tributaries that are tremendous white-water streams. Mill Creek joins the North Fork at Mount Jackson, Stony Creek joins at Edinburg, Cedar Creek joins below Strasburg, and Passage Creek joins near Buckland. Few other rivers have streams with the beauty and the rapids of these four creeks.

Smith Creek

INTRODUCTION

Smith Creek is one of the north-flowing tributaries of the North Fork Shenandoah. It does not have the scenery or the rapids like the other streams of the North Fork (such as Mill Creek, Stony Creek, Cedar Creek) or even the east-flowing section of the Upper North Fork. It is more like the North Fork in the Mount Jackson area, near where Smith Creek enters the North Fork Shenandoah, flat and meandering.

Section 1. Endless Caverns (Rte 793) to North Fork Shenandoah River

Gradient	Difficult	Distance	Time	Width	Scenery	Map
8	1	15.5*	6	20-30	Good	22

*plus 1.5 miles on the North Fork to Rte 698

Trip Description: The steam flows through one of the prettiest parts of the Shenandoah Valley, past neat farms, lush fields, and big barns. Since the banks are low and clear of vegetation in most parts, it is possible to see the scenery. It has a sand and gravel bottom for most of the trip and the faster portions are narrow and twisting. It has all of the usual small stream hazards, such as fences, low-water bridges, mill dams, cattle in the stream, cattle gates, trees blocking the stream. These minor obstacles require an ability to control the boat and a willingness to jump out of the boat without hesitation.

The careful observer will see the steel traps set along the bank, many of which will have already caught the unwary muskrat; this is a favorite stream for trappers who hike the banks and do not canoe. Warning: do not tamper with the traps; they may not lynch trap-raiders, but they may blast away with rock-salt.

The length of the trip can be varied by selecting any one of a number of bridges as putins or takeouts. The preferred takeout is Route 793; just upstream from the North Fork; the next takeout is 1.5 miles downstream on the North Fork at Mount Jackson (Route 698).

Hazards: Many low-water bridges, most of which are easy to lift over. Fences and cattle gates. Remains of old mill dam. Trees/debris in main passage of stream. Cows crossing the stream or just standing in it.

Water Conditions: Canoeable in winter and spring normally or during the early summer following an extended wet spell or very heavy rain.

GAUGE

None. If riffles at putin are canoeable, there is enough water.

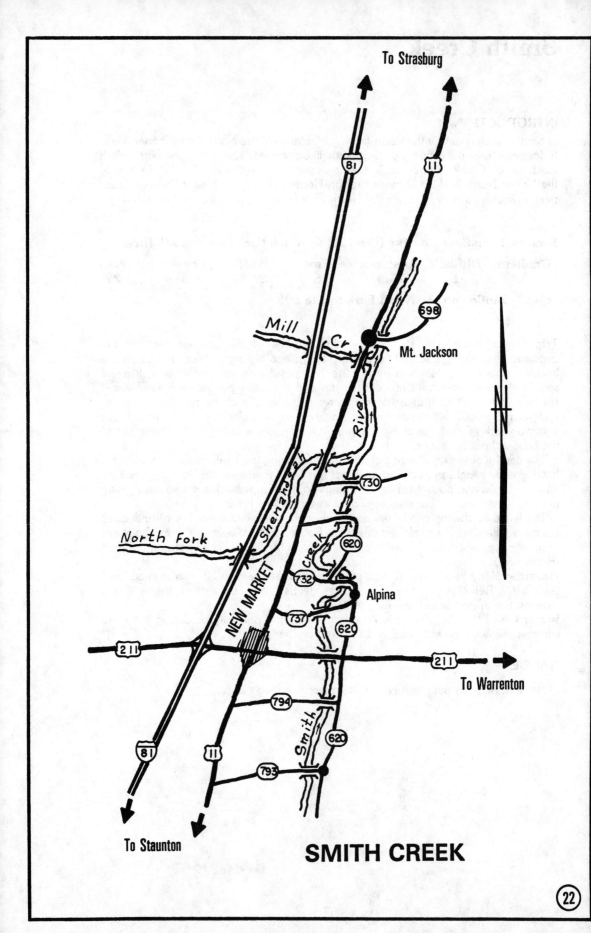

To Strasburg

81

11

Mill Cr

598

Mt. Jackson

River

Shenandoah

North Fork

730

Creek

620

732

Alpina

NEW MARKET

737

620

211

211

To Warrenton

794

81

11

Smith

620

793

To Staunton

SMITH CREEK

22

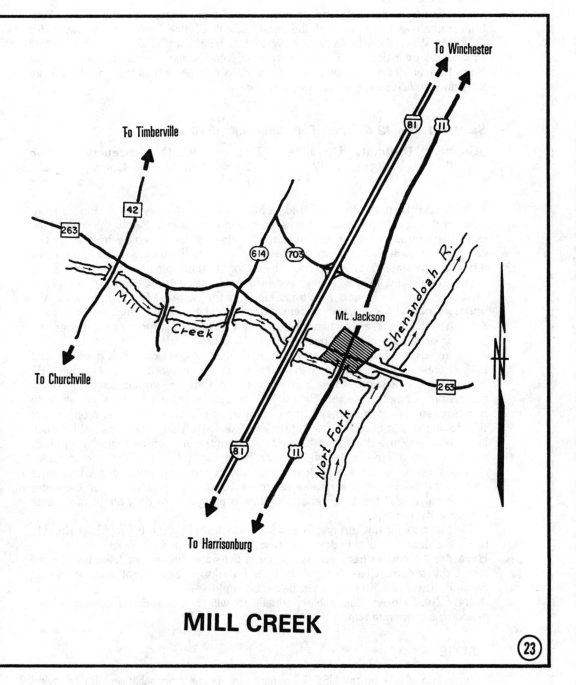

MILL CREEK

23

Mill Creek

INTRODUCTION

Mill Creek is probably the smallest canoeable tributary of the North Fork Shenandoah and it is one of the most difficult to find with enough water for canoeing. When there is water, however, this tiny stream is really a canoeists delight as it passes over dozens, if not hundreds, of small ledges before it drops into the North Fork at Mount Jackson over a horrendous falls. Action all the way. If you like tangling with wildcats, you will love this stream.

Section 1. Rte 42 to North Fork Shenandoah River

Gradient	Difficulty	Distance	Time	Width	Scenery	Map
30	1-35	7	2	20-50	Good	23

Trip Description: At Route 42 Bridge, Mill Creek is not as wide as a canoe is long, so point the bow of the canoe downstream upon unloading. Below the bridge, the creek tears through bushes and over small ledges at an extremely brisk rate. The current is so swift that downstream paddling is not really necessary for quite some distance. The water is clear and cool; the bottom is sand, gravel, and solid rock; the banks are low and lined with trees and bushes. Within the first two miles, however, there are two fences and two trees blocking the stream. One fence is on the upstream side of a low-water/underwater bridge where canoes must be lifted over. After the bridge, there are fewer obstacles and the terrain is more open. Farms line both banks and a number of bridges cross Mill Creek.

The rapids are fairly steady with frequent small ledges, long rock gardens, and swift chutes at gravel bars. On the outskirts of Mount Jackson, just above I-81 bridge, there is a strong Class 3 rapid that is a series of sloping ledges in quick succession. Complex. Great. Below I-81 bridge, a scouting trip is an absolute necessity, so approach the next drop cautiously. It is a man-made chute on the left side down the face of an 18' sloping rock wall (ledge). It is a tough one, with a rock in the middle of the chute, but the canoeist (or nut) will wash through the rapid, in all probability. It is not a risk-of-life rapid, but it damn sure is a risk-of-boat rapid. Rescue suggestions: have a rescue team ready in the short pool below, know the route to the nearest hospital, plan a return trip to pick-up the canoe when the water goes down. And if this is not enough, there is a seven-foot dam about 500 yards downstream; portage.

The takeouts for this trip are: Below I-81 bridge, before the big rapid; at Rte 11, below the dam; Rte 698 bridge on the North Fork Shenandoah River.

Hazards: Numerous trees across stream. Low-water bridge. At least two fences across the stream. Class 5 rapid at Mount Jackson. Seven-foot dam in Mount Jackson, just above Route 11, just below big rapid.

Water Conditions: Canoeable normally in winter and spring following a wet period or a moderate rain.

GAUGE

A reading of 5.0' on the USGS Cootes Store gauge is probably zero for canoeing this stream.

Cedar Creek

INTRODUCTION

Cedar Creek may be the prettiest steam in the Shenandoah watershed as well as the most popular white-water stream in Virginia. More canoeists have paddled on Cedar Creek than any other stream in the state. Cedar Creek begins as a tiny stream in the foothills of the Appalachian mountains, passes through mountain gaps and rolling foothills, and then drops into the North Fork Shenandoah River. The water is clear and unpolluted, the shuttles are easy, the scenery is outstanding, the rapids are frequent, and the hazards are few. Furthermore, the Cedar Creek area has a rich and fascinating history that cannot fail to capture the imagination.

Section 1: Star Tannery (Rte 55) to Stephens Fort (Rte 628)

Gradient	Difficulty	Distance	Time	Width	Scenery	Map
12	1-2₃	9.5	4	25-35	Good	25

Trip Description: From Star Tannery to Stephens Fort, Cedar Creek is a small stream moving swiftly over a bottom of sand and gravel. It starts at a shallow gravel bar, barely 20' wide, with cool, clear, sparkling water. In the first three miles, the left bank is fairly open country, mostly farmland, but the right bank has high bluffs. At a number of spots, the stream becomes very narrow and funnels directly against huge rock formations on the right, requiring quick, precise, left turns. Then Cedar Creek goes through a gap in North Mountain, and there are bluffs on both sides; and the rapids change from gravel bars to rock gardens and one rapid is at least 200 yards long (Class 2).

When Cedar Creek is almost out of the gap, the terrain becomes more open, and the first man-made rapid, a four-foot ledge, is reached. This is a Class 3 drop, and an honest Class 3 too. Just below this rapid, just far enough to get a swamped canoe ashore and dump it, there is another man-made rapid, a more gentle four-foot Class 3 drop. These ledges were created by dams built by property owners; paddlers should never look at these rapids in dead low water, as it is too horrifying to see what one has paddled over in complete innocence.

Below the two ledges, there are two low-water bridges in fast water that cannot be negotiated; the portages are easy. Then below the second bridge, there is a fascinating rock formation on the right bank; a dark rock with holes and passages throughout. At this point, the geography of the area changes completely, for the stream is in the rolling foothills. Just before the Stephens Fort takeout, there is a beautiful waterfall where a small stream enters on the left bank. This waterfall is just below a mill, it is within sight of the takeout, and canoeists can paddle under and behind the waterfall.

Hazards: Two low-water bridges.
Water Conditions: Canoeable normally in winter and spring following a wet period or moderate rain.

Section 2. Stephens Fort (Rte 628) to Rte 11 Wayside

Gradient	Difficulty	Distance	Time	Width	Scenery	Map
11	2	10.5	4	30-40	Very Good	25

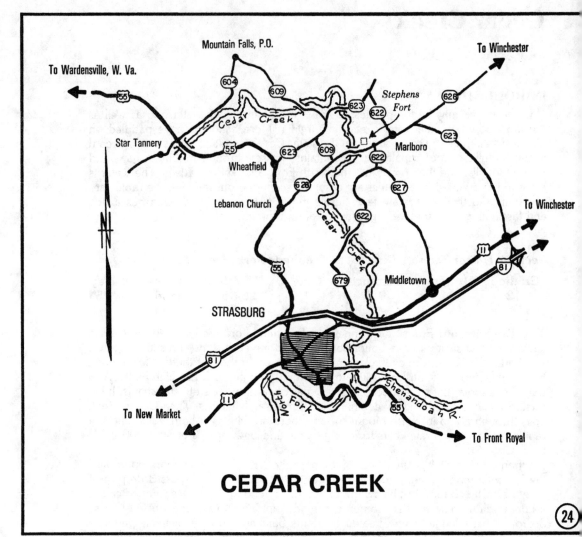

CEDAR CREEK

(24)

Trip Description: From Stephens Fort to Middletown (Rte 11 Wayside), Cedar Creek is a beautiful white-water stream for advanced beginners and intermediate paddlers. The trip begins just below a scenic waterfall and an old mill on the north bank, close to an old colonial fort. The riffles start immediately and the rapids are fairly closely spaced; in the upper part of this trip, the rapids are mostly rock gardens, gravel bars, narrow chutes, and a few small ledges. There are very scenic rock formations along the bank, there is an old graveyard with markers dating back to 1802, and there are fords that have been used since the 1700's. In the quiet stretches, the cool clear water still moves swiftly over a sand, gravel, and broken rock bottom, so it does not become boring.

There is a mid-point high bridge (Route 622) and there is a low-water bridge, which might be runnable, depending on water level. There are more signs of civilization below this bridge as there is a railroad bridge, the ruins of an old mill, and the overburden from a mining operation. The rapids tend to be stronger, with a nice set of small ledges just before a narrow chute being the best rapid on this section. There is a massive cave, named Panther Cave, on the left bank and there are the abutments of a bridge on the Valley Pike, the colonial road from Staunton to Winchester. The Route 11 Wayside is a most convenient takeout.

Hazards: Low-water bridge. One tree across stream, maybe.

Water Conditions: Canoeable in winter and spring normally or during the early summer following an extended wet spell or very heavy rain.

Section 3. Rte 11 Wayside to North Fork Shenandoah River

Gradient	Difficulty	Distance	Time	Width	Scenery	Map
13	13	3	1	30-40	Good	25

Trip Description: The section of Cedar Creek from Rte 11 Wayside to the North Fork Shenandoah is a short trip that very few padlers make more than once. It meanders a bit over riffles (small ledges) before dropping over a 4 foot sloping ledge (Class 3). This rapid is not too super, but the low-water bridge just below it increases the risk factor a lot and decreases the margin for error. The takeout can be the low-water bridge or alongside the road on the left as Cedar Creek approaches the North Fork.

The scenery on this section does not compare with the upper section, but it is still good. The banks are low so the terrain can be seen, the bottom is sand and gravel for the entire trip, and the current is fast.

Hazards: Low-water bridge

Water Conditions: Canoeable in winter and spring normally or during the early summer following an extended wet spell or very heavy rain.

GAUGE

A reading of 3.8' on the USGS Cootes Store gauge is zero for canoeing. There is a RC gauge on the Route 11 bridge.

HISTORY

Cedar Creek is located in the heart of the Shenandoah Valley and many events have occurred in its valley. It was settled in the 1700's by Germans from Pennsylvania who travelled from Sheperdstown to Winchester to Middletown. There was a low grade of iron ore in the area and a bountiful supply of wood for fueling the furnaces, so iron furnaces were built along Cedar Creek. Stephens Fort, a small five-sided fort with three floors, was built for the early colonists. By the 1800's, the Indians were gone from the valley and the area prospered. As a mark of progress, a whiskey distillery was built along Cedar Creek to keep the workers happy.

The Valley Pike crossed Cedar Creek just upstream of the Route 11 bridge; this road was built on an old Indian trail. Now Route 81 follows this historic route. It was along the Valley Pike on the north shore of Cedar Creek that the Civil War battle of Cedar Creek was fought in 1864. General Sheridan's forces were deployed along the creek with the right flank under command of General George C. Custer; Custer was camped at Stephens Fort. The Confederate forces under General Jubal Early, although outnumbered by 2 to 1, crossed the North Fork Shenandoah over two fords just below where Cedar Creek joined the North Fork. The Union forces were completely surprised by the attack and were almost routed, but General Sheridan rallied the Union troops and drove the Confederates back beyond Strasburg. The Union forces loss was 5665 men, the Confederate 2910; the Union forces, however, captured most of the Confederate artillery, baggage/forage weapons, ammunition, and ambulances. The Confederate defeat virtually ended the fighting in the Shenandoah Valley.

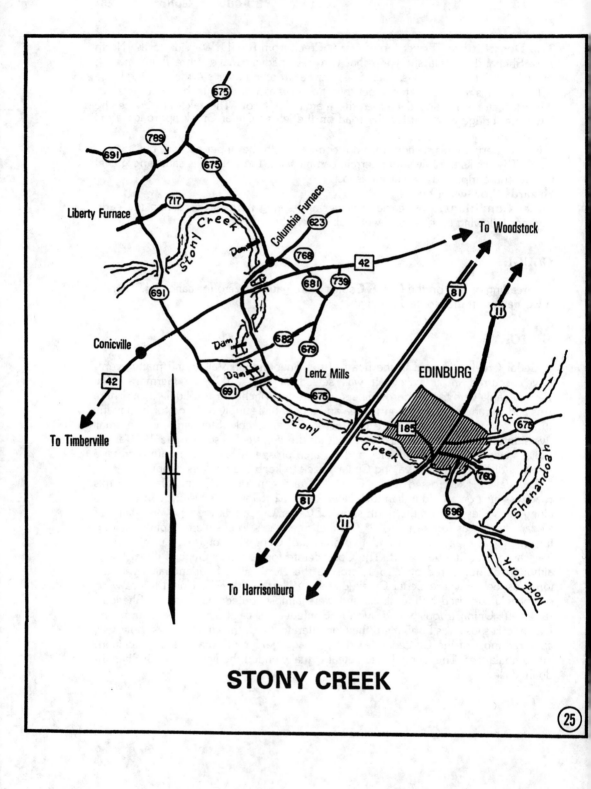

STONY CREEK

Stony Creek

INTRODUCTION

Stony Creek may be the most beautiful tributary in the entire Shenandoah watershed, even better than Cedar Creek. It is a very small stream from start to finish, a distance of about 16 miles, and it passes through one of the prettiest valleys in Virginia. It is unfortunate that the stream has dams and low-water bridges, but these disadvantages are insignificant when compared with its good features.

Section 1. Liberty Furnace (Rte 691) to North Fork Shenandoah River

Gradient	Difficulty	Distance	Time	Width	Scenery	Map
20	2-3	15.5	5	30-50	Very Good	24

Trip Description: Stony Creek is a very small stream near Liberty Furnace, with crystal clear water rushing over a rock and gravel bottom. It has long stretches of Class 2 rapids with very short pools between rapids and there should be at least six Class 3 rapids to add real spice to an already delightful fare. The rapids are comprised of small rock gardens, small ledges, and gravel bars beyond count. In many of the upper stretches, the right bank has high rock bluffs with magnificent formations; below Columbia Furnace, it is mostly rolling hills or open farmland.

There is a 3' dam about 1.5 miles above Columbia Furnace that is usually runnable with care/precautions. There is a low-water bridge and a high bridge (Rte 42) at Columbia Furnace, which is about the mid-point of the trip. Below Columbia Furnace and above Edinburg, there is a 5' to 6' dam; portage on the left. This dam is about 200 yards above Route 710. There is also a 3' dam just above Rte 710 that is runnable with due care and all precautions. And there are four low-water bridges below Columbia Furnace, all in fairly swift water.

The preferred takeout is Route 760 bridge in Edinburg, about 50 yards from the North Fork Shenandoah. Other takeouts are alongside Route 675 and Route 185 west of Edinburg and at the Route 11 and Route 698 bridges at Edinburg.

Hazards: Two three-foot dams that are usually runnable. One five-foot dam that is not runnable; portage. Five low-water bridges.

Water Conditions: Canoeable normally in winter and spring following a wet period.

HISTORY

The Stony Creek area has a history that includes old iron furnaces (Liberty Furnace, Columbia Furnace); old mills (Lantz Mills and one near the putin that is still operational); battles with Indians; and volunteers for the 1st Virginia Brigade. Shenandoah County provided the "Independent Greys", "Page Greys", "Mount Jackson Rifles", and "Emerald Guards" to the 33rd Regiment of the "Stonewall Brigade" (1st Virginia Brigade CSA).

Shenandoah county was originally named Dunmore County by Lord Dunmore, royal governor of Virginia. After five years of problems with the inhabitants of the county, Lord Dunmore became so exasperated that he decided the county did not deserve his name. So it was renamed Shenandoah County. Three cheers for the valley people.

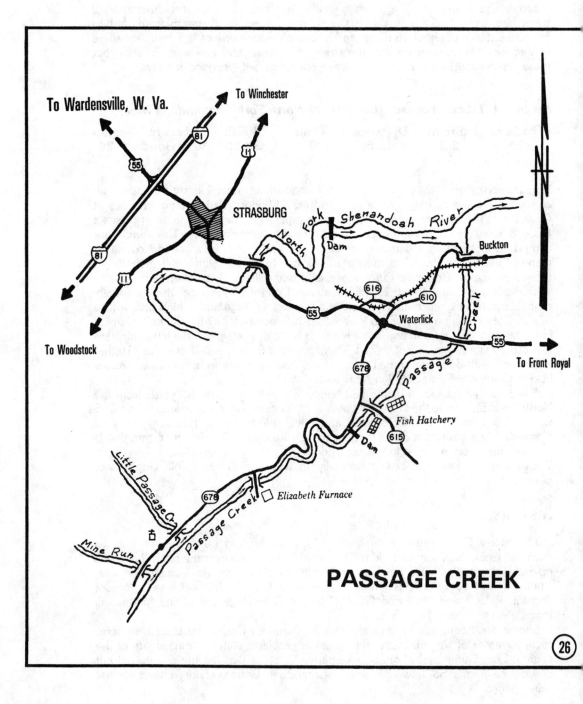

To Wardensville, W. Va.

To Winchester

STRASBURG

North Fork Shenandoah River

Dam

Buckton

To Woodstock

Waterlick

To Front Royal

Fish Hatchery

Dam

Little Passage Cr.

Elizabeth Furnace

Mine Run

Passage Creek

Passage Creek

PASSAGE CREEK

26

Passage Creek

INTRODUCTION

Passage Creek drains a valley that is a geological phenomena. The Massanutten Mountains begin near Elkton and Harrisonburg and range north to the Strasburg-Front Royal area; it divides the upper Shenandoah Valley and separates the North Fork and the South Fork of the Shenandoah. As it reaches its northern extremity, the Massanutten Mountain divides and forms a most secluded valley. Passage Creek drains this valley. The valley was called Powell's Fort in colonial days; today it is called Fort Valley.

Section 1. Little Passage Creek to Elizabeth Furnace

Gradient	Difficulty	Distance	Time	Width	Scenery	Map
12	1-2	5	2	20-30	Very Good	26

Trip Description: Passage Creek is a small meandering stream in the upper reaches of the valley, moving swiftly over sand and gravel bars through some of the most beautiful farmland in Virginia. It does not have sufficient gradient for major rapids, and its meandering means that it is, at best, a pleasant, low tension trip through a wide valley. The water is clean and unpolluted. The rapids are mostly gravel bars, the banks are low, and the terrain is flat. The mountain range on each side of the narrow valley give it a character of its own. There is at least one low-water bridge and there are a number of barbed/woven fences.
Hazards: Barbed/woven wire fences. Low-water bridge.
Water Conditions: Canoeable normally in winter and spring following a wet period or a moderate rain.

Section 2. Elizabeth Furnace to Waterlick (Rte 55)

Gradient	Difficulty	Distance	Time	Width	Scenery	Map
35	2-4	6	1.5	25-35	Very Good	26

Trip Description: When Passage Creek leaves the wide valley area and arrives at the Elizabeth Furnace recreation area, the valley begins to close in on the stream and it stops its meandering. And Passage Creek becomes a little terror that delights the heart of the white-water canoeist. For the benefit of the weak hearted and the inexperienced paddlers, there are a number of points to takeout at picnic areas, camping spots, or old fords prior to entering the gorge section.

Starting from the picnic area, Passage Creek becomes a very fast steam over Class 1 and 2 gravel bars, small ledges, and rock gardens for about 1.5 miles. In this area, it is away from the road which is high on the left (west) bank. When the stream comes back to the road, the rapids really begin with an honest Class 3 that has about three separate drops of 1-2 feet each with maneuvering required. These rapids are typical of those rapids that will be encountered in the next two miles above the fish hatchery. The next rapid is a difficult S or Z turn, followed by small ledges. When the river moves away from the road again, and the right bank is a sheer rock cliff, Out-of-Sight Rapid is next; a Class 4 with a complicated entry.

Below Out-of-Sight Rapid is a Class 3 followed by a narrow, fast difficult passage to the left of an island; this passage is close to the road on the left bank. Then a good Class 3 rapid alongside a high rock wall, a few riffles, and then the fish hatchery dam. Let down on the left side of the dam; canoeists have done much damage to the right side and the hatchery personnel prohibit portaging on the right bank. Try to stay on the dam itself close to the left bank.

Below the dam, the creek resumes its dash to the North Fork Shenandoah, past steady, long Class 2 rapids. It really becomes interesting and dangerous below the hatchery, where there are trees growing helter-skelter over an ill-defined stream bed. A slalom with immovable gates. Plan for at least one carry around a downed tree, a number of scratches on body and boat, and a couple of heart-stopping intricate passages.

The normal takeout is Route 55 bridge at Waterlick but there is still 1.5 miles of white-water action all the way to the low-water bridge at Buckton; this bridge is just below a high railroad bridge. Do **not** miss your eddy turn above the low-water bridge. An easy takeout if you get to takeout, that is.

Hazards: Seven foot dam above fish hatchery. Tree blocking the stream below the fish hatchery.

Water Conditions: Canoeable in winter and spring normally or during the early summer following an extended wet spell or very heavy rain.

GAUGE

A reading of 5.0' on the USGS Remington gauge or 3.5' on the USGS Cootes Store gauge is zero for canoeing. There is a RC gauge on the Route 55 bridge.

HISTORY

Many stories have been told about Fort Valley and the mountains that surround it. General Daniel Morgan is said to have retreated into the valley during the Revolutionary War; Morgan was from Berryville and knew of the valley, so it is a reasonable tale. George Washington considered retreating into Fort Valley as a final stronghold if everything went bad; Washington had surveyed this area for Lord Fairfax, so he had first hand knowledge of the valley. In colonial days, a settler named Powell established the valley as his fort and defended it from the Indians who used the valley of North Fork Shenandoah for their hunting and war parties. Another story tells that a Confederate general had planned to refuse surrendering, to fortify the valley, and to continue fighting the Union forces. In the Civil War, Confederate officers overlooked the Union forces deployed along Cedar Creek and planned their attack against vastly superior (numerically) Union troops under Sheridan. The progress of the battle was observed and controlled from observation points on Signal Knob, the high point west of Passage Creek and south of Route 55; a trail leads up to this point from Fort Valley.

South Fork Shenandoah River

INTRODUCTION

The South Fork of the Shenandoah River flows northward from the confluence of the South River, North River, and Middle River at Port Republic to meet the North Fork of the Shenandoah River at Front Royal to form the main Shenandoah River. It meanders through a narrow valley between the Blue Ridge Mountains and the Massanutten Mountains, forming at least twenty-seven bends that resemble big "S's" Its valley is less populous than the valley of the North Fork, but the river is bigger, clearer, and swifter. There are few rivers that offer over a hundred miles of canoeable waters through a land of history and romance.

Section 1. Port Republic (Rte 865) to Island Ford (Rte 649)

Gradient	Difficulty	Distance	Time	Width	Scenery	Map
5.5	1-2	10.5	4	40-60	Good	27

Trip Description: Starting at Port Republic, the preferred putin is on the North River, just above its confluence with the South River. At this point the river is fairly wide and flows over a bed of sand, gravel, cobble, and rocks; the water is fairly clear because of the water from the Middle river and North River. About one mile below Port Republic is Great Island, the biggest island on the South Fork; the right passage is the best. While passing around the island, there is a passage to the left of another, smaller island. Below Great Island, the backwater for the Lynnwood Dam begins; this eight-foot dam cannot be run. Portage on the left or run the mill race on the right -- after scouting to make sure it is clear of trees and debris; there are two good drops in this mill race.

The section from Lynnwood to Island Ford is much similar to the upstream section, with one exception. There is the remains of the Harrisonburg Power Plant dam about five miles below Lynnwood. This washed out dam is a jumble of concrete, steel, and debris that presents a definite risk-of-life situation. Do not try it unless your will is already filed and you have had last rites -- or you have exceptionally poor judgment. Other than this hazard, the river only has occasional riffles and small ledges to break up the flat stretches.

Hazards: Remains of power dam. Eight-foot dam at Lynnwood.

Water Conditions: Canoeable in winter, spring, and early summer, except following periods of little precipitation. Canoeable after a heavy rain in the summer and fall.

Section 2. Island Ford (Rte 649) to Elkton (Rte 33)

Gradient	Difficulty	Distance	Time	Width	Scenery	Map
5.0	1-2	7.0	3	45-60	Good	27

Trip Description: From Island Ford to Elkton, the river enters a scenic portion of the valley as the southern extremity of the Massanutten Mountains are approached. The gradient is only 5 fpm, so there are not many rapids. It is a scenic trip, however, through beautiful farmlands with mountains to the east and to the west. The water is clear and the bottom is sand and gravel.

About a mile below Island Ford, there is a ledge of about three feet, followed by riffles. About one-quarter mile below Route 33, there is a nice rapid formed by the

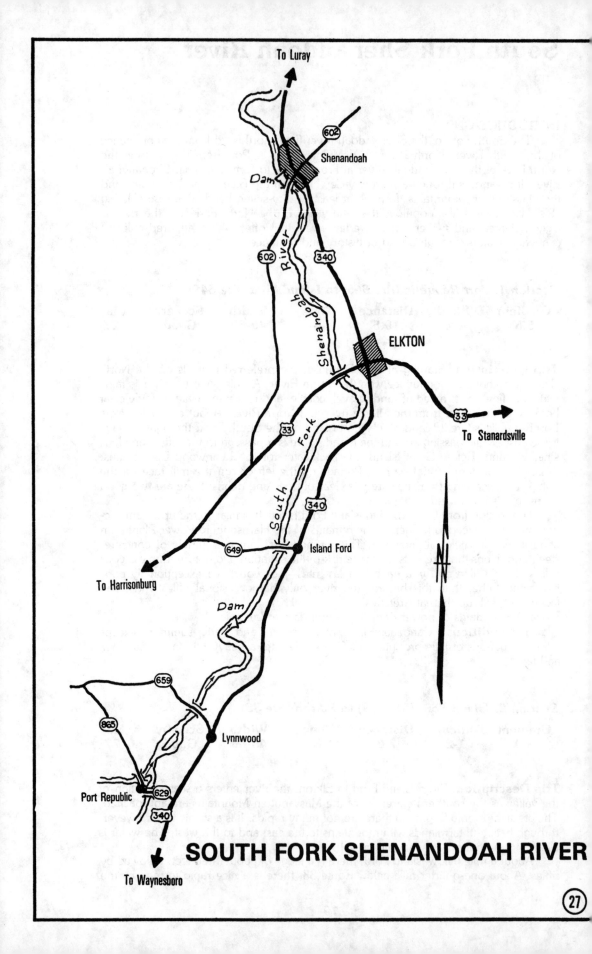

To Luray

602

Shenandoah

Dam

602

340

Shenandoah River

ELKTON

33

To Stanardsville

South Fork

340

649

Island Ford

N

To Harrisonburg

Dam

659

865

Lynnwood

629

Port Republic

340

SOUTH FORK SHENANDOAH RIVER

To Waynesboro

27

remains of an old four-foot dam; run in the center. Since much of the gradient in this section is absorbed in these two rapids, the rest of this section has only a moderate current. The takeout is the Virginia Game Commission Landing on the right bank.
Hazards: None.
Water Conditions: Canoeable in winter, spring, and early summer, except following periods of little precipitation. Canoeable after a heavy rain in the summer and fall.

Section 3. Elkton (Rte 33) to Shenandoah (Rte 602)

Gradient	Difficulty	Distance	Time	Width	Scenery	Map
6.5	1-2	7.0	3	50-70	Good	27

Trip Description: The trip from Elkton to Shenandoah is a leisurely trip through a pleasant part of the valley. The river is fairly wide. The current is not too fast, and there are not too many rapids. About two miles below Elkton there are some ledges, a few ledges in the next two miles downstream; the dam at the putin is a nice rapid. There is a ten-foot dam at Shenandoah that has a two mile backwater; portage on the right to takeout at the parking area below the dam on the right or takeout about 400 yards above Shenandoah on an unpaved road (Route 602) on the right.

This section of the South Fork has gravel bar rapids and small ledges; the banks are about 4' to 5' high; the Blue Ridge mountains are fairly close to the river at the takeout; and the river flows close to both the Massanutten Mountains on the left and the Blue Ridge Mountains on the right going downstream.
Hazards: None.
Water Conditions: Canoeable in winter, spring, and early summer, except following periods of little precipitation. Canoeable after a heavy rain in the summer and fall.

Section 4. Shenandoah (Rte 602) to Newport (Rte 340 at Folz Mill)

Gradient	Difficulty	Distance	Time	Width	Scenery	Map
7.0	1-2	14.5	6	60-80	Good	28

Trip Description: From Shenandoah to Newport (Foltz Mill) is a fairly long trip (14.5 miles) that requires a lot of paddling for a one-day trip. The gradient is much similar to the sections upstream, so there is only a moderate amount of current. The rapids are the gravel bar type, for the most part, although a number of little ledges appear in low water. There is a good ledge about 2 miles below Shenandoah, a set of ledges just before reaching Route 340 bridge at Grove Hill, and there is a good set of ledges just below Grove Hill. There is a Virginia Game Commission landing on the right on Route 650 for an easy takeout.

From Grove Hill to Newport is a pretty dull trip. There are only a few riffles of the gravel bar type before reaching the backwater of the Massanutten power dam. This is a high dam (16 feet) that backs up water for about 2.5 miles, one of the longest, flattest stretches on the South Fork. The best thing that can be said for this stretch is that there are some memorable rock cliffs and bluffs in the backwater. Portage the dam on the right. The takeout is at Kite's Store; a private campground that charges a very modest fee to putin or takeout.

The South Fork in this section is much similar to the section just upstream in many respects. It alternates between the Massanutten Mountains on the left and the Blue Ridge on the right as it meanders back and forth.
Hazards: Sixteen-foot dam one mile upstream from Newport.
Water Conditions: Canoeable in winter, spring, and early summer, except follow-

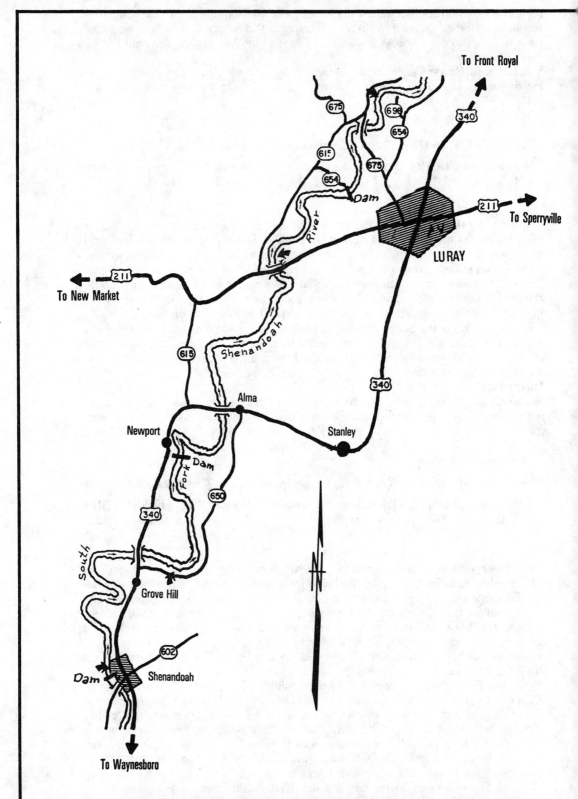

SOUTH FORK SHENANDOAH RIVER

28

ing periods of little precipitation. Canoeable after a heavy rain in the summer and fall.

Section 5. Newport to Luray (Rte 211)

Gradient	Difficulty	Distance	Time	Width	Scenery	Map
8	1-2₃	9.0	3.5	60-80	Very Good	28

Trip Description: The trip from Newport to White House Landing just west of Luray, under Route 211 bridge, is probably the prettiest section of the South Fork. The gradient (8 fpm) is the steepest of any section of the South Fork, it has the best current, and the rapids are more frequent. The rock formations along the bank are memorable, the water is clear and moves fast, and the farms along the bank are well-tended. The trip starts with a nice rapid at the remains of the Old Foltz Mill dam; stay away from the left, where there are some remains of old steel gears and axles. In the first three miles, above Rte 340 bridge, there are some nice ledges that create long rapids that require manuevering. There are small ledges and riffles most of the way to Route 211, so it is not an unpleasant trip.

There is a lot to see and learn about this area. There is one named cave and a number of smaller, unnamed caves; there is the site of a colonial fort built by a family during the Indian days; there are the remains of old dams and old mills -- which are hard to recognize. The trip can be extended about a mile to a takeout on an unpaved road on the right; this section has the remains of an old dam and an old mill. The dam itself is easily runnable or the mill race on the far right is runnable; make sure it is clear of trees and debris.

Hazards: Left side of old dam rapid at putin.

Water Conditions: Canoeable in winter, spring, and early summer, except following periods of little precipitation. Canoeable after a heavy rain in the summer and fall.

Section 6. White House Landing (Rte 211) to Bixler's Bridge (Rte 675)

Gradient	Difficulty	Distance	Time	Width	Scenery	Map
5.5	1	8	4.5	60-100	Fair	28, 29

Trip Description: The trip from White House Landing to Bixler's Bridge is not really a canoeing stream. The dam and mill race about one mile below Route 211 bridge is the best rapid on the section; below there is a three to four mile backwater from the 20-foot dam just west of Luray. This may be the longest, flattest stretch of the South Fork. The portage on the left bank is not easy and there are only a few riffles between the dam and Bixler's Bridge, so a takeout on the left bank at the Massanutten Public Landing on Route 615 is preferred. There is a reconstructed colonial fort on the left bank below the dam, and the area immediately above the dam is called Egypt Bend.

Hazards: Twenty-foot dam. Low-water bridge at takeout.

Water Conditions: Canoeable most of the year except following a long dry spell. Canoeable after a moderate rain in the summer.

Section 7. Bixler's Bridge (Rte 675) to Good's Mill (Rte 684)

Gradient	Difficulty	Distance	Time	Width	Scenery	Map
4.0	1-2	11.5	5	70-90	Good	29

Trip Description: From Bixler's Bridge, a low-water bridge on Route 675 with a public landing, to Goods Mill is a fairly long trip -- not in distance, but in time. But it is probably one of the prettier canoeing sections on the South Fork, particularly the last four miles. The trip starts with small riffles over gravel bars, through open farmland; the river is fairly narrow at the putin, but it widens quite a bit downstream. If one is alert, there is the underwater bridge (which appears as just another small ledge), a restored colonial fort, a number of caves along the river banks, and an overhead cable with pulley on this section above Bealers Ferry. While there are occasional small ledges in this section, there are not many rapids, and the current is fairly slow; the gradient is only about 4 fpm.

At Bealers Ferry, where Route 661 comes to the river, there is a nice set of riffles; then there are continuous ledges (Goods Falls) for one mile above Goods Mill; they are small ledges that require a lot of maneuvering and an ability to read water. The takeout at Good's Mill is on private property and there is a fee; so either pay up or takeout at Bealers Ferry (there is no fee there) or continue downstream at least another four or five miles.

Hazards: None.

Water Conditions: Canoeable most of the year except following a long dry spell. Canoeable after a moderate rain in the summer.

Section 8. Good's Mill (Rte 684) to Burners Ford (Rte 664)

Gradient	Difficulty	Distance	Time	Width	Scenery	Map
4.5	1-2	9	4	80-100	Very Good	29

Trip Description: The trip from Good's Mill to Burners Ford, where Route 664 ends at the river, is probably the best section of the middle South Fork. There is just one way to describe the farmland, the riffles, the islands, the wildlife, the rock cliffs, the fish dams, the clear water -- beautiful. For many years, the snowy egrets and grey herons were always in the shallow riffles during the summer. The big pool and high rock cliff at Compton is a distinctive feature and the many enchanting spots for a lunchstop make it even more pleasant.

The rapids in this section are the ledge type, small ledges that extend across the river, requiring a lot of maneuvering and a sharp eye for reading water. The two-foot ledge at the starting point is the best ledge, but the biggest rapid (Class 2) is at Compton, recognized by the high bluff and the railroad track high above the river. At least one rapid is the remains of an old Indian fish dam, recognized by the V-shaped dam that points downstream. The takeout at Burners Ford which is not easy to recognize, is at the end of a long set of little ledges, just beyond a large willow tree on the right bank. This trip can be shortened by taking out above Compton on Route 663, but you will miss some of the best of the South Fork.

Hazards: None.

Water Conditions: Canoeable most of the year except following a long dry spell. Canoeable after a moderate rain in the summer.

Section 9. Burners Ford (Rte 664) to Bentonville (Rte 613)

Gradient	Difficulty	Distance	Time	Width	Scenery	Map
7.0	1-2	7.0	3	100-120	Good	29

Trip Description: From Burners Ford to Bentonville Bridge, a low-water bridge with access to the river, is the last of the best of the South Fork. The river moves fairly swift (compared to other sections) as the gradient increases. There is one two-foot ledge about two miles downstream from Burners Ford and there is at least one Indian fish dam. The Hazard Mill Recreation area is on the left bank about four miles

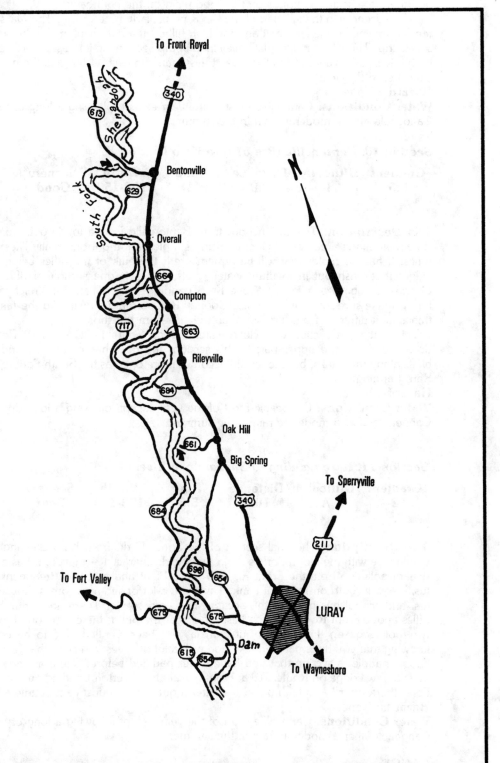

To Front Royal

340

613

Shenandoah

Bentonville

629

South Fork

Overall

664

Compton

717

663

Rileyville

684

Oak Hill

561

Big Spring

To Sperryville

340

684

211

To Fort Valley

699

654

675

675

LURAY

Dam

615

654

To Waynesboro

N

SOUTH FORK SHENANDOAH RIVER

29

downstream, there are archeological excavations at the sites of old Indian villages, and there are scattered ponds on the flood plain on the right bank.

The scenery in the last part of the trip is particularly noteworthy. The Massanutten Mountains on the left bank and the high hill on the right bank make this a most scenic trip. There is very little flat valley land in this section, so it is a secluded section of the river. It has a lot of small ledges, it has clean and clear water, and there is very little litter in the area.

Hazards: None.

Water Conditions: Canoeable most of the year except following a long dry spell. Canoeable after a moderate rain in the summer.

Section 10. Bentonville (Rte 613) to Karo Landing

Gradient	Difficulty	Distance	Time	Width	Scenery	Map
5.5	1	9.0	4	100-150	Good	30

Trip Description: The South Fork from Bentonville Bridge to Karo Landing, a state maintained area beside Gooney Run, is a pleasant trip if one really likes small riffles. It has no rapids that will be remembered, the bulk of the riffles being small ledges that wash out in medium water levels. There is one section of riffles that extends for about a mile just above Karo Landing, with a flat, flat stretch at the finish. Make sure that you recognize Gooney Run so that you will find the takeout; things look different from the river than they do from the shore.

This is the last section with clean water on the South Fork, as Front Royal is downstream. In the upper part of this section, the river has mountains and high bluffs along the banks, but the terrain becomes more open as the South Fork reaches Karo Landing.

Hazards: None.

Water Conditions: Canoeable most of the year except following a long dry spell. Canoeable after a moderate rain in the summer.

Section 11. Karo Landing to Shenandoah River

Gradient	Difficulty	Distance	Time	Width	Scenery	Map
2	A	10.5	5.5	120-150	Poor	30

Trip Description: The final section of the South Fork, from Karo Landing to its confluence with the North Fork is a trip that builds character -- maybe. It has a great deal of pollution from the Front Royal Viscose Plant and a sewage treatment plant just below it, both on the right bank. There are a lot of summer homes, house trailers, and school bus hulks in this section. Not very scenic. There are a number of riffles above Front Royal, but the best rapid is at the putin; there is reported to be a two-foot ledge on this section, but that has not been verified. Try to be content knowing that you have paddled a section with a lot of caves, a section that few other people paddle, a section that you have never paddled before. There are two takeouts: a new bridge on Route 619 at Front Royal and Riverton Landing on the North Fork: the former has a high bank, the latter a quarter-mile upstream paddle.

Hazards: None.

Water Conditions: Canoeable most of the year except following a long dry spell. Canoeable after a moderate rain in the summer.

GAUGE

A reading of 1.2' to 1.3' on the USGS Front Royal gauge is zero for canoeing on all sections. There are RC gauges on Rte 211 bridge near Luray and Rte 340 bridge near Alma.

86

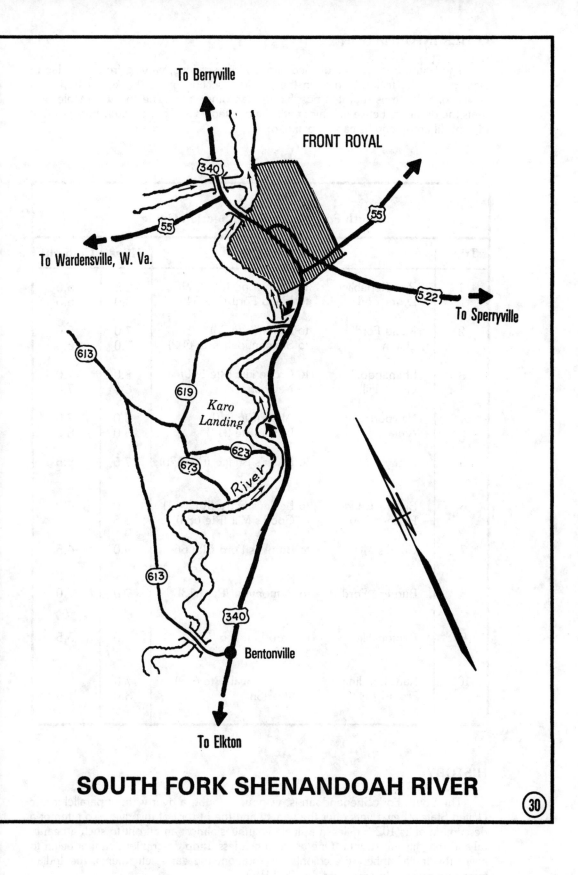

To Berryville

FRONT ROYAL

340

55

To Wardensville, W. Va.

55

522

To Sperryville

613

619

Karo Landing

623

673

River

613

340

Bentonville

To Elkton

SOUTH FORK SHENANDOAH RIVER

30

OTHER INFORMATION

The South Fork can be divided into a variety of trips, varying from one day to eight days. The technical data in the previous section broke the South Fork into eleven one-day trips, but it is possible to plan other trips. The following table presents the distances between major putins and takeouts along the South Fork, so that trips of different lengths can be planned.

Trip #	Section		Miles	Gradient
1	Port Republic	to Lynnwood (Rte 659)	2.5	5.5
	Lynnwood	to Island Ford (Rte 649)	8.0	5.5
2	Island Ford	to Elkton (Rte 33)	7.0	5.0
	Elkton	to Shenandoah (Rte 602)	7.0	6.5
3	Shenandoah	to Grove Hill (Rte 340)	8.0	7.0
	Grove Hill	to Newport	6.5	7.0
4	Newport	to Alma (Rte 340)	3.0	8.0
	Alma	to Luray (Rte 211)	6.0	8.0
5	Luray	to Bixler's Bridge (Rte 675)	7.5	5.5*
6	Bixler's Bridge	to Bealer's Ferry (Rte 661)	8.0	4.0
	Bealer's Ferry	to Good's Mill (Rte 684)	3.5	6.0
7	Good's Mill	to Burner's Ford (Rte 664)	9.0	4.5
8	Burner's Ford	to Bentonville (Rte 613)	7.0	7.0
9	Bentonville	to Karo Landing	9.0	5.5
10	Karo Landing	to Front Royal (Rte 619)	7.0	2.0
	Front Royal	to Riverton	3.0	1.5

Table 3
South Fork Shenandoah Section Guide

HISTORY

The South Fork Shenandoah is, without a doubt, a river without parallel in the United States. Few rivers offer the variety and the history of this river. To attempt a description of its 102.5 miles in a single volume is almost an affront to such a beautiful and magnificent stream. One book, much less a trip description, cannot begin to cover the Indian tribes, the colonial exploration, the early settlements, the Indian wars, the early industries, and the Civil War.

The exploration of the South Fork of the Shenandoah began with John Lederer, who was followed by Spotswood and other adventurers. It is a narrower valley than the North Fork and it is more susceptible to flooding, due to the lower elevation of the land and the larger watershed, so the early settlers did not colonize the South Fork Valley as much as the North Fork. The North Fork had the Valley Pike, from Strasburg to Lexington, built over an old Indian trail. The South Fork did not have a valley that afforded a good road without frequent fords and/or bridges. People tended to build towns at the lower end, Front Royal, and the upper end, Waynesboro; on the North Fork, towns were built at regular intervals and the population was always greater in that valley.

The South Fork valley was settled during the later 1600's and it had its share of colonial forts, Indian massacres, mills and factories, iron furnaces and mines, farms and industries, caves and archaelogical sites, fords and ferries. River navigation was a very important means of transporting farm products, flour, pig iron, lime, and ores to the tidewater area by way of Harpers Ferry and the Potomac River; the river was the principal means of travel in the South Fork valley until the arrival of the railroads. "The Shenandoah River: An Illustrated Trip Log", by Matacia and Cecil describes the mills, furnaces, industries, mines, forts, and settlements in detail; this guidebook is filled with the history and folklore of the South Fork valley and the river.

During the Civil War, a bloody battle was fought at Port Republic/Cross Keys in 1862, one of the many battles during Jackson's valley campaign. General Freemont (USA) had marched south through the North Fork valley and General Shields marched south through the South Fork valley. Stonewall Jackson's forces first engaged Freemont's forces at Cross Keys, just northwest of Port Republic; the Confederates held Freemont's forces and kept him from joining the other Union column by burning the bridges across the South Fork. The fiercest battle was fought on the east bank at Port Republic, with both forces taking heavy casualties; over ten percent of each force were killed, wounded or captured, a very heavy loss for a one-day battle.

During Jackson's Valley Campaign, a Union detachment of over 1,000 men was forced to withdraw from Front Royal and was overrun and captured by the Confederate forces. In that battle, the 1st Maryland Regiment (CSA) engaged the 1st Maryland Regiment (USA) at Riverton and captured the Union Force. A Union attack three weeks later drove the Confederates from Front Royal and captured a large number of troops.

One of the most depressing chapters in the Civil War was the hanging of captured prisoners by General Sheridan (USA) and Colonel Mosby (CSA). Mosby's force was such a thorn in the side of the Union forces that the headstrong Sheridan ordered the hanging of six Confederates captured near Front Royal; the hanging was conducted in the presence of General Custer, who had a sign attached to the swinging bodies that read, "This shall be the fate of all of Mosby's men." Some weeks later, 26 of Custer's troopers were captured, twenty-six slips of paper were placed in a hat, six troopers drew their death notice. Battle-hardened veterans wept openly as they watched the troopers pay the price for policies of generals. Fortunately, the hanging stopped when the score was even, but not in time for twelve good men.

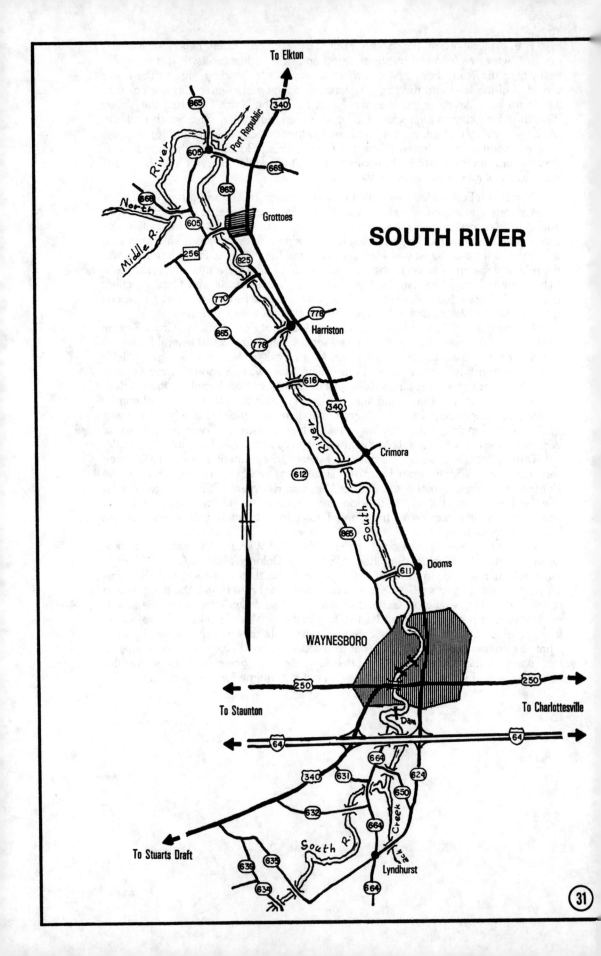

SOUTH RIVER

To Elkton

865 · 340 · Port Republic · 669 · 605

North River · 668 · 605 · 865 · Grottoes

Middle R. · 256 · 825

770 · 778 · Harriston · 865 · 778

616 · 340

River · Crimora

612 · South · 865

611 · Dooms

WAYNESBORO

250 · 250

To Staunton · Dam · To Charlottesville

64 · 64

340 · 631 · 664 · 624

532 · 650

664 · Creek

To Stuarts Draft · South R. · Lyndhurst

639 · 635 · 664

635

South River

INTRODUCTION

The South River is one of the three major tributaries of the South Fork of the Shenandoah River. It has its headwaters in the vicinity of Lynhurst where three small streams converge, but its principal tributary is Back Creek which joins it just below Lynhurst. Back Creek begins in the Blue Ridge Mountains in the George Washington National Forest, above Sherando and contributes most of the water in the South River. The South River then flows north for about 34 miles to Port Republic to join the Middle River and North River to form the South Fork.

Section 1. Lynhurst (Rte 632) to Dooms (Rte 611)

Gradient	Difficulty	Distance	Time	Width	Scenery	Map
10	1-2-3	12	6	20-40	Poor	31

Trip Description: The South River from Lynhurst to Dooms is basically three different sections: a good white-water section through a scenic valley; a section with dams and pollution in a small city; and a flat, meandering stream with high banks. The upper (white-water) section offers good canoeing, the middle (urban) section offers hazards, and the last (flat-water) section offers tedium. While variety is the spice of life, this type/degree of diversity does little to delight the heart of a canoeist.

Between Lynhurst and Waynesboro, the river is a small, fast flowing stream over a bed of gravel and sand. The current is moderate in most parts and moves at a uniform rate, as the gradient of 10 feet/mile is fairly steady. The first two miles has light riffles followed by small ledges. The final four miles to Waynesboro has more white-water, small ledges, rock gardens, gravel bars, small chutes, fast turns. The terrain is mostly open farmland and the banks are low; it is difficult, however, to see past the trees/bushes/briars on the banks. There are usually a number of trees blocking the stream. The takeout at Waynesboro is the city park on the left bank. If continuing, portage around the right side of a seven-foot dam about ½ mile downstream.

The section from the Waynesboro City Park to Dooms is not recommended, but if canoed, it should be done with caution and scouting and portaging. The river has a weir at the start of the industrial area that has a strong and dangerous hydraulic. Two dams, one of which is 12 feet high, add to the hazards. The scenery, which includes factories, abandoned mills, warehouses, and storage areas, is not worth the trip. The current varies from fast to none, the water quality from good to terrible, the banks from low to high.

Below Waynesboro, there is no convenient takeout before Dooms. This section has high banks, polluted water, flat water, and urbanization. The bottom is sand and gravel; the riffles are the gravel bar or rock garden variety. The current is slow. There is very little to say good about this part of the South River.

Hazards: Three dams in Waynesboro. One weir with hydraulic in Waynesboro. Trees/fences across stream in upper part.

Water Conditions: Canoeable normally in winter and spring following a wet period or a moderate rain.

Section 2. Dooms (Rte 611) to Harriston (Rte 778)

Gradient	Difficulty	Distance	Time	Width	Scenery	Map
9	1-2	13	4.5	50-60	Good	31

91

Trip Description: The South River from Dooms to Harriston looks as if it should be a white-water stream. It flows through a narrow valley between the Blue Ridge Mountains on the east (right) bank and high hills on the left (west) bank. There are few rapids, however, as the river merely meanders over a very gradual gradient through a fairly flat valley. It flows over a sand bottom with a few gravel bar or rock garden rapids/riffles; the stronger rapids are the remains of old mill dams. One old dam, just below Crimora, fed the mill whose canal and concrete work can be seen on the left bank.

The water is of poor quality in this area because of the industrial pollution in Waynesboro, the current is very slow, and the flat stretches seem very long. The best riffles are near Harriston. The scenery is fair, nothing exceptional, and the high banks (6' to 8') block the view from the stream.

Hazards: A couple of trees blocking the main passages.

Water Conditions: Canoeable in winter and spring normally or during the early summer following an extended wet spell or very heavy rain.

Section 3. Harriston (Rte 773) to Port Republic (Rte 865)

Gradient	Difficulty	Distance	Time	Width	Scenery	Map
7.5	1-2₃	8	3.5	50-70	Good	31

Trip Description: The industrial pollution has cleared up a great deal (Remember: The Solution to Pollution Is Dilution -- U.S. Army Corps of Engineers) by the time the South River reaches Harriston. So from Harriston to Port Republic, the water is much clearer and the trip is more pleasant. It flows over a bed of sand and gravel, between high banks that are tree-lined for most of the distance. The riffles/rapids are the small rock garden and gravel bar type for the most part. There are a few small ledges and one Class 3 rock garden about 200 yards above Route 256 near Grottoes. Watch this rapid which dashes between VW size rocks and large trees. Below Grottoes, there are many good riffles.

The scenery on the left bank is fairly good; there are rock formations and high bluffs in many stretches. At Harriston and Grottoes, there are a number of industries, but they do not discharge effluents into the river. The takeout can be at Route 669 on the South River, but Route 865 on the North River is easier; the 200 yard upstream paddle is not too tough.

Hazards: None.

Water Conditions: Canoeable in winter, spring, and early summer, except following periods of little precipitation. Canoeable after a heavy rain in the summer and fall.

GAUGE

A reading of 2.0' on the USGS Front Royal gauge is about zero for canoeing on Section 1; a reading of 1.5' for the lower sections.

HISTORY

The final battle in Jackson's Valley Campaign in 1862 was fought at Port Republic. Fremont's forces (USA) moved from Harrisonburg to Cross Keys, just north of Port Republic, and Sickles (USA) forces moved south along the valley road (now Route 340) toward Port Republic. Jackson's forces fought skirmishes with and then turned back a half-hearted attack by Fremont's forces; then Jackson attacked Sickles forces in strength just NE of Port Republic. The Union forces were driven to Elkton and then across Swift Run Gap (Rte 33) to the east. During this battle, Jackson held the bridges and fords on the North River, South River, and South Fork so that he could prevent the Union force from joining and could attack either force.

Union losses totaled about 1,200 killed and wounded; Confederate, about 1,100 killed and wounded.

The final battle of Sheridan's raid on the Shenandoah Valley occurred at Waynesboro, when General George Custer captured the remainder of Jubal Early's force. The Union forces captured almost 1,600 Confederates and seventeen battle flags with few Union casualties, crossing the South River at Waynesboro and at fords/bridges north and south of Waynesboro. Confederate prisoners were held for a short time along the west bank of the South River between Waynesboro and Crimora.

There were a number of mills along the South River in colonial days, and there is one magnificent building still standing on the left bank. There are a number of caves near Grottoes, the best known being Grand Caverns; the others include Madison's Cave, the Weast's Cave.

OTHER INFORMATION

When the water is very high, the putin can be as far up as Route 634, although the normal putin on the upper section is Route 664. If the water is not high enough for the upper-upper section, the putin can be Route 650, just below the confluence with Back Creek. The takeout on the upper sections should be on the outskirts of Waynesboro, about where the backwater of the first dam begins, as it is not a very pretty thing to see what happens to the South River for the next seven miles. Below Waynesboro, the first putin is at Dooms, for a flat water paddle to Crimora; only one riffle can be remembered. The eleven mile section from Crimora to Grottoes is the best of the South River in many respects, although it is not really white-water. This section can be extended to Port Republic, an addition of about four miles; it has a number of small ledges and gravel bar type rapids just below Grottoes, but it then becomes rather flat with only riffles.

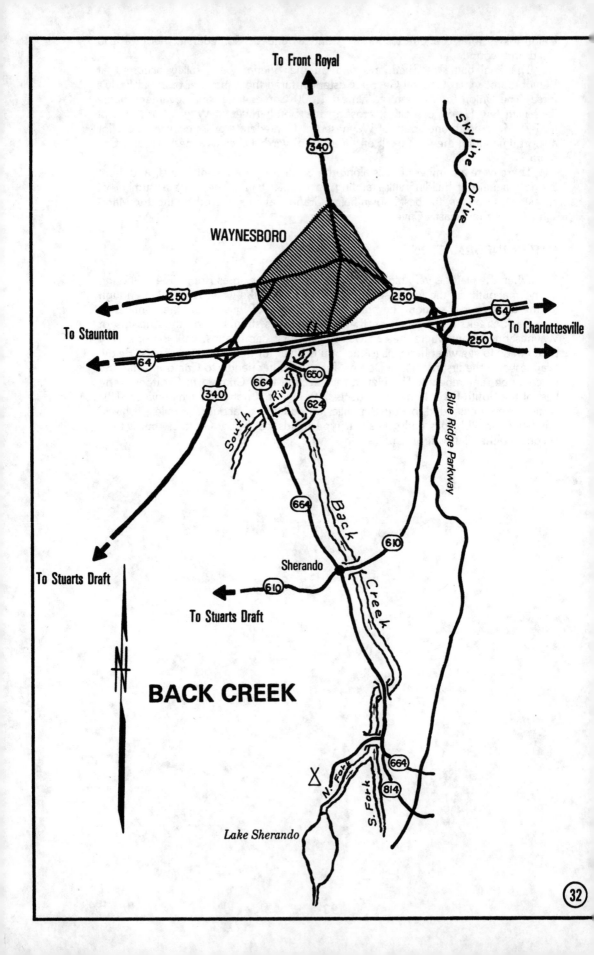

Back Creek

INTRODUCTION

Back Creek is the uppermost and the biggest tributary of the South River above Waynesboro. It is a very small stream that dashes through a gorge in its upper reaches and moves swiftly through rolling country before joining the South River. It offers plenty of white-water action and thrills.

Section 1. Lake Sherando (Rte 664) to South River

Gradient	Difficulty	Distance	Time	Width	Scenery	Map
36	2-3	9	3	20-40	Good	32

Trip Description: The putin is just below the confluence of the North Fork and South Fork of Back Creek, where the road goes to Lake Sherando. The gradient in the first five miles is 50 feet/mile, a rather impressive rate of drop, but the gradient is fairly steady. There are gravel bar rapids, rock garden rapids, and small ledges for most of the way to Sherando (Route 610 bridge). The stream moves very fast and there are no major rapids until a three-foot ledge is reached just above Sherando. There are three low-water bridges (underwater in high water) that are a major hazard, and there have been trees and debris blocking the stream at a couple of spots.

Below Sherando, the gradient drops to about 30 feet/mile, and the stream begins to moderate a bit. The current is still swift. There are fewer chances of the stream being blocked, and the country is more open. The bottom is mostly sand, rock, and cobble in this section, and the rapids are mostly cobble bars and scattered rock gardens. The takeout is normally at Route 624, but the trip can be extended by one mile on Back Creek to the South River and one mile on the South River to the Route 650 bridge. There is very little to recommend about this additional two miles, but it may be worth doing to some canoeists.

Hazards: Trees blocking the stream in upper portion. Low-water bridges. Below one bridge are a set of abutments with tree/debris blocking the stream.

Water Conditions: Canoeable normally in winter and spring following a wet period or a moderate rain.

GAUGE

A reading of 3.0' on the USGS Front Royal gauge is zero for canoeing.

HISTORY

The town of Sherando was named after the Iroquois chief Sherando who was killed by the son of Powhatan, who was the chief of the fierce and powerful Powhatan Conferacy. Opecananough, the son, had driven the Iroquois from the valley area, and left his son, Shewanee, in charge. When Shewanee was driven back to the tidewater, Opecananough killed Sherando in a lightning attack and reinstalled his son. The valley Indians were then known as Shawnees thereafter and the Shawnees were always known for their cruelty and their warlike ways.

In the Back Creek area, there are the ruins of an old iron furnace, Mount Torrey Furnace, which produced iron in the 1880's. There are two unusual stone heaps just south of Sherando, near Route 664; their origin and purpose is unknown, but it is apparent that they were constructed by man. There is Lake Sherando on the North Fork of Back Creek and a camping ground, and there is the Blue Ridge Parkway about a mile to the east of the putin.

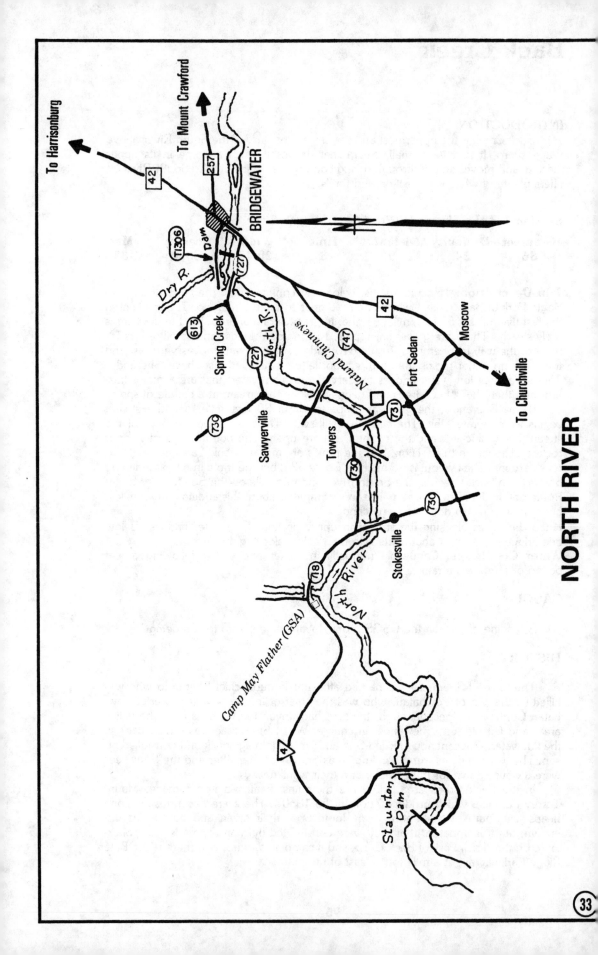

NORTH RIVER

North River

INTRODUCTION

The North River is one of the most interesting and the most diversified tributaries in the Shenandoah watershed. The upper section may be the best white-water canoeing in the Commonwealth of Virginia; the lowest section near Port Republic is some of the flattest water in the state; the other sections have varying degrees of white-water. The scenery varies from a spectacular mountain gorge to rolling foot-hills to beautiful Shenandoah farmlands. From Class 4 rapids to flatwater, from rocky cliffs to mud banks, from dense woodlands to open farmlands, from swift currents to meandering floating. It is all there.

Section 1. Staunton Dam to Stokesville (Rte 730)

Gradient	Difficulty	Distance	Time	Width	Scenery	Map
46	2-4	7	2.5	20-40	Excellent	33

Trip Description: The North River gorge section, starting at the Staunton Dam and ending at Stokesville, is truly a jewel of a white-water stream. It begins with rock garden rapids, clear water, and a bottom of sand and rocks; it is very swift with many blind turns; its width is about 30 feet. After about a mile, the rapids are more of the small ledge type, increasing to 1 to 2 feet, ever continuous. On one trip, a downed tree blocked the main passage, so look out for this hazard. About one mile from the takeout, just above the Girl Scout Camp, there are two major ledges that must be scouted. The first is a 5 foot ledge that funnels left with a hard right turn; the second is a six foot drop that is run close on the left side. Below the two ledges, there are small ledges, then gravel bars to the bridge at Stokesville. This section is a genuine gorge without a road alongside except for a short distance at the beginning and the end.
Hazards: Two major Class 4 rapids. Possible tree across stream.
Water Conditions: Canoeable normally in winter and spring following a wet period or a moderate rain.

Section 2. Stokesville (Rte 730) to the Spring Creek (Rte 727)

Gradient	Difficulty	Distance	Time	Width	Scenery	Map
28	2₃	19	3.5	30-40	Good	33

Trip Description: From Stokesville to Spring Creek, the North River is a fast moving stream with a very good gradient. It moves swiftly over a bed of broken rocks, gravel, and sand; it has swift chutes, small ledges, rock gardens, and gravel bars for a variety of rapid types. It flows through farmland but the trees along the bank block the view in most parts. There are a few houses along the bank and there are a number of bridges; in a few spots, it runs close to a paved road. There are few difficulties in this section; but there are trees growing in the stream, and there is a low-water bridge. All in all, it is quite enjoyable. While this section cannot begin to compare with the rapids and scenery of the gorge section, it is still a good white-water stream that is comparable to the Brocks Gap section of the North Fork Shenandoah.
Hazards: Low-water bridge. Possible blockage of stream by tree.
Water Conditions: Canoeable normally in winter and spring following a wet period or a moderate rain.

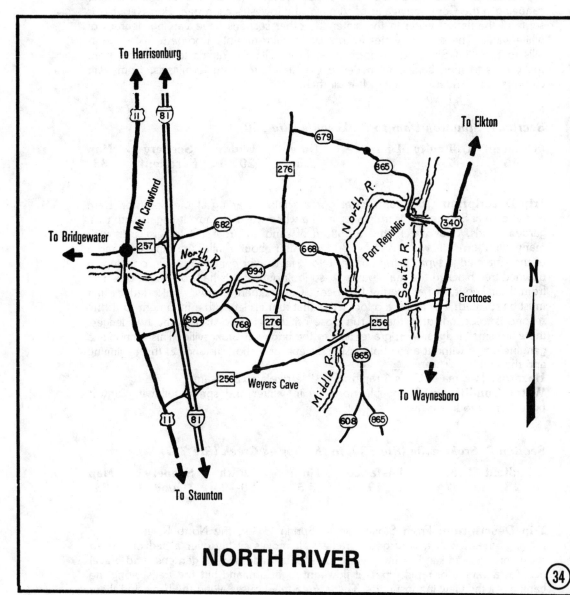

To Harrisonburg

To Elkton

Mt. Crawford

679

276

865

North R.

To Bridgewater

257

682

668

North R.

340

Port Republic

994

South R.

Grottoes

994

768

276

256

256

Weyers Cave

865

To Waynesboro

Middle R.

608

865

N

To Staunton

NORTH RIVER

34

Section 3. Spring Creek (Rte 727) to Bridgewater (Rte 42)

Gradient	Difficulty	Distance	Time	Width	Scenery	Map
9	1-2	9.5	3.5	40-50	Good	33

Trip Description: From Spring Creek to Bridgewater (Rte 42), the North River is a Class 1-2 run in which there are few rapids. The river is reaching the valley area and is just starting to meander a bit. The current is moderate, the rapids are mostly of the gravel bar type, and the terrain is more open. About 600 yards above the Route 42 bridge, there is an 8 foot dam; portage. Or takeout at the low-water bridge across the Dry River on the left bank about a mile above the dam.

This section of the North River is the transition between the white-water stretches and the flat, meandering stretches. In places it seems to be a white-water stream, particularly near the section where the Dry River enters, but it never makes it. The valley through which it flows is ringed by high hills and, near the Dry River, the hills on both banks are very close up. A good trip for beginners.

Hazards: Eight foot dam just above Bridgewater (Route 42)

Water Conditions: Canoeable in winter and spring normally or during the early summer following an extended wet spell or very heavy rain.

Section 4. Bridge water (Rte 42) to Port Republic (Rte 865)

Gradient	Difficulty	Distance	Time	Width	Scenery	Map
4.5	1-2	15.5	6	40-60	Good	34

Trip Description: From Bridgewater to Port Republic, the North River is much like its sister, the Middle River. There is not much of a gradient, so the current is slow and the paddling is tiring. There are very few rapids and only a few riffles, so there is little to say about the white-water canoeing. The scenery is beautiful farmland and the small towns are collections of large, well-kept, white houses. The only difficulties on this trip is the work required for paddling and remains of a six foot mill dam about mid-way on the trip. The dam can be run where a ten foot section is broken out; scout it carefully as there is a strong hydraulic in high water; it is close to Route 276 bridge and can be seen from the roadway.

This is a very long trip that can be shortened by taking out at any of three bridges. Considering the flatness of the stream, it might be wise to make this two separate trips.

Hazards : None

Water Conditions: Canoeable in winter and spring normally or duing the early summer following an extended wet spell or very heavy rain.

GAUGE

There is an RC gauge on Rte 730 Bridge at Stokesville. A reading of 4.5' on the USGS Cootes Store gauge should be zero for the upper sections. A reading of 2.0' on the USGS Front Royal gauge should be zero for canoeing on the lower sections.

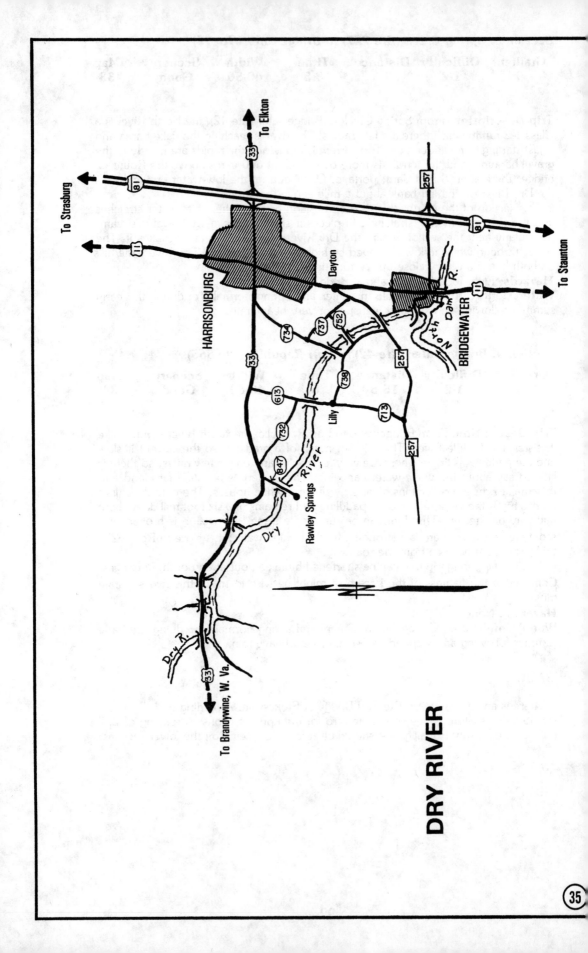

DRY RIVER

Dry River

INTRODUCTION

The Dry River, from the park area to Rawley Springs is one of the best named rivers in the Common wealth of Virginia. During the summer and fall months, there is virtually no water; in fact, water flows steadily for only a few months during the year. It is probably canoeable fewer days per year than any stream in Virginia. But if it has water, it is a must trip for all intermediate/advanced paddlers.

Section 1. Rte 33 bridge to Lilly (Rte 613)

Gradient	Difficulty	Distance	Time	Width	Scenery	Map
52	2-4	10	3.5	25-35	Excellent	35

Trip Description: The putin at Route 33 bridge (5.4 miles above Rawley Springs) is just above the point where a major tributary joins the Dry River; so if there is enough water at this point, there is enough on all points of the river. The river is best known for its cobble bottom, and most of the rapids at the start are of the cobble bar type. The river is quite close to Route 33, but it seems more remote, particularly in the section above Rawley Springs. The banks are low, so the scenery can be observed; the water is clear, and usually very cold; the trees seem to have been there forever. The gradient in the upper section is 50 fpm, but it is a steady drop and not too awesome.

As the mountain pass begins to narrow, about three and one-half miles downstream, there is a series of four good rapids and a 6 foot dam. The rapids are fairly complex (Class 3-4) and the dam should be portaged. There are two fish ladders on the dam, one close to the right bank and one near the middle; these have been run by canoeists at ideal water levels. The rapids and the dam are not the only hazards, however; the river stream bed has trees and bushes growing in the middle of the river.

It is an eerie feeling to be paddling through trees and bushes, like the Dry Gorge section of Lost River, only more so. Also, the river divides into a maze of small passages that are most intricate and have a tendency to run out of water. There is a beaver dam of about one-foot in height in the upper part; it is easy to run, but the thicket below it is a real challenge.

Below Rawley Springs bridge, there is a strong, long, complex rapid (Class 4); then the river passes through the Dry River Gap and the terrain begins to become more open, the banks become higher, and the briar bushes on the bank more dense. The scenery is less impressive as there are shanties along the bank, litter/trash along the banks, and there are numerous trees across the river. The gradient is still about 45 fpm, so there is still very good current over the gravel bars and through the small chutes. The takeout at Lilly is fairly obvious and quite easy.

Hazards: Trees/bushes in the stream bed and blocking the stream. Six-foot dam just above gap.

Water Conditions: Canoeable only in winter and spring following a prolonged wet period or very heavy rain.

Section 2. Lilly (Rte 613) to North River

Gradient	Difficulty	Distance	Time	Width	Scenery	Map
45	2-3	6	2	30-40	Good	35

Trip Description: Between Lilly and the North River at Bridgewater, the Dry River continues its dash over a bed of cobbles at a rate of 45 fmp. It divides around small islands, sweeps against high banks, and turns abruptly at small chutes. It is still a very fast current and there is sufficient action to interest the intermediate paddler. One ledge is really a paved ford where the road crosses about half-way down. The takeout is a steel low-water bridge 25 feet above the North River in fast water; beware of sudden swim calls.

The water is still clear, cool, and unpolluted; the banks are low and covered with bushes, briars, and trees; the terrain is largely flat, open farmland; and there is less litter/trash. The current is very fast and the bottom is mostly cobble and gravel. The rapids are mostly small ledges, gravel bars, and rock gardens.

Hazards: Steel low-water bridge at the takeout. Trees blocking the stream.

Water Conditions: Canoeable normally in winter and spring following a wet period or a moderate rain.

GAUGE

A reading of 4.5' on the USGS Cootes Store gauge is probably zero for canoeing on this section. There is an RC gauge on Route 613 bridge; deduct 6" to determine the water level at Route 33 bridge.

OTHER INFORMATION

The most memorable things about this river are the composition of the river bottom — cobbles and stones, billions of them — and the scenery in the upper areas. Owen Cecil, a canoeist/engineer/geologist, commented on the instability of the river bottom, how the cobbles shift and tumble downstream. This means that the passages change frequently and that the river is continually cutting a deeper passage through the mountain gap. It also means that at low water levels, the water tends to seep through the rocks and not run off on the surface. This makes a rather dry stream bed in periods of low water.

Camping is prohibited in this watershed because of possible contamination of the water supply for the town of Harrisonburg; this, and other constraints, means that the water quality is good. The scenery is magnificent in the upper gorge area, from the canoe and from the car. It is such a beautiful area that words are inadequate and it must be seen to be believed.

Middle River

INTRODUCTION

The Middle River is the least well-known of the three major tributaries of the South Fork Shenandoah River and it is certainly the least frequently canoed section. It begins meandering in the George Washington National Forest west of Staunton and continues meandering for the next 55 miles. It does more winding than almost any other river/creek/stream in Virginia.

Section 1. West View (Rte 254) to Churchville (Rte 250)

Gradient	Difficulty	Distance	Time	Width	Scenery	Map
20	1-2	8	3.5	20-30	Good	36

Trip Description: The Middle River at West View is a tiny stream flowing swiftly over a sand and gravel stream bed. It is very hard to find this section with water, so few people have canoed it. It has gravel bar rapids, barbed wire fences, and many trees blocking the stream. The scenery is open farmland and can be seen over the low banks. The river can be canoed above Route 254, but there is a veritable barrage of trees across the stream, even more than below Route 254. The fast current on this section is more than neutralized by the need to portage around or over the trees. This is a trip for canoeists who enjoy pain or find challenges in strange ways.

Hazards: Many, many trees blocking the stream.

Water Conditions: Canoeable normally in winter and spring following a wet period or a moderate rain.

Section 2. Churchville (Rte 250) to Verona (Rte 11)

Gradient	Difficulty	Distance	Time	Width	Scenery	Map
11	1-2	17	6	30-50	Good	36

Trip Description: From Route 250, west of Staunton, to Route 11, near Verona, is the best section of the Middle River of the South Fork Shenandoah. It begins as a very small stream over a bed of sand, gravel, and cobble, but it soon begins to meander to the point that you actually paddle south on a section that generally flows in a northerly direction. In the last four miles, you paddle to the east and west more than to south, even though the river now flows in a southerly direction. The trip can be broken up into a shorter trip by any one of four bridges that cross the middle river. At Frank's Mill (Route 732 bridge) there is an old mill dam that is 9' high, and there are signs of other dams at most of the other bridges. At Route 11, under the bridge, there is a seven foot dam; many people have driven over the bridge, but few realize the dam is there. Portage on the left.

Hazards: Nine foot dam just above Route 732, three miles downstream. Seven foot dam at takeout. Low-water bridge. Cows in the stream. Trees blocking the passage.

Water Conditions: Canoeable normally in winter and spring following a wet period or a moderate rain.

Section 3. Verona (Rte 11) to Damtown (Rte 616)

Gradient	Difficulty	Distance	Time	Width	Scenery	Map
6	1	14	5.5	40-60	Good	36

MIDDLE RIVER

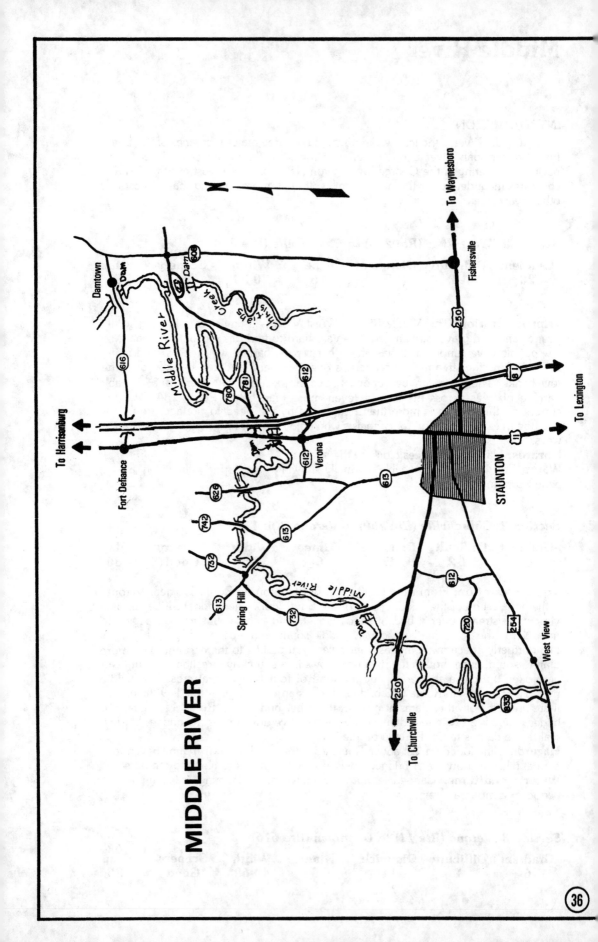

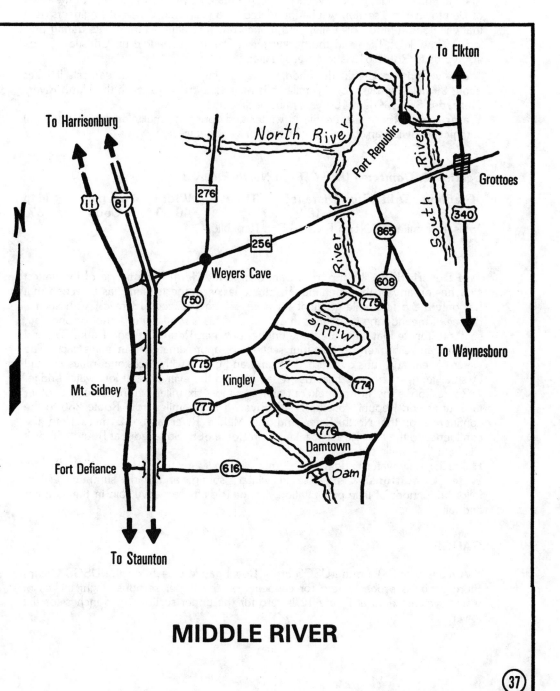

MIDDLE RIVER

Trip Description: There is a pleasant little rapid just below Route 11, just enough to stimulate the imagination, but the trip from Verona to Damtown does not have very much more in the way of rapids. The gradient (6 fpm) is not really enough to produce more than gravel bar rapids and small ledge rapids, separated by flat water. The final mile is a lot of backwater paddling, created by the six foot dam at the town of Damtown. This section will be inundated by a proposed Corps of Engineers dam that will flood a lot of this valley and, concurrently, create big mud flats during periods of low flow. To avoid the backwater at Damtown, paddle up Christian Creek 400 yards to Route 612 and an easy takeout.

Below Christian Creek, the Middle River begins meandering in earnest. It takes about 29 miles by river for 8.5 miles of straight line travel to reach the North River.
Hazards: Six-foot dam 100 yards above takeout.
Water Conditions: Canoeable in winter and spring normally or during the early summer following an extended wet spell or very heavy rain.

Section 4. Damtown (Rte 616) to North River

Gradient	Difficulty	Distance	Time	Width	Scenery	Map
2.5	1	18*	9	40-60	Good	37

*plus 4.25 miles on North River to Port Republic.

Trip Description: The trip from Damtown to the North River is one of the flattest stretches on any of the Shenandoah tributaries; no other stream has a section that has only a 2.5 feet/mile gradient for such a long distance (18 miles) with such a degree of meandering (five loops in 16 miles). This is too long of a trip for one day, so it is fortunate that there are three bridges between Route 616 and Route 256 and the trip can be broken up into four sections of approximately four miles each. The water is clear and runs over a bed of sand and gravel with occasional riffles created by small ledges. The only hazards are fatigue and the ever-present low water bridge.

Route 256 is the normal takeout as it is almost six miles before there is another takeout at Port Republic on the North River. It is 1.5 miles from Route 256 to the confluence of the North River and the Middle River and 4.2 miles from the confluence to the Port Republic takeout on Route 865. So takeout at Route 256 or it will be a 22 + mile trip.
Hazards: Low-water bridge. Boredom.
Water Conditions: Canoeable in winter, spring, and early summer, except following periods of little precipitation. Canoeable after a heavy rain in the summer and fall.

GAUGE

A reading of 2.0' on the USGS Front Royal gauge or 4.5' on the USGS Cootes Store gauge is probably zero for canoeing on the upper sections. Eight inches of water over the dam at Route 11 is zero for the upper sections, two inches for the lower.

Christians Creek

INTRODUCTION

Christians Creek is a small, fast, meandering stream that flows into the Middle River of the Shenandoah. It meanders more than the Middle River and the Middle River meanders as much as the North Fork Shenandoah. Christians Creek is typical of the north and northeast flowing streams in the Shenandoah basin. Fairly flat, sand and gravel bars, low banks, remains of mill dams, picturesque farmlands, many cattle, and pleasant people.

Section 1. Fisherville (Rte 250) to Middle River

Gradient	Difficulty	Distance	Time	Width	Scenery	Map
15	1₂	11	4	20-30	Good	38

Trip Description: Christians Creek is a fast-flowing small stream that has a good gradient, passes through a beautiful valley, and has excellent scenery. It has a sand and gravel bottom; the rapids are mostly gravel bar rapids, swift chutes, and quick turns. The water is clear, but it is polluted a bit by the cows who stand in it; it has low-water bridges at the good riffles; and the banks are low enough to enjoy the country side. It flows through a fairly wide valley with mountains to the east and to the west; the farmlands along the banks are well-tended and there is little sign of litter.

The normal takeout is Route 612 (new or old bridge), about 400 yards above the Middle River. This takeout is just below a five-foot dam. If continuing to the Middle River, the next takeout is at Damtown, two miles downsteam.

This stream will be flooded back up to Rte 254 by a dam that the Corps of Engineers has proposed for the Middle River. While the stream would not be missed by canoeists, the residents whose roots go back to the early 1700's would miss their farms and their homes.

Hazards: Five-foot dam. Low-water bridges. Fences and cattle gates. Trees blocking part of the stream.

Water Conditions: Canoeable in winter and spring normally or during the early summer following an extended wet spell or very heavy rain.

GAUGE

None. If the riffles at Route 250 are runnable, there is plenty of water for the trip.

107

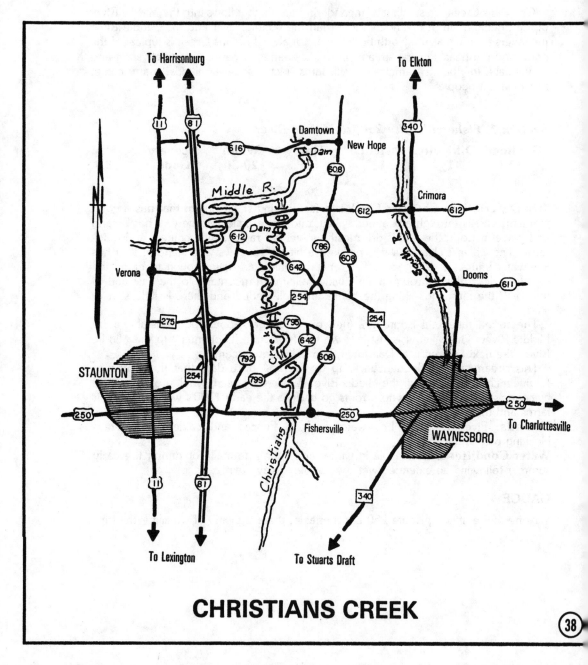

CHRISTIANS CREEK

38

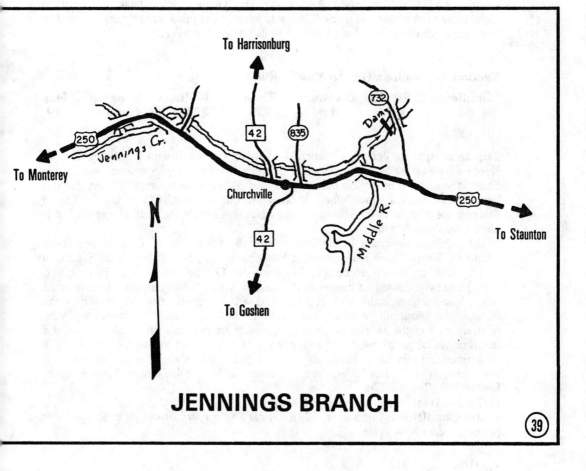

To Harrisonburg

To Monterey

Jennings Cr.

Churchville

To Goshen

Dam

Middle R.

To Staunton

JENNINGS BRANCH

39

Jennings Branch

INTRODUCTION

Jennings Branch is a very small and exceptionally fast mountain stream that flows into the Middle River of the Shenandoah near Churchville. It begins high in the mountains, rushes through a narrow mountain valley, slows a bit in the foothills, and empties into a slow, meandering river — all in the space of 8 miles. It flows close alongside Route 250 for the entire distance: while on the south side of the road, it is a terror of a little stream; while on the north side, it is more respectable. It is strictly a high-water stream that can be paddled only when most other streams are in flood; it does not hold water very long because of its limited watershed.

Section 1. Jennings Gap to Middle River

Gradient	Difficulty	Distance	Time	Width	Scenery	Map
64	1-3	8.0	2.5	20-30	Good	39

Trip Description: Jennings Branch is a little terror of a stream that flows close to Route 250 west of Staunton, dashing over small ledges, rock gardens, and cobble bars in the upper part, cobble bars in the lower part. It is such a small stream that it is barely wider than a canoe where it breaks through Jennings Gap. By the time it reaches the Middle River, about 2 miles below Churchville, it is bigger and it is almost flat, unrecognizable.

The putin is alongside Route 250, about six miles west of Churchville, about where Buckhorn Creek joins Jennings Branch. At this point, it is only 15 feet wide and flowing very swiftly, so be prepared for a JATO-style takeoff — to 15 mph in 5 feet. Then be prepared for bushes in the stream, water flowing around/among small trees, low-hanging limbs and bushes, and an occasional tree/fence across the stream. Jumping out of the canoe without hesitation may be necessary, unpleasant as it might be. Below Lone Fountain, there are no such problems — just a different set of problems, such as barbed wire fences and low-water bridges. The recommended takeout is Route 801, about 600 yards above the Middle River. If continuing to the Middle River, the trip is extended by 3 miles (and a 9 foot dam) to Franks Mill (Route 732).

Hazards: Trees and fences across the stream. Low-water bridge.

Water Conditions: Canoeable only in winter and spring following a prolonged wet period or very heavy rain.

GAUGE

None.

Martin's Mill, Lock, Dam Just above RR bridge at Remington. Located on left bank. Dam was wood cribs with stones. Stone foundations still apparent.

Wheatley's Mill, Lock, Canal. Located at head of Kellys Ford Rapids. Lock and canal on left bank. Canal is apparent. Dam was wood cribs with stones. Canal of two miles. Mill canals on right bank.

Mountain Run Dam, Lock, Canal. Dam was wood cribs with stones. Canal on left bank is apparent, cut through bedrock. Wooden locks. Dam was nine feet high.

Kimper's Ford Lock, Dam, Canal. Located about four miles below Mountain Run. Only a riffle remains at this site.

Snake Castle Lock, Dam, Canal. Canal on right bank. Timbers from lock still there. Rock ledge excavation obvious. Mill race on left. Large rock and blasted opening on left.

Skinkers Dam, Lock, Canal. Guard lock and canal on left bank. Mill foundation midway on ½ mile long canal. Lift lock (No. 14) of stone.

Deep Run Dam, Lock, Canal. Just above Deep Run which enters on left. Four locks and 1½ mile canal on right. Canal entry is Lock 13 at bluff on right. Stone wall of canal along river.

Powells Dam, Lock, Canal. Canal of ½ mile. Guard lock at dam. Three locks of 25 foot lift at end of canal. About ¾ mile above Rapidan River.

Rapidan Dam, Lock, Canal. Four stone locks and 1½ mile canal on right. Four locks of 32 foot lift. Stone wall, stone locks still in good condition — impressive. Gold mine along canal.

Scott's Lock, Dam, Canal. Stone locks on right bank in good condition. ¼ mile canal on right in fair condition.

Ballard's Lock, Dam, Canal. One mile canal on left bank. Guard lock in good condition. Lift lock with 11 foot lift at end of canal in good condition.

Banks Dam, Lock, Canal. Near Motts Run Landing. Two excellent stone locks (Nos 2 & 3). Remains of dam now a riffle.

Taylor's Dam, Canal, Lock. Canal and lock on right bank. Lock in excellent condition. Canal is 2¼ miles long, ending in a basin in Fredericksburg. Now a VEPCO canal.

Rappahannock River Canal System

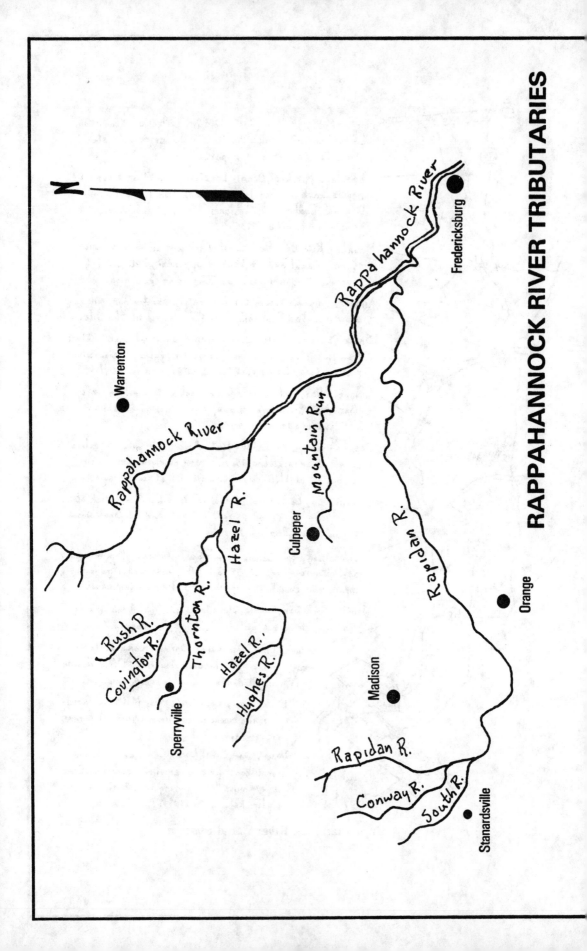

RAPPAHANNOCK RIVER TRIBUTARIES

Chapter 4

The Rappahannock River Watershed

The Rappahannock River watershed is entirely in Virginia, reaching from the eastern slopes of the Blue Ridge Mountains to the Chesapeake Bay. It drains about 2850 square miles, about 7.0 percent of the state. It's principal tributaries are the Hazel River and the Rapidan River, each of which have many tributaries. The Rappahannock River is the first river south of the Potomac River; the next river south of the Rappahannock River is the York River.

The following streams, whose locations are shown on Figure 6, are described in this chapter:

Rappahannock River
Hazel River
Hughes River
Thornton River
Rush River
Covington River
Mountain Run
Rapidan River
South River
Conway River
Robinson River

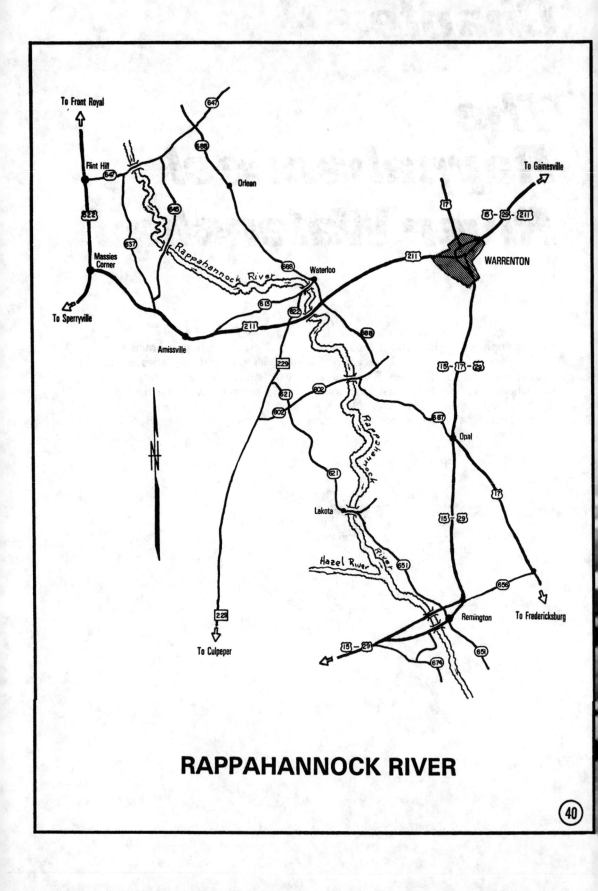

RAPPAHANNOCK RIVER

40

Rappahannock River

INTRODUCTION

The Rappahannock River. There is so much to say about this magnificent stream that it would require a book to describe it and its place in Virginia history. No other river or watershed in the Old Dominion can rival its role during the Civil War where the Army of the Potomac (USA) and the Army of Northern Virginia (CSA) fought many bloody engagements. Its history includes the Indian tribes (one of which gave the river its name), a major canal system, colonial settlements, and Indian/settler wars. At present the Rappahannock River and its tributaries can be summarized as wild, unpolluted streams that offer superlative white-water, outstanding fishing, and beautiful scenery. Not all elements on all sections of all streams, of course.

Section 1. Orleans (Rte 647) to Waterloo (Rte 211)

Gradient	Difficulty	Distance	Time	Width	Scenery	Map
7	12	13.5	5	30-50	Good	40

Trip Description: The Rappahannock River has its beginning in the Blue Ridge mountains at Chester Gap, where Route 522 crosses from Flint Hill to Front Royal. It is a mere trickle of a stream above Huntley, but it picks up volume from a lot of small runs. It is joined by the Jordan River just east of Flint Hill, 50 yards upstream from the Route 647 bridge; at this point, it becomes a canoeable stream. From Route 647 to Route 211, it is a small, fast, unpolluted stream with clear water, a sandy bottom, distinctive rock formations, and outstanding spots for lunch. It has a few rock garden rapids, many gravel bar riffles, and a number of small, swift chutes. There are the remains of a number of old beaver dams on this upper section and local trappers take a lot of beaver and muskrats. About 2 miles above Route 211, there are the ruins of Fox's Mill; stop and look at these ruins, as the keystone sills above the windows are classics. This mill is at Waterloo, the upstream terminus of the old Rappahannock canal; it was burned during the Civil War and was never rebuilt.

Hazards: Trees blocking the stream.

Water Conditions: Canoeable in winter and spring normally or during the early summer following an extended wet spell or very heavy rain.

Section 2. Waterloo (Rte 211) to Remington (Rte 29)

Gradient	Difficulty	Distance	Time	Width	Scenery	Map
3.5	A,1	18	8	60-90	Good	40

Trip Description: The trip from Rte 211 to Remington is the longest stretch of flat water on the Rappahannock. The gradient is small, so there is very little current; so prepare for long distance paddling or shorten the trip by one bridge. See Map. There is no white-wate in this section, just a few gravel bar riffles. The banks are fairly high, the bottom is sand and mud, the banks are tree-lined, and the land is very good for farming. There are a number of old fords, the ruins of old mill dams, the remains of old canal dams, and a lot of cattle grazing on the banks. The gradient picks up a little for the last two miles, beginning about where the Hazel River enters, but not enough for rapids.

Hazards: None

Water Conditions: Canoeable in winter and spring normally or during the early summer following an extended wet spell or very heavy rain.

Section 3. Remington (Rte 29) to Kellys Ford Bridge (Rte 620)

Gradient	Difficulty	Distance	Time	Width	Scenery	Map
10	1-2₃	4.5	1.5	70-90	Good	41

Trip Description: The Rappahannock River between Remington and Kellys Ford Bridge is one of the most popular canoe trips in the Old Dominion. It is convenient to Washington, Richmond, and Charlottesville; it is served by good roads; it usually holds water throughout the year; and it offers a challenge to both the white-water canoeist and the float fishermen. It is a fairly short trip that includes flat water and white water; good fishing spots and good swimming holes; ruins of an old canal and ruins of a large dam; big rocks for sunning and lunch stops; challenging rapids and trophy-size bass. The worse thing that can be said about this section is that it is too short. The rapids include: (1) the remains of the old canal dam just below the railroad bridge; (2) the first riffles at the start of the rapids, the riffles being the remains of Wheatleys Dam and locks; (3) steady rock garden rapids (Class 1-2) for ½ mile; (4) a broken ledge rapid (Class 3) formed by big rocks (Sandy Beach Rapid); (5) small ledges and rock garden rapids (Class 1-2) to the takeout, about one mile. The last 2 miles of white water more than compensate for the first 2½ miles of flat water.

The water is clear (except when high) and unpolluted, the bottom is coarse sand, the banks are moderately high and tree-lined, the terrain is open and flat farmland. The trace- of a 1½ mile long canal can be seen on the left (north) bank just upstream of the takeout bridge.

Hazards: None

Water Conditions: Canoeable in winter, spring, and early summer, except following periods of little precipitation. Canoeable after a heavy rain in the summer and fall.

Section 4. Kellys Ford Bridge (Rte 620) to Motts Run Landing

Gradient	Difficulty	Distance	Time	Width	Scenery	Map
6	1-2₃	24.0	10	80-120	Good	41,42

Trip Description: It is 15.5 miles from Kellys Ford Bridge to the Rapidan River and 8.5 miles from the Rapidan River junction to Motts Run Landing. Definitely an overnight canoe trip. And once the trip is started at the Kellys Ford Bridge, there are no bridges or public landings until one arrives at the Motts Run Landing. There are very few houses that can be seen from the river and there are few signs of civilization in this section. So be prepared to go the entire distance once you start, unless you know the area real well. There are numerous remote spots for camping along the river, but they are on private property. So do not abuse the property.

The Rappahannock is a beautiful river, and this is a beautiful section. It begins with light riffles below the putin and it continues with occasional rock garden rapids (Class 1-2). There are numerous sand bars and occasional rock formations that are ideal for lunch stops and swim calls. Many of the rapids are the remains of old canal dams, which were built at intervals of two miles or less. There are the remains of old locks and bypass canals at many of these dams, and there are fords below most of the old dam sites. The rapids/riffles, the sandy bottom, the clear/clean water, the remoteness of the area, and the absence of litter make this an ideal float trip.

There is a ½ mile rock garden rapid (Class 2) just before the Rappahannock River joins the Rapidan River. Then there is a ½ mile rock garden rapid (Class 2) just

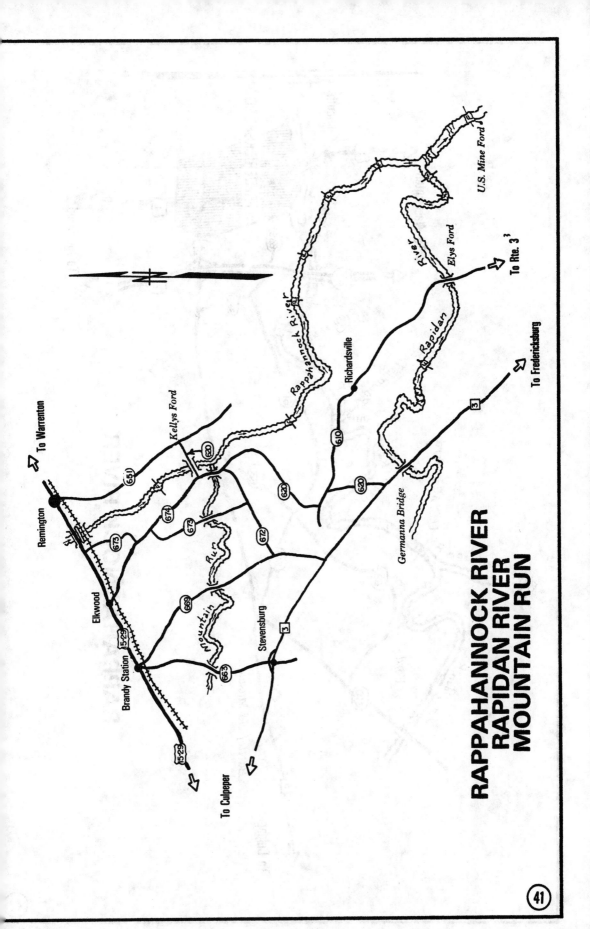

RAPPAHANNOCK RIVER
RAPIDAN RIVER
MOUNTAIN RUN

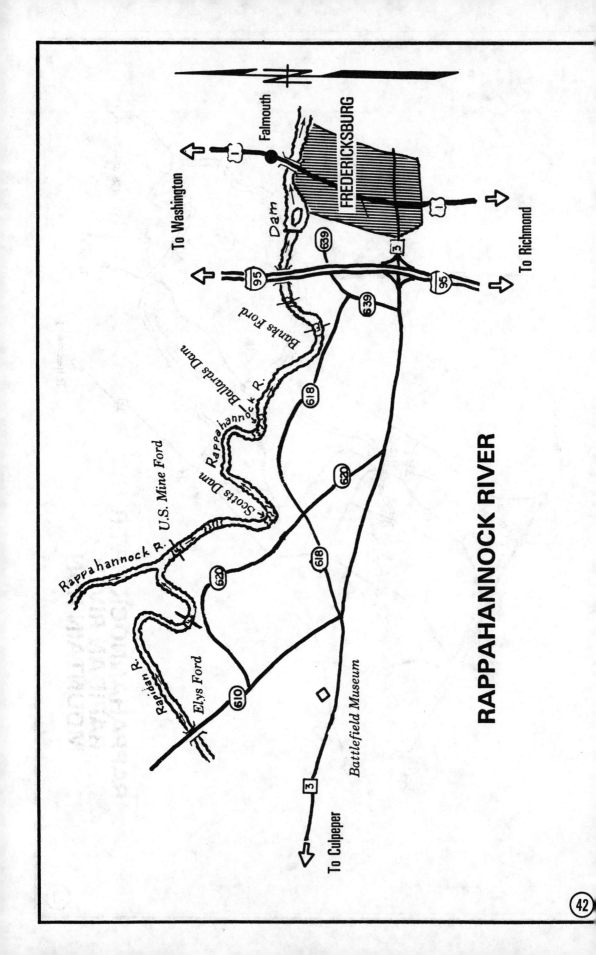

RAPPAHANNOCK RIVER

below the confluence; this rapid is the remains of the Rapidan Dam, part of the canal system, and it was the largest dam in the entire system. On the right bank, there is the bypass canal that has stone locks, the entrance to a gold mine (U.S. Mine), and stone walls. About three miles below the Rapidan, there is a Class 2 rapid that is the remains of Ballards Dam.

There is an access/egress point just below the confluence with the Rapidan River, at the site of the colonial road that went to Scotts Dam; the road is on the right (south) bank; the road is not visible from the river and it has deteriorated a lot; this takeout/putin is a sandy beach facing a 50 foot rock bluff across the river, at the end of set of riffles after 1.5 miles of flatwater. It is reached from Rte 620, the first road east of two bridges in close succession. There may be a number of places that can be used for putins/takeouts in this section, as a number of farmers in the area permit canoeists to cross their property for a $2 fee. Check the local fisherman or bait shops for specific information.

Hazards: None

Water Conditions: Canoeable most of the year except following a long, dry spell. Canoeable after a moderate rain in the summer.

Section 5. Motts Run Landing to Fredericksburg (Rte 1)

Gradient	Difficulty	Distance	Time	Width	Scenery	Map
13*	1-34	4.5	4	100-120	Good	42

*1 mile at 30 feet/mile

Trip Description: The trip from Motts Run to the VEPCO dam has a few rapids that end in a two mile stretch of backwater. Portage around the left side of the dam for a relatively easy carry and a chance to walk under the dam without danger and have water pouring over you without being wet. It is well worth the effort to paddle this section at least one time for that experience. Note: the diversion canal on the right side of the dam is extremely dangerous and the portage is difficult. Stay away from it. This dam was built long before the Civil War and was used with the canal system; Civil War photographs show a 12' to 15' dam with a lot of water flowing over it. VEPCO just took over an existing dam and enlarged it.

The section below the Fredericksburg dam begins with simple riffles, but the river changes its nature quickly. Most of the water flows to the right against a high bluff and then drops over a three foot ledge with a hole on the downstream side, at least four feet total drop. This ledge will be a Class 4 rapid in high water, and it will swamp open tandem boats in moderate or high water levels. Below this ledge, there are four Class 2-3 rapids and a few riffles before the takeout immediately below the U.S. Route 1 bridge on the Fredericksburg side of the river.

Hazards: Twenty foot dam just above Fredericksburg.

Water Conditions: Canoeable most of the year except following a long, dry spell. Canoeable after a moderate rain in the summer.

GAUGES

The USGS Remington gauge and the RC gauge on Rte 29 bridge can be used to estimate water levels on the Rappahannock River. The water level is for canoeing at the following gauge levels.

Section	RC Remington (Rte 29)	USGS Remington (Rte 29)
Section 1	1.5'	4.8'
2	1.0'	4.3'
3	0'	3.3'
4	0'	3.3'
5	-.6"	2.8'

HISTORY

When Captian John Smith sailed up the Rappahannock River to a small island in the Fredericksburg/Falmouth area, the Indian tribes of the Powhatan Confedracy lived in the lower portions, generally from the Fredericksburg area to the Chesapeake Bay; this included the Rappahannock, Tappahannock, Nantaughta-cuad, Cytlawpaum, and Payankatank tribes. The river itself was named after a tribe with which Captain Smith had a small skirmish in the vicinity of Falmouth. In the upper reaches, the Indian tribes were of the Monocan Confederacy, a group that was largely in the upper James River Basin. The Indians of the lower Rappahannock were of the Powhatan Confederacy; they were warlike and had frequent clashes with the white settlers and the area was the scene of numerous massacres, betrayals, and broken treaties.

A fort was established where Fredericksburg now exists after John Lederer explored the river and its falls and was able to convince the House of Burgesses that it was a desirable area for settling. By 1680, the upper and lower valley of the Rappahannock was relatively free of hostile Indians and settlement had begun. During the Revolutionary War, Fredericksburg provided an adopted Scotchman to the Navy of the colonies, John Paul Jones; other Virginians from this area fought as Morgan's Riflemen in battles from Massachussetts to South Carolina. These Virginians had fought under Braddock in the French and Indian War during which they learned that the frontiersmen were equal to the continental regulars when fighting in the woodlands and wilderness of the colonies. It is reported that George Washington predicted to the Fredericksburg Masonic Lodge, of which he was a member, that New York could some day surpass Fredericksburg as a seaport and commercial center if the city of Fredericksburg did not continue its growth and industry.

Between the Revolutionary War and the Civil War, the citizens of Fredericksburg chartered a series of companies for the purpose of building a canal from Fredericksburg to Waterloo. This would provide a means for conveying the agricultural products to the coastal markets and for shipping finished goods to the inland areas. After a series of abortive efforts, construction on the canal was begun at Fredericksburg-Falmouth in 1829 after eighteen years of dreaming and planning. It was planned that there would be 28 lift locks, eighteen dams, and three canals over the fifty miles in which there was a fall of 323 feet. The initial work began at the dam which diverted water through a canal into Fredericksburg; the works still remain. In the first two years, locks were constructed in Fredericksburg, at Kellys Mill, at Wheatley's Mill, and just below the junction with the Rapidan; canals were constructed at the Kellys Ford rapids and the Falmouth rapids.

The canal system was comprised of a series of dams across the river with lift-locks on the banks; the dams provided calm water navigation in lieu of occasional rapids. The astute observer can deduce their location from the location of the dams and locate the canals associated with these locks. There were three dams just downstream from the confluence of the Rappahannock with the Rapidan; Rapidan Dam, United States Dam, and Scotts Dam. The Rapidan Dam extended over 1000' downstream and was the largest in the system. The canal on the right (south) bank is still there and is a magnificent example of stone wall dams and stone locks; it is over a mile in length and is worth a stop for inspection. Other dams were at Bank's Ford, Scott's Ford, Burrows Ford, Richards Ford, and Kelly's Ford. When finished, the system included: 47 locks, 25 of which were built with stone and are visible today; twenty dams that varied in height from six to twelve feet and in length from 200 to 1000 feet; and over fifteen miles of canals.

The Rappahannock canal system failed for a variety of reasons. First, it never was properly funded. Next, it was never supported by the up-river people. Finally, the railroad arrived about the same time the system became operational.

During the Civil War, the Rappahannock served as a barrier for Union forces and for Confederate forces, since it was located about mid-way between Richmond and Washington. In 1862-1863, major battles were fought at Fredericksburg and

Chancellorsville, during which time the dams and fords became the crossing places for Union forces. The battle of Chancellorsville began with Union forces crossing at U.S. Ford (remains of U.S. Dam), Kellys Ford and Banks Ford on the Rappahannock, and Elys Ford and Germanna Ford on the Rapidan in a maneuver to encircle the Confederate forces at Fredericksburg. In that battle, which was considered as the most masterful employment of troops by General Rovert E. Lee, there were over 20,000 casualties, one of whom as General T.J. (Stonewall) Jackson. Although other battles were fought at the Wilderness and Spotsylvania in 1864, there were no more attempts to cross the lower Rappahannock by either forces. The fords in the upper reaches of the Rappahannock River between Kelly's Ford and Waterloo, however, were crossed many times by Union and Confederate forces marching to and from Manassas, Front Royal, Culpepper, and Gordonsville. When the Confederate forces were marching to the Second Battle of Bull Run, there was fire-fight at Kelly's Ford. During this battle, the Union paymaster is reported to have buried his gold coin to avoid it being seized. It is supposed to still be there and many people have tried to find it.

Two of the most pleasant news items about the Rappahnannock River in recent years were the end of the plans to build the Salem Church Dam and the acquisition of land for a Kellys Ford Park by the Commonwealth of Virginia. The high dam would have been built by the Corps of Engineers just above the I-95 bridge near Fredericksburg; it would have created a lake that would have extended almost to the Kellys Ford bridge during maximum impoundment. In low water, the impoundment would have been used to maintain a minimum flow below the dam, which would have resulted in miles and miles of mud flats upstream. Randy Carter was one of the principal opponents of this dam, fighting it almost alone for many years. It was 1975 before the plans were withdrawn after it was found that there was not a real need for a high dam and that the cost-benefit ratios used in the USACOE studies were not realistic.

In 1976, the state executed an option to purchase the land on the south (right) bank of the Rappahannock River from Wheatleys Dam (where the riffles start) to below Kellys Ford Bridge. In addition, options were secured for land on the north bank. The good people in that area wanted to deal with the state and the state bought the property for less than the normal market price. It just goes to show that there are good people and good things in this life — occasionally.

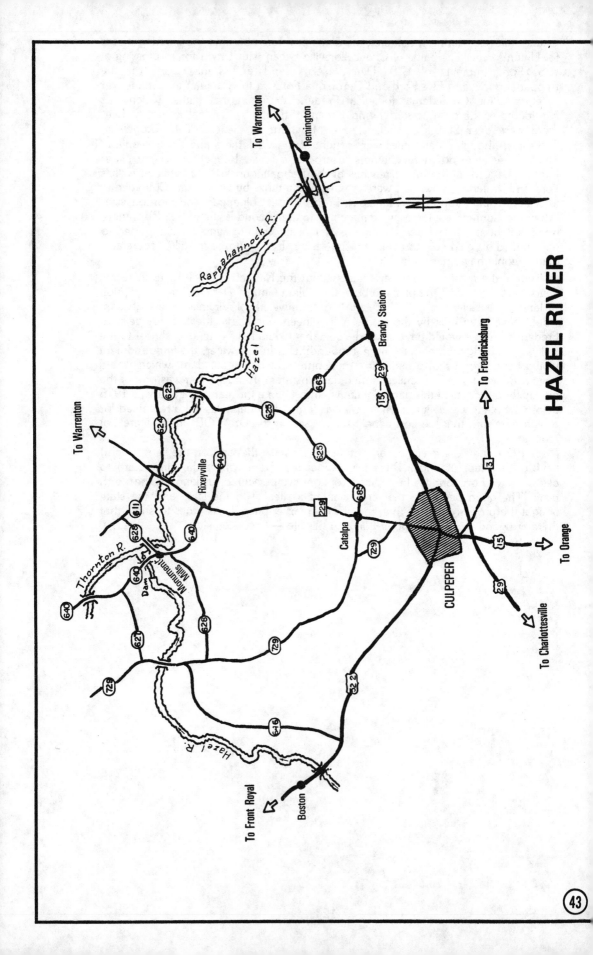

HAZEL RIVER

Hazel River

INTRODUCTION

The Hazel River is the second largest tributary of the Rappahannock River, and it is certainly the flattest of all the tributaries. It is the most meandering stream in the Rappahannock watershed, winding constantly while flowing to the east, the north, the northeast and the southeast. The people who live along the Hazel have a strong affection for it, for it is an unspoiled, underdeveloped natural stream that is crossed by few bridges.

Section 1. Boston (Rte 522) to Monument Mills (Rte 640)

Gradient	Difficulty	Distance	Time	Width	Scenery	Map
7	1	12.5	5	30-40	Good	43

Trip Description: From Boston to Monument Mills, where the Thornton River joins it, the Hazel River is a fairly flat Piedmont stream that wanders through a farming area. It does not have much gradient, so the current is fairly slow; in low water, there is a lot of hard paddling on the flat pools between gravel bar riffles. The clay banks are very high and are tree-lined, so the surrounding scenery is blocked from view. The only points of major interest are the remains of an old canal system that existed in the early 1800's. The major hazard is the abandoned power dam at Monument Mills, just upstream from Route 640. This dam was a mill dam in the 1700's, then a mill and canal dam in the 1800's, and an electrical power dam in the early 1900's. It is still in good shape although an abutment had to be rebuilt after a recent hurricane washed it out. Takeout at Route 628, about 400 yards downstream from Route 640 where the Thornton River joins the Hazel; it is an easier spot at a bridge that may be a low-water bridge in moderate water.
Hazards: Ten-foot high power dam about ½ mile from takeout. Possible wire fences. Occasional trees across stream.
Water Conditions: Canoeable in winter and spring normally or during the early summer following an extended wet spell or very heavy rain.

Section 2. Monument Mills (Rte 640) to Rappahannock River

Gradient	Difficulty	Distance	Time	Width	Scenery	Map
2.5	A	12.5*	6*	40-70	Good	43

*Plus 2.5 miles (and one hour) on Rappahannock to Rte 29.

Trip Description: The Hazel River, from Monument Mills to the Rappahannock River and then to Route 29 at Remington, is one of the flattest trips in Virginia. Only the Willys River can rival this section of the Hazel for the least gradient. Both the Hazel and the Rappahannock sections (12.5 miles, 2.5 miles) requires a lot of long, hard paddling. There is very little current, there is very little to see, there are no rapids, and the bottom is sandy with some clay. Again, the only points of significance are the sites of the old canal system where the ruins of dams make light riffles. The Rappahannock River is about 100 feet wide but there is no danger, even in high water. The takeout is old Route 29 bridge (now Route 29 Business) at Remington.
Hazards: None
Water Conditions: Canoeable in winter and spring normally or during the early summer following an extended wet spell or very heavy rain.

GAUGE

A reading of 1.8' on the USGS Culpepper or 4.4' on the USGS Remington gauge is zero for canoeing on Section 1; 1.6' and 4.2' for Section. 2. A reading of -2" on the RC gauge on Route 522 or 10" on the RC gauge on Route 29 is zero for canoeing.

OTHER INFORMATION

After the Fredericksburg to Waterloo canal passed the confluence of the Hazel, a series of dams and locks were constructed on the Hazel River. It was the slack-water type of canal in which the dams backed the water between each dam and the barges/boats/bateaux/canoes were always on flat water. Lift locks were constructed at the mill dams so that the various craft could continue without unloading and reloading the cargo. A power plant was built on the dam at Monument Mills sometime in the 1920-1930 period; it has been long abandoned, but the dam is still there. Other dams, now washed out, can be recognized only in low water by the careful observer. Chapter 7 has a map prepared by Wm Trout that depicts the sites of the dams/locks/canals that were operating in the early 1800's and the remains that can be found by the perceptive canoeist.

There are a number of old fords in the area, particularly near Boston; these fords were used by Union and Confederate forces moving between Warrenton and Culpepper and Front Royal and Culpepper. But it seems that history and nature did not look kindly on the Hazel, in many respects, as there are no colonial forts, no major battles, no Indian massacres, no caves.

The tributaries of the Hazel River are white water streams that offer challenge, scenery, and excitement to paddlers of all types and abilities. Few other rivers can compare with the Hughes River, the Thornton River, the Rush River, and the Covington River, streams that begin in the Blue Ridge Mountains and flow into the Hazel River after leaving the foothills. These streams are in such close proximity that it is easy to paddle two of them in a single day. Below the juncture with the Thornton, the Hazel River has only one tributary that could be canoed, Muddy Run, but it is not a white water stream.

The upper reaches of the Rapidan River are quite similar to the upper reaches of the Hazel River. The upper Rapidan River, the Conway River, the South River are all good white water streams that begin in the Blue Ridge Mountains. Shortly after the Rapidan is joined by its two tributaries, it leaves the foothills and it is a flat Piedmont stream that has few, if any, tributaries that are canoeable.

Thornton River

INTRODUCTION

The Thornton River is such a small stream that it would be named Thornton Creek or Thornton Run in most other parts of the country. It begins as a series of cascades down the mountainside at Thornton Gap, where Route 211 crosses the Blue Ridge Mountains, and ends as a flat, slow-moving stream when it joins the Hazel River at Monument Mills. Between Thornton Gap and Monument Mills, a distance of less than thirty miles, the river displays every possible mood and offers almost every challenge that a small stream can offer.

Section 1. Above Sperryville to Fletchers Mill (Rte 620)

Gradient	Difficulty	Distance	Time	Width	Scenery	Map
58	2-3	2.5	1	15-20	Fair	45

Trip Description: Starting about a mile above Sperryville, alongside Route 211, the Thornton River dashes down the mountainside to Sperryville, through Sperryville to join the other Thornton River, and through a half-dozen barbed-wire fences to Fletchers Mill, where there is a heavy, wooden cattle-gate. This brisk run is for open boaters who can/will jump out of their canoes on a frequent basis to avoid the fences; decked boat paddlers should be cautious about this section.

The current is exceptionally fast, the banks are low, and the bottom is solid rock or broken rock. The rapids are mostly ledges for the first mile; rock gardens, the remaining distance. The scenery is not particularly good, as it has many houses along the bank in the upper parts and a town in the middle. Like canoeing through front yards and back yards.

Hazards: Numerous wire fences. One wooden cattle gate.

Water Conditions: Canoeable only in winter and spring following a prolonged wet period or very heavy rain.

Section 2. Fletchers Mill (Rte 620) to Rock Mills (Rte 626)

Gradient	Difficulty	Distance	Time	Width	Scenery	Map
24	2₃	7	2	20-30	Very Good	45

Trip Description: Below Fletcher's Mill, the Thornton River starts with a good Class 2 rapid with good wave action and then enters a series of long, swift, straight runs with overhanging trees/bushes, limbs. After about ¾ mile, a cattle gate is portaged on the right; the next cattle gate sometimes has a narrow opening that requires a good eye and steely nerves. When the river forms a pool and then runs up against a rock cliff on the right, there is a good Class 3 rapid with a sneaky hydraulic about 30 feet downstream. From there to Rock Mills, the river is much tamer and the rapids are shorter, less frequent, and less difficult.

The Thornton may well be the most popular white-water canoe trip in Northern Virginia and may have been canoed by more beginners than almost any other small stream. There is a good reason for its popularity, as it has an easy putin, has a mid-point bridge for a convenient takeout, offers steady rapids, and has beautiful scenery. The current is very fast, the water is cold and clear, the bottom is sand or sand and rock, the banks have rock cliffs and evergreen trees, and there are few signs of civilization.

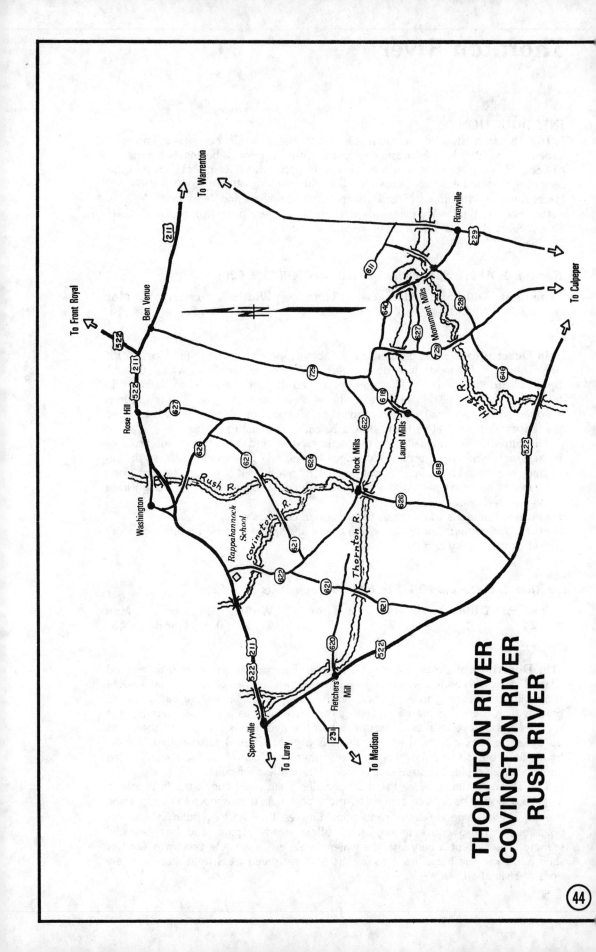

THORNTON RIVER
COVINGTON RIVER
RUSH RIVER

44

Hazards: Two wooden cattle gates. Possible tree across the stream.
Water Conditions: Canoeable normally in winter and spring following a wet period or a moderate rain.

Section 3. Rock Mills (Rte 628) to Hazel River

Gradient	Difficulty	Distance	Time	Width	Scenery	Map
7	1-2	14	5	30-40	Good	45

Trip Description: The Thornton River from Rock Mills to Monument Mills is quite a change from the upper sections. It is now a flat, meandering stream with very little current and very few rapids. The bottom has changed to sand and clayey sand, the riffles are mostly gravel bars, and the banks are quite high. The terrain is mostly open farmland, but the banks are treelined for most of the distance. It is a good trip for beginners, but it is not white-water. The takeout is on the Hazel River, about 400 yards after the Thornton joins the Hazel; this bridge, Route 628, may be too low to negotiate. Be careful.
Hazards: Maybe a tree blocking the stream.
Water Conditions: Canoeable normally in winter and spring following a wet period or a moderate rain.

GAUGE

A reading of 2.6' on the USGS Culpepper gauge is minimum for Section 1; a reading of 2.0' is zero for Section 2; 1.8' for Section 3. There is a RC gauge on Route 620 Bridge at Fletchers Mill.

OTHER INFORMATION

The Thornton River and its tributaries were the principal sources of power for mills in the Sperryville area. Fletcher's Mill (which was on Beaver Run), Rock Mills, Laurel Mills, and Monument Mills were all active in colonial and antebellum days. The woolen mill at Laurel Mills was operating as late as the 1930's; it was powered from a low dam (now a Class 1 riffle) about 1/3 mile upstream that diverted water into a canal on the right bank. It is worth a visit to Laurel Mills to see the magnificent old mansion on the hill that belonged to the mill owners. The old mill building (name unknown) at Route 621 Bridge was reassembled after moving to this location from another site; some timbers still have the identification markings.

Rush River

INTRODUCTION

The Rush River is probably named after the fact that its water is in a terrible rush to join the Thornton River. The stream is so fast that it is difficult to remember more than its speed, which does not lessen until it is joined by the Covington River. It joins the Thornton River at Rock Mills, where it looks deceptively placid.

Section 1. Washington (Old Rte 211) to Rock Mills (Rte 622)

Gradient	Difficulty	Distance	Time	Width	Scenery	Map
32	2-4	6	2	15-30	Good	45

Trip Description: The Rush River trip normally begins at the old mill on old Route 211, just east of Washington. In low water, it is hard to believe that this stream is canoeable. When there is water and the canoeist is fighting for his boat and his ego, it still does not seem canoeable. The rapids are continuous rock gardens with occasional ledges; the water is extremely fast, flowing over a rock, gravel, and boulder bottom. The scenery is best described as a blur of greenery of some sort on banks that might be high or low in an area that could be wooded or open farmland — you will have to hike it to get a better description.

There are no major rapids with distinctive features, but there are many very long, very fast, very narrow sections that seem like mill races. Most of the fences or trees across the river seem to be on blind turns, at the end of long rapids, or at the deepest spots on the stream; hard to see, hard to stop, hard to jump out of your boat. Notwithstanding, the Rush River is a must for every open boat white-water canoeist that wants to test himself.

Hazards: Electric wire fence. Barbed/woven wire fences. Wooden cattle gates. Trees across the stream.

Water Conditions: Canoeable only in winter and spring following a prolonged wet period or very heavy rain.

GAUGE

A reading of 5.0' on the USGS gauge at Remington is probably zero for canoeing. A reading of 2.05' on the USGS gauge at Old 211 Bridge is zero. A reading of 1.3' on the RC gauge at Fletchers Mill on the Thornton is about 3" on the Rush.

Covington River

INTRODUCTION
The Covington River is a tributary of the Rush River, which is a tributary of the Thornton River. It begins at Jenkins Mountain, just north of Sperryville, passes under Route 211, and drops a total of 155 feet in the short distance of 4.5 miles. It has some of the biggest rapids (and more of them) than any small stream in the Northern Virginia area.

Section 1. Rappahannock School (Rte 622) to Rush River.

Gradient	Difficulty	Distance	Time	Width	Scenery	Map
34	2-4	4.5*	2	15-30	Good	45

*plus 1.5 miles on Rush River to Rock Mills

Trip Description: The Covington River trip normally begins at Route 622 although it is possible to start at Route 211. The section from Route 211 to Route 622 drops at a horrendous 50 feet/mile through briars and low bushes that increase the difficulty rating at least one level. Be prepared to fight your weight in wildcats on this section.

At the Route 622 bridge, the Covington is about as wide as a canoe is long. The current is very fast, and the trip begins with a nice 400-yard Class 2 rock garden, followed by a 4-foot Class 3 drop that appears to be the ruins of an old mill dam. Then the action begins to really pick up; you are out of the flat water. From here to the Rush River, there are at least eight rapids of Class 3 or higher rating. Between the big drops, the river dashes though complex rock garden and small ledges. One Class 4 rapid is particularly memorable; the water funnels to the left, drops to the right, splitting about a VW-size rock; the S-turn to the left is extremely difficult, the chute to the right is not too desirable. But both choices are better than the other alternative.

The river has fairly high banks, and many trees and bushes along the side, so the scenery is blocked from view — when one has the time to look, that is. The bottom is almost solid rock; there are large rock formations along the side; and there are waves, hydraulics, and crosscurrents galore. This is not a stream for the inexperienced, the faint-hearted, the hesitant, the out-of-shape canoeist.

After joining the Rush River, which enters on the left, there is about 1.5 miles of Class 1-2 water. Takeout on the left just before entering the Thornton River.

Hazards: Possible barbed/woven wire fence. One very tough Class 4 rapid.

Water Conditions: Canoeable only in winter and spring following a prolonged wet period or very heavy rain.

GAUGE

A reading of 1.3' on the RC gauge at Fletchers Mill on the Thornton or 2.0' on the USGS gauge at Washington on the Rush River will be about 3" on the Covington. There is an RC gauge on the Route 622 bridge.

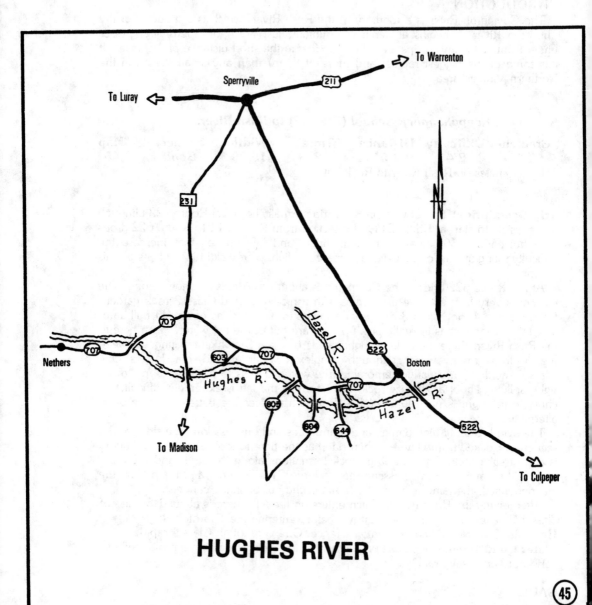

To Warrenton

To Luray

Sperryville

211

231

Hazel R.

522

707

707

603

707

Boston

Nethers

707

Hughes R.

707

805

Hazel R.

804

644

522

To Madison

To Culpeper

HUGHES RIVER

45

Hughes River

INTRODUCTION

The Hughes River starts at Old Rag Mountain as a series of waterfalls that can be only described as spectacular and non-canoeable. Since the hiking trail to Old Rag begins beside the Hughes, more hikers, have seen this stream than have canoeists. Below the settlement of Nethers, it becomes canoeable, but in only eight miles, the Hughes joins the Hazel River and it is no more.

Section 1. Nethers to Rte 231 Bridge

Gradient	Difficulty	Distance	Time	Width	Scenery	Map
62	2-3	3	1	15-25	Good	44

Trip Description: The upper reaches of the Hughes River are canoed only by the brave, the foolish, the unwitting, and those who love pain. The river makes a mad dash through near continuous rapids (ledges, rock gardens, and cobble bars), punctuated by a large number of barbed wire fences. It is exciting, challenging, and competitive, but it requires the canoeist to jump out of his boat in fast water to avoid the fences. Not normally run by canoeists, but runnable if proper precautions are exercised.

Hazards: Numerous barbed wire fences, one or more wooden cattle gates, possible tree across stream, briars on the bank.

Water Conditions: Canoeable only in winter and spring following a prolonged wet period or very heavy rain.

Section 2. Rte 231 to Boston (Rte 522)

Gradient	Difficulty	Distance	Time	Width	Scenery	Map
16	2-3	12*	3	30-40	Good	44

*includes 4 miles on Hazel River

Trip Description: The Hughes River from Route 231 to Boston is one of the better white-water canoeing streams in the eastern United States. The first 1.5 miles of this section was renowned for its briars and thorny bushes, so the trip usually begins alongside Route 601, near the chicken farm. The takeout is on the Hazel River at the Route 522 Bridge near Boston.

The trip begins with a fairly steady Class 2 rock garden that does not offer many eddies. The bottom is sandy where it is not solid rock or cobble; it has clear, unpolluted water with a fast current; and it has rocky bluffs and scenic spots galore. The rapids are mostly of the ledge type; there must be at least ten Class 2 ledges, all low-risk. The river is crossed by three bridges, one of which is a low-water bridge slightly more than six miles downstream.

Below the low water bridge, the Hughes River is joined by a small stream on the left; this is the Hazel River and Hughes River then becomes the Hazel River for the final four miles. The current becomes moderate, the banks are higher, and the bottom is beginning to change from sand and gravel to clayey sand with occasional gravel. There are nice Class 2 rapids until the last mile, which is mostly fast current and narrow passages.

It is difficult to say anything uncomplimentary about this trip. The ledges are exciting without being overly complicated; the current is fast and the pools between

131

rapids are few and short; and there are more beautiful spots for lunch stops than one can count. The putins and the takeouts are easy, short, and convenient; and there are a number of convenient bridges for walking out, if necessary. And there are no signs of pollution, trash, habitation, or cheap riverside camps.

Hazards: Low-water bridge, one barbed wire fence, at least one tree across stream.

Water Conditions: Canoeable normally in winter and spring following a wet period or a moderate rain.

GAUGE

A reading of 2.6' on the USGS Culpepper gauge is zero for the upper section, 2.0 for the lower section. The RC gauge on Rte 522 bridge indicates the level for Section 2. Add 8" for Section 1.

OTHER INFORMATION

Below the confluence of the Hughes and the Hazel Rivers, there is a magnificent mansion overlooking the river on the left bank; this is the Freedom Studies Center, a training center for officials from the third world nations. It is a quasi-governmental activity that assists the emerging nations by educating their executives and administrators in the methods for countering subversion and maintaining democratic institutions. The guest speakers include Heads of Executive Departments, retired military and diplomatic leaders, executives of international organizations, (World Bank, etc.), and business leaders.

The old store at Boston, near the Route 522 bridge, is a priceless example of the country general store that has a little bit of everything that one could want, but appears too disorganized for one to find it. The proprietor is one of the most independent women in Virginia and she is a no-fuss-and-no-nonsense type of the first order. A real example of rural Americana. Priceless.

About three miles below the low-water bridge, there is a small cave in a rock formation on the left bank that appeared to merit exploration. It seemed harmless enough from a distance, but upon closer inspection, it appeared that the entrance was almost blocked by sand pushed up from inside. Naturally, this aroused curiosity, until a canoeist with credible hunting expertise identified the tracks in the vicinity of the cave as belonging to one or more bears. Discretion overcame curiousity at that point.

The section of the Hughes River above the parking lot for the hike up Old Rag Mountain is a series of small, non-canoeable waterfalls in a magnificant mountain setting. There is a trail alongside the falls up to the Appalachian Trail/Skyline Drive area that is described in the literature of the Potomac Appalachian Trail Club. This is not an easy hike going uphill or downhill, but it is a hike worth taking.

Mountain Run

INTRODUCTION

Mountain Run is a stream that more canoeists have seen and passed over but have not paddled than any other in Virginia. In its upper reaches, it is a lake just west of Culpepper alongside Rte 29, from which it flows through the town of Culpepper, under Rte 29 Business and Rte 29 Bypass. It can be seen from Rte 29 Bypass, just east of Culpepper as a fair sized stream, but since it has no rapids at this point, it does not attract any attention. When viewed from Rte 620 Bridge near Kelly's Ford, it is a fast moving stream the size of the Hughes River, flowing over a nice riffle, just before it joins the Rappahannock.

Section 1. Brandy Station (Rte 663) to Rappahannock River

Gradient	Difficulty	Distance	Time	Width	Scenery	Map
6	1	14	6	20-30	Good	41

Trip Description: Mountain Run is a small stream that flows almost parallel to the Rappahannock River and enters it about ½ mile below the Kelly's Ford Bridge. It flows through fairly hilly country and fairly flat country, and its banks seem to be tree-lined for the entire distance. It has a moderate current in some sections, but there are many flat sections. Its bottom is sandy with gravel bar riffles in some sections; there are a few riffles of the gravel bar and rock garden type; and there are a few swift, narrow passages. The better whitewater is at the remains of old mill dams, and the riffle just above the Route 620 takeout. Those paddlers continuing below Route 620 face an upstream paddle of 600 to 800 yards or a downstream paddle of 28 miles for a takeout.
Hazards: Trees blocking the stream.
Water Conditions: Canoeable in winter and spring normally or during the early summer following an extended wet spell or very heavy rain.

GAUGE

A reading of 4.3' on the USGS Remington gauge or a 1.0' reading on the RC Route 29 — Remington gauge is zero for canoeing on Mountain Run.

HISTORY

Most of the bridges across Mountain Run were built at the locations of colonial fords or early grain mills. For example, the Route 620 bridge is the site of the ford on the road from Kellys Ford to Elys Ford, a major route in the early/mid 1800's. Union forces crossed at the Route 620 ford and the Route 672 ford while they were marching to the bloody battle of Chancellorsville.

Mountain Run was the locale for the Battle of Brandy Station in 1863. Union columns crossed the Rappahannock at Kellys Ford and at Beverly Ford, just below the confluence of the Hazel, in an early morning surprise attack. A bloody battle continued throughout the day, with cavalry units fighting at Stevensburg (on Route 3), at Fleetwood Hill (just north of Brandy Station), at Elkwood (on Route 29), and at Brandy Station. While Union losses were twice the Confederate losses, the Union cavalrymen gained the confidence in themselves and their leaders that enabled them to fight so fiercely in the later battles of 1863.

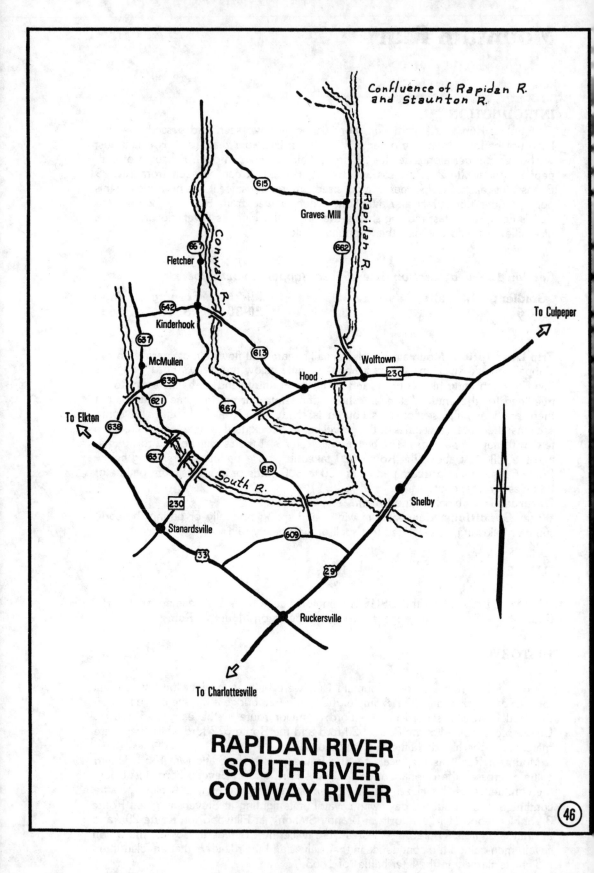

Confluence of Rapidan R. and Staunton R.

615

Graves Mill

Rapidan R.

662

667

Conway R.

Fletcher

642

Kinderhook

637

613

McMullen

638

Wolftown

230

To Culpeper

Hood

621

667

To Elkton

638

637

819

South R.

230

Stanardsville

609

Shelby

33

29

Ruckersville

To Charlottesville

N

**RAPIDAN RIVER
SOUTH RIVER
CONWAY RIVER**

46

Rapidan River

INTRODUCTION

The Rapidan River has its headwaters in one of the most beautiful areas in Virginia -- Madison County. It begins in the Shenandoah National Park in an area called Hoover Camp, where President Hoover escaped from the heat of Washington summers. From "President's Camp" to the Rappahannock River, a distance of almost 100 miles, the Rapidan passes through a countryside that has a history rivaled by few other rivers. The numerous fords, old mills and remains of mill dams, and the old iron furnaces testify to its rich and varied history. In its upper reaches, the Rapidan varies from impossible waterfalls to exciting white-water; in its lower reaches, it is a flat, meandering, slow moving Piedmont River; between, it is a pleasant, enjoyable, fast moving stream. On all sections, it is still a special river to Virginians.

Section 1. Shenandoah Park to Graves Mill

Gradient	Difficulty	Distance	Time	Width	Scenery	Map
35	2-4	2	1	15-25	Excellent	46

Trip Description: The first canoeable section of the Rapidan River begins within the Shenandoah National Park where the Staunton River joins the Rapidan River. This is the place where the Forest Service road, an extension of Route 662, leaves the river on a left turn. The putin is about 150' upstream. For the next two miles, to the first ford/bridge just below Graves Mill, there is no break in the rapids, so be prepared when taking on this little terror. It is almost inconceivable to imagine canoeing on the Rapidan above the putin for this trip; it is a continuous series of small waterfalls between large boulders.

The river starts with two complex drops between large boulders (Class 4) just below the putin; these rapids produced seven wipeouts from six highly experienced paddlers, one rapid claiming five in a row. There is one tortuous turn close to the right bank through a 4' wide passage, followed by a big drop. This passage should be scouted first time or the rapid should be run to the left of the big rock, scraping a lot. It is a Class 4, and risk-of-boat, for sure. Then there is an island to be passed in the right passage, plus a lot of other competitive action. Then it lets up a barely perceptible amount for the next mile After leaving the park, it is a more respectable stream with only one significant (Class 3) rapid which can be seen from the road. The bottom starts out as solid rock but changes to cobble; the rapids vary from boulder fields, big ledges, rock gardens, to cobble/gravel bars; the scenery includes parkland and farmland. The water is unbelievably cold and fast. The scenery is excellent, rock bluffs and evergreens, but paddlers do not get a chance to look at the scenery.
Hazards: At least three Class 4 rapids. Continuous Class 3 rapids. Trees/bushes extending over the stream.
Water Conditions: Canoeable only in winter and spring following a prolonged wet period or very heavy rain.

Section 2. Graves Mill to Wolftown (Rte 230)

Gradient	Difficulty	Distance	Time	Width	Scenery	Map
24	2-3	6	2	25-50	Good	46

Trip Description: Between Graves Mill and Route 230, the river changes its temperament, its size, and its hazards. It becomes a very fast flowing stream of increased

135

volume whose rapids are largely of the gravel bar type with sharp turns and narrow passages; the wave action is still good and there are a few ledges and rock gardens. At one spot, the river runs through a wide, wooded stretch with a lot of debris among the trees; all passages are equally good/bad. The principal hazards are a couple of trees that block the stream, the cattle gates under the bridges, a couple of fences, and a three-foot dam. The dam is a serious hazard with a difficult portage on the right. A number of canoeists have run this dam close to the right, but this is not a good policy.

The Rapidan has been channelized a bit in this section, but not enough to change its character. It is still a swift stream with clear water, flowing over a bottom of sand and gravel/cobble. It has fairly low banks that give a good view of the farmlands, except for the tree-lined sections.

Hazards: Three-foot dam midway between Route 662 bridge and Route 230 bridge; bad hydraulic. Big trees blocking stream in same section. Trees/debris two miles below Graves Mill. Electric/barbed/woven wire fences. Wooden cattle gates beneath private bridges. Fence below takeout bridge.

Water Conditions: Canoeable normally in winter and spring following a wet period or a moderate rain.

Section 3. Wolftown (Rte 230) to Shelby (Rte 29)

Gradient	Difficulty	Distance	Time	Width	Scenery	Map
16	2	7	2	40-60	Good	46

Trip Description: Below the Old Mill Museum at Wolftown, the Rapidan leaves the flat farming valley and enters an area with heavily wooded, rolling hills. The gradient increases to 27 feet/mile and for three miles, it is an enjoyable Class 2 white-water trip. The current is quite fast, the rapids/riffles are fairly constant, the scenery is quite good, the water is clear and cool, and the bottom is sand and gravel.

The Conway River enters on the right about 3 miles downstream, followed 2 miles later by the South River on the right. Between the Conway and the South Rivers, the Rapidan becomes a tame, fast-flowing stream over gravel bars, small ledges, and rock gardens. Below the South River, the Rapidan is fairly flat and the current is slow; the gradient is only 5 feet/mile. The banks are high and clayey, the bottom is sand and clay, the water is not quite as clear as it was upstream. The Rapidan is now entering the Piedmont area. The takeout at Route 29 is a welcome sight.

Hazards: Possibly a barbed/woven electric wire fence.

Water Conditions: Canoeable in winter and spring normally or during the early summer following an extended wet spell or very heavy rain.

Section 4. Shelby (Rte 29) to Liberty Mills (Rte 231)

Gradient	Difficulty	Distance	Time	Width	Scenery	Map
8.5	1-2	11	4.5	50-60	Good	47

Section 5. Liberty Mills (Rte 231) to Madison Mills (Rte 15)

Gradient	Difficulty	Distance	Time	Width	Scenery	Map
4	1-2	10.5	4	50-60	Good	47

Trip Description: The Rapidan River below Shelby tries to be a white-water stream, but it never succeeds. The rapids/riffles are too infrequent to keep up interest, the flat stretches are almost too long for comfort, and the current does not provide a lot of help. The bottom is mostly sand and gravel with signs of clay, the clay banks are high, the water is becoming more of a yellow color, and the banks are treelined. The terrain is fairly open and flat, great for farming but not very scenic.

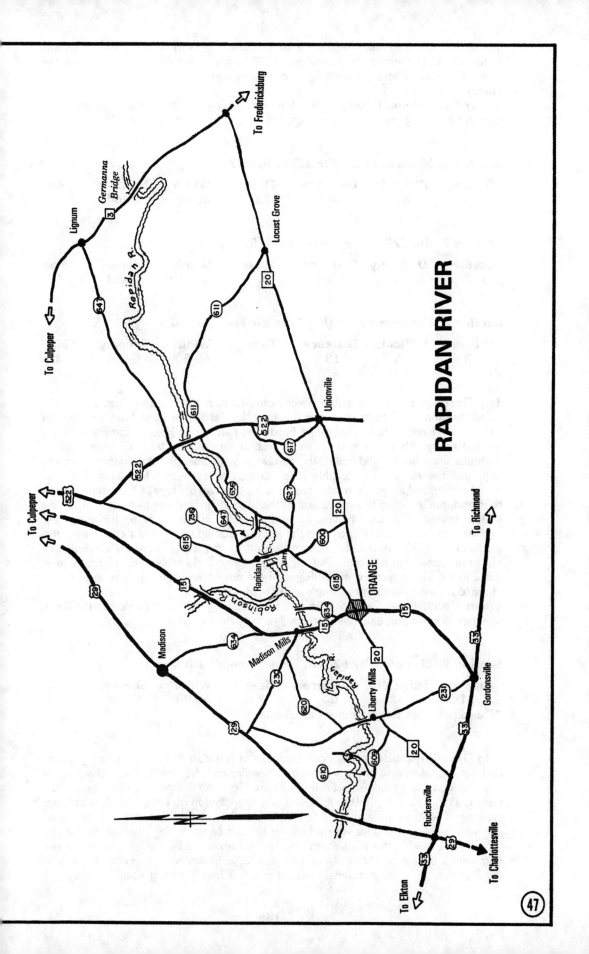

RAPIDAN RIVER

The more interesting riffles/rapids are the remains of old mill dams. There was a mill at the town of Liberty Mills, where Route 231 crosses the river, and one near the Route 610 ford. There are no mills or mill dams now.

Hazards: None.

Water Conditions: Canoeable in winter and spring normally or during the early summer following an extended wet spell or very heavy rain.

Section 6. Madison Mills (Rte 15) to Rte 522

Gradient	Difficulty	Distance	Time	Width	Scenery	Map
5	A,1	14.5	6.5	50-60	Good	47

Section 7. Rte 522 to Germanna Ford (Rte 3)

Gradient	Difficulty	Distance	Time	Width	Scenery	Map
3	A	13.5	6	50-70	Good	47

Section 8. Germanna Ford (Rte 3) to Ely Ford (Rte 620)

Gradient	Difficulty	Distance	Time	Width	Scenery	Map
3	A	13.	6	60-80	Good	42

Trip Description: The Rapidan River from Madison Mills to Elys Ford can be divided into many different trips, but the most logical sections are Madison Mills to Route 522, Route 522 to Germanna Ford, and Germanna Ford to Ely Ford. There are not many differences in these three sections of the Rapidan. All three sections are quite flat (about 4 feet/mile), the current is quite slow, the river banks are quite high, and the water is a noticeable yellow color. There are very few signs of rapids, and the riffles, what few there are, are mostly the gravel bar type. The terrain is open farmland, but it is hard to see because of the high banks and the trees along the side of the stream. The only hazard of note is a seven-foot dam at Rapidan, just upstream of Route 615. Portage on the left or let down on the right center over the old fish ladder. This is one of the prettiest spots on this river. There are a number of old fords across the Rapidan, and there are signs of old mills and old roads near these fords. These sections of the Rapidan are not white-water trips; so be warned.

Hazards: Seven-foot dam at Rapidan Mills. Boredom.

Water Conditions: Canoeable in winter and spring normally or during the early summer following an extended wet spell or very heavy rain.

Section 9. Ely Ford (Rte 620) to Rappahannock River

Gradient	Difficulty	Distance	Time	Width	Scenery	Map
11	1-2	6*	2	60-90	Good	42

*Plus distance on Rappahannock to takeout

Trip Description: Below Ely Ford Bridge, the Rapidan has an increased gradient and is more interesting to the white-water paddler and the serious float fisherman. It has one good ledge about three miles below Ely Ford Bridge, following two small rapids, all in a stretch of 200 yards; this was the location of Todd's Ford, a colonial crossing. There is a riffle about one mile below the putin bridge that appears to be the remains of an old dam with a lock on the left bank; at the entrance to the last rapid before joining the Rappahannock, there appears to be the remains of an old dam with a bypass on the right. The longest rapid in this section occurs just before the Rapidan joins the Rappahannock, a steady Class 2 rock garden for about ½ mile. Immediately upon joining the Rappahannock, there is a 400 yard long Class 2 rock garden (the remains of Rapidan Dam), so be prepared.

When starting on the Rapidan River at Elys Ford, the trip must end on the Rappahannock, as there are no more takeouts on the Rapidan. One can continue eight miles downstream on the Rappahannock to Motts Run Landing, which is about four miles above Fredericksburg, for an easy, well recognized takeout; or one can takeout just below Scotts Dam, about 2.5 miles after reaching the Rappahannock. This is a tough takeout that is hard to find with a poor road, but it may be better than paddling six miles against a wind or walking out.

This is the nicest section of the lower Rapidan River, as it has nice scenery, particularly in the last two miles, it has a good current, and it has nice rapids. The bottom is mostly sand; the banks are very high (10'-12') near the putin; and there are convenient, scenic lunch stops. After reaching the Rappahannock, a stop to inspect the canal and locks on the right is an imperative. Don't miss this engineering masterpiece.

Hazards: None.

Water Conditions: Canoeable most of the year except following a long dry spell. Canoeable after a moderate rain in the summer.

GAUGES

The Rapidan River has at least three gauges that can be used to estimate how much water is in each section. Use the following table to convert the gauge readings for a canoeist's zero level:

Section	USGS Culpeper	Gauge Location USGS Remington	RC Rte 29 (Shelby)
1	4.0'	5.5'	1½'
2	3.3'	5.2'	1'
3	2.8'	4.6'	6"
4	2.0'	4.3'	0"
5	1.8'	4.1'	-4"
6	1.6'	4.0'	-6"
7	1.4'	3.5'	-8"
8	1.2'	3.3'	-10"

HISTORY

The Rapidan River has its scenic or historical points. The mill museum at Route 230 is worth a visit; never have you seen such a fascinating array of belt conveyors, belt drives, millstones, and storage/transfer chutes. It is well worth the nominal admission fee. A number of rapids are the remains of the colonial mills that supported a largely agricultural citizenry. At one time, there was a mill about every 8 to 10 miles along the river. Most of the bridges across the Rapidan are where old mills were located.

The Rapidan River was the locale for one of the earlier, if not the earliest, industrial activities in Virginia. In 1714, Governor Spotswood, probably the most able of the colonial governors, brought 12 German miners with their families to Virginia and settled them on the south bank of the Rapidan. They established the settlement of Germanna, named for the German Queen Anne, where Virginia Route 3 now crosses the Rapidan, the site of Germanna Ford. In 1732, Spotswood, no longer governor, was still operating an iron furnace, a foundry, and a mill at this site. The ruins of Spotswood Furnace are about 400 yards upstream on the small run just west of the road to the Scotts Dam takeout.

When Governor Spotswood and his "Knights of the Golden Horseshoe" made their exploratory trip to the Shenandoah valley, they followed the Rapidan to the three forks area (Conway, South, and Rapidan) and then crossed the Blue Ridge at Swift Run Gap. Swift Run is a tributary of the North Fork Rivanna, about three miles from the South River of the Rapidan, the exact spot where Route 33 crosses the Blue Ridge. There is a monument at Swift Run Gap commemorating this trip of Spotswood and his "Knights", a trip that was marked more by parties, late risings, and hangovers than by diligent exploration.

In 1864, Union forces crossed the Rapidan River in pursuit of the Confederate forces under General Lee, using Germanna Ford, Skinners Ford, Culpeper Mine Ford, and Ely's Ford to cross the river; they briefly paused at the small crossroads of Old Wilderness Tavern. There was little indication that one of the fiercest and bloodiest battles of the Civil War was to be fought in an area known for its dense woods and difficult terrain. Two days later, Grant's forces has suffered 17,666 casualties in a force of 101.895; the Confederates had lost 7,750 from a force of 61,025. Uncontrolled brush fires were a major problem and fighting stopped at several points by mutual consent so that the soldiers could cooperate in saving the wounded; nevertheless, over 200 wounded soldiers were known to have been suffocated or burned to death.

There have been gold mines in the Rapidan and Rappahnnock valleys since 1831, principally in Orange county, but also in Spotsylvania County and Culpeper County. The existence of gold in Virginia was known as early as 1782, when Thomas Jefferson gave a description of a lump of ore weighing four pounds. This gold seam is an extension of the Montgomery seam that was mined extensively in Maryland near Great Falls. The more important mines at the time of the Civil War were located near the juncture of the Rapidan and the Rappahannock River (United States Mine and Culpeper Mine). There have not been any gold mines in operatiion in Virginia since the 1930's but there has been renewed interest in reopening some of the mines near the Rapidan since the price of gold has risen.

South River

INTRODUCTION

The South River is the smallest of the three rivers that flows together in the headwaters of the Rapidan River. It begins in the Shenandoah National Park, flows through a beautiful farming valley, and joins the slow-flowing Rapidan just above Route 29 bridge. It is best known as a trout-fishing stream and is seldom canoed.

Section 1. McMullen (Rte 638) to Rapidan River

Gradient	Difficulty	Distance	Time	Width	Scenery	Map
41	2	9.5*	3	15-25	Good	46

*Plus 2 miles on Rapidan River to Rte 29

Trip Description: The South River is best described as a nine-mile long Class 2 gravel-bar/rock-garden rapid. It is barely 12 feet wide at the putin and rarely exceeds 25 feet in width at any point. It has a very steady gradient and there are no major rapids or big ledges, just mile after mile of waves and maneuvering. The current is quite fast; the water is cool and clear; the bottom is mostly gravel in the upper part, sand and gravel on the lower part. There are two low-water bridges in this section, one on a state road, one on a private road; both are upstream from Route 231. It is frequently stocked with trout, so do not attempt to paddle this stream on opening day of trout season, regardless of the water level and your desires.

The trip can end at Route 619, about one mile above the Rapidan River, thereby missing two miles of the Rapidan. The Rapidan has a gradient of only 5 feet/mile below its junction with the South River, so it is quite flat and fairly slow. The trip can be lengthened by starting further upstream if there is enough water, a definite improvement over extending the trip by continuing three miles below Route 619 to the Route 29 bridge on the Rapidan.

The South River is hard to scout from the road alongside, as there are high cobble banks and there are trees along the bank for practically the entire distance. When the stream was channelized and cleared of briars, bushes, downed trees (a good operation, this time), the cobble/rocks were used to build up the banks. But the channelizing did not affect the stream too adversely, as the bottom is almost solid rock and the water velocity has already started reshaping the stream bed. Besides, who is going to look at the scenery.

Hazards: Two low-water bridges.

Water Conditions: Canoeable only in winter and spring following a prolonged wet period or very heavy rain.

GAUGE

A reading of 3.5' on the USGS Culpeper gauge should be zero for canoeing. A reading of 8" on the RC gauge on the Route 230 bridge over the Conway or 14" on the RC gauge on the Route 29 bridge over the Rapidan should be zero for canoeing. There is an RC gauge on Route 230 bridge over the South River.

Conway River

INTRODUCTION

The Conway River, also known as the Middle River, begins high in the Shenandoah National Park, dashing over waterfalls between Cliff Mountain and Bluff Mountain to reach a narrow valley below. It then rushes through this narrow valley, which is ringed by small mountains and high hills, until it joins the bigger and more sedate Rapidan River. It is a white-water stream for those canoeists who want to "whip their weight in wildcats", said Randy Carter.

Section 1. Above Fletcher (Rte 667 Low-water bridge)

The two-mile section above the low-water bridge (formerly a paved ford) at Fletcher drops at a rate of 150 feet/mile; above that section, it drops at an even more furious rate. It is doubtful if the stream is canoeable in the very upper part, but it will be near impossible to find out; when there is enough water to canoe at Fletcher, the ford upstream is too deep to cross.

Section 2. Fletcher (Rte 667) to Hood (Rte 230)

Gradient	Difficulty	Distance	Time	Width	Scenery	Map
70	2-3₄	5.5	2.5	25-35	Very Good	46

Trip Description: The Conway River between Fletcher and Kinderhook drops at a rate of 100 feet/mile for two miles, dashing over ledges, through boulder fields, over rock gardens, and past gravel bars, in that general sequence. The rock garden below the putin at the new low water bridge is too tough, so start a little downstream. And be prepared for continuous action. This is no place for the inexperienced, the hesitant, or the out-of-shape paddler. There are low-water bridges, continuous rapids, trees blocking part of the stream, and few eddies.

Below Kinderhook, the Conway River drops at a more modest gradient, only 60 feet/mile. There are many rock garden rapids plus one major sloping ledge with a hydraulic that eats boats; this ledge is easily recognized: about two miles downstream, right turn to enter, left turn for the four foot drop, big rock formation on the left, Class 4 in high or moderate water. There is one major log jam that is a risk-of-life hazard and at least one barbed wire fence at an S-turn.

The scenery in the first two miles above Kinderhook is excellent. The left bank is a high rock bluff in many parts, the right bank is lined with evergreens. Near Kinderhook, the valley opens and there are farm houses; below Kinderhook the valley is all farmland. The stream is treelined and the banks are high virtually all the distance, so there is little scenery to see -- if there were time to see the scenery. The water is exceptionally fast for the entire 5.5 miles and it is clear, cool, and unpolluted. The river bottom is almost solid rock in the first mile, broken rocks and sand/gravel for the next mile, sand and gravel for the next three miles, and mostly sand for the last half-mile.

Hazards: One barbed wire fence. One major log/debris jam -- risk-of-life. Cattle gate at Route 230 bridge. Trees blocking part/all of the stream, one big ledge with hydraulic.

Water Conditions: Canoeable only in winter and spring following a prolonged wet period or very heavy rain.

Section 3. Hood (Rte 230) to Rapidan River and Rte 29 Bridge

Gradient	Difficulty	Distance	Time	Width	Scenery	Map
31	2-3	2.5*	1	25-35	Good	46

*plus 5 miles on the Rapidan River

Trip Description: The Conway River from Route 230 to the Rapidan River is still lively, but it is quite a change from the upper sections. It has a more modest gradient, it is a bigger stream, the terrain is more open, and the rapids are not as continuous or as strong. Upon joining the Rapidan River, however, the entire river changes. The Rapidan has a gradient of only 8 feet/mile for five miles below the point where the Conway joins and it is something of a drag. The takeout at Route 29 is a welcome sight.

The lower Conway section is characterized by: clear, fast water; sand and gravel bottom; high tree-lined banks; open farmland. The rapids are small ledges, rock gardens, and gravel bars. The Rapidan River has very high banks (6'-8') and a slow current; the water is usually muddy, and the bottom is sand. The rapids are mostly gravel bars.

Hazards: Maybe a wire fence. Otherwise, none.

Water Conditions: Canoeable normally in winter and spring following a wet period or a moderate rain.

GAUGES

A reading of 3.5' on the USGS Culpeper gauge is zero for canoeing on Section 2; a reading of 3.2 is zero for Section 3. There is an RC gauge on Route 230 bridge and the Kinderhook bridge.

OTHER INFORMATION

In the mid-1960's, a group of canoeists, assisted by a large number of Scouts, worked to clear the many trees that blocked the Conway River. All went well until the final mile where the two work parties split. One group worked upstream from Route 231 bridge to an island with a ford crossing the river and the island, stopping at the ford. The other group worked downstream to the island with the ford, stopping at the ford. It was agreed by the two parties that the channel to the right side of the island would be cleared. So the upstream group worked up to the ford, clearing the channel on the right looking upstream. The downstream group worked down to the ford, clearing the right channel — looking downstream. Both parties left thinking that the river was clear. The following spring, a group of canoeists had a very rude shock; those going to the right met trees across the stream in shallow, swift water; those going to the left of the island met trees across the river in deep, swift water. Only the author, who was on the work trip, had figured out what had happened on the work trip; he paddled down to the ford in the right channel, stopped at the ford, carried his boat over the island, and paddled down on the left channel. He waited at the takeout for the others, who were wet, puzzled and mad (in that sequence).

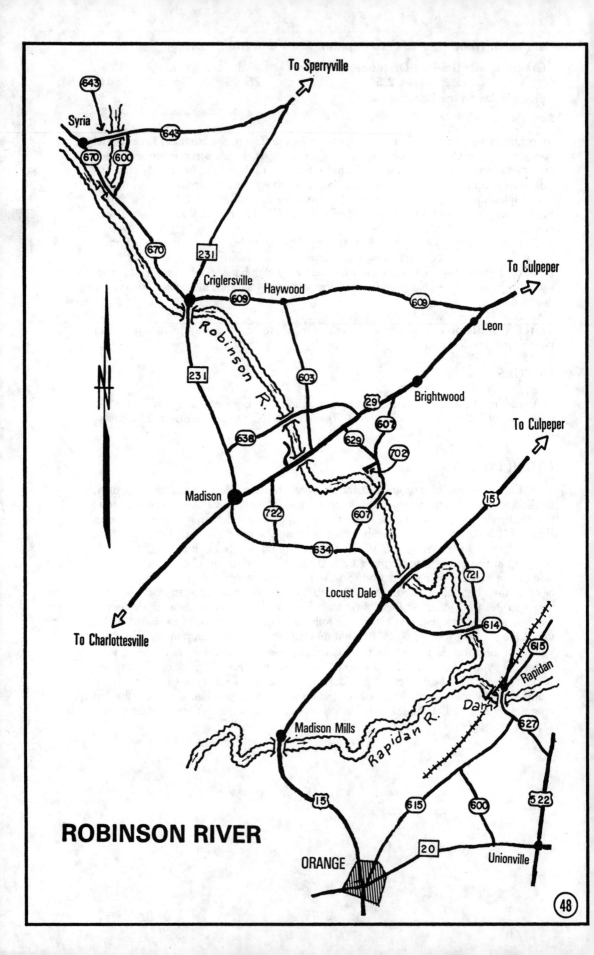

ROBINSON RIVER

Robinson River

INTRODUCTION

The Robinson River is one of the finest white-water streams in the Rappahannock watershed, and it is one of the major sources of pride in Madison County. It begins in the Shenandoah Park, not too far from the "President's Camp", as a brook cascading over a series of small waterfalls. It passes through a small valley with open farmland and apple orchards, joining the Rapidan River near the town of Rapidan.

Section 1. Syria (Rte 643) to Rte 29

Gradient	Difficulty	Distance	Time	Width	Scenery	Map
31	2-3	9.5	3.5	20-40	Very Good	48

Trip Description: The trip can begin on the Robinson River at Route 643 bridge near Syria or on the Rose River alongside Route 670 near Syria. At these putins, both streams are tiny brooks flowing swiftly over a gravel-bar bottom. Until reaching the confluence of the Rose River and the Robinson River near Route 670 bridge over the Robinson, the gravel bar rapids are Class 2, the water is clear and fast, and the scenery is very good. Below the confluence, which is a good putin at slightly lower water levels, the rapids include gravel bar rapids, rock gardens, and small ledges. There is more water as many side streams pour in, and the action is better. There is a paved ford at Criglersville, followed by a couple of Class 2 rapids, followed by a footbridge that blocks the river, followed by a low-water bridge that is runnable on the right side of a small island.

Just below the Route 231 bridge, there are three ledges, 2 to 3 feet high, in quick succession; these are Class 3 with water over 6". From Route 231 to Route 29 bridge, the current begins to slow, the bottom is mostly sand, the banks are higher, and the canoeist can relax. There are signs of channelizing in this section, good since it removed trees blocking the river, bad because the river loses its character. In a few years, however, it will return to a more natural state. The takeout is alongside Route 636, just upstream from Route 29 on the south (right) bank.

Hazards: Occasional barbed/woven wire fence. Low water bridge and low foot bridge.

Water Conditions: Canoeable only in winter and spring following a prolonged wet period or very heavy rain.

Section 2. Rte 29 to Locust Dale (Rte 15)

Gradient	Difficulty	Distance	Time	Width	Scenery	Map
6	1-23	9.5	4	30-40	Good	48

Trip Description: Between Rte 29 and Rte 15, the Robinson River is a Piedmont stream, flowing through farmlands over a bed of sand and gravel. There are a few small ledges, a few rock gardens, and a lot of gravel bars. The best rapid is below the dam, about two miles downstream, a Class 3 drop through cement chunks and boulders; the 12-foot dam was washed out on the right side during the 1969 flood. Just below the dam, on the north (left) bank there is a convenient takeout on Route 702. About a mile below the dam is a low-water bridge; the culverts are a challenge. Beware.

The current is moderate, the banks are high (very high just above the dam), the bottom is mostly sand, the water is becoming a bit yellow-colored, the rapids are less frequent, and the gradient is very slight (6 feet/mile). It is quite a change from the upper section.

Hazards: Low-water bridge. Occasional fence.

Water Conditions: Canoeable normally in winter and spring following a wet period or a moderate rain.

Section 3. Locust Dale (Rte 15) to Rapidan (Rte 615)

Gradient	Difficulty	Distance	Time	Width	Scenery	Map
6	12	6.5*	3.5	30-50	Good	48

*includes two miles on Rapidan River

Trip Description: The Robinson River begins its final meanderings below Route 15 bridge, and the canoeist will travel in every direction on the compass before reaching the Rapidan River. The river has only a moderate current, the bottom is mostly sand with traces of clay, the banks are too high to see over, and trees line the river for much of the distance. About two miles below Route 15, Cedar Mountain rises on the north (left) bank, but there are not many rapids. This is good farmland, there are few signs of littering, and it is pleasant canoeing. But it is not white-water. After joining the Rapidan, the trip must be extended for 2.2 miles to the town of Rapidan. There is a 6-foot dam at Rapidan Mill, 100 feet upstream from Route 615; portage on the left or let down over a rickety fish ladder on the right. Careful.

Hazards: Six-foot dam at takeout bridge.

Water Conditions: Canoeable in winter and spring normally or during the early summer following an extended wet spell or very heavy rain.

GAUGE

A reading of 2.1' on the USGS gauge at Culpeper is zero for the upper section; a reading of 1.9' is zero for the middle section; a reading of 1.7' for the lower section.

HISTORY/OTHER INFORMATION

During the early phases of the battle of Second Manassas (Second Bull Run), Jackson's Corps advanced from Gordonsville and crossed the Rapidan and the Robinson to engage Federal troops advancing on Culpeper. A fierce battle was fought at Cedar Mountain, just north of the Robinson and in the vicinity of Route 15. The U.S. casualties numbered 2,350; the Confederate; 1,340. When General Lee bypassed the Union forces who were deployed from Cedar Mountain to the Rapidan River to the east, the stage was set for the second major battle at Manassas Junction.

There is a beautiful lodge just north of Criglersville that has offered fine food, good lodgings, and southern hospitality for many years. Many newly-weds spend their honeymoons in this beautiful inn.

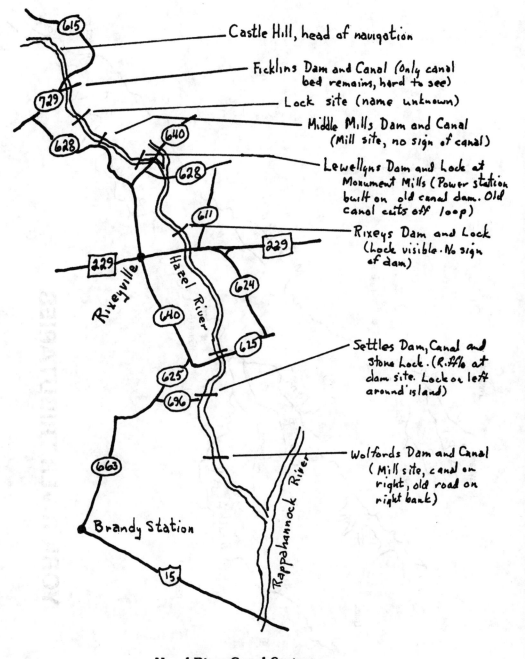

Castle Hill, head of navigation

Ficklins Dam and Canal (only canal bed remains, hard to see)

Lock site (name unknown)

Middle Mills Dam and Canal (Mill site, no sign of canal)

Lewellyns Dam and Lock at Monument Mills (Power station built on old canal dam. Old canal cuts off loop)

Rixeys Dam and Lock (Lock visible. No sign of dam)

Settles Dam, Canal and Stone Lock. (Riffle at dam site. Lock on left around island)

Wolfords Dam and Canal (Mill site, canal on right, old road on right bank)

Rixeyville

Hazel River

Brandy Station

Rappahannock River

Hazel River Canal System

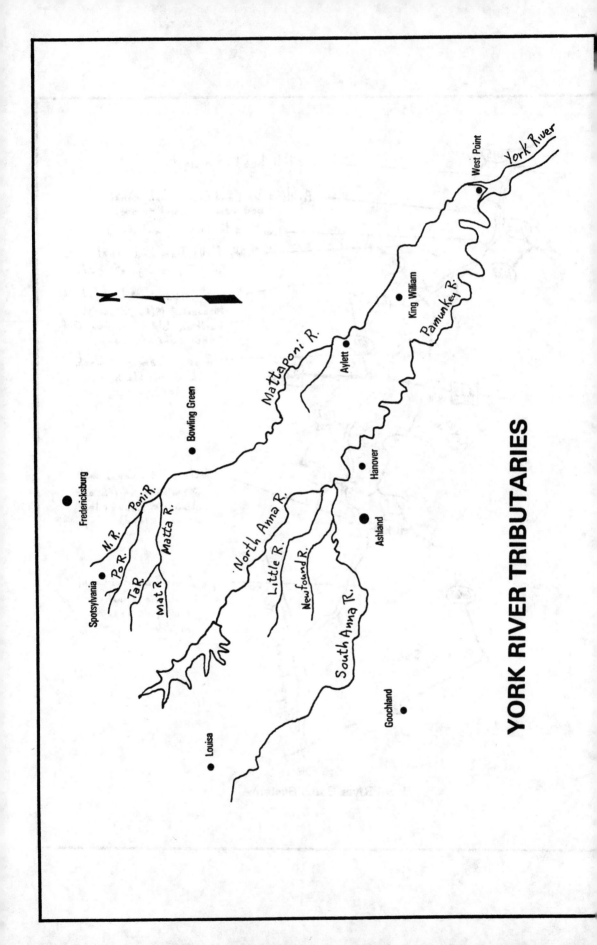

YORK RIVER TRIBUTARIES

Chapter 5

The York River Watershed

The York River watershed is entirely in Virginia, draining the Piedmont area and the coastal plains area between the Rappahannock River and the James River. The York River itself is a tidewater river, formed by the Pamunkey River and the Mattaponi River; it is not included in this book, only its tributaries. The York River drains about 2660 square miles in Virginia, about 6.6% of the state.

The following streams, whose locations are shown on Figure 7, are described in this chapter:

> Pamunkey River
>> North Anna
>>> Little River
>> South Anna
> Mattaponi River
>> Matta River
>> Po River

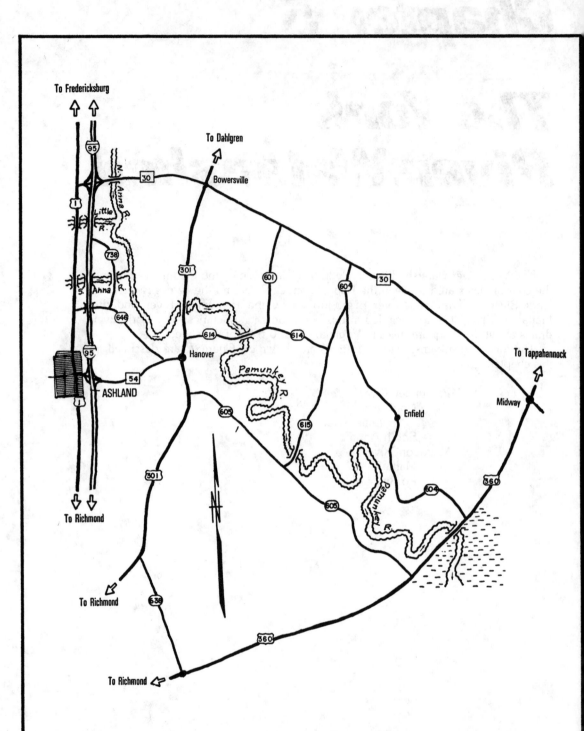

PAMUNKEY RIVER

49

Pamunkey River

INTRODUCTION

The Pamunkey River is formed by the North Anna and South Anna Rivers near Ashland. It is a typical river of the coastal plains, deep, winding, and fairly constant in width. It joins the Mattaponi River at West Point to form the York River. For about 40-45 miles, the Pamunkey has a current, then it becomes a tidewater river.

Section 1. Hanover (Rte 301) to Rte 360

Gradient	Difficulty	Distance	Time	Width	Scenery	Map
2	A	33	16	60-100	Good	49

Trip Description: The Pamunkey River is formed shortly after the North Anna and South Anna drop from the Piedmont to the coastal plains. The confluence is about 1 mile below the last bridge (Rte 738) on the South Anna and about 6 miles below the last bridge (Rte 30) on the North Anna. So the preferred putin to canoe the Pamunkey from the confluence to Route 301 is on the South Anna. From the confluence to Route 301 bridge is approximately 7 miles.

The most popular canoe trip on the Pamunkey is from Route 301 to Route 360. It is a winding river of fairly constant width with small, slow flowing streams feeding it at regular intervals. It does not become much wider as other streams flow into it; it just seems to get a bit deeper. The water is surprisingly clear and has a beautiful color as it is thoroughly scoured by the clean sandy bottom. The current is steady and the trees across the stream present few problems.

There is no way to escape the fact that the Pamunkey River is not a white-water trip. It is, however, a beautiful trip if one appreciates a pure wilderness that shows few signs of civilization, if one wants to see more wild animals and birds than ever before, and if one likes the silence that is achieved only in a wilderness. It is as if time has stood still for many years and only the movement of the canoe gives a feeling of time and space.

Below Route 360, the Pamunkey River enters a swamp area before joining the Mattaponi River at West Point. The swamp, in itself, is a beautiful swamp, if one has an appreciation for swamps. Many years ago, this area was the scene of extensive logging, but it has recovered. On the north bank, below Route 360, is the Pamunkey Indian Reservation. The Pamunkey tribe was one of five tribes that lived along the York River watershed; the others included the Mattaponi, Youghtayjnd, Werono-comico, and Chickahominys, all members of the powerful and warlike Powhatan Confederacy.

This trip can be shortened or broken into two one-day trips by paddling the section from Route 301 to Route 615 and from Route 615 to Route 360. Route 615 divides the trip almost equally. The trip can also be lengthened if the trip is started at Route 738 on the South Anna, the distance to Route 301 is about 8 miles; from Route 30 on the North Anna, about 13 miles to Route 301 bridge.

Hazards: None.

Water Conditions: Canoeable most of the year except following a long, dry spell. Canoeable after a moderate rain in the summer.

GAUGE

There is an RC gauge on the North Anna bridge (Route 1). A reading of 1.2' on the USGS Culpeper gauge should be zero for canoeing.

North Anna

INTRODUCTION

The North Anna River is best known for its Fallsline Rapid, but it is a river of many things. It had many mills and mill dams during colonial days, a major Civil War battle was fought on its banks, and the upstream reaches have been inundated by the VEPCO dam. Its rapids are quite competitive and the scenery is good; it is truly a pleasant white-water experience.

Section 1. Lake Anna (Rte 601) to Butler Ford Bridge (Rte 601)

Gradient	Difficulty	Distance	Time	Width	Scenery	Map
3	12	14.0	5	50-80	Good	50

Trip Description: The Lake Anna Dam of the Virginia Electric Power Company has dammed most of the upper reaches of the North Anna. Consequently, the upper North Anna trip begins at the first bridge downstream, Smith Mill Bridge, where Route 601 crosses the river. In this section, the river has a moderate current, the water is frequently muddy, the banks are 5' to 8' high, the bottom is sand and clayey sand, the banks are treelined. About six miles downstream, about 1/4 mile above Route 738 bridge, there is an abandoned power plant dam that has a drop of 10 feet and the machinery of the plant in the rapids below; just look at this rapid, don't try it. The next bridge is Route 603, the location of the Jericho Mill of colonial/antebellum days. The takeout for this upper trip is Butler Ford Bridge, site of the Old Quarles Mill. There are other putins and takeouts on this section, as the river is crossed by many bridges.

The rapids on this section are in the final two miles; they are mostly small ledges, although there is one good set of Class 2 rapids. The scenery is mostly a wilderness and there is very little litter/trash on the banks or in the river.

Hazards: Ten-foot power dam.

Water Conditions: Canoeable in winter, spring, and early summer, except following periods of little precipitation. Canoeable after a heavy rain in the summer and fall.

Section 2. Butler Ford Bridge (Rte 601) to Carmel Church (Rte 1)

Gradient	Difficulty	Distance	Time	Width	Scenery	Map
8	2-34	9.5	3.5	80-100	Good	50

Trip Description: The trip through the North Anna fallsline begins at Butler Ford Bridge, and ends at Chesterfield Bridge (Route 1). There are no convenient takeouts or putins between these two points, but there is one long, steep takeout walkout point on the left (north) bank at the Fallsline Rapid. The normal takeout is on the right bank, just below Route 1; try to be the first boat there, as that mud bank becomes rather slippery (and ego deflating) after two or three boats have wet it properly.

There are two rapids of note on this section of the North Anna. The first is a very long rapid (about 400 yards) that begins with small ledges in quick succession that increase to a three foot drop, followed by a complex rock garden. The second is the Fallsline Rapid (Class 4) which is comprised of two quick three-foot drops close on the right side, followed by a big drop (5') close on the right. There is more gradual

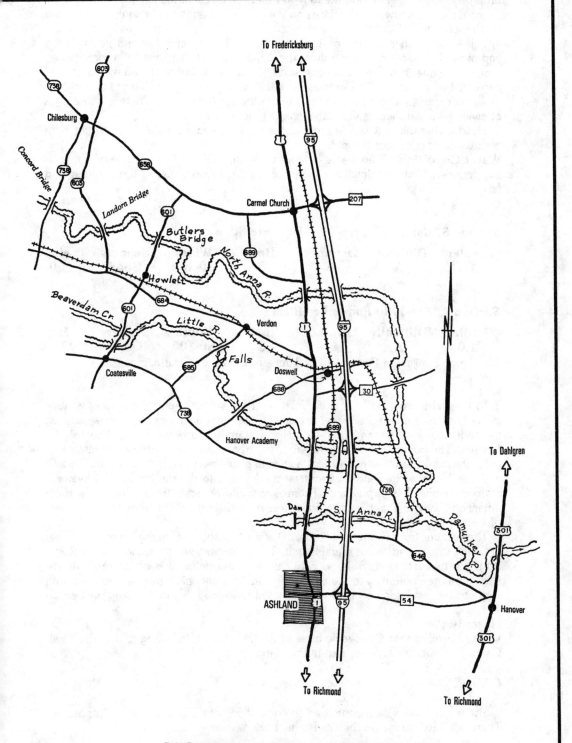

NORTH ANNA RIVER
LITTLE RIVER

50

drop on the left side in moderate to high water, followed by the big drop on the right or a couple of narrow, deadly drops on the left. Scout on the right bank or line down on the left side.

This is the prettiest section of the North Anna. The water is fast and flows over a bed of sand. The rapids are mostly of the ledge type, but there are good rock garden rapids. The river has clean sandbars, small islands, rock formations on the bank, and narrow, fast passages. The area is a virtual wilderness, owned by major lumber/timber companies who have planted trees in the cut-over areas. There are few signs of civilization and there is very little litter on the banks.

Hazards: One major (Class 4) rapid at the fallsline, about 1 mile above Route 1. In high water, it is a Class 5 rapid.

Water Conditions: Canoeable in winter, spring, and early summer except following periods of little precipitation. Canoeable after a heavy rain in the summer and fall.

Section 3. Carmel Church (Rte 1) to Rte 30

Gradient	Difficulty	Distance	Time	Width	Scenery	Map
1.5	A	6	3	80-100	Good	50

Section 4. Rte 30 to Pamunkey River

Gradient	Difficulty	Distance	Time	Width	Scenery	Map
1.0	A	6*	3	80-100	Good	49, 50

*plus 7 miles on Pamunkey or 1 mile upstream on South Anna

Trip Description: The river is very flat on these sections, and the current is quite slow. The riffles are of the gravel bar or sand bar type with long, flat pools between them. It is a good stream for fishing, for swimming, for sunning, and for picnic-lunches. The bottom is hard yellow sand, the trees have changed from hardwood to pine, the banks are lower. It is now a coastal plains river. There are islands, shoals, and beaches of white sand that contrast markedly with the dirt banks. The water is fairly clear and it is unpolluted. There is virtually no litter/trash. The Little River enters on the right about 3 miles downstream from Route 30, increasing the volume of water perceptibly.

The sections from Route 1 to Route 30 and from Route 30 to the Pamunkey River are quite similar and are of equal length. The problem with the section below Route 30 is the takeout, as there is no convenient access point. It is seven miles downstream on the Pamunkey to the next bridge and it is one mile upstream on the South Anna to the last bridge on it. So be prepared for a long day of paddling on Section 4.

Hazards: None.

Water Conditions: Canoeable most of the year except following a long dry spell. Canoeable after a moderate rain in the summer.

GAUGE

The water level is dam-controlled so correlation with USGS gauges is impossible. There is an RC gauge on the US Route 1 bridge.

HISTORY

The North Anna had a place in history in 1846 when the Confederates under General Lee were defending Richmond from the Army of the Potomac under Generals Grant and Meade. The Confederate forces were deployed generally on the southern bank of the North Anna River from Butler Ford Bridge (Route 601) to

Chesterfield Bridge (Route 1), with a force on the north side of Chesterfield Bridge; the center of their lines was at Ox Ford. Union forces crossed at Jericho Mill (Route 603), flanking the Confederates on the left and forcing a withdrawal; other Union forces drove the Confederates from the north side of Chesterfield Bridge. The main battle was then fought with the Confederate forces deployed in an east-west line on the south bank from Chesterfield Bridge to Ox Ford, and a north-south line from Ox Ford through Verdun to the Little River along Route 685. Over 150,000 men participated in this battle, and losses were heavy on both sides. The Confederates were forced to withdraw to Cold Harbor where one of the bloodiest battles of the war was fought.

There were many colonial mills along the North Anna; there were at least four mills on the section from Lake Anna Dam to the Fallsline Rapid. At Butler Ford Bridge, you can examine some ruins from the Old Quarles Mill, north bank, beside roadway. Examine these ruins while waiting for the shuttle. Then, about 4 miles downstream from Butler Ford Bridge, where there is a big flat rock formation (lunch stop) in midstream, there are the ruins of an old mill and a number of houses on the left (north bank). Take time to examine the stonework, the chimneys, the spring-house; let your imagination soar. You are at Ox Ford where Anderson's First Corps (CSA) was defending high bluffs along the right (south) bank against Burnside's Ninth Corps (USA) on the left (north) bank. Less than one hundred and twenty years ago, lunch stop rock was no-man's land amid shot and shell.

During Sheridan's Richmond raid in 1864, the Union forces crossed the North Anna at Butler Ford bridge and attacked a Confederate force at Beaver Dam Station, destroying locomotives, box cars, medical supplies, and rations and recapturing Union Troops who have been captured at the Battle of the Wilderness. This force, led by Custer's Brigade, then marched south across the Little River, and crossed the South Anna at Squirrel Run Bridge (now Route 33), fighting off fierce but ineffectual Confederate attacks. Part of the Union force captured Ashland while the main force moved to Yellow Tavern for a major cavalry engagement, where General J.E.B. Stuart was killed. Sheridan's forces then moved SE along the Chicohominy River to join other Union forces at Haxall's Landing on the James River.

Lake Anna is an impoundment for the North Anna Power Plant of the Virginia Electric and Power Company. This power plant is a nuclear plant and it has been the subject of much debate in recent years. It seems that the power plant was built on a geological fault that could result in a major shift in the earth below the plant. VEPCO had knowledge of this fault but built there anyway, citing the probability of a catastrophe being extremely low. Game theory (and common sense) will tell anyone that a strategy that includes the possibility of an unacceptable disaster, even with a very low probability, is a very poor strategy, particularly when the other strategies had few penalties (cost or time) and no possibility of that type of danger.

Little River

INTRODUCTION

The Little River is a very small river that is the principal tributary of the North Anna. It is a small, flat, slow winding stream for many miles, before it drops over a most impressive fallsline. Then it is a small, fast-moving stream to its junction with the North Anna just below Route I-95.

Section 1. Route 601 to Verdun (Rte 685)

Gradient	Difficulty	Distance	Time	Width	Scenery	Map
3	A-1	9.0	4	20-30	Good	50

Trip Description: The Little River above Verdun is a small, meandering stream through a very remote area. The putin at Route 601 is alongside the old road, just below the ruins of an old mill and old dam (2'). At the putin, the current is swift and the stream looks interesting, but it slows down appreciably (a 3-feet/mile gradient) and there are some trees down across the stream. In fact, there has been one tree just upstream of Route 685 bridge for many years.

The river has a sandy bottom, 2' to 4' high banks, dense vegetation along the banks, and a fairly slow current. The riffles are mostly of the gravel bar, swift chute, and quick turn type. There are not very many rocks in the river until Route 685 is approached.

Hazards: Trees across the stream.

Water Conditions: Canoeable normally in winter and spring following a wet period or a moderate rain.

Section 2. Verdun (Rte 685) to Doswell (Rte 1)

Gradient	Difficulty	Distance	Time	Width	Scenery	Map
12*	1-35	5.5	2	25-40	Very Good	50

*1 mile drops 40 feet

Trip Description: At the Route 685 bridge, the Little River changes its nature dramatically in many respects. The sand bottom and clay banks change to a rock bottom and high bluffs, the current picks up, the stream widens, and honest-to-goodness rapids begin. For the next 400 yards, the rapids increase in complexity and the drops are bigger. In one section, the rapids increase to three and four foot drops; one passage near the left bank, has a one-foot and two three-foot drops in the space of thirty feet -- just before the waterfall. Virtually all rapids above the waterfall are of the ledge type; below, rock gardens and gravel bars.

Waterfall Rapid is not really a waterfall in the classic sense although it is not a rapid in the normal sense. It is comprised of two portions which should be scouted from the island in the center of the river (very little water goes to the right of the island). Most canoeists portage on the right side; canoeists with an urge for self destruction will run the rapid. It is too complex a rapid to describe easily, but the secret to the first part is to enter close to the island, turn hard left for a small drop, turn a hard right for a five foot drop over a washboard rock (60 degree slide) into a pool with strong cross currents/eddies. The second drop is about 30 feet downstream; it is a five foot drop that would be simple except for the strong jet of water hitting the boat from the left side right in the middle of the drop. But don't let that stop you from

156

taking on an exciting drop which should be considered even if the first part is too much.

Below Waterfall Rapid, the stream is comparatively tame. It has high banks, very fast current, small riffles, and at least three trees that require lifting over or carrying around. Frankly, the lower part is so anti-climatic after the section with rapids that it s hard to enjoy a real nice run down to Route 1 wayside. So many people terminate their trip at Route 688, the midpoint.

Hazards: One Class 5 rapid about 400 yards below Route 685 bridge.

Water Conditions: Canoeable in winter and spring normally or during the early summer following an extended wet spell or very heavy rain.

Section 3. Doswell (Rte 1) to North Anna River

Gradient	Difficulty	Distance	Time	Width	Scenery	Map
3	A	4.0*	2	30-50	Good	50

*plus distance on North Anna and Pamunkey Rivers

Trip Description: Below Route 1, the Little River is still a small, winding stream over a sandy bottom with gravel bar rapids. Very few canoeists have been on this four mile section, as there is no convenient access to the Little River or the North Anna. So a trip below Route 1 on the Little River is really a 15 mile trip to the first takeout on the Pamunkey River or a 9 mile trip (one mile of which is upstream) to the last bridge on the South Anna River. If there were rapids in this stretch, it might be worth the long trip; but slow, flat water holds few attractions.

Hazards: One major Class 5-6 rapid 600 yards below Route 685 putin. Trees across the stream.

Water Conditions: Canoeable in winter and spring normally or during the early summer following an extended wet spell or very heavy rain.

GAUGE

There is an RC gauge on Route 685 bridge. A reading of 1.8' on the USGS Culpeper gauge should be zero for canoeing.

HISTORY

During the Civil War, a major battle was fought in 1864 at the North Anna, a few miles to the north of the Little River. During that battle, Confederate forces fell back to a line along the Little River; this defensive line was not assaulted, however, as the Confederates withdrew to the Cold Harbor area toward Richmond. The outlines of old redoubts, trenches, and field fortifications are still seen in the area of the bridge at Vedun.

There was a mill on the Little River at the waterfall in colonial days. One of the mill stones, all 200 pounds of it, is still there, on the right bank along the portage route.

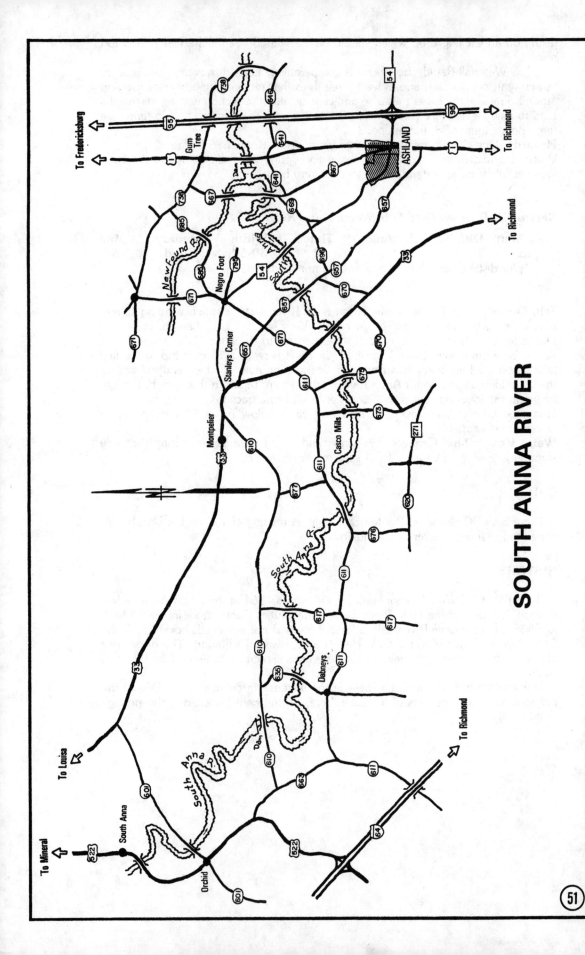

SOUTH ANNA RIVER

51

South Anna

INTRODUCTION

The South Anna is one of the longest canoeable small rivers in Virginia. It begins almost at Charlottesville and it seems that it should have been a tributary of the James River. Instead it flows southeast, parallel to the James River, and joins the North Anna River to form the Pamunkey River near Ashland. It is a pretty river that had many mills and mill dams, many fords and crossings, and good farmlands along the bank.

Section 1. South Anna (Rte 522) to Dabneys (Rte 635)

Gradient	Difficulty	Distance	Time	Width	Scenery	Map
2	A	17	8	30-50	Good	51

Section 2. Dabneys (Rte 635) to Casco Mills (Rte 673)

Gradient	Difficulty	Distance	Time	Width	Scenery	Map
3	A-2	12.5	5	40-50	Good	51

Trip Description: The South Anna River from the town of South Anna to Casco Mills is about 30 miles of a beautiful Piedmont river through an area that is almost a wilderness. There are numerous bridges crossing the river, but there are few signs of civilization along the banks. The area is wooded, the terrain is rolling, and there are farmlands nearby. The clay banks are high for most of the way, varying from 3 feet to 8 feet, and there are high bluffs in a number of spots.

There are very few rapids/riffles on these sections of the South Anna; most are the Class 1 gravel bar type. A couple of old mill dams, 2' to 3' high, might be runnable in moderate water levels; during high water, they are dangerous. The current is very slow, as the gradient is almost flat. Any less current would mean a swamp. The water is yellow in color from the Piedmont clay, but it has no industrial or sewer plant pollution -- just agricultural. The bottom is mostly sand, with gravel in a few spots. There are a few islands, a few swift/narrow chutes, and a few rocks along the bank. The broken dam just above Casco Mills and the rapid under the bridge are Class 2 and the best of this thirty miles.

It is possible to start further upstream on the South Anna, preferably at Route 646 bridge, just below the Yanceyville dam. The distance from Route 646 to Route 522 is about 17 miles but it is crossed by three highway bridges (Route 605, Route 699, Route 647), so it can be divided into shorter trips. The gradient is about 2 feet/mile, so it is flat and slow like the section below Route 522. The scenery is much similar. Just more of the same, but with trees blocking the stream.

Hazards: Low mill dams, two to three feet high. Almost every bridge has a dam/mill just upstream.

Water Conditions: Canoeable in winter and spring normally or during the early summer following an extended wet spell or very heavy rain.

Section 3. Casco Mills (Rte 673) to Ashland (Rte 54)

Gradient	Difficulty	Distance	Time	Width	Scenery	Map
6.5	1-2	10.5	4	40-60	Good	51

Trip Description: The section of the South Anna River between Casco Mills and Ashland is the best white-water, the best scenery, and the most accessible. It is a small river that has clean and clear water, sandy bottoms, small islands, sand bars/beaches, and intricate passages. The rapids are mostly long rock gardens, but there are a few small ledges and many gravel bars. The stream bed varies from solid rock in the upper sections to solid rock and sand, to rocks and sand, to sand and gravel, to sand. The banks are fairly high, 4' to 6' and they are treelined for the entire distance.

The Class 2 rapid at the putin starts the trip well, but there is little white-water until reaching a 3-foot ledge about 2.5 miles downstream. This ledge was also a mill dam at one time; there is a bridge about 100 yards downstream. The river has only light riffles until Route 33 (which is about mid-point) and then it is flat for about a mile. For the next four miles below Squirrel Run Bridge (Route 33), there are fairly continuous Class 1-2 rock gardens with a couple of small ledges. Then it has only light riffles for the last mile to the takeout at the pumping station. This is truly one of the most pleasant trips in Virginia.

Hazards: None.

Water Conditions: Canoeable in winter, spring, and early summer except following periods of little precipitation. Canoeable after a heavy rain in the summer and fall.

Section 4. Ashland (Rte 54) to Rte 738

Gradient	Difficulty	Distance	Time	Width	Scenery	Map
3	A	14	5.5	50-60	Good	51

Trip Description: The South Anna is once again a flat, uninspiring river. It is in the coastal plains but it seems more like it is in the Piedmont area; the terrain has low hills, and the banks are high and clayey, much similar to the upstream sections. The bottom is mostly sand, the banks are heavily wooded, and the current is only moderate. There are a couple of caves to explore, there is a side trip up the Newfound River, and there is a lot of wildlife. It does not have any rapids, however.

There is a major dam (20') just above Route 1 at the Ashland Flour Roller Mill; this dam has a backwater that seems to be at least four miles long. Portage on the left. Below U.S. Route 1, the river flows over gravel bars and sandy beaches with a moderate current. It has a few scenic spots, such as where Falling Creek cascades into the South Anna just below Route 1; this is a picturesque staircase adjacent to an exquisite rock hillside with hollows, caves, and interesting formations.

The South Anna joins the North Anna to form the Pamunkey River about 1 mile below Route 738. It is seven more miles of flat water on the Pamunkey to the next takeout point, so do not continue below Route 738 unless prepared for a long paddle.

Hazards: Twenty-foot dam just above Route 1.

Water Conditions: Canoeable in winter, spring, and early summer except following periods of little precipitation. Canoeable after a heavy rain in the summer and fall.

GAUGE

There is an RC gauge on the abutments of the weir at the pumping station. Two inches of water over the Ashland Mills dam is zero for canoeing upstream.

Mattaponi River

INTRODUCTION

The Mattaponi River System is many different rivers that are named in the most logical system that one could ever perceive. It includes the Mat River and the Ta River which flow together and become the Matta River; it includes the Po River and the Ni River which flow together and form the Poni River; and it becomes the Mattaponi River itself after the Matta and Poni Rivers join. The Mattaponi, in turn, unites with the Pamunky River to form the York River at West Point.

Section 1. Confluence Poni/Matta Rivers to Milford (Rte 207)

Gradient	Difficulty	Distance	Time	Width	Scenery	Map
1	A	10.5*	5	40-60	Fair	53

*Plus 2 miles on Poni River

Trip Description: The Mattaponi River begins at the junction of the Matta River and the Poni River, about two miles above Route 626. To paddle the section above Route 626, the putin must be on the Poni River (Route 606, near Guinea) or on the Matta River (Route 632); the putins add about 2 to 2.5 miles to the trip, all flatwater miles. So the trip normally begins at Route 626, where there is a very good swimming hole.

Below Route 626 and upstream of Route 207, the Mattaponi is a very, very flat (about 1 foot/mile) stream that passes through a major swamp. It is of great interest to paddlers who like swamps, trappers of beaver and muskrat, birdwatchers looking for waterfowl or birds that inhabit swamps, and marine biologists studying the role of swamps in our food chain. So, if any of these are your thing, then this is your stream.

The current is extremely slow, the water is clear, the banks are not very high, the terrain is flat and swampy. The trees across the stream are too numerous to count, the streams wind in many directions, there are a lot of beaver cuttings and a few beaver dams. The river looks fast, clear, and inviting at the putin, but it changes all too soon.

Hazards: Many, many trees across the stream.

Water Conditions: Canoeable most of the year except following a long dry spell. Canoeable after a moderate rain in the summer.

Section 2. Mattaponi River-Milford (Rte 207) to Aylett (Rte 360)

Gradient	Difficulty	Distance	Time	Width	Scenery	Map
2.5	A,1	30	12	50-100	Good	52

Trip Description: Below Milford, the Mattaponi is a beautiful stream for an overnight canoe trip. The water is a surprisingly clear green color, the bottom is sandy, it has high and low banks and occasionally high bluffs. It abounds in fish, birds, and mammals, and it has a reasonably good current. There are no major problems although there will be numerous spots where trees block the stream, particularly in the upper parts. There are numerous camping sites, and the trip length can be adjusted to the requirements of the paddler as there are crossings about every eight miles. The takeout at Aylett is about where tidewater begins, and it is a town of truly friendly people.

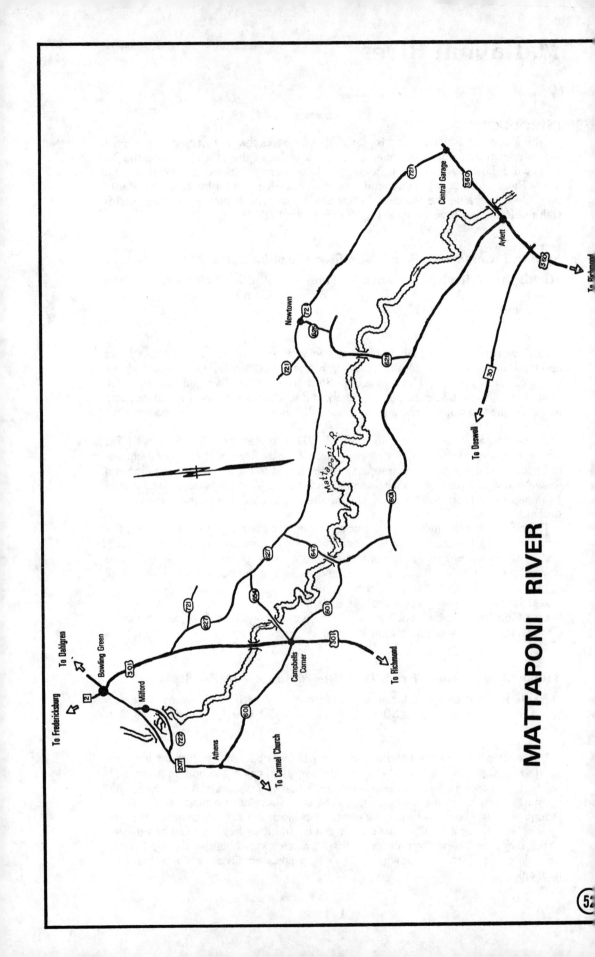

MATTAPONI RIVER

Below Aylett, the Mattaponi River enters another swamp area and then passes the Mattaponi Indian Reservation. It joins the Pamunkey River at West Point to form the York River. But the section below Aylett is for motorboats or marathon canoeists, as it is tidewater. A takeout at Herring Creek shortens the trip by about five miles; this creek enters on the right (south) bank.

Scenery: Wet clay glistens like solid rock; the clay changes from a red color to a grey color in one area. Exposed tree roots protrude where the water has washed away the bank. The bottom is a hard reddish sand for the most part. Often, black gravel lines the shallows and the sandbars. The trees over the river block the light and it is like paddling in a tunnel. The banks are up to ten feet high for long distances.

Hazards: A couple of trees across the stream.

Water Conditions: Canoeable most of the year except following a long dry spell. Canoeable after a moderate rain in the summer.

GAUGE

A reading of 1.5' on the USGS Culpeper gauge should be zero for canoeing on Section 1.

OTHER INFORMATION

The Mattaponi River watershed can be best described as flat meandering streams that flow through numerous swamps. The streams and swamps formed a major barrier to the construction of roads during colonial days and during the Civil War. Most of the battles in Northern Virginia were fought north, west, and south of this network of rivers/swamps. Only the battle of Spotsylvania Courthouse was in this watershed; the upper Ni River was crossed by many regiments in an encircling movement in this battle. After this bloody battle, the Confederate forces fell back to the North Anna for the next bloody engagement.

The Washington Post newspaper published a series of articles in 1975 about the Indian reservations in Virginia. It highlighted the problems that the Pamunkey and Mattaponi Indians were having in trying to provide an environment in which their heritage and tribal ways could be preserved but one in which they could reap some of the benefits of our modern society. The Indians are largely dependent on fishing and farming for a livlihood, with other income from the sale of home-made Indian articles. It is a hard life on these reservations and it takes a hardy people to survive.

Matta River

INTRODUCTION

The Matta River is one of the two principal tributaries of the Mattaponi River. It is formed by the Mat River and Ta River flowing together in the midst of a beautiful Piedmont swamp; later, it flows through a coastal plains swamp. There is only one rapid on the entire river, so the swamps are twice as numerous as the rapids.

Section 1. Snell (Rte 738) to Jarrells Mill (Rte 1)

Gradient	Difficulty	Distance	Time	Width	Scenery	Map
3.5	A	8.5	6.0	20-30	Good	52

Trip Description: The Mat River is just too small for canoeing from Route 647 to its junction with the Ta River. It is so small that a road map with mileage data is needed to identify which small stream is really the Mat River. The Ta River, however, is a nice size stream at Snell where it passes under a new, high concrete bridge. It is about 20 feet wide and five feet deep at the putin, and it doesn't get any wider in the next 2.5 miles, where it joins the Mat River to form the Matta River. The stream is very narrow, winding, and frequently very deep; the water flows rather slowly (the gradient is only 2 feet/miles) and is very dark in color.

The Mat and Ta flow through one of the most beautiful Piedmont swamps that you could imagine; the starkness and desolation of the swamp will impress you and leave you a richer person for having been there. It is not an easy canoe trail, however, as there are many trees across the only passage. It may be difficult to determine which passage should be taken, there will be occasional beaver dams (low dams that make nice ledges), and the banks are typical for swamps. The stream has a deep, silty/boggy bottom in the swamp area and a sandy bottom in the area below the swamp. The banks in the swamp are low, so the view is not obstructed.

It is very difficult to determine the stream bed in the swamp area and a lot of back-tracking is quite likely. It is even more difficult to tell where/when the Mat enters, as it appears to be just another branch of the Ta rejoining the main stream.

Shortly after the Mat and Ta Rivers join, the Matta River leaves the scenic swamp and enters the rolling Piedmont area. It also enters a stretch with at least fifteen big trees blocking the stream, and that does not count the trees that the canoeist goes over or under. It winds through a heavily wooded area with high banks and thick bushes/vines. The current is slow, the water is dark colored, and the bottom turns to sand. There is one gravel bar riffle and one spot with some rocks in the river -- that's all for six miles. Below Route 1 bridge, there is a good Class 3-4 rapid at the ruins of an old dam. Get permission to land on the sandy beach below the dam and scout the rapid before attempting it.

Hazards: Many trees across the stream.

Water Conditions: Canoeable in winter and spring normally or during the early summer following an extended wet spell or very heavy rain.

Section 2. Jarrell's Mill (Rte 1) to Mattaponi River

Gradient	Difficulty	Distance	Time	Width	Scenery	Map
9	1	7*	5	20-30	Fair	52

*Plus 2 miles on the Mattaponi to Route 626

Trip Description: Below Jarrell's Mill, the gradient on the Matta increases and it becomes a more interesting trip; it has more gravel bars, more frequent riffles, and small passages. It is still a small stream, however, and it still has a lot of trees across it. The scenery is still about the same; high banks, slow current, sandy bottom, light brown water, dense vegetation on banks. Don't let the beautiful sand beach at Jarrell's Mill give a false impression of the river; see it at Route 632 before attempting it and remember that there is another swamp below Route 632.

Once the Matta joins the Poni River, it has a lot more water, is much wider, and is quite improved. But it will be a long day from Route 1 to Route 626, longer than any nine miles should be.

Hazards: Numerous trees across the stream.

Water Conditions: Canoeable in winter and spring normally or during the early summer following an extended wet spell or very heavy rain.

GAUGE

A reading of 2.0' on the USGS gauge should be zero for canoeing. There should be enough water to run the ruins of the dam just below Route 1 to canoe either section.

OTHER INFORMATION

There is a large swamp that extends for about two miles or more below Route I-95. While the swamp on the upper section is a Piedmont swamp, this is a coastal plains swamp. The trees on this section have not been ravaged by a forest fire like the upper swamp, and there are more plants normally associated with the coastal swamps. There is definitely more current in this section, but the river is just a narrow as it is in the upper section. During the summer, this area should be teeming with water birds, beaver, and water moccasins.

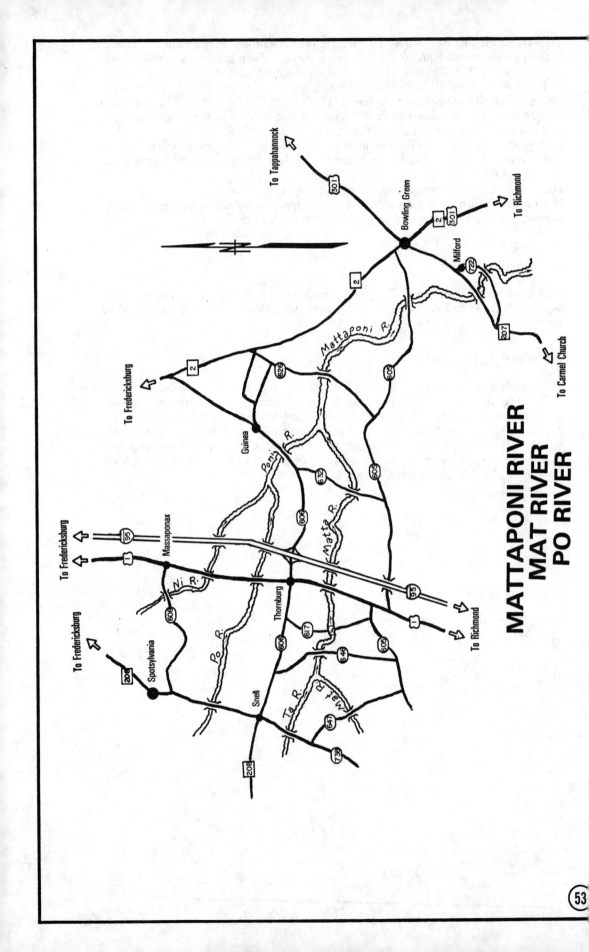

MATTAPONI RIVER
MAT RIVER
PO RIVER

Po River

INTRODUCTION

The Po River is the largest and longest tributary in the Mattaponi watershed. It begins near Spotsylvania and flows southeast to join the Ni river and form the Poni River. It is a fairly flat stream, start to finish, with the only excitment being at a dam millrace.

Section 1. Spotsylvania (Rte 208) to Massaponax (Rte 1)

Gradient	Difficulty	Distance	Time	Width	Scenery	Map
2	A	5.5	3.5	20-40	Fair	52

Trip Description: From Spotsylvania to Route 1, the Po River is about as flat as the Ta River, and that is really flat. It has very little current, the banks are fairly low and wooded, the water is fairly clear, and the bottom is sand and clayey sand. There is a nice riffle at the Indian Acres Campground, but very little else of a challenging nature. There are a few trees across the stream.
Hazards: Trees across the stream.
Water Conditions: Canoeable in winter and spring normally or during the early summer following an extended wet spell or very heavy rain.

Section 2. Massaponax (Rte 1) to Poni River

Gradient	Difficulty	Distance	Time	Width	Scenery	Map
10	1-2	4.5*	3	30-60	Fair	52

*Plus 1 mile on Poni River to Route 606 near Guinea

Trip Description: From Route 1 to the junction of the Po River and the Ni River, the Po River has it best gradient, the most riffles, and the best current. But it is not a white-water river. The best action is the mill race of a dam about 500 yards below Route 1, just above I-95. The stream then winds through a heavily wooded area into a swampy area; the bottom is sandy and clayey at the start but it gradually changes; the banks are high at the start but are lower further downstream. The current is slow and the water is clear.

The Ni River enters on the left, a very small stream, and the Poni is a moderate-size stream. At the Route 606 bridge, where there is an easy takeout, the river is wide and deep, probably because of dredging.
Hazards: Dam just below Route 1. Trees blocking the stream.
Water Conditions: Canoeable in winter, spring, and early summer, except following periods of little precipitation. Canoeable after a heavy rain in the summer and fall.

GAUGE

A reading of 2.0' on the USGS Culpeper gauge should be zero for canoeing.

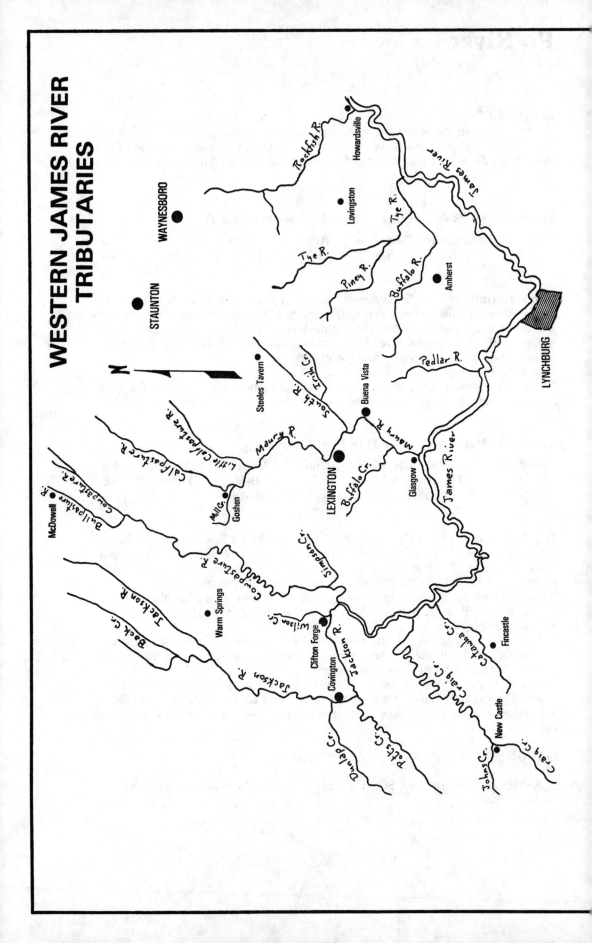

WESTERN JAMES RIVER TRIBUTARIES

Chapter 6

The James River Watershed

The James River Watershed is virtually an all-Virginia watershed (less than .1% is in West Virginia), and it has the largest watershed in the state. It drains the central part of the state, from the West Virginia line to the Chesapeake Bay. Its drainage area is about 10,100 square miles, comprising about 24.9% of the state. It has more tributaries, big and small, than any other two rivers in Virginia and it crosses more geologic regions than any other river in the state.

The following streams, whose locations are shown on Figures 8 and 9, are described in this chapter:

James River
    Jackson River
        Back Creek
        Dunlap Creek
        Potts Creek
        Wilson Creek
    Cowpasture River
        Bullpasture River
        Simpsons Creek
    Craig Creek
        Johns Creek
        Catawba Creek

    Jennings Creek
    Maury River
        Calfpasture River
            Mill Creek
        Little Calfpasture
        South River
            Irish Creek
        Buffalo Creek

Pedlar River
Tye River
    Piney River
    Buffalo River
Rockfish River
    North Fork Rockfish River
Hardware River
    North Fork Hardware River
    South Fork Hardware River
Rivanna River
    North Fork Rivanna River
    South Fork Rivanna River
        Moormans River
        Mechums River
Slate River
Willis River
Appomatox River
    Swift Creek
Chicohominy River

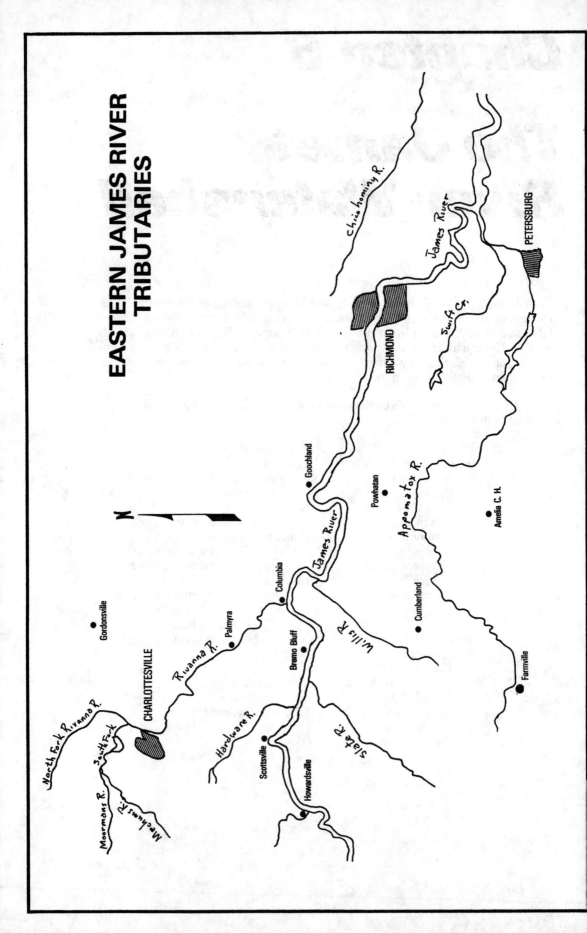

EASTERN JAMES RIVER TRIBUTARIES

James River

INTRODUCTION

The James River is the longest and the largest river in Virginia, draining over one-quarter of the state. It begins in the Appalachian Plateau, crosses the Valley of Virginia, breaks through the Blue Ridge, winds through the Piedmont, and drops down to the Coastal Plains. Its history is the history of Virginia and it has played a major role in the development of the state. Its major tributaries include the Jackson River, the Cowpasture River, the Maury River, the Tye River, and Rivanna River,· and the Appomatox River. It is unfortunate that it has industrial/municipal pollution, abandoned dams, and towns/cities that have abused such a magnificent river.

Section 1. Iron Gate (Rte 727) to Eagle Rock (Rte 220)

Gradient	Difficulty	Distance	Time	Width	Scenery	Map
4	1	16	6.5	90-100	Good	54

Trip Description: The first putin on the James River is at Route 220, about ½ mile below the confluence of the Jackson River and the Cowpasture River. The trip should begin at Route 727 just below Iron Gate on the Jackson River, about ½ mile above the beginning of the James River, so that the paddler can include this upper stretch. It is interesting to start at the Iron Gate bridge if for no other reason than to see the difference in the water from the Jackson and the water from the Cowpasture Rivers. Words cannot really convey the shock.

From Iron Gate to Eagle Rock, a rather interesting set of names for a trip title, the James River begins its trip of over 400 miles to the Chesapeake Bay. The river is quite wide, the current is quite slow, and the rapids are few and far between. The north (left) bank is preempted by the C&O railroad, the south (right) bank is largely farmland. The water is still polluted from the Jackson River, so swimming is not encouraged. The rapids are short rock gardens that cross the entire river, Class 2 or less; most of the rapids are the remains of the dams that were constructed between Buchanan and Covington when an extension of the James River and Kanawha Company canal was planned.

Hazards: None.

Water Conditions: Canoeable in winter, spring, and early summer, except following periods of little precipitation. Canoeable after a heavy rain in the summer and fall.

Section 2. Eagle Rock (Rte 220) to Springwood (Rte 630)

Gradient	Difficulty	Distance	Time	Width	Scenery	Map
5.5	1₂	16.5	7	90-110	Good	54

Trip Description: From Eagle Rock to Springwood, the James River is still fairly flat with a few more riffles/rapids. The rock garden rapids are the remains of old low dams built as part of the James River and Kanawha Canal system when it came upstream from Buchanan. Again the C&O is on the left, farmlands on the right. By the time the James gets to Springwood, the pollution is not noticeable, as aeration and dilution take effect. This is a nice, relaxing, pleasant flat trip good for beginners, fishermen, and escapists.

The current is moderately slow, the banks are high, the water is becoming clearer,

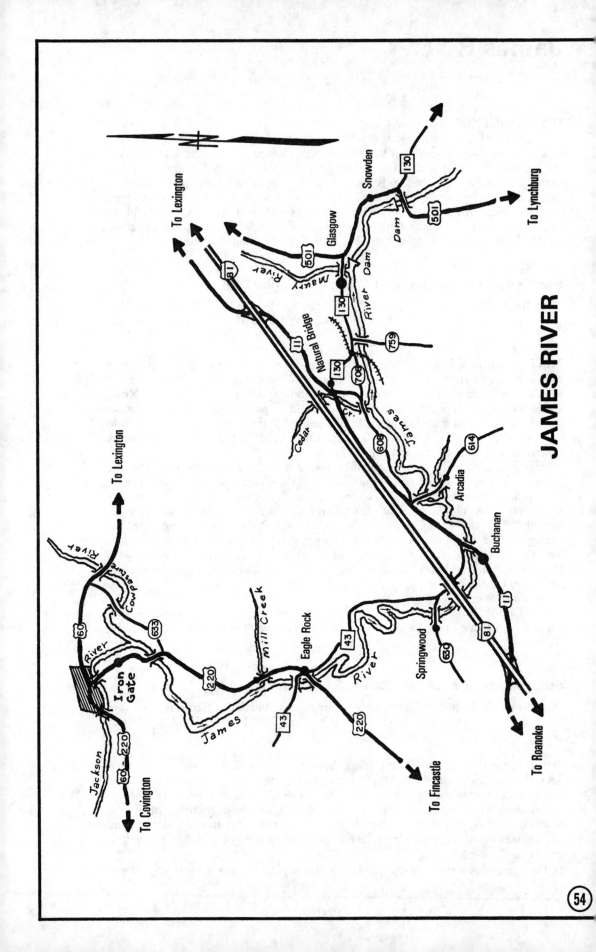

JAMES RIVER

the fishing is better. The river flows through rolling terrain in a surprisingly remote area; there are few signs of houses and there is no litter. The sandy bottom and the gravel bar riffles are definite plus factors.

Hazards: None.

Water Conditions: Canoeable in winter, spring, and early summer, except following periods of little precipitation. Canoeable after a heavy rain in the summer and fall.

Section 3. Springwood (Rte 630) to Arcadia (Rte 614)

Gradient	Difficulty	Distance	Time	Width	Scenery	Map
4	1	11.5	4	90-110	Good	54

Section 4. Arcadia (Rte 614) to Natural Bridge Station (Rte 759)

Gradient	Difficulty	Distance	Time	Width	Scenery	Map
5	1	13	5	90-110	Good	54

Section 5. Natural Bridge Station (Rte 759) to Glasgow (Locher Landing)

Gradient	Difficulty	Distance	Time	Width	Scenery	Map
2	A	3.5	1.5	100-110	Good	54

Trip Description: From Springwood to Arcadia, from Arcadia to Natural Bridge Station, and from Natural Bridge Station to Glasgow (Locher Landing), the James River changes very little. The gradient ranges from 2 feet/mile to 5 feet/mile, so there are very few rapids; all are Class 2 (or less) gravel bars. In the first section above Arcadia, the river passes under Route I-64 and Route 11 bridges near Buchanan, an industrious, pleasant little town. It is also crossed by railroad bridges. Below Buchanan and at Buchanan, the rapids, such as they are, are mostly the remains of old dams built for the James River and Kanawha Canal Company. On the section between Arcadia, and Natural Bridge Station, the river is fairly wide, the current is moderate, there are a few small islands, and the water is ideal for swimming and fishing. Before reaching the RR Bridge at Natural Bridge, Cedar Creek enters on the left; this creek passes under Natural Bridge, a geological wonder and a major tourist attraction. Natural Bridge is a limestone arch cut by water, 215 feet high and 90 feet long; Route 11 is built over Natural Bridge. From Natural Bridge Station to Glasgow, the river is very flat, as it is saving its energy for the plunge over Balcony Falls, the mighty rapids where the James breaks through the Blue Ridge Mountains. There are a few riffles, Class 1, in this section, but, at best, it builds a lot of character. The take-out is normally at Locher Landing on the Maury which joins the James River at Glasgow; it may be a hard paddle up to Locher Landing in high water, as there is a short rapid in the 200 yards between the landing and the James River.

Hazards: None.

Water Conditions: Canoeable most of the year except following a long dry spell. Canoeable after a moderate rain in the summer.

Section 6. Glasgow to Snowden

Gradient	Difficulty	Distance	Time	Width	Scenery	Map
11	2-4	5	2	110-130	Very Good	54

Trip Description: From Glasgow to Snowden, the James River passes through a gap in the Blue Ridge Mountains; this is the famous Balcony Falls section. The putin at Glasgow is at the end of Route 648, at Locher Landing, just above the point where the Maury River joins the James River; an alternate putin is Route 130 bridge across the Maury, a difficult putin. The takeout is alongside Route 501 at Snowden; there is no town at Snowden, only a sign and a couple of houses; the takeout is not too obvious; so watch for a trail to the river. The major portion of this trip can be seen from Route 501 wayside high on the north bank; it really looks easy from a 1000' elevation.

Just below Glasgow is the remains of the old VEPCO power dam; this dam is the site of the old Mountain Dam, which was built around 1840 as part of the JR&K Canal system. The upper structures of this dam were removed by an explosion in 1975 and a gap was created on the right side of the dam. Do not be tempted to run this gap, as the entire James River flows through this gap over a 9' to 10' drop into a lot of debris, metal work and steel reinforcing rods. It is a challenge only to paddlers with a death wish.

The rapids below the dam start with a series of small river wide ledges, none of which are above Class 2. Then there is the falls, a major ledge with a five foot drop; the passage is on the left or left center portion and has very big, very strong waves. It is a fairly honest Class 4 rapid at all levels. Below the big rapid, there are Class 2-3 ledges and rock gardens for about a mile or less. Then there is the backwater of the dam at Snowden; and character building begins again. The rapids in this area are named: White Rock Rapid, the Great Balcony Falls, the Little Balcony, and Tobacco Hills Rapid.

Hazards: One major rapid, Balcony Falls. Ten-foot drop in breakout of 18' dam.

Water Conditions: Canoeable most of the year except following a long dry spell. Canoeable after a moderate rain in the summer.

Section 7. Snowden to Six-Mile

Gradient	Difficulty	Distance	Time	Width	Scenery	Map
5	1-2	29	•	100-200	Poor	55

Trip Description: The James River between Snowden and Six Mile has a total of seven dams in a distance of 29 miles. The dams vary in height from 9 feet to 30 feet for a total height of 131 feet; the total drop in the river from the top of Snowden dam to the river below the last dam is only 155 feet, so almost 85% of the drop in the river is absorbed behind the dams. The dams include the Snowden Dam, Bedford Power Dam, Big Island Dam, Holcombs Rock Dam, Coleman Falls Dam, Ruesens Dam, and Lynchburg Dam. *Table 4 is a summary description of these dams. These are not easy dams to portage around; as a general rule, the only safe portage is on the right bank. This area is not recommended for paddling, but if one loves pain, it should be considered.

The scenery in this area is not very good, as the C&O railroad is along the banks and RR bridges cross occasionally. The river is polluted heavily in Lynchburg, a heavily industrialized city with steel foundries, paper mills, and chemical plants. The only rapids are the ledges and rock gardens just below the upper dams; these rapids end all too quickly in the backwater of the next dam, usually less than ½ mile downstream.

Hazards: Seven high dams, varying from 9 feet to 30 feet.

Water Conditions: Canoeable most of the year except following a long dry spell. Canoeable after a moderate rain in the summer.

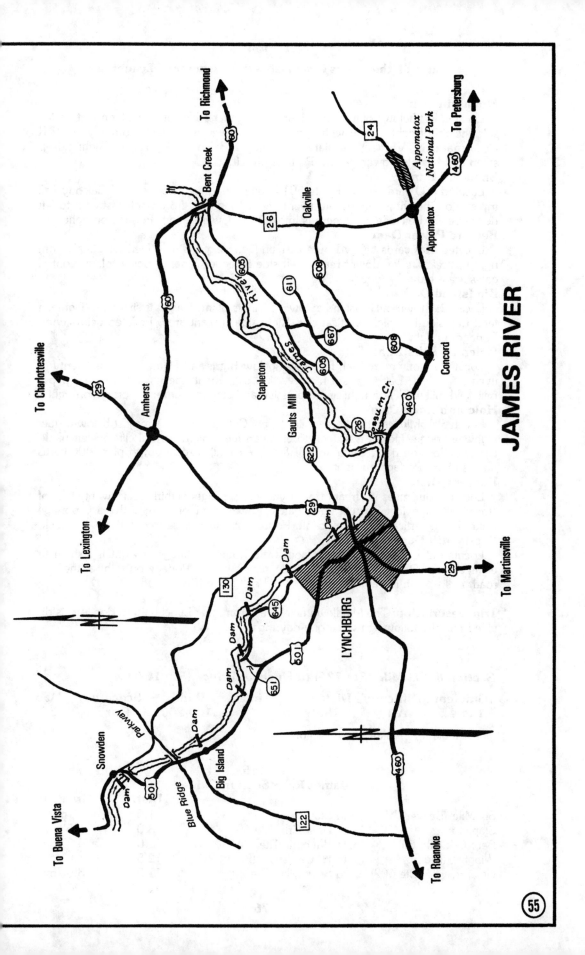

JAMES RIVER

55

Table 4
Dams on the James River Between Glasgow and Lynchburg

Mountain Dam

Located just below point where Maury River enters. Height is eighteen feet on left side; height of right section with upper part removed is ten feet. Formerly a JR&K Co. canal dam; VEPCO dam later. Just above Balcony Falls Rapid. Right side is steep and has old power station. Portage on left.

Snowden Dam

Located 300 yards above Route 501 bridge; one mile below end of Balcony Fall trip section; height is eighteen to twenty feet. Diagonals from right upstream to left downstream. Left side is dangerous intake to a power station. Portage on right.

Bedford Power Dam

Located 800 yards below Route 501 bridge. Height is nine feet. Diagonals from right upstream to left downstream. Left side is feeder canal to power plant; control gates are a hazard. Portage on right.

Big Island Dam

Located at town of Big Island at Owens-Illinois plant. Height is sixteen to eighteen feet. Left side is a high, vertical cliff. Right side is plant area. Polluted below dam. Portage on right.

Coleman Falls Dam

Located slightly more than four miles below Big Island Dam. Height is twenty to twenty-two feet. Left side is a high, vertical cliff. Right side has ruins of old paper mill. Old mill works on right are impressive and can be a hazard. Portage on right.

Holcomb Rock Dam

Located slightly less than three miles below Coleman Falls Dam; just below a state highway bridge. Height is sixteen to eighteen feet. High, vertical cliff on left bank. Diversion lock on right. Canal (old JR&K Co. canal) feeds a power plant 400 yards downstream. Portage on right.

Ruesens Dam

Located four miles upstream from Lynchburg. Height is thirty feet; twenty feet of stone dam, ten feet of steel flood gates. Power plant on right with easy portage route. High, vertical cliff on left bank. Portage on right, close to old JR&K Co. lock.

Scotts Mill Dam

Located at Lynchburg, ½ mile above old Route 29 bridge. Height is sixteen to eighteen feet. Dam anchored in right center on island. Portage on right at the railroad tracks or on left at the remains of old mill along River Road.

Trip Description: The Middle James River, from near Lynchburg to Bon Air, is divided into the following twelve one-day trips.

Section 8. Six Mile (Rte 726) to Hugenot Bridge (Rte 147)

Gradient	Difficulty	Distance	Time	Width	Scenery	Map
1 to 4.5	A-12	135*	*	100-200	Fair	56

*see table for breakdown of section

Table 5
James River Section Guide

		Dist.	Gradient
Six Mile (Beaver Crk)	to Stapleton	11.0	3'/mi.
Stapleton	to Bent Crk (Rte 60)	13.0	4.5'/mi.
Bent Crk (Rte 60)*	to Wingina (Rte 56)*	15.0	4.5'/mi.
Wingina (Rte 56)*	to Howardsville (Rte 602)*	12.5	3.0'/mi.
Howardsville (Rte 602)*	to Scottsville (Rte 20)	11.5	3.0'/mi.

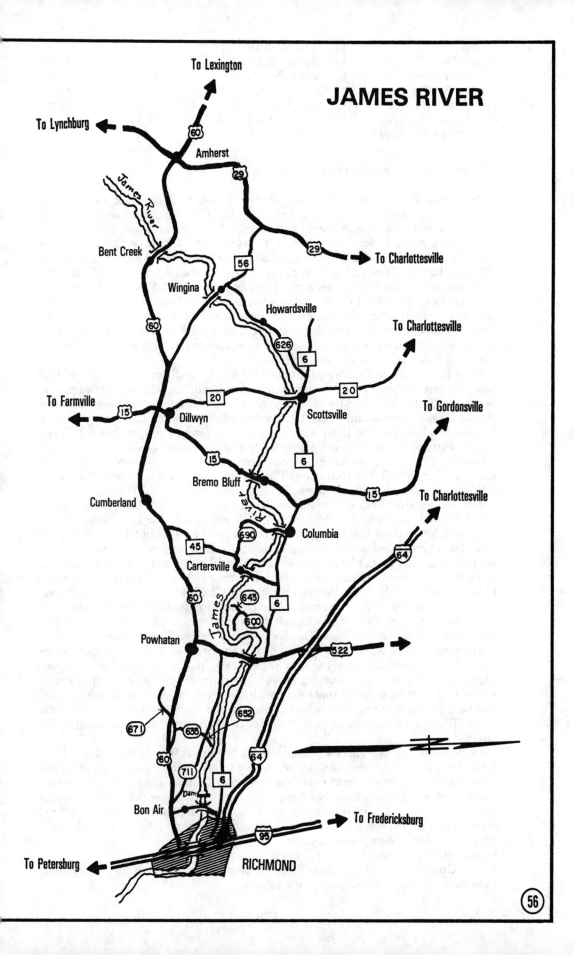

JAMES RIVER

To Lexington

To Lynchburg

60

Amherst

29

James River

Bent Creek

56

Wingina

Howardsville

To Charlottesville

29

626

6

To Charlottesville

20

To Farmville

15

Dillwyn

20

Scottsville

To Gordonsville

15

6

Bremo Bluff

River

15

To Charlottesville

Cumberland

690

Columbia

64

45

Cartersville

60

James

645

6

600

Powhatan

522

671

652

635

60

64

711

6

Dam

Bon Air

95

To Fredericksburg

To Petersburg

RICHMOND

56

Scottsville (Rte 20)	to Bremo Bluff (Rte 15)	12.0	4.5'/mi.
Bremo Bluff (Rte 15)	to Columbia (Rte 690)*	10.5	2.0'/mi.
Columbia (Rte 690)*	to Cartersville (Rte 45)	9.0	2.0'/mi.
Cartersville (Rte 45)	to West View (Rte 643)*	6.0	1.0'/mi.
West View (Rte 643)*	to Goochland (Rte 522)	12.0	1.5'/mi.
Goochland (Rte 522)	to Vests Store (Rte 652)*	12.5	1.0'/mi.
Vests Store (Rte 652)*	to Bon Air (Rte 147)	10.0	1.0'/mi.

*Virginia Game Commission Landing at this site.

The James River from Six Mile (near Beaver Creek) to Bent Creek is a long trip, about 24 miles, that drops a total of only 100 feet. This means an average gradient of about 4 feet/mile; the gradient varies from 3 feet/mile to 5 feet/mile, so don't expect very many rapids. The trip can be broken into shorter sections by taking out at Galts Mill, Stapleton, or Riverville, all on the left bank. The putin is on Route 726 over Beaver Creek with a short carry (or drag) to the James; Galts Mill is about 8 miles downstream, Stapleton is about 11 miles downstream, Riverville is about 4.5 miles upstream from Bent Creek. In this stretch, the river begins to recover from the industrial and municipal pollution from Lynchburg and it is fairly nice by the time the Virginia Game Commission landing at Bent Creek is reached. There are a few riffles and small rapids in a few spots that are not noticeable except in low water. All rapids are Class 2 or less; most are near Bent Creek.

From Bent Creek to Goochland (Route 522) the James River can be paddled with ease, as there are six Virginia Game Commission Landings (Wingina, Howardsville, Scottsville, Columbia, Cartersville, and West View) and two major bridge crossings (Route 20 at Scottsville and Route 15 at Bremo Bluff). Other takeouts are possible at Norwood, where the Tye River joins the James; Warren Ferry at Route 627 and Hatton Ferry at Route 625; and a couple of secondary roads near the major bridge crossings. The average distance between each of these access points is about 11 miles, varying from 5.7 to 15.0 miles. The average gradient is less than 3 feet/mile, with some sections having gradients of only 1 foot/mile.

The James River from Cartersville to Goochland is very flat; its gradient is only about 1 to 1.5 feet/mile. From Route 522 at Goochland to Hugenot Bridge (Route 147), the James River is still very flat, as the gradient is still about 1 to 1.5 feet per mile. The river has many islands, one of which is about 4 miles long, and there is a long backwater to Bosher Dam. Bosher Dam is a 14 to 16 foot high dam about 1.5 miles above Hugenot Bridge, and it backs water up for about ten miles -- or it seems to be ten miles. In this area, the river is big and wide, and in high water, it is awesome. The scenery, while nice, cannot compensate for the flat water, however.

The best sections of the Middle James River are from Stapleton to Wingina and from Scottsville to Bremo Bluff. The Scottsville to Bremo Bluff section is the most popular section for white-water paddling. It starts as a wide flat river that begins dropping over small ledges as the river approaches some islands. This is the Seven Islands area, but there are more than seven Islands there; one island, Big Island, is almost two miles long. In this one mile stretch, the river drops about 15 feet; the left side is easy; the right side is a rock garden rapid that is a Class 4 with certain water levels. There is a long easy rapid at the takeout. High water wipes out most of the rapids.

From Six Mile to Bon Air, the James River is a big river flowing through the Piedmont Province of Virginia. There are numerous small, sleepy towns along its banks, most of which are where small rivers enter, such as Columbia at the Rivanna River. There is no doubt at any time that there is strength in the water even where there is very little gradient. The banks are tree-lined for the most part, but most of the flood plain alongside is devoted to farmland. The terrain is mostly rolling hills and all the tributaries seem to dump muddy water into it.

Hazards: Sixteen foot dam near Bon Air.

Water Conditions: Canoeable most of the year except following a long dry spell. Canoeable after a moderate rain in the summer.

Section 9. Bon Air (Rte 147) to Mayo Island

Gradient	Difficulty	Distance	Time	Width	Scenery	Map
14*	2-45	6.5	3	250-300	Fair	57

* ½ mile # 30 feet/mile

Trip Description: Between Hugenot Bridge and Mayo Island Bridge, the James River enters its falls line, where the river drops 90' in a distance of 6.5 miles while passing from the Piedmont to the Coastal Plains. This section has a number of dams and heavy rapids that should not be undertaken by the beginning paddler. The first dam at Williams Island is about 3 feet high on the right channel and about 5 to 9 feet high on the left channel. It is not easy or safe to run this dam; so portage or start just below the dam. The putin along Riverside Drive on the south (right) bank from a parking lot will eliminate a lot of flat water and a portage. Try it, you'll like it.

The rapids below Williams Island Dam are of the Class 1 rock garden type with a few Class 2 chutes interspersed. There are fairly long flat stretches between the rapids until the first two bridges (Route 195 and a railroad bridge) are reached. Then the action picks up a bit for the next 1.5 miles with rock garden rapids (Class 2 in low water, Class 3 in high water). Keep to the right or right center of the river as Belle Island is approached; Belle Island is in mid river just across from the big apartment building on the right bank and a strange stairway. The dam on the right (south) side of Belle Island does not have water over it at normal levels; if it does, maybe you shouldn't be there. Look at the massive rock formations below the right side and imagine what a powerful, terrifying rapid that used to be. Then cross over to the break in the Belle Island Dam close to the island.

The chute in the broken section of the Belle Island Dam is the first of the heavy rapids that continue most of the way to the takeout. It is a five foot drop (Class 4) into a hydraulic that swamps most open boats and gobbles up decked boats. It can be sneaked to the left a bit or run fast through the center by decked boats. Most boats, gear, and paddlers are picked up on a set of rocks about 50 yards downstream. Below the dam, there are two strong Class 3 rapids before Hollywood Rapid (Class 4); this big, complex, deadly rapid is entered on the right, close to the island. Scout this one on your first trip or you may join a rather large club of those paddlers who have had trouble there. Below Hollywood Rapid, the rapids are Class 2 for about 300 yards, to the point where a pipeline/weir is crossed. Then there is a flat stretch for about 400 yards.

There is a rapid to the north of Hollywood Rapid that can be reached by paddling upstream and across the river after running Belle Island Dam. This is Cemetery Rapid, and it is a long, strong, complex rapid that contains all of the drop associated with the entrance rapids to Hollywood, the rapids below Hollywood, and Hollywood Rapid. The drops, the waves, the cross currents, and the holes are impressive. Rescue is difficult in this rapid because of its length and its strength.

The next rapid below Tredegar Street and the ferry to Belle Island is the remains of an old dam. At the left center, where there are rocks below the 2' drop, it can be run easily. But 200 yards below this rapid/dam is the VEPCO dam which has a 20' wide break with a five foot drop. This is a genuine Class 4 rapid with a most unusual wave at the top and a most interesting hydraulic below. Skirt the wave and the hydraulic by staying to the left.

Below the VEPCO dam, paddle toward the north (left) bank; part of this trip is upstream and is a lot of work, but it is worth it. For close to the left bank, near a railroad and a pipeline that parallel the river, is Pipeline Rapid, a series of drops varying from two to three feet. There are at least three good drops and about three lesser drops in a space of 100 yards; all are exciting. In high water, this stretch of closely spaced ledges is rather awesome, if not terrifying. Below these rapids is the Mayo Island Bridge, the takeout, and flat/tide water.

Hazards: Williams Island Dam, 3 feet to 9 feet high. Rapids at Belle Island Dam and below, at least three Class 4 rapids.

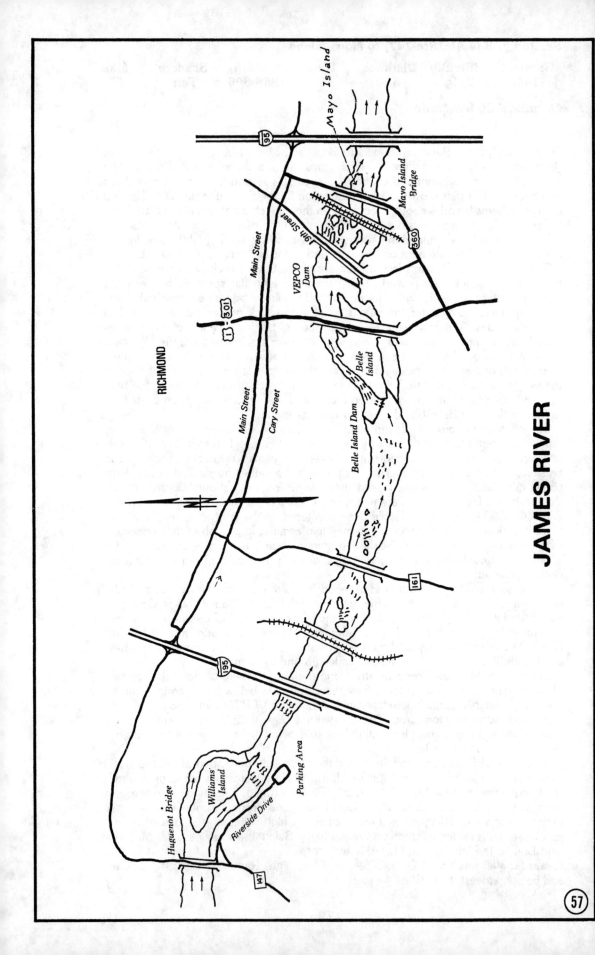

JAMES RIVER

Water Conditions: Can be canoed throughout the year, even following a long, dry period. Do not attempt at normal spring and winter water levels.

HISTORY

The history of the James River in the 1600's is a story of the trials, and despair, the privations, and the adversities of the English Colonists in the new world. It includes the settlement of Jamestown, the first permanent English settlement; the great Indian massacre of 1622; the explorations of Captain John Smith; the marriage of Pocahontas, daughter of the mighty Chief Powhatan, and John Rolfe; the introduction of indentured servants and slaves to work the plantations; and the establishment of the College of William and Mary. Few areas in the United States have the rich history and heritage of the lower James River valley.

The falls of the James River at Richmond were first explored by Captain John Newton; since this was the limit of navigation, this was the limit of colonization in the early 1600's. The James River valley above Richmond was rapidly settled, however, once the land in the Tidewater area was exhausted or became unavailable. Charlottesville, Lexington, Buchanan, Lynchburg and Covington became major centers of commerce and the river provided the transportation necessary to carry their products downstream and to bring finished goods upstream. Great barges, fifty to ninety feet long, propelled by a crew of three, made the trip from Lynchburg to Roanoke. Over 500 of these barges/batteaux plied the James River between these two cities, taking a week to go downstream and ten days to return.

The need for a canal system along the James River was recognized by the colonists, and a canal was proposed within the House of Burgesses in 1774. It was 1785, however, before the James River Company was organized to open the river for navigation above Richmond. George Washington was the company's first president, and he was an avid supporter of canals/waterways to the west. For the first 20 years the James River Company was a poor investment for the stockholders, but things gradually improved, and, in 1820, the state took it over. By 1840, there was 146 miles of canal open between Richmond and Lynchburg and by 1851 the section from Lynchburg to Buchanan was operating. Over 195 freight boats made three trips a week between Lynchburg and Richmond; there were daily departures for passengers between these cities. An extension from Buchanan to Covington was begun, using slackwater navigation (like most of the river from Glasgow to Buchanan), but this upper section was not completed.

As the James River and Kanawha Canal progressed, navigation on the James River tributaries improved. Canals were constructed on the Willis River, the Slate River, the Rivanna River, and the North (Maury) River. The Rivanna River canal and the North River canal were successful and provided transportation for goods between the James River and Lexington/Charlottesville. Other streams along the James River were crossed by viaducts that carried the canal above the tributaries; many of these viaducts are still standing and are used by the C&O railroad. The canal was heavily damaged during the Civil War, and after the Civil War, the railroads brought about the end of the canal.

The great Indian warpath through the Valley of Virginia crossed the James River near Buchanan at a ford near Looney's Creek. For many years, the settlers in this area lived in peace with the Indians who expected and received generous entertainment/food from the colonists. This accommodation ended at the time of the French and Indian War, when the Indians joined the French in making war on the Colonists. A surprise raid by sixty Shawnee warriors, a tribe known for its cruelty and fighting ability, almost wiped out the settlers along the James River in the Valley.

One of natures marvels, the Natural Bridge, is near the James River. This limestone arch, towering 215 feet above Cedar Creek was first bought by Thomas Jefferson from King George III. According to an Indian legend, the Monocans were fighting desperately against the Shawnees when they were forced to a great chasm. At the moment they faced annihilation, the Great Spirit erected a bridge for them. After sending the women and children across to insure that it was safe, the Monocan warriors fell back and defended at Natural Bridge. They escaped and gave credit to the Great Spirit for the bridge.

It was on the Balcony Falls section in 1854 that a canal boat with over 40 crewman/passengers broke loose from a tow line on the North (Maury) River during high water. The canal boat, the Clinton, washed over the Mountain Dam, as the river was too deep for the poles of the crewmen to touch bottom. The boat did not capsize when it ran over the dam, but the unfortunate souls on the boat still had the worse to face. It was at White Rock, just above Balcony Falls, that the captain and five people jumped from the boat to the rocks in midstream. Then the Clinton washed downstream through all of the rapids and, by some miracle, lodged gently on a rock near Snowden without damage or loss of life. A rescue of the people on the rock was undertaken, and a slave, Frank Padgett, lost his life making two attempts to remove the men from the rock during freezing weather on a flooded river. There is a monument alongside the C&O railroad to Frank Padgett's memory.

During the Civil War, the James River had its role. Belle Island, at Richmond, was used as a POW camp for Union enlisted men. The JR&K canal provided the means for transporting goods from the Valley of Virginia to Richmond until a Union raid by Custer on Lynchburg, Scottsville, and Glasgow damaged the canal.

The river is crossed by 29 bridges between the confluence of the Covington and Jackson Rivers and the Chesapeake Bay. Two ferries cross the James River between Howardsville and Scottsville. There are at least 14 dams of four feet or higher and its islands are too numerous to count. The river crosses the Valley of Virginia, the Blue Ridge Plateau, the Piedmont, and the Coastal Plains of Virginia. Its major tributaries included the Jackson, the Cowpasture, the Maury, the Tye, the Rivanna, the Slate, the Willis, the Appomattox, the Chicohominy, and the Rockfish Rivers.

Jackson River

INTRODUCTION

The Jackson River has its beginnings near the town of Monterey, Virginia, but it is not canoeable until it has travelled at least fifteen miles downstream. From just above the Little Mountain Gorge to its confluence with the Cowpasture River, where it forms the beginning of the mighty James River, the Jackson River travels about 71 miles through gorges and valleys, through white-water and quiet water, past farms and towns. It changes from free-flowing to a massive dam impoundment, from clear and clean to dark and polluted, from remote wilderness to urban complexes, from country crossroads to industrial giants. Its tributaries, Back Creek, Potts Creek, Dunlap Creek, Wilson Creek, and its gorges, Little Mountain Gorge, Richardson Gorge, and the Jackson Gorge, give the Jackson River a place in the heart of all paddlers.

Section 1. Starr Chapel (Rte 220) to Warm Springs (Rte 39)

Gradient	Difficulty	Distance	Time	Width	Scenery	Map
22*	2-3	11	4	25-40	Very Good	58

*4 miles at 50 feet/mile

Trip Description: From Route 220 bridge north of Warm Springs to Route 39 bridge west of Warm Springs, the Jackson River travels between Little Mountain and Warwick Mountain. This is not a gorge of the magnitude of the two gorges downstream, but it is certainly a mountain pass for about six miles. At the putin, the river is about 30'-40' wide, the water is clear and fast, and the bottom is rock and gravel. The rapids start as rock gardens and gravel bars, changing to rock gardens, boulder fields, and small ledges as it enters the gorge. While the overall gradient on this section is 22 feet/mile, four miles of the gorge drops at 50 feet/mile. It is good that the Jackson is a fairly small stream in this area. The rapids are at least Class 2-3, they are frequent and fairly long, but they are fairly continuous. One three-foot ledge across the entire river is quite interesting; it is at a spot where there is a high cliff on the left in a right turn which masks it. Good sport. Stay awake. Below this gorge, the terrain opens into Hidden Valley and a mansion formerly owned by W. R. Grace; there is a concrete low-water bridge to portage and good spots to camp along the river. Below the low-water bridge, the rapids change to the cobble bar type, the current becomes moderate, and the scenery is very good. This section has real white-water and beautiful scenery.
Hazards: Low-water bridge.
Water Conditions: Canoeable normally in winter and spring following a wet period or a moderate rain.

Section 2. Warm Springs (Rte 39) to McClintic Bridge (Rte 603)

Gradient	Difficulty	Distance	Time	Width	Scenery	Map
25*	2-3	5.5	2	30-50	Excellent	58

*2 miles at 40 feet/mile

Trip Description: From Route 39 bridge to McClintic Bridge below Back Creek, the Jackson River begins with a bit of meandering in a valley/farmland area. After three miles of riffles, Class 1-2 rapids, the Jackson enters the Richardson Gorge,

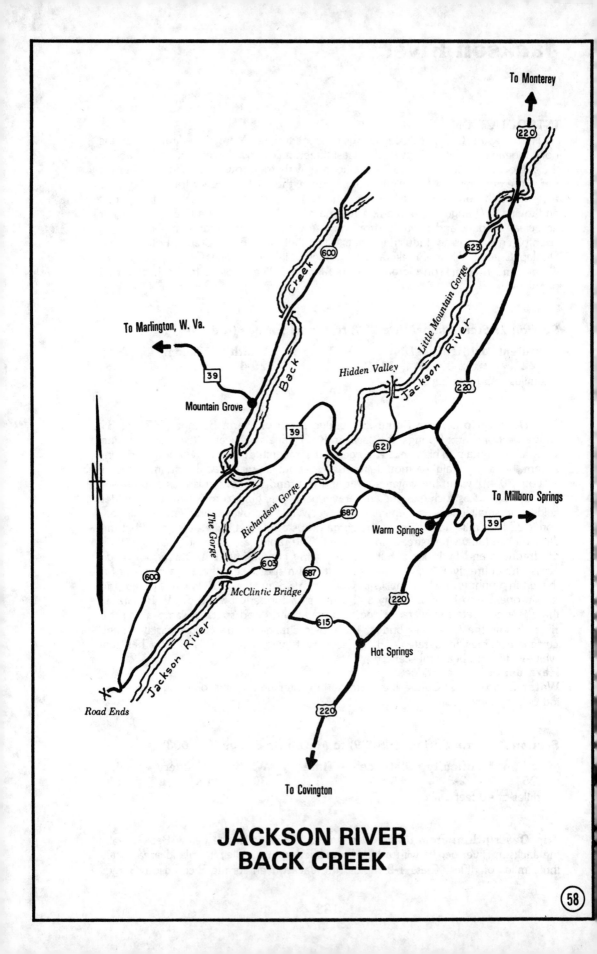

JACKSON RIVER
BACK CREEK

where it drops at 40 feet/mile for two miles. The rapids include rock gardens, boulder fields, and ledges, Class 2-3 or slightly better; the rapids are fairly continuous, the pools are rather short, and the action is exciting. Again, it is good that the Jackson is still a fairly small stream, for it would be a nightmare to face this gradient in a narrow gorge on a big river. The ledges are less than 3 feet, the maneuvering is demanding, and the scenery is spectacular. The water is still clear, the bottom is almost solid rock, and the cliffs are awesome. The gorge ends as Back Creek joins the Jackson from the right (west) about 200 yards from McClintic Bridge. Route 603 bridge is at the beginning of the backwater from the Garthright Dam.

Hazard: Low-water bridge at start of gorge.

Water Conditions: Canoeable in winter and spring normally or during the early summer following an extended wet spell or very heavy rain.

Section 3. McClintic Bridge (Rte 603) to Garthright Dam

Gradient	Difficulty	Distance	Time	Width	Scenery	Map
*	*	12.5	6	50-300	Good	59

*Backwater of dam

Trip Description: The Jackson River from Route 603 to the Gathright dam will be flat water for 12.5 miles upon completion of this Corps of Engineers dam. In its natural state, the Jackson had about 11.5 miles of Class 1-2-3 riffles and rapids before it entered the Jackson gorge. In the gorge, the river dropped at 40 feet/mile over tremendous rapids (Class 3-4). It was a much bigger river, as Back Creek had doubled the water in the Jackson, and the strength/power of the water was evident. Now it is only a memory, for the dam is in the middle of the gorge.

Hazards: None.

Water Conditions: Not applicable to backwater of a dam.

Section 4. Garthright Dam to Clearwater Park (Rte 687)

Gradient	Difficulty	Distance	Time	Width	Scenery	Map
11	1-2	13	5	50-80	Fair	59

Trip Description: From the foot of Gartright dam to Clearwater Park, the Jackson River is flowing through a narrow valley, close to the bluffs on the right and then close to the bluffs on the left. It is a mild white-water stream with occasional Class 1-2 gravel bar rapids; there is one rapid that might be a low Class 3. The water is still clear, the current is moderate, but the stream has had its spirit broken by the dam and is meekly proceeding to the pollution from the WESVACO plants in Covington. Roads touch the river on both banks and there are a couple of bridges, so the trip can be broken into segments. The banks are fairly high, the bottom is sand and gravel, there are more signs of litter, and there are houses along the banks.

Hazards: None.

Water Conditions: Subject to releases from Garthright Dam (U.S. Army Corps of Engineers).

Section 5. Clearwater Park (Rte 687) to Idlewilde (Rte 18)

Gradient	Difficulty	Distance	Time	Width	Scenery	Map
7	1-2	11.5	5	60-80	Poor	59

Trip Description: From Clearwater Park to Idlewilde (Rte 18), the destruction at the Jackson River is completed. It is a fairly wide stream at the start of this section, flowing over a sand bottom and passing Class 1-2 rock gardens and gravel bars until it reaches the backwater of the WESVACO Dam in Covington. The dam is about 7 feet high and is easily spotted; portage on the right. Below this plant, the river is not fit for man or fish and the air is not much better. The river is joined by Dunlap Creek, passes under Route 60, under a city street bridge, under Route 220 bridge, and then another bridge before arriving at Potts Creek on the right and the takeout bridge. Few people canoe this section because of the air and water pollution and the lack of a good gradient (which means a lack of rapids).

Hazards: Seven foot dam at WESVACO plant in Covington.

Water Conditions: Subject to releases from Garthright Dam (U.S. Army Corps of Engineers)

Section 6. Idlewilde (Rte 18) to James River

Gradient	Difficulty	Distance	Time	Width	Scenery	Map
11	1-2	18	7	70-90	Fair	59

Trip Description: The trip from Idlewilde (Rte 18) to the James River is one long trip (18 miles) that could be broken up into two short trips. The entire stretch has a gradient of 11 fpm, but the best rapids are in the first five miles where it passes between Horse Mountain and Fore Mountain, ending just before Lowmoor and the airport. These rapids are a strong Class 2 for the most part and many are quite long, enjoyable rock gardens. From Lowmoor to Clifton Forge, the Jackson River makes a series of loops/bends away from the highway (which is Routes 220, 60, and I-64). The rapids in this section are mostly Class 1 or a low Class 2.

Between Clifton Forge and the Cowpasture River, the Jackson tries to become a white-water stream again. In Rainbow Gap, between Clifton Forge and Iron Gate, the towering sheer rock cliffs on each side are magnificent. A perfect setting for a river to break through a mountain pass in a series of major rapids. But, alas, there are only Class 1-2 riffles in a setting of trash dumps on both banks. Virginians should never allow fellow Virginians to desecrate a river like this. Below Iron Gate, a town on the right bank, there is the final bridge (Route 727) over the Jackson, about ¼ mile before the dark, smelly Jackson joins the clear, pure Cowpasture to form the James River. It is worth the ½ mile trip to the James River and then to the next Route 220 bridge just to see the difference in streams. You will always remember it.

Hazards: None.

Water Conditions: Canoeable in winter, spring, and early summer, except following periods of little precipitation. Canoeable after a heavy rain in the summer and fall.

GAUGE

There is an RC gauge on Route 39 bridge at Warm Springs, a USACOE gauge at Garthright Dam may be available in the future.

OTHER INFORMATION

The Garthright Dam is a prime example of the way the Corps of Engineers becomes the willing pawn of construction companies and industrial giants. The true reason for the dam is to assist in the abatement of WESVACO pollution, which becomes near intolerable during low flow periods on the river. Also, the dam provides the Corps with more empire building, an important thing for military and civil service types. Now, the dam is threatened by limestone caves and fissures in both banks, geological flaws that may cause the dam to fail like the 1976 failure of the Glen Torrey dam.

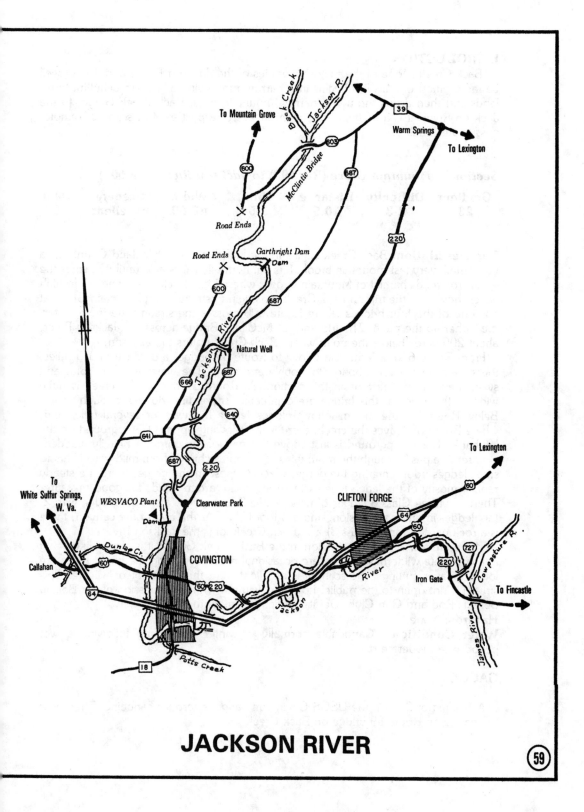

JACKSON RIVER

Back Creek

INTRODUCTION

Back Creek is one of the major tributaries of the Jackson River, and it may well be the prettiest one also. It begins in a narrow mountain valley with beautiful farmlands and then drops through a narrow mountain pass, Back Creek Gorge, to the Jackson River. It is a magnificent stream in every respect--rapids, scenery, remoteness, water quality.

Section 1. Mountain Grove (Rte 600) to Jackson River (Rte 603)

Gradient	Difficulty	Distance	Time	Width	Scenery	Map
23	2-3	10.5	3.5	40-60	Excellent	58

Trip Description: Back Creek begins in the higher parts of Highland County as a very small, very fast mountain brook. It is not normally canoeable until it reaches the small crossroads hamlet of Mountain Grove, where Little Back Creek joins it. In high water, however, the trip on Back Creek can begin upstream from Mountain Grove at any one of the four bridges where Route 600 crosses the stream; the more water, the higher up the putin. The trip ends at McClintic Bridge across the Jackson River, about 200 yards below the point where Back Creek enters the Jackson.

From Route 600 at Mountain Grove to Route 39 bridge, a distance of 1.5 miles, the stream flows over a bottom of cobble and sand. The water is clear, cold, and swift; there are no hazards in this section. At Route 39 bridge, the creek is quite wide; if the riffles at this bridge are canoeable, the entire trip has enough water. Below Route 39, the stream follows alongside the highway for several miles and, where Route 39 leaves the creek, there is the Blowing Springs Campground on the left bank. This campground is just above the start of the gorge, a heavily wooded, very remote pass through the mountains. The rapids change from mild gravel bars to small ledges upon entering the gorge, Class 2 types. In the gorge, there are steady rapids, mostly of the ledge type, with strong rock garden rapids for good measure. There are three Class 3 ledges of note, a 2½-3 foot ledge, a two-step ledge with 2-foot ledges in quick succession, and a 3-foot ledge. At the end of the canyon, there is a rock garden rapid (Class 3) and Back Creek joins the Jackson River.

There are few signs of civilization in the Back Creek Gorge; it is almost like being in a complete wilderness. There are occasional rock cliffs along the bank, there are lots of beaver cuttings, the scenery is excellent, and there is a lot of wildlife. This stream is not open to the public, however, without written permission of the Boiling Springs Rod and Gun Club. Get it in writing or meet the local fuzz.

Hazards: None.

Water Conditions: Canoeable normally in winter and spring following a wet period or a moderate rain.

GAUGE

A reading of 2.5' on the USGS Covington gauge is zero for canoeing. There is a RC gauge on Route 39 bridge on Back Creek.

Dunlap Creek

INTRODUCTION

Dunlap Creek is the most western stream in the James River watershed, flowing northeast through a narrow valley to join the Jackson River at Covington. It is a very small stream in its upper reaches, but it is a moderate size creek by the time it reaches the Jackson. In its course, it goes through narrow valleys and farmlands past high rock bluffs, and over a bottom of sand and gravel.

Section 1. Crows (Rte 311) to Jackson River

Gradient	Difficulty	Distance	Time	Width	Scenery	Map
20	1-2₃	12.5	4	25-40	Good	60

Trip Description: The putin is at Route 311 bridge, 3 miles west of Crows; Crows is the settlement at the junction of Route 159 and Route 311. At this point, two small streams join Dunlap Creek and it is all of 30' wide. The bottom is solid rock and it starts with a nice riffle. About one mile downstream, the creek becomes much narrower, with swift chutes and deep pools. Then it becomes a bit flatter with longer pools broken by gravel bars and small rock gardens. By the time the Route 159 bridge at Homatite is reached, the stream is 40' to 50' wide and the rapids are small ledges and gravel bars with long flat pools between them. The gradient is such that there is a moderately swift current; at high water levels, the current increases but the rapids are washed out.

The Dunlap Creek Valley is not a particularly scenic valley. It is not really a farming valley, and it is heavily wooded and narrow in many parts. The high hills, rock bluffs, and gradient lead the paddler to expect more action, but none really materializes. Below the second Route 159 bridge, the third bridge from the putin, there is the remains of an old dam; the dam was about 6' high, but it is washed out on the right abutment. There is a flood gate, about 4½' wide in the middle, that makes an exciting chute. Careful, careful.

After reaching the vicinity of Route I-64, Dunlap Creek really picks up. The gravel bar rapids, the solid rock bottom, and the small ledges make for steady Class 2 rapids. There are a couple of Class 2-3 rapids around the Route 60 bridge, just before reaching Humpback Bridge. Humpback Bridge is a wooden covered bridge of a most unusual design: unlike most other covered bridges, the roadway is built along the arch. For the next two miles, Dunlap Creek flows over a sandy bottom with gravel bar rapids before passing under Route 700, the road to the Episcopal Boys Home; this is the recommended takeout, about ½ mile above the Jackson River. If continuing to the Jackson River, takeout at Route 60 or the next bridge downstream.

Hazards: Trees blocking stream in upper region.

Water Conditions: Canoeable in winter and spring normally or during the early summer following an extended wet spell or very heavy rain.

GAUGE

If the riffles at Humpback Bridge are canoeable, there is sufficient water for this trip.

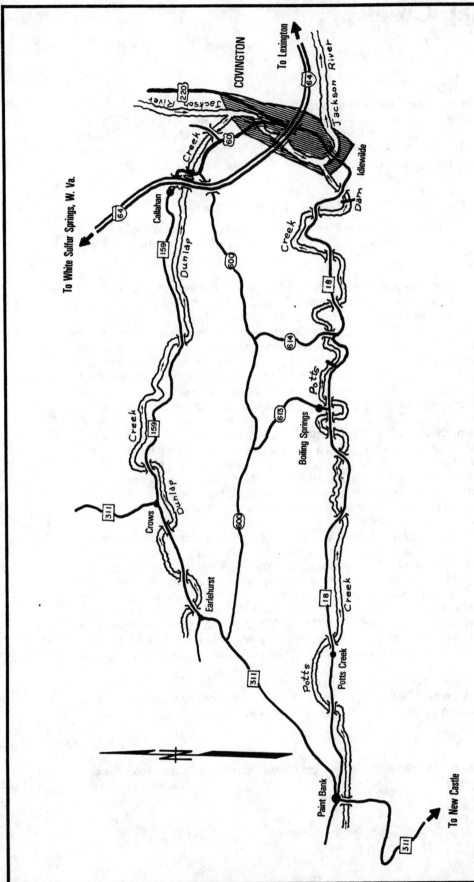

**POTTS CREEK
DUNLAP CREEK**

Potts Creek

INTRODUCTION

Potts Creek is one of the finer white-water streams on the James River watershed, and it offers such a wide variety of rapids that it can be broken up into advanced trips, intermediate trips, and beginner trips. It flows through a beautiful valley, the water is clear and clean, the current is fast flowing, the scenery is quite good, and there is a campground beside the creek. It is crossed by Route 18 bridge a total of 13 times between Paint Bank and Covington, so it can be divided into any length of trip desired.

Section 1. Paint Bank (Rte 311) to Potts Creek (Rte 18)

Gradient	Difficulty	Distance	Time	Width	Scenery	Map
36	2-3₄	6.5	2	30-40	Excellent	60

Trip Description: From Paint Bank (Route 311 bridge) to the second Route 18 bridge downstream, Potts Creek is the delight of the white-water canoeist. It begins as a 40 foot wide stream over a canalized gravel bed, moves through a farming area over gravel bar rapids, and passes high bluffs on each side. About a mile downstream the remains of a low-water bridge make a Class 2 rapid; about 2.5 miles downstream, Potts Creek becomes a genuine trout stream. The rapids become long, intricate, rock gardens; there are Class 3 sloping rock ledges; there are series of ledges in quick succession; there are intricate chutes with strong currents and complicated entries. Everything one could want in continuous white-water. The current is swift, the water is clear and cool, the bottom is solid rock or gravel, the scenery is natural. From the first Route 18 bridge to the second Route 18 bridge, there is more of the same, but the rapids are more Class 2 than Class 3. There is a campground alongside Potts Creek above the first bridge, in the part with the super white-water.
Hazards: None.
Water Conditions: Canoeable in winter and spring normally or during the early summer following an extended wet spell or very heavy rain.

Section 2. Potts Creek (Rte 18) to Boiling Springs (Rte 613)

Gradient	Difficulty	Distance	Time	Width	Scenery	Map
19	23	11	4	40-60	Very Good	60

Trip Description: From the second Route 18 bridge to Boiling Springs (Route 613 bridge), Route 18 crosses Potts Creek four times, so the length of this trip can be varied easily. The stream is wider, the current is fast, the scenery is good, and the water is clear. The rapids are mostly Class 1-2 gravel bars and rock gardens, with occasional small ledges, and there are chutes where the creek narrows down to 15 to 20 feet. The bottom is sand with rocks or just rocks, there are many swimming holes, and the flat stretches are longer and more frequent. The rock bluffs on the left side in one stretch are particularly memorable.
Hazards: None.
Water Conditions: Canoeable in winter and spring normally or during the early summer following an extended wet spell or very heavy rain.

Section 3. Boiling Springs (Rte 613) to Idlewilde (Rte 18)

Gradient	Difficulty	Distance	Time	Width	Scenery	Map
14	1-2	15	5.5	40-60	Good	60

Trip Description: From Boiling Springs to the Covington city limits, Potts Creek is a pleasant, relaxing, scenic stream that has enough rapids to challenge the beginner. It is crossed by Route 18 about six times, so the trip can be planned about a variety of takeouts. At the first Route 18 bridge below Boiling Springs, there is a sloping 3' ledge, and there are a few ledges of 1' to 2' in the upper part of this stretch. About three miles below the putin, there is a 5' dam; exercise caution. Most of the rapids below the dam are the gravel bar and rock garden variety, Class 1-2; the ledges are so low, however, that they do not quite succeed in creating good rapids. At one point, there is a massive, beautiful multicolored rock formation on the left, and it appears to be an ideal spot for super ledges -- but no such luck. By the time the 4 foot dam at Covington is reached, the current is moderate, the pools are longer and more frequent, and there is a low-water bridge for spice/variety. The dam at Covington might be runnable, but scouting and last rites (during high water) are appropriate.

This trip can be continued down to the Jackson River, and then down the Jackson River to Route 18 bridge (sound familiar?), a distance of about ½ mile. There is really nothing to recommend this section other than to be able to say one has paddled on the Jackson.

Hazards: One 5' dam near Boiling Springs, one 4' dam at Idlewilde (Covington city limits).

Water Conditions: Canoeable in winter, spring, and early summer, except following periods of little precipitation. Canoeable after a heavy rain in the summer and fall.

GAUGE

If the riffles at Route 311 are canoeable, there is plenty of water for all sections.

Wilson Creek

INTRODUCTION

Wilson Creek is a very small stream that flows through the Douthat State Park and joins the Jackson River just below Clifton Forge. It is canoeable only for a very short distance below the high dam in the park and then only during periods of heavy precipitation. It has more dams per mile than any other little stream in Virginia.

Section 1. Below Douthat Park Dam to Jackson River

Gradient	Difficulty	Distance	Time	Width	Scenery	Map
53	2-3	7.5	2.5	15-30	Fair	61

Trip Description: The Wilson Creek trip begins just below the high (30') dam in the Douthat State Park, where it is a very small stream that is not more than 15' wide. It flows swiftly, very swiftly, over a bottom of solid rock for most of the first four miles; and the scenery in the park is excellent. About two miles downstream, it flows over a paved ford and shortly thereafter it passes under Route 629 bridge. Below this bridge, the rapids change from small ledges and rock gardens to rock gardens and gravel bars.

About 2.5 miles below the putin, just after leaving the park, there is a private campground on the left bank; 50 yards below the bridge to this campground, there are two 6' dams in quick succession. About 400 yards below these dams, there is another campground with another bridge and another 6' dam. Below this second campground, the current begins to slow and the banks are higher. Just below I-64, there is a nice Class 2 rapid. The takeout is about 1.5 miles below the I-64 bridge, just before the creek enters the Jackson River, on one of the streets of Clifton Forge; it takes a bit of imagination to find the logical takeout. It is easier to continue on the James River; the next takeout is the Route 220 bridge near Iron Gate, about 1/2 mile downstream.

Hazards: Three six-foot dams near the mid-point, at the private campgrounds.

Water Conditions: Canoeable only in the winter and spring following an extended wet period or heavy precipitation.

GAUGE

None. Strictly a target-of-opportunity.

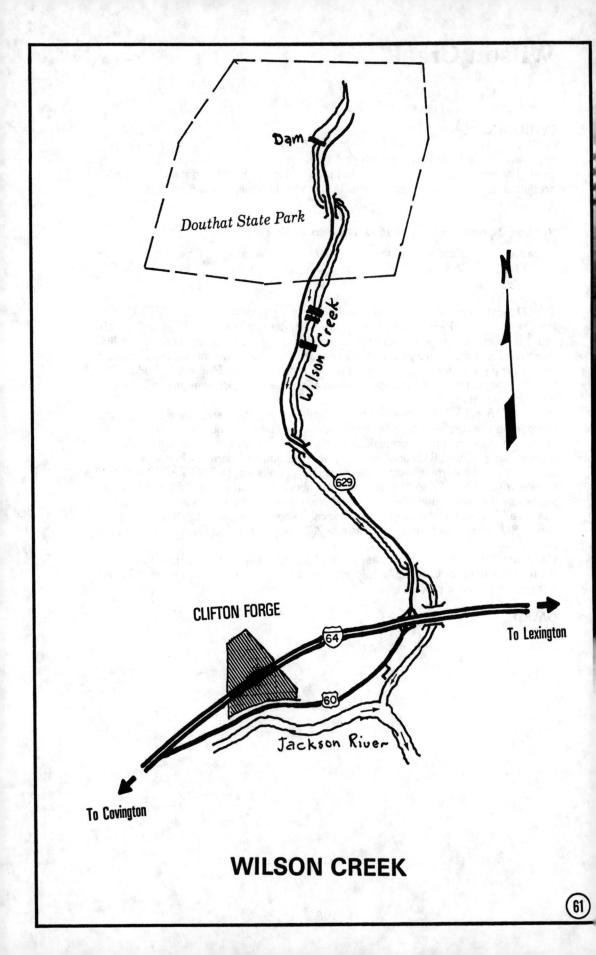

Dam

Douthat State Park

Wilson Creek

629

CLIFTON FORGE

64

60

To Lexington

Jackson River

To Covington

WILSON CREEK

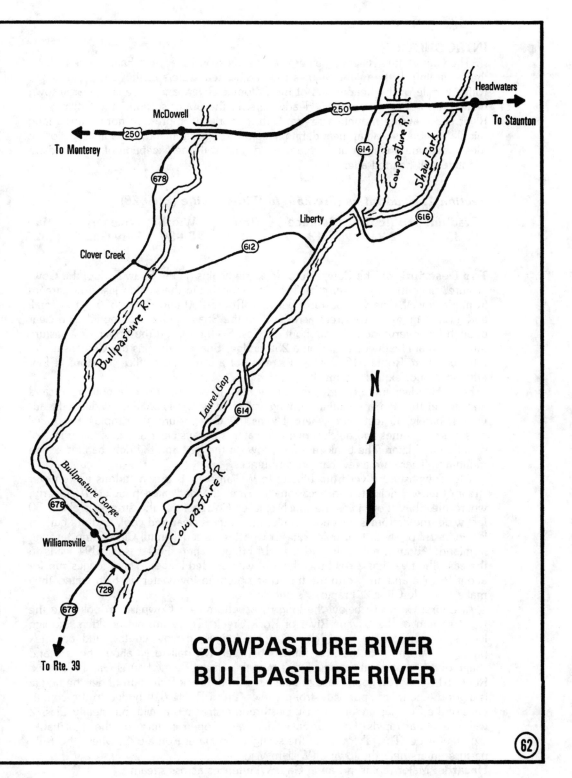

**COWPASTURE RIVER
BULLPASTURE RIVER**

Headwaters

To Staunton

McDowell

To Monterey

250

250

678

614

Cowpasture R.

Shaw Fork

Liberty

616

Clover Creek

612

Bullpasture R.

Laurel Gap

614

Cowpasture R.

Bullpasture Gorge

678

Williamsville

728

678

To Rte. 39

N

62

Cowpasture River

INTRODUCTION

The Cowpasture River combines with the Jackson River near Eagle Rock to form the beginning of the mighty James River. The headwaters of the Cowpasture start within a mile of the headwaters of the Potomac River, and there is a nearby town named, appropriately enough, Headwaters. In the upper sections, the Cowpasture River is a brawling mountain stream with a short but impressive gorge; in its long middle section, it is a flat meandering stream through farmland; in its final section, it tries to become a white-water stream again, but, with the exception of two rapids, it is only a half-hearted attempt.

Section 1. Headwaters (Rte 250) to Williamsville (Rte 628)

Gradient	Difficulty	Distance	Time	Width	Scenery	Map
35	2-3₄	13	4.5	20-30	Very Good	62

Trip Description: The Cowpasture River trip begins on the Shaw Fork of the Cowpasture, since the Cowpasture itself is not canoeable in the section just downstream from McDowell. The Cowpasture, between Route 250 and Route 616 is too small and has too many fences/trees across it; but the Shaw Fork is big enough and clear enough for a very good trip of about 4 miles. So the trip on the upper Cowpasture must begin at Headwaters, at Route 250 bridge. Shaw Fork joins the Cowpasture at Liberty, where Route 616 crosses; there is not a town, post office, or store at Liberty, so do not expect too much.

From Headwaters to Liberty, the Shaw Fork flows swiftly over a bottom of sand and gravel through a beautiful farming valley. It is barely 20 feet wide at Headwaters, barely 30 feet wide where it joins the Cowpasture. The rapids are gravel bars, narrow chutes and quick turns; the water is always clear and is virtually free of pollution and litter. The banks are fairly low on the left, and the right bank is a high mountain. There are a few barbed wire fences.

The Cowpasture River from Liberty to Williamsville is a tremendous white-water stream that will delight, and occasionally scare, the dedicated paddler. At Liberty, where the Shaw Fork joins the much smaller Cowpasture, the stream is about 30 feet wide, the bottom is rock and cobble, the water is clear and cool, and the current is very fast. For about four miles, the Cowpasture is a delightful Class 2 trip through farmland. About a mile below Route 614 bridge, where Forest Road 394 leads to the east, the river has a solid rock bottom with eroded ledges. These ledges run for about ½ mile and are worth the trip to see them in low water; in high water, they make a steady Class 2-3 rapid. It's unbelievable.

At Laurel Gap, just below the long rock bottom, the Cowpasture looks like the worst section of the Savage River or Rock Creek. There are big boulders, sloping ledges, horrendous rock gardens, diagonal ledges, narrow chutes, and complex passages. At one spot the river funnels between two tall rocks about the size and shape of two-seater out-houses. Don't miss this chute! Below Laurel Gap is the next Route 614 bridge, a good place to take a break; the rock formation under the bridge is a good lunch/rest spot with strong eddies. From Route 614 bridge to the confluence of the Cowpasture and the Bullpasture, the stream is a mild, but steady Class 2 with gravel bar rapids. Fast current, clear water, open country on the right bank, sixty feet wide. The takeout is at the swinging bridge at Route 628, where the Bullpasture enters near the town of Williamsville.

Hazards: Major rapids in Laurel Gap. Wire fences across stream.

Water Conditions: Canoeable normally in winter and spring following a wet period or a moderate rain.

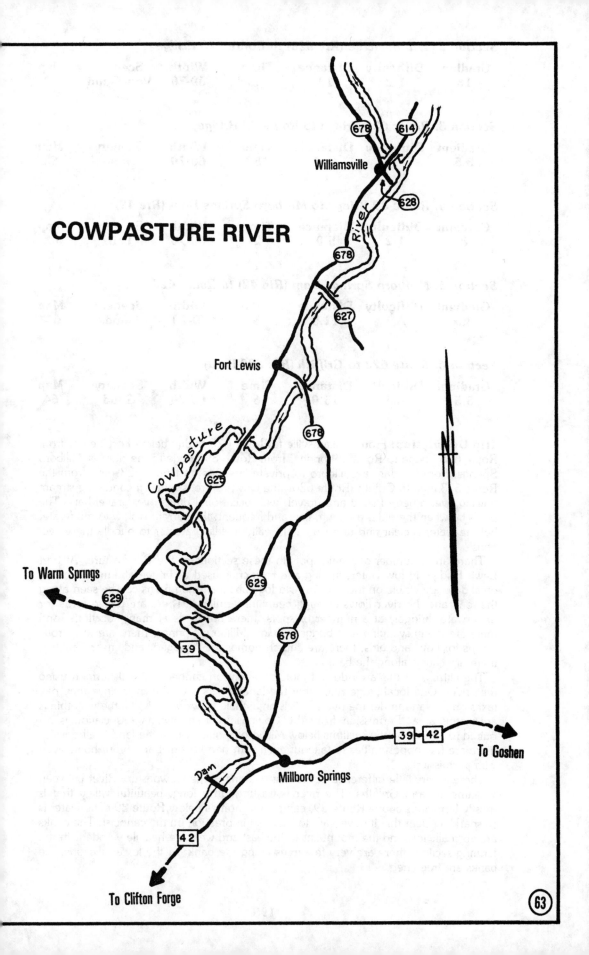

COWPASTURE RIVER

Williamsville

678 614

628

River

678

627

Fort Lewis

678

Cowpasture

625

To Warm Springs

629

629

678

39

39 42

To Goshen

Dam

Millboro Springs

42

To Clifton Forge

Section 2. Williamsville (Rte 628) to Route 625 Bridge

Gradient	Difficulty	Distance	Time	Width	Scenery	Map
13	1-2	10	3.5	50-70	Very Good	63

Section 3. Route 625 Bridge to Route 39 Bridge

Gradient	Difficulty	Distance	Time	Width	Scenery	Map
5.5	1	13.5	5	60-70	Good	63

Section 4. Route 39 Bridge to Millboro Springs Dam (Rte 42)

Gradient	Difficulty	Distance	Time	Width	Scenery	Map
8	1-2	5.0	2	60-70	Fair	63

Section 5. Millboro Springs Dam (Rte 42) to Route 623

Gradient	Difficulty	Distance	Time	Width	Scenery	Map
3.5	A,1	11.5	5	60-70	Good	64

Section 6. Route 623 to Griffith (Rte 630 Ford)

Gradient	Difficulty	Distance	Time	Width	Scenery	Map
5.5	A,1	15.0	6	60-70	Good	64

Trip Description: From Williamsville to Route 625 bridge below Fort Lewis, from Route 625 bridge to Route 39 bridge, from Route 39 bridge to the dam at Millboro Springs, from the dam at Millboro to private landings off Route 623, and from the Route 623 area to Griffith (Route 630), the Cowpasture is a flat, meandering stream flowing over a bed of sand and gravel, with occasional riffles over gravel bars. The pools between the riffles are long, flat, and frequent; the current is slow to moderate; but the water is clear and unpolluted. It really builds character to paddle these sections.

There are a number of scenic spots in these sections of the Cowpasture. At Fort Lewis Bridge, in low water, the log and rock cribs used as bridge abutments in colonial days are visible on the bottom. Old log cabins and log barns can be seen along the road and the river flows through beautiful farmland. There are paved fords (or underwater bridges) at a number of spots, there are fords at many locations, and there are many swinging foot bridges. Below Millboro Springs, there are numerous camps for boys and girls, there are church homes for the aged, and, near Griffiths, there are cabins along the bank.

The citizens of this area do not look favorably on canoeists and fishermen using their river. One local judge ruled that the landowners own the river since they pay taxes on the land under the river. This is an archaic view, but it is still the way things are in this area. Permission from the Cowpasture Landowners Association is required to paddle on the sections below Millboro Springs. Since the land is all posted, there are few opportunities to takeout even with permission. Eat in your boat, even with permission.

There is very little difference in the five sections of the Cowpasture River between Williamsville and Griffiths. The river flows through a long, beautiful valley that is mostly farmlands above Route 39, camps and homes below Route 39. The water is so sparkling clear that it never fails to leave an impression on the canoeist. The banks are normally low and the mountains to the east and west are heavily wooded. In the farming section, there are very few trees along the bank; in the lower sections, the banks are tree-lined.

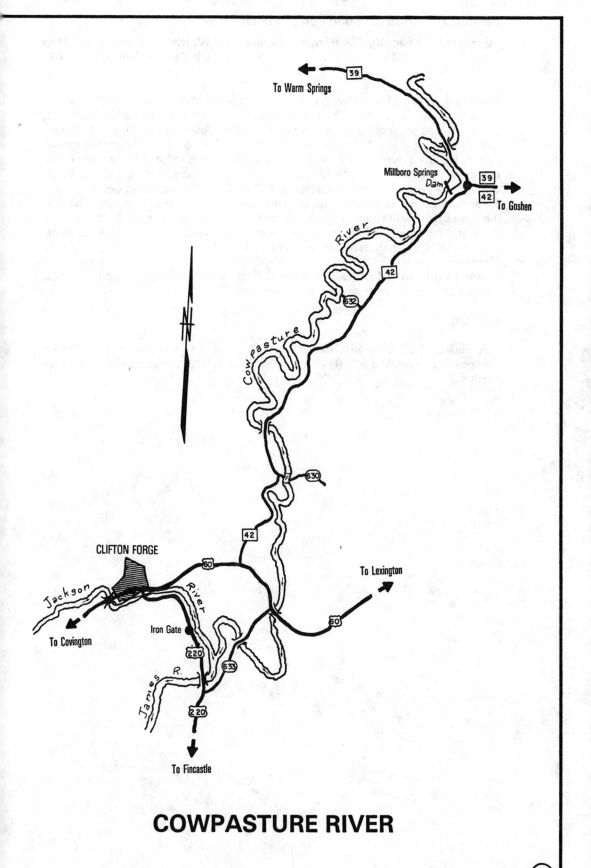

COWPASTURE RIVER

Section 7. Griffith (Rte 630 Ford) to James River

Gradient	Difficulty	Distance	Time	Width	Scenery	Map
12	1-23	13.5	5	60-80	Good	64

Trip Description: From Griffiths to the James River, the Cowpasture River begins to become more interesting. The gradient picks up, the water volume has increased, and the rapids are more frequent. About two miles downstream, there is a Class 3 rapid, just beyond the RR bridge and tunnel. About a mile below Route 60 bridge, there is a Class 3 rapid. The water is still clear, the area is rather remote, the current moves at a moderate rate, the rapids are mostly gravel bars, there are a few islands with narrow passages, and the rapids are Class 1-2. The recommended takeout is Route 633 bridge; to continue means flat water paddling for almost three miles to the James River and about one half mile on the James River to landings above Eagle Rock. It is probably worth the trip to the James River to see the clean, clear Cowpasture meet the polluted, dark Jackson River.

Hazards: None.

Water Conditions: Canoeable most of the year except following a long dry spell. Canoeable after a moderate rain in the summer.

GAUGE

A reading of 1.5' on the RC gauge on the Route 60 bridge is zero for canoeing on Sections 2, 3; a reading of 1.0' is zero for Sections 4, 5, 6; a reading of 6" is zero for Section 7.

Bullpasture River

INTRODUCTION

The Bullpasture River is the principal tributary of the Cowpasture River, and it is one of the prettiest tributaries in the James River watershed. It is the only James River tributary that begins in West Virginia; according to the USGS topographic maps, it begins year around flow about 300 yards into Pendleton County, West Virginia. It is a lively stream throughout its short, but entire length, never pausing in its rush to the calm and serene Cowpasture.

Section 1. McDowell (Rte 250) to Williamsville (Rte 628)

Gradient	Difficulty	Distance	Time	Width	Scenery	Map
19*	2-4	15	5	25-40	Excellent	62

*4 miles at 45 feet/mile

Trip Description: From McDowell to Williamsville, the Bullpasture is a white-water stream, intermediate in the upper part, advanced in the final stretch. It begins as a trout stream with a width of 25 to 30 feet, dashing over a bottom of solid rock, broken rock, and gravel. The water is very clear and unpolluted, the right bank is open farmland for ten miles, and the left bank has high bluffs and mountains throughout. The rapids between McDowell and the Bullpasture Gorge are gravel bars, rock gardens, and small ledges. The rapids start as Class 1-2 in the first part, but become better and stronger (Class 2-3) when the Route 612 ford is passed, about 5 miles below Route 250; as the road approaches the river and the mountains close in on each side, about four miles below the Route 612 ford, after a couple of creeks enter on the right, the rapids are stronger and are Class 3 on occasion.

Shortly after passing the open terrain, there is another ford, Route 609 from Route 678, just above the Bullpasture Gorge. This is a convenient takeout for the weak in heart and a convenient putin for those who want big white-water only. From this point on, the paddler is committed to Class 3, Class 4, and Class 5 rapids for the next three miles. There are few pools, the rapids are near continuous, the drops are complex and big, the turbulence and cross currents are strong, and the waves are big. There are few landmarks to reference and the rapids do not have names, so look out for anything and everything, particularly the 8' ledge. Just above Williamsville, there is a complex Class 3 rock garden, which can be seen from Route 614 bridge. From Route 614 bridge to the Cowpasture River is about ½ mile of Class 2-3 rapids; the takeout is easy. Do not run the Bullpasture Gorge if there is the slightest belief that the water is high.

Hazards: Fences and low-water bridges in upper stretches. Major ledges in gorge.

Water Conditions: Canoeable normally in winter and spring following a wet period or a moderate rain.

GAUGE

A reading of 2.5' on the USGS Covington is zero for canoeing. A reading of 1.5' on the RC gauge on Route 60 over the Cowpasture is zero for canoeing.

201

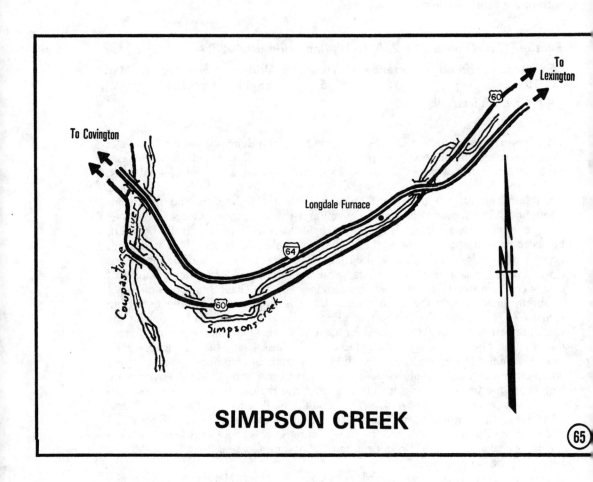

To Lexington

To Covington

Longdale Furnace

Cowpasture River

Simpsons Creek

SIMPSON CREEK

Simpsons Creek

INTRODUCTION

Simpson Creek appears to be little more than a drainage ditch alongside Route 60 between Lexington and Clifton Forge. It is a very small, very swift, and very challenging creek that drains a narrow valley between North Mountain and Brushy Mountain. Very few people have paddled this stream, as it does not hold water very long.

Section 1. Ponderosa Truck Stop (Rte I-64) to Cowpasture River (Rte 60)

Gradient	Difficulty	Distance	Time	Width	Scenery	Map
62	2-3	6.5	1.5	15-25	Fair	65

Trip Description: The trip on Simpson Creek normally begins in the vicinity of the I-64 and Route 60 interchange near the Ponderosa Truck Stop; it can begin about 1.5 miles further upstream, water conditions permitting, at the next Route 60 bridge. The takeout is alongside Route 60 where the creek joins the Cowpasture River at Route 60 bridge.

At the upper putin, the creek is about 15' wide, flowing over a bottom of solid rock. The bottom is almost solid rock for the first five miles; only in the final stretches is there any sand or small gravel. The water is clear and cool, but it may be polluted from the many septic tank drainfields of houses along its bank. The rapids are fairly continuous and are of the small ledge and rockgarden type; the biggest drops are where they cannot be seen from Route 60, which parallels Simpson Creek for the entire distance. The gradient is fairly steady, so there are not any waterfalls or major ledges/drops; there are few eddies until the final two miles. The banks are fairly high and there are many private bridges crossing the stream, particularly in the Longdale Furnace area. There are many houses along the stream, so the scenery is, at best, that of looking at front yards.

Harzards: Fence and footbridge across the stream.

Water Conditions: Canoeable only in winter and spring following a prolonged wet period or very heavy rain.

GAUGE

A reading of 2.5' on the RC gauge on the Route 60 bridge over the Cowpasture River is probably zero for canoeing.

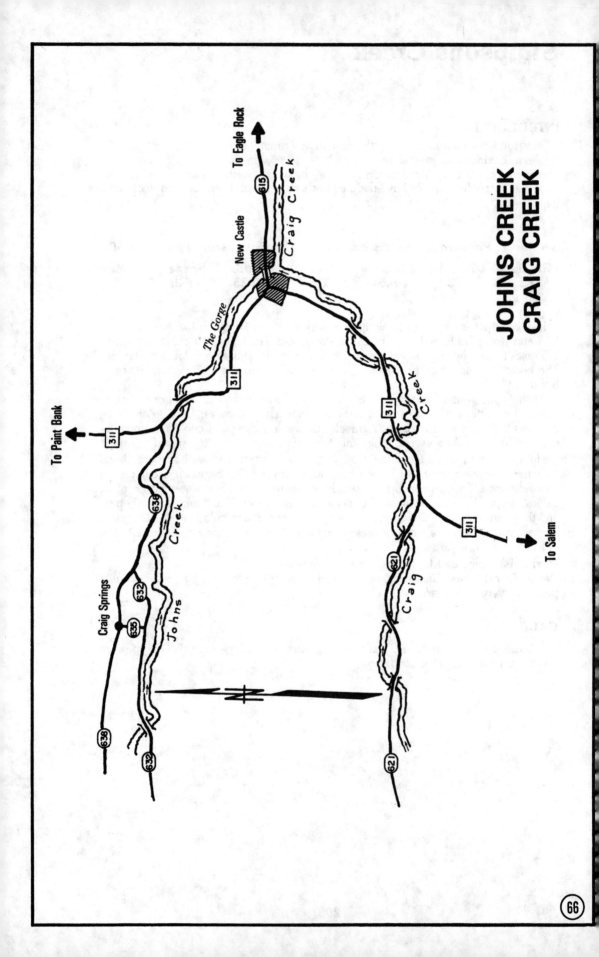

JOHNS CREEK
CRAIG CREEK

Craig Creek

INTRODUCTION

Craig Creek is the largest creek that feeds into the James River in its upper reaches; if it were east of the Blue Ridge Mountains, it would be called a river. It is canoeable in its lower sections throughout the year, even in dry weather, as a general rule. It meanders through a beautiful farming valley and there are few bridges across it. There are a lot of fords and a lot of stretches where it is close to a paved road, but, for the most part, it shows few signs of civilization. It has numerous deep spots for swimming, sand bars for sunbathing, swinging bridges for walking across the creek, and fords for driving across the creek.

Section 1. Old Rte 311 Bridge (Nr Rte 621) to Newcastle

Gradient	Difficulty	Distance	Time	Width	Scenery	Map
16	1-2₃	7	2.5	20-30	Fair	66

Trip Description: From the old Route 311 bridge (near Route 621) to Newcastle, Craig Creek is a swift stream flowing over a bed of rocks and solid rock. It seems to flow through the back yards of houses as it approaches Newcastle, but for the most part, the stream flows through a farming area. The rapids are mostly Class 1-2 gravel bars with a few rock gardens and ledges, also Class 1-2. The river is only about 25' wide at the putin, although it is 40' wide in spots. Route 311 crosses Craig Creek three times, one very close to the putin, so the length of the trip can be varied easily. The trip can be extended by putting in upstream along Route 621, but the stream is very small, there are many fences, and there are numerous low-water bridges. The best takeout is a ford about 1 mile downstream from where Johns Creek joins Craig Creek; there is a swinging foot bridge and a ford just off Route 615.
Hazards: Fences. Low-water bridges. Trees across stream.
Water Conditions: Canoeable normally in winter and spring following a wet period or a moderate rain.

Section 2. Newcastle to Given (Rte 606)

Gradient	Difficulty	Distance	Time	Width	Scenery	Map
5	1	12.5	5	30-40	Good	67

Section 3. Given (Rte 606) to Oriskany (Rte 705 Ford)

Gradient	Difficulty	Distance	Time	Width	Scenery	Map
5	1	11.5	4.5	40-50	Good	67

Section 4. Oriskany (Rte 705 Ford) to Parr

Gradient	Difficulty	Distance	Time	Width	Scenery	Map
6	1	15.5	6	40-60	Good	67

Section 5. Parr to James River

Gradient	Difficulty	Distance	Time	Width	Scenery	Map
6	1	12.5	5	50-60	Good	67

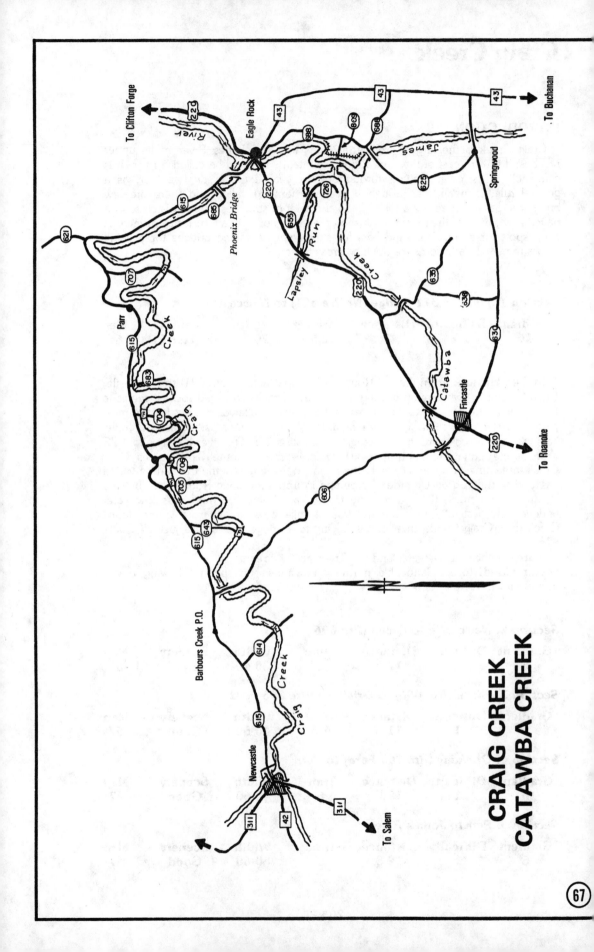

CRAIG CREEK
CATAWBA CREEK

67

Trip Description: From Newcastle to Given, from Given to Oriskany, from Oriskany to Parr, and from Parr to the James River, Craig Creek meanders for a distance of 42 miles. It is crossed by a couple of bridges near Newcastle and near the James River, but for a distance of more than 30 miles, it is crossed only by fords and low-water bridges. Most of the fords are fairly deep and should be attempted only by farm vehicles, pickup trucks, and four-wheel drive vehicles; it is best to have someone walk across the ford prior to driving across, as the clear water makes it difficult to judge depth.

The creek has a fairly uniform width for the entire 42 miles, although the water gets rather thin at wide gravel bars. Most of the rapids/riffles are gravel bars, small rock gardens, small ledges, and swift chutes around islands. There are enough rapids/riffles to break up the monotony, but not enough to consider it a white-water trip. The water is clear and unpolluted most of the time, the scenery varies from open farm lands to rocky cliffs, and the high mountains to the north and west are always in sight. There is a classic example of an anticline, an arch of layered rock, on the right bank in the lower section; there are numerous swimming holes and sunbathing beaches, and there are wonderful fishing spots. There are so many fords and other access points that the trip length can be varied quite easily.

The bridge on Route 685, near the James River, is a beautiful one-lane steel truss bridge with ornate steelwork. It was built by the Phoenix Bridge Company and they had reason to be proud of their work. The spires on the corners, the company plaque, the intricate scrollwork in the steel, the embellishments — all combine to make it a memorable bridge.

This valley seems to have been abandoned and have fallen into disrepair. There are very few gasoline stations, no general stores, no bait shops, no motels, and only a few houses. Almost eerie. But it is still a stream to canoe, for the creek is so beautiful.

Hazards: Low-water bridges. Maybe a fence in the upper section

Water Conditions: Section 2: Canoeable in winter, spring, and early summer, except following periods of little precipitation. Canoeable after a heavy rain in the summer and fall.

Section 3,4,5: Canoeable most of the year except following a long, dry spell. Canoeable after a moderate rain in the summer.

GAUGE

Check the water levels at any of the riffles/fords. If there is enough at any of the fords, there is enough for any/all sections.

Johns Creek

INTRODUCTION

Johns Creek is a small stream that joins Craig Creek at Newcastle. In its upper reaches, it is a mild, relaxing, pleasant trip through farmland; in the final section, it is a short, thrilling white-water challenge that will test the abilities of the best paddlers. Throughout, it is a remote stream that is crossed by only one bridge (Route 311) between the upper putin and the bridge at Newcastle. There are no other convenient takeouts and most (if not all) of the property in that area is posted. The creek is a uniform width, 25 to 35 feet, start to finish, flatlands and gorge.

Section 1. Rte 632 Bridge to Rte 311 Bridge.

Gradient	Difficulty	Distance	Time	Width	Scenery	Map
12	1-2₃	15	4.5	25-35	Very Good	66

Trip Description: Below Route 632, southwest of Craig Springs, Johns Creek is a small stream that passes through a beautiful farming valley. It starts with Class 1 gravel bar riffles at the putin and within a mile enters a small gorge and builds up to Class 2 ledges and rock gardens. The remains of a low-water bridge ½ mile, downstream is a hazard and an alternate putin point. At a white farmhouse with a private bridge, the rapids are Class 2-3; there is a good access point below these strong rapids and above the easiest stretches. The creek flows for 10 miles on the south side of the valley, on the opposite side of the valley from the road. The right bank has high bluffs, rock cliffs, and hills/mountains for almost the entire distance. Only in one place are there farms/fields on the right (south bank). The valley almost seems deserted as many houses and barns are abandoned; it is hard to understand how anyone would want to leave such a beautiful valley. The swift current, the clear water, the remote farmlands, the uncut forests, the steady riffles, the sand and gravel bottom, the small ledges — all make a jewel of a stream.
Hazards: Low-water bridge. Trees across stream. Barbed/woven wire fences.
Water Conditions: Canoeable normally in winter and spring following a wet period or a moderate rain.

Section 2. Rte 311 Bridge to Newcastle (Rte 615)

Gradient	Difficulty	Distance	Time	Width	Scenery	Map
63	2-5₆	5.5	5	25-35	Excellent	66

Trip Description: From Route 311 bridge to Newcastle, Johns Creek flows through a gorge that will challenge the best of canoeists/kayakers. The one Class 2 rapid at the bridge is enjoyable, but it is also deceptive — it is the easiest rapid for the next five miles. Below the trash pile on the left bank, the rapids start with 2 foot ledges in quick succession and rock gardens/boulder fields, all Class 2-3 rapids. Then it turns into a steady Class 4-5 terror for about 4 miles. There are sections with continuous 1' to 3' ledges for 100 yards; one rapid drops 6' to 7' in two steps with a complex maneuver required; most rapids involve "S" turns through narrow passages. There is one long rapid with at least eight drops of 2' each and then a turn around a VW size rock, through a narrow passage. Many passages are less than 5' wide with intricate turns, fierce currents, and strong eddies; many rapids involve total drops of 6' to 8' through chutes that come too fast for a neat plan. It is mostly a reaction type of river. For example, one rapid has a 3' drop, followed quickly by a 2' drop, followed by a 3' drop, a turn through a passage flanked by big rocks, over a 4' drop with a nasty hydraulic.

There are occasional pools in the gorge and in these pools, the paddler will have all of forty feet of flat water in which to regain lost composure. Then the rapids start again. Big ledges, boulder fields, rock gardens, hydraulics, big waves, strong cross currents, excrutiating turns, occasional trees across the stream — they are all there. Near the end of the gorge, there is a 10-foot drop into a rock garden; this is not runnable at any level. At the zero level, it took a five boat group 7 hours to canoe 5.5 miles; at 14", it was a nightmare for a group of Kayaks and C-1's; at 3"-4", it was almost too much for good open boaters. One good intermediate paddler wiped out three times at the zero level.

The gorge is a magnificent creation. Clear water, big rock formations, overhanging cliffs, uncut forests. By the time the gorge ends, the last mile of Class 2 rapids are a blessed relief. By the time Newcastle is reached, Route 615 bridge is a most welcome sight.

Hazards: Plenty of complex, strong rapids in gorge.

Water Conditions: Canoeable in winter and spring normally or during the early summer following an extended wet spell or very heavy rain.

GAUGE

The footing on the abutments of Route 311 bridge is zero for canoeing.

OTHER INFORMATION

Johns Creek is one of those small mountain streams that is not paddled very often for a variety of reasons. First of all, there is no gauge that can be used to determine if there is enough water for canoeing or if there is too much water for canoeing. Then, it is so very far from the metropolitan areas where most of the white water canoeists and kayakers live and work; it is a four hour drive from Washington, three hours from Richmond. Next, there has been very little information published about the putins, the takeouts, the shuttle routes, the distances, and the difficulties of the rapids. Finally, the paddlers have not known about alternate streams in the area in the event that Johns Creek cannot be paddled; there was little information about other streams in that same area.

The alternates to Johns Creek are Craig Creek, Potts Creek, Dunlap Creek, the lower Cowpasture River, the Jackson River, Catawba Creek, and the upper James River, with sections for the beginner, intermediate, and advanced paddler. Johns Creek should not be neglected in the future.

Catawba Creek

INTRODUCTION

Catawba Creek is the smallest of the canoeable white-water streams coming into the James River from the south. It starts above the town of Catawba on Catawba Mountain, but it is not normally canoeable until it reaches the vicinity of Fincastle. It drains Fincastle Valley, which is one of the prettier valleys in the Valley of Virginia.

Section 1. Fincastle (Rte 220) to James River

Gradient	Difficulty	Distance	Time	Width	Scenery	Map
7	1-2	11.5	4	25-35	Good	67

Trip Description: It is possible to start on Route 606 NW of Fincastle but the preferred putin is Route 220 bridge north of Fincastle, where the creek is about 20' to 25' wide. Below Route 220, Catawba Creek flows about 9.5 miles to the James River over a bed of sand, gravel, and rock. Below Route 635, a bridge near the midpoint, the gradient increases a bit, the terrain is more closed, and the rapids increase in frequency and difficulty. The final set of rapids is almost 2 miles of steady Class 2 rock garden white-water.

The preferred takeout is at either a low-water bridge off Route 726 or at the confluence of Lapsley Run and Catawba Creek, about one-half mile above the James River, alongside Route 726 at a swimming hole. If the trip is extended to the James River, it means a four mile plus paddle to Springwood Bridge (Route 630) or a "Mission Impossible" type of takeout across the river where Route 809 comes to the railroad tracks on the north bank. Good luck with that takeout.

This tiny stream should be considered as an alternate when other streams are too high or when one is compelled to paddle something that few others have even heard about. While it flows fairly fast in the lower part, it is not very fast in the upper part. It is quite clean, however, and it has wooded banks most of the way. The rapids are mostly gravel bars, small rock gardens, and a few ledges in the last part.

Hazards: Low-water bridge. Tree blocking the stream.

Water Conditions: Canoeable in winter and spring normally or during the early summer following an extended wet spell or very heavy rain.

GAUGE

None.

Jennings Creek

INTRODUCTION

Jennings Creek is a very small mountain stream that begins in the Jefferson National Forest and ends in the James River after a distance of less than ten miles. It flows through a remote area of the Blue Ridge Mountains that is a pure paradise to hunters and fishermen. It has wilderness areas and beautiful campsites; there is no litter, pollution, or commercialization. It has a number of tributaries, all quite small, that are canoeable under certain conditions, including North Creek, Middle Creek, and McFalls Creek.

Section 1. Crawford Store (Rte 614) to James River

Gradient	Difficulty	Distance	Time	Width	Scenery	Map
64 *	2-34	4.5	1	15-30	Very Good	68

* ½mile at 90 feet/mile

Trip Description: The trip on Jennings Creek normally begins at the store/station where McFalls Creek joins Jennings Creek, although it can begin higher upstream on either stream when there is enough water. But from this point to Arcadia is enough white-water for most people. It begins as a steady Class 2 white-water stream flowing swiftly through a most beautiful forest; the bottom is solid rock and the scenery is magnificent for the next three miles; it has a sand and gravel bottom and high banks only after passing the bridge at Arcadia. The rapids in the first 3.5 miles are mostly small ledges and rock gardens, usually Class 2, but there are occasional Class 3 rockgardens to add spice to an already well-seasoned trip.

Middle Creek enters on the right about 1.5 miles from the putin, and North Creek enters about 3 miles downstream on the right. Then the stream makes its final plunge into the James River valley. There are two Class 4 rapids with big drops about 400 yards below the point that North Creek enters. Both rapids have sharp ledges that slope from the rock cliffs on the right, pushing water and paddlers to the left; after a steep drop on the left (its a lot higher on the right), a hard right turn is required. Scout these rapids from the road and then be prepared to recover boats and paddlers from the river just below the rapids.

It is possible to takeout at Route 622 in Arcadia, about 200 yards below the big rapids or at Route 614 bridge about 400 yards further downstream. If continuing to the James River, the next takeout is Route 614 bridge over the James River, but this adds ½ mile to the trip and a tough takeout. There is an old iron furnace in Arcadia, close to the Route 622 bridge; it can be seen from Route 614.

Hazards: Two major (Class 4) rapids between Arcadia and North Creek.

Water Conditions: Canoeable normally in the winter and spring after a moderate rain or following a wet period.

Section 2. North Creek: Campground to Jennings Creek

Gradient	Difficulty	Distance	Time	Width	Scenery	Map
110	2-3	2.5	.5	15-25	Very Good	68

Trip Description: The trip from North Creek Campground to Jennings Creek may take less time to canoe than it does to check the map data and write the trip description. It begins as a small terror dropping over ledges and dashing through

211

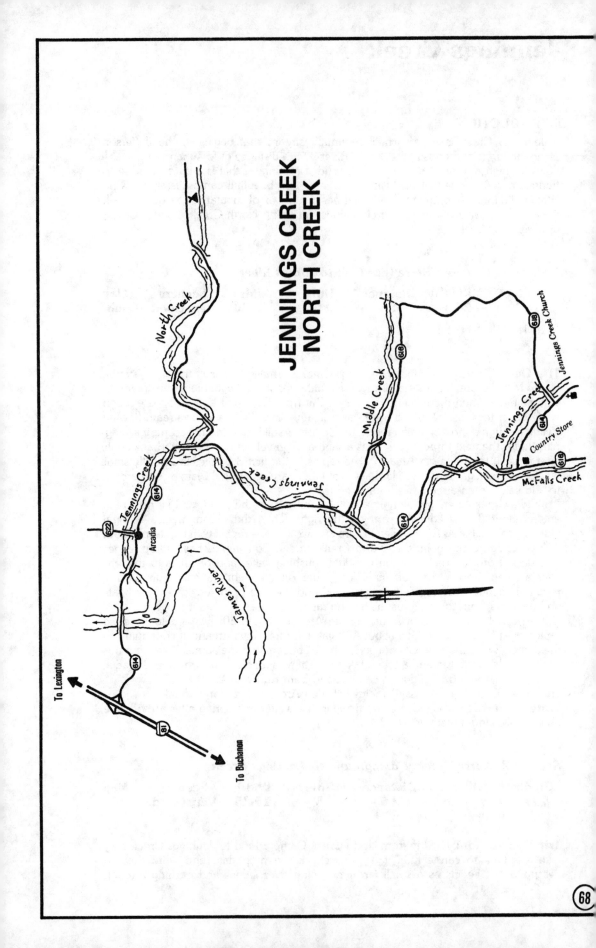

JENNINGS CREEK
NORTH CREEK

rock gardens at a horrendous pace. There are no eddies, the rapids are continuous, the scenery is just a blur, and there is no time or place for scouting. If a paddler does not have experience, good instincts, and quick reactions, there will be trouble for sure. The stream is the same width as there are few tributaries enroute; the bottom is solid rock with a few traces of coarse sand; the bridges are frequent and high enough to pass under comfortably. The scenery is largely the slopes of steep mountains on each side of the road/stream, but it will have to be admired while on the shuttle. If continuing on Jennings Creek, prepare for two complex, tough rapids — in addition to the action where the two streams join. There are few, if any, distinctive or memorable rapids in this section; it just looks like waves, rocks, and small hydraulics without respite for the entire distance.

Hazards: None

Water Conditons: Canoeable normally in the winter and spring following a wet period or after a moderate rain.

GAUGE

None available.

OTHER INFORMATION

Jennings Creek drains the northern and western slopes of the Blue Ridge Mountains near Peaks of Otter. The southern and eastern slopes in this area drain into Little Otter Creek and Big Otter Creek which, in turn, drain into the Roanoke River near Bedford. The Blue Ridge Parkway is reached from Jennings Creek by driving steadily uphill along McFalls Creek to Powell Gap. Just to the east of Powells Gap is the large, beautiful lodge area where Route 43 meets the Blue Ridge Parkway; this is a small, flat mountain valley between Sharp Top Mountain and Flat Top Mountain— the two peaks that form the Peaks of Otter.

The campground alongside North Creek is an enchanting spot that few people have ever seen. The camping sites along the stream are wooded, the water is clear and refreshing, and the high rock bluffs block the cold wind. Of course, if one prefers a more commercial atmosphere with more conveniences, there is the Yogi Bear Jellystone Campground on Middle Creek nearby. Jennings Creek, Middle Creek, North Creek, and McFalls Creek are trout streams that are stocked by the state; do not attempt these streams on opening day of trout season, as the difficulty rating may change to risk of life— and not because of the rapids. During deer season, try to wear bright clothing and avoid using a white handkerchief (it may look like the rear end of a white-tail deer), as this area is quite popular with hunters, particularly during November and December.

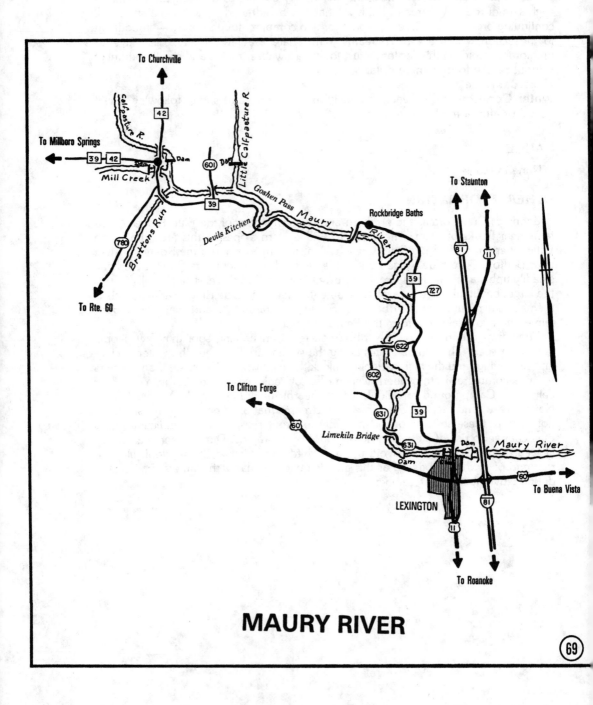

MAURY RIVER

Maury River

INTRODUCTION

The most exciting and the most scenic white-water river in Virginia is, without a doubt, the Maury River in its Goshen Pass section. No other stream has rapids of such strength and complexity, no other stream has such magnificent rock cliffs along both banks, and very few other streams are so easily accessible for rescue or walkout. There is only one Goshen Pass.

Section 1. Above Goshen Pass to Rockbridge Baths (Rte 39)

Gradient	Difficulty	Distance	Time	Width	Scenery	Map
36	2-45	6.5	2.5	50-70	Excellent	69

Trip Description: The Maury River begins at the confluence of the Calfpasture River and the Little Calfpasture River, about ¼ mile above Goshen Pass, but the trip through Goshen Pass begins at a convenient putin alongside Route 39 at the western end of the pass. This section is for only those paddlers interested in heavy white-water, and this putin should be a takeout for the less experienced who started on the Calfpasture River and do not want to risk boat and gear.

The river starts out with Class 2-3 rock gardens, a good warm-up for things to come. At the first of the stronger rapids, the water funnels to the right and builds up in strength and cross-currents; it may swamp open boats that do not stay left. Then there is the Devils Kitchen Rapid, a monstrous Class 4-5 rapid that must drop twenty-five feet in less than two hundred feet; this rapid is entered on the left and requires the paddler to successfully negotiate at least eight two-to-three foot drops while working to the right bank at the bottom. Scout this complex, powerful rapid from the right bank downstream to see the tortuous path. At the foot of the rapid, the waves build up and there are big rocks waiting for the unwary or the wipeouts. This is one of the most difficult rapids in Virginia.

Below Devils Kitchen, there are a number of strong, complex rapids, usually on right turns. There are rock garden rapids that require a lot of quick maneuvering and frequent bailing (by open boat paddlers). At high water levels, this section is a nightmare of big waves, big holes, and strong crosscurrents; at low water levels, it is difficult to pick a route, but no major problem. Just below the main picnic area, there are two very good ledges, riverwide Class 3-4 ledges, that is; they are more impressive than they are dangerous. Then there is a two step ledge that has strong hydraulics and a rock at the bottom that eats swamped boats. Then things become milder and the river gets rather shallow around a couple of islands.

The river still has good strong Class 3 rapids before reaching Rockbridge-Baths, but most of the remaining section has Class 2 rock garden rapids. Just before the takeout bridge, there is a runnable 5' drop, a natural rock ledge that may have been used as a dam; there is a 5' drop on the left through an easy but exciting, S-turn. Great, man, great. From that drop to the bridge is quiet water. "Thank you, Lord, for getting me through again."

Hazards: Plenty of big (Class 4-5) rapids.

Water Conditions: Canoeable in winter and spring normally or during the early summer following an extended wet spell or very heavy rain.

Section 2. Rockbridge-Baths (Rte 39) to Limekiln Bridge (Rte 631)

Gradient	Difficulty	Distance	Time	Width	Scenery	Map
15	1-2	13	4.5	50-60	Good	69

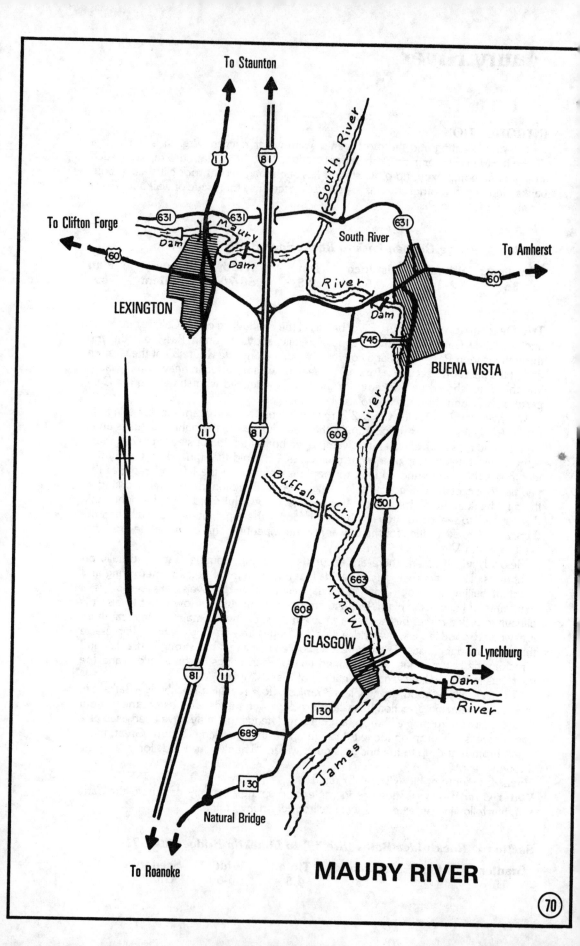

MAURY RIVER

⑦⓪

Trip Description: The Maury River between Rockbridge Baths and Limekiln Bridge is a pleasant Class 1-2 white-water trip in the upper half but it has only Class 1 riffles in the final half of the trip. In high water, the first mile could have two Class 3 rapids, but that is the only section where the rapids increase in difficulty as the water level increases. By the time Limekiln Bridge is reached, there will be many tired canoeists. The trip has a lot of pleasant aspects, such as low banks, sandy bottoms, rock cliffs, gravel bars, small ledges, and rock gardens. The water is usually clear, the current is fast to moderate, and, there are no hazards. But it really is not white-water; it is canoeing and relaxation in a scenic, remote area.

Hazards: None.

Water Conditions: Canoeable in winter and spring normally or during the early summer following an extended wet spell or very heavy rain.

Section 3. Limekiln Bridge (Rte 631) to Ben Salem Wayside (Rte 60)

Gradient	Difficulty	Distance	Time	Width	Scenery	Map
5	12	10	4	50-60	Good	69, 70

Trip Description: Between Limekiln Bridge and Route 11 Bridge in Lexington, there are two dams and a lot of quiet water and flat water. One mile below Limekiln Bridge, there are the remains of a four-foot mill dam, with a canal along the left bank to a mill 400 yards downstream. This dam is just a good rapid and is runnable. About 50 yards above Route 11, about 5 yards above the old RR bridge footings, is the Lexington dam; it is 8' high and must be portaged. There is a mill on the left about 2 miles above Lexington, right beside the road, that operated until the 1930's. There are occasional riffles, the bottom is sandy, and the swimming is good. The banks are low, the water is clear and clean, the terrain is rolling woodlands, and the current is moderately slow. It is pleasant and scenic, but it is not white-water.

Between Lexington and the Ben Salem Wayside, about 3 miles downstream from Lexington, there is a 12' to 14' old navigation dam. It is truly a beautiful structure, built from 2'x4'x3' limestone blocks; it has a backwater of about 2 miles. The ruins of an old mill and locks are on the left bank. About three miles farther downstream is a Class 2 rapid at the remains of the South River dam; the remains of the lock are on the right bank. Just below this rapid, the South River enters on the left (north) bank. The Class 1-2 rapid at the takeout is the remains of the Ben Salem navigation dam. The remains of a magnificent lock are right beside Route 60 at the wayside.

Hazards: Twelve-foot dam three miles below Lexington, eight-foot dam at Lexington.

Water Conditions: Canoeable in winter and spring normally or during the early summer following an extended wet spell or very heavy rain.

Section 4. Ben Salem Wayside (Rte 60) to James River

Gradient	Difficulty	Distance	Time	Width	Scenery	Map
11	1-2	13.0	5	60-80	Good	70

Trip Description: The Maury River between Ben Salem Wayside and Glasgow (Locher Landing) had many dams in the early 1800's, but only the Moomaw dam just west of Buena Vista remains. This dam is 12-14' high, and was originally constructed in the 1800's with limestone blocks (2'x4'x3'); a concrete slab was placed on top of the dam in the 1900's and it was used as a power dam. Some of the original navigation dams below Buena Vista have been removed for their stone (Buffalo Creek Dam), have broken away (Goose Neck Dam), or have been washed out.

From the Wayside to the Moomaw Dam is about two miles; the dam is about 400 yards below the Route 60 bridge. Above the dam, there are a few riffles over a sandy bottom; below the dam there are more riffles while passing by the back streets and waterfront of Buena Vista. Just below the 10th Street Bridge and the Glen Maury Park, there are the remains of an old dam; it is now an easy 2'-3' ledge.

About four miles below Buena Vista, there was a high dam which was part of the old canal system and later a power dam. This dam (Gooseneck Dam) has been washed out on the right side, a 30' wide gap, and only a Class 2 rapid remains. Below this dam, there are fairly continuous riffles, small ledges, and gravel bars to the take-out. The current is moderate, the scenery is good, the swimming is excellent. Buffalo Creek enters on the right, three miles from the takeout; the Lone Jack Quarry discolors the river with a lot of particulates two miles from the takeout; there are signs of the old canals on the left bank; and there are occasional islands with swift channels. There is a takeout at Rte 130 bridge but there is an easier takeout 400 yards downstream at Locher Landing, at the end of Route 684.

Hazards: Twelve-foot dam at Buena Vista.

Water Conditions: Canoeable in winter, spring, and early summer, except following periods of little precipitation. Canoeable after a heavy rain in the summer and fall.

GAUGE

There are two USGS gauges for the Maury River and one RC canoeing gauge. The USGS gauges are at Rockbridge-Baths and at Buena Vista. The RC gauge is on the Rte 39 bridge at Buena Vista. The following table compares these gauges and indicates the canoeing levels.

Table 6
Maury River Gauges

CFS	RC Gauge	USGS-RB	USGS-BV	Difficulty
255	0"	2.0		—
	6"	2.25	2.9	3-4
510	1'	2.5		3-5
820	1.8'	3.0		3-5
1,380	2.4	3.7		4-5

The minimum water level for Goshen Pass is 6" to 8" on the RC gauge, 2.25' USGS Rockbridge Baths gauge, and 2.9' on the USGS Buena Vista guage. The maximum water level for open boats is about 3.9' USGS-BV, 1.5' RC. For deck boaters, the limit is only that which the mind will establish and ego will permit; levels of 4500 CFS (6.5' on the USGS-RB gauge) have been run by decked boaters of dubious sanity. Sections 2 and 3 can be run with 6" less water; Section 4, with 1' less water.

HISTORY

The Maury River is formed by the Calfpasture River and the Little Calfpasture River between the town of Goshen and the beginning of Goshen Pass. Prior to the 1870's, the Maury River was named the North River and the records in the Virginia Legislature in the early 1800's refers to it by that name. The river was renamed in 1873 in honor of Matthew Fontaine Maury; Commander Maury was a famous oceanographer who headed the hydrographic office of the U.S. Navy, served in the Confederate Navy, served with Maximillian in Mexico, and taught at VMI. Maury loved Goshen Pass and the river, and after his death, his remains were marched through the pass by the VMI cadets.

Lexington is a very historic town. Its citizens provided riflemen in the Revolutionary and Civil War; the VMI cadets, teenagers, marched to and died in the battle of New Market. Stonewall Jackson taught at VMI prior to serving the Confederacy. Robert E. Lee served as president of Washington and Lee College after the war of Northern

Aggression; George C. Marshall graduated from VMI and went to the highest military and diplomatic positions.

The leading citizens of Rockbridge County were determined to extend river navigation to Lexington from the James River and to "build in the most permanent and substantial canal possible." The construction which was begun in 1851 was so good that navigation could be easily reopened today if some of the work had not been deliberately torn down. Each section, upon completion, became a major commerce center; Buffalo Creek, Thompson, Moomaw's, South River, and Anderson Landings each had its day in the sun. In 1860 navigation was opened to Lexington largely because the JR&KC Company had bought the North River Navigation Company in 1858. At this time, the system was comprised of 9 dams, 16 locks, and a system of canals that included one canal over 4½ miles long. Only the North River canal system was capable of handling the largest canal boats from the James River Canal.

The first landing was Millers Landing, opposite the boat yard at Buffalo Creek where the canal boats and bateaux were built. This section included a 4.5 mile canal with 6 locks, 2 aqueducts, and a dam, completed in 1857. By the time the system was completed, another canal of 2½ miles length, 15 more locks, and 9 dams were constructed. This canal system, which prospered until the early 1880's, was probably used until 1895 when the Shenandoah Valley (now N&W) RR built a dam across one of the canals. Most of the dams have been torn out and some of the locks have been covered over by the RR or completely removed for their stones, but their locations can be discovered from the nearby roads or the river.

OTHER INFORMATION

While canoeing on the Goshen Pass section of the Maury River on a crisp spring day, a group of canoeists met a group of college students from Lexington. As part of their fraternity initiations, the students were required to make a trip on this section using inner tubes. The canoeists wore wet suits, the students wore bathing suits; the paddlers had hot coffee/chocolate/soup, the students had a few cold beers; the paddlers had waterproof packs and throw lines; the students had prayers and optimism. It makes one cold to even think of that type of hazing; streaking seems to be a saner option.

During Hurricane Camille, the Maury River was an unbelievable sight. It crested at Lexington Dam twenty-six (26) feet above zero. At places, the river appeared to be a gigantic lake, flooding fields on each bank and reaching widths of one-half mile below Lexington. The roads near the Maury were washed out by the water; at one place, sections of asphalt as large as 20 by 30 feet were lifted from the road bed and deposited in farmers' fields. The devastation was staggering.

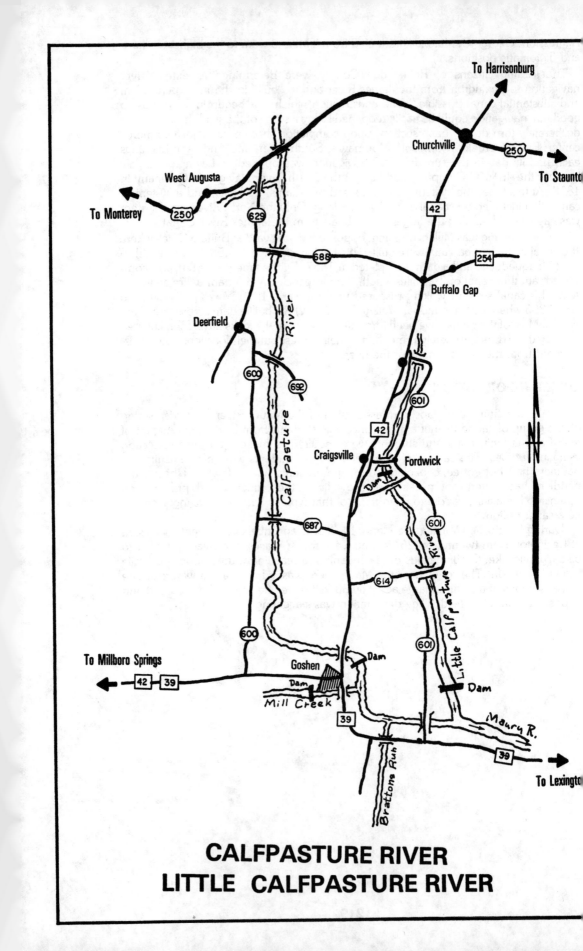

CALFPASTURE RIVER
LITTLE CALFPASTURE RIVER

Calfpasture River

INTRODUCTION

The Calfpasture River begins in the Virginia Highlands at Bald Ridge, just north of Route 250, and it flows in a southwesterly direction toward the town of Goshen. Below Goshen, it is joined by the Little Calfpasture River to form the Maury River, just before the Maury enters Goshen Pass. Throughout its entire length, the Calfpasture is a pleasant, beautiful, relaxing, enjoyable stream that flows through a farming valley with high mountains on each side. It is the principal tributary of the Maury River; its tributaries include Mill Creek, Bratton Run, Ramsey Draft, Hamilton Draft, and the Little Calfpasture.

Section 1. West Augusta (Rte 250) to Deerfield (Rte 692)

Gradient	Difficulty	Distance	Time	Width	Scenery	Map
24	2₃	10	3	20-35	Good	71

Trip Description: The four sections of the Calfpasture River, Rte 250 to Deerfield, Deerfield to Ramsey Gap Bridge, Ramsey Gap Bridge to Goshen, and Goshen to the Maury River, are quite similar in many respects. The biggest difference is in the size of the stream and the volume of water in the stream as it travels through a narrow valley. From Route 250 to just below Goshen, it travels in a southwesterly direction; below Goshen it turns to the east until it ends at the Little Calfpasture River.

At Route 250 bridge, the Calfpasture River is about 20'-25' wide, flowing over a bed of gravel/stones; the water is very clear and is without pollution. It is usually too shallow to start canoeing at this point, except after a long wet spell, so the next bridge downstream is the preferred putin. Ramsey Draft enters from the west and provides a lot more water above this bridge (Rte 688). From Route 250 to Deerfield, the rapids are mostly of the cobble bar type with occasional ledges that are less than 2 feet in height. It is a fairly steady Class 2 trip, the current is moderately fast, there are not many pools or flat stretches, and the banks have stretches with evergreen stands that will be remembered.

There are limestone and slate formations that form a solid rock bottom in this section, with ledges parallel to the water flow, diagonal to the waterflow, and perpendicular to the water flow. These ledges make very interesting Class 2 rapids that have strange waves and unusual currents. About three miles below Route 688 bridge, there is a spot that may be the most beautiful scene on any river in Virginia.
Hazards: Low-water bridge about 4 miles downstream. Barbed/woven wire fences. Trees across the stream.
Water Conditions: Canoeable normally in winter and spring following a wet period or a moderate rain.

Section 2. Deerfield (Rte 692) to Ramsey Gap Bridge (Rte 697)

Gradient	Difficulty	Distance	Time	Width	Scenery	Map
15.5	1-2	8	2.5	25-35	Very Good	71

Section 3. Ramsey Gap Bridge (Rte 697) to Goshen (Rte 42)

Gradient	Difficulty	Distance	Time	Width	Scenery	Map
11	1-2	11.5	4	30-60	Good	71

Trip Description: From Deerfield to Goshen, a distance of 19.5 miles, the Calfpasture River is a pleasant stream flowing through a narrow mountain valley. It meanders a bit between the Great North Mountain to the east and Walker Mountain to the west, but it travels very close to the Great North Mountain for most of the trip. In this section, it receives water from many little streams entering on both sides and it changes from a small stream to a small river. The rapids are mostly gravel bar rapids with either swift chutes or wide shallow areas; there are a few small ledges and a number of abrupt turns below small chutes; all are Class 2 or less. The water is still clear, the current is moderate, there are a number of beautiful rock bluffs, the scenery is mostly farmland, the road is nearby at many spots, and there are no hazards (no dams, fences, trees, low-water bridges). There are the remains of a low dam just below Route 42 at Goshen; it is about four feet high and might be runnable in the left/left-center section in low water; in high water, it is dangerous. The trip can be divided into many lengths by taking out or putting in alongside Route 600 or at the Route 692 bridge.

Hazards: None.

Water Conditions: Canoeable in winter, spring, and early summer, except following periods of little precipitation. Canoeable after a heavy rain in the summer and fall.

Section 4. Goshen (Rte 42) to Maury River

Gradient	Difficulty	Distance	Time	Width	Scenery	Map
15	1-2	4	1.5	50-70	Fair	71

Trip Description: From Goshen to the Maury River, the Calfpasture River increases in width and volume as Mill Creek, Brattons Run, and the Little Calfpasture River feed into it. The rapids are still Class 1-2, but the paddler can feel the strength of the water increasing. By the time the Little Calfpasture is reached, where the Maury River begins, it is a good size mountain river. The rapids are still gravel bars and rock garden rapids, but they have become stronger -- no longer riffles. The water is still fairly clear and green colored, but it now has been exposed to a small town, a creosote plant, and a log yard. The last takeout before Goshen Pass is at the Maury River alongside Route 39 on the right, just as the Maury begins to leave the open valley. Only the advanced or expert paddler should continue beyond this point.

Hazards: None.

Water Conditions: Canoeable in winter, spring, and early summer, except following periods of little precipitation. Canoeable after a heavy rain in the summer and fall.

GAUGE

A reading of 4.0' on the USGS Buena Vista gauge should be zero for canoeing on the upper sections, 3.5' on the lower section. A reading of 1' on the RC gauge at Rockbridge Baths over the Maury should be zero for canoeing the upper sections, 6" for the lower sections. There are RC gauges at Route 692 and Route 688 bridges on the Calfpasture.

Little Calfpasture River

INTRODUCTION

The Little Calfpasture River is a beautiful stream that flows for about sixteen miles through a narrow mountain valley to join the Calfpasture River to form the Maury River. The valley is bordered by high mountains to the east and low mountains to the west, so close that the stream cannot meander very much. The valley appears to have been bypassed by time and progress, and only a few local people appreciate its beauty.

Section 1. Augusta Springs (Rte 601) to Maury River (Rte 39)

Gradient	Difficulty	Distance	Time	Width	Scenery	Map
16	1-2	16	6	15-30*	Good	71

*Very wide in backwater above second dam

Trip Description: The Little Calfpasture River is a very little river in its upper reaches; in fact, it does not even appear big enough to be called a creek or a run. From Augusta Springs to Fordwick, it flows swiftly over a rock bottom through fairly continuous riffles/rapids---steady Class 2. It is difficult to observe the scenery in this stretch because of the dense vegetation along the banks, but the stream is in a very narrow valley. About four miles downstream, it enters Estaline Valley, a most beautiful farming area. The bottom has changed to sand and gravel, the terrain is open farmland, and the current is fairly fast. Below Bells Valley, where Route 601 crosses the stream, the river is fairly flat and there are only a few gravel bar riffles. The scenery is strictly that of good farmland in a narrow valley between high mountains.

There are a few interesting points along this river. Near Craigsville, there was a settlement named Fordwick, where the Lehigh Portland Cement Co. had a very big operation. The plant is on the left (east) bank and it is still impressive, even though closed; the quarry area on the right bank just below the bridge has high white cliffs along the stream for about a mile, the area mined by the plant. There is a dam about 200 yards below the Fordwick bridge; this 12' dam must be portaged and both sides are difficult. The town of Craigsville was hit hard by the plant closing, but the good people did not allow their town to fall into disrepair. It is a pretty town well worth seeing.

Below Route 601 bridge, which is almost the midpoint of the trip, the Little Calfpasture is free-flowing for about four miles. Then the river becomes a 400 acre lake that extends for a distance of about four miles, or so it seems. Below the high dam, it is about one mile to the Maury River; then it is about 300 yards to a takeout alongside Route 39 at the start of Goshen Pass. It would be wise to takeout just above the lake on the road to the Boy Scout Camp and avoid the flat water and the portage.

Hazards: Twelve-foot dam 200 yards below Route 684 near Craigsville. Forty-five foot dam one mile above the Maury River. Trees/fences blocking the stream in the upper reaches.

Water Conditions: Canoeable normally in the winter and spring following a prolonged wet period or heavy rain.

GAUGE

A reading of 3.5' on the USGS Buena Vista gauge or 1.0' on the RC gauge on the Maury River at Route 39 is probably zero for canoeing. A reading of 8" on the RC gauges on the Calfpasture River is zero for the upper stretches of this stream.

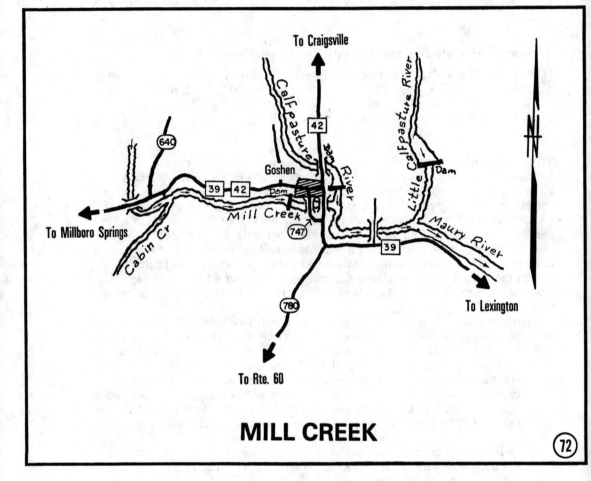

To Craigsville

Calfpasture River

Little Calfpasture River

640

42

Goshen

Dam

39 42

Dam

Mill Creek

747

Cabin Cr

Little Calfpasture River

Dam

Maury River

39

To Millboro Springs

N

To Lexington

780

To Rte. 60

MILL CREEK

72

Mill Creek

INTRODUCTION

Mill Creek is an untamed terror of a small stream that flows down a steep mountain valley from atop a mountain to a flat mountain valley. It drains such a small area and its gradient is so steep that it is very difficult to find it with water. Even though it flows fairly close to Route 39/42, it seems to flow through a remote area.

Section 1. Route 42 Wayside to Goshen (Rte 39)

Gradient	Difficulty	Distance	Time	Width	Scenery	Map
31	2-3	7.5	2	25-35	Good	72

Trip Description: The Mill Creek trip begins at a roadside turnout on Route 39 & 42, just west of Panther Gap, midway between Millboro Springs and Goshen. The putin is about 300 yards east of a truckstop/gas station/restaurant, where the creek is barely wider than a canoe length. The toughest section, which is close to Route 39 & 42, is a Class 3 slalom course that should be undertaken only by the experienced white-water paddler. The gradient is fairly steady and most of the rapids are small ledges and complex rock gardens. There is a 3' ledge about 100 yards after the stream leaves the road; it looks like a low dam and it usually has a stream-wide hydraulic that can be formidable in high water; this ledge is just after passing through Panther Gap where the power lines cross overhead.

This river is very fast and there are very few eddies; in fact, it may be too narrow for an eddy turn. The maneuvering requirements are most demanding, and boats will take a severe beating if swamped. There are a few trees and/or fences that block the stream, so open boaters must be prepared to jump out without hesitation and decked boaters must have a very good eddy turn or a superior back stroke. There is an 8' dam just before the town of Goshen that must be portaged. Then there is the takeout, a low water bridge in the town of Goshen that presents a hazard in itself; looking at it on the shuttle could save a lot of embarrassment, financial loss, and bodily harm.

This stream is so fast and the action is so continuous that a canoeist will not have time to observe the scenery or to look for the stream's namesake, i.e. the mill. Again, this is a trip for only the brave and the foolhardy, who must also be very good paddlers.

Hazards: Trees/fences across the stream. Eight-foot dam at Goshen. Low-water bridge at Goshen.

Water Conditions: Canoeable only in winter and spring following a prolonged wet period or very heavy rain.

GAUGE

A reading of 6.0' on the USGS Buena Vista gauge or 3.0' on the RC gauge at Rockbridge Baths Bridge will be zero for canoeing this stream.

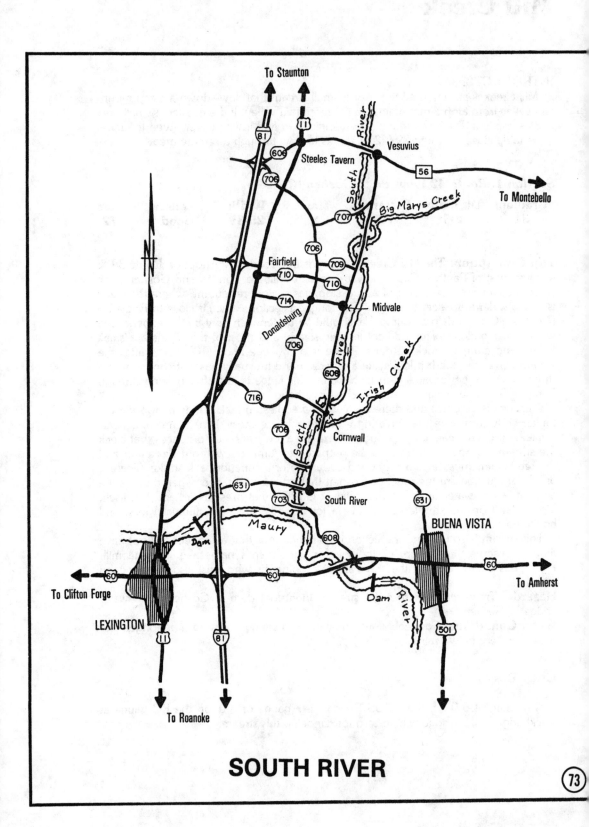

SOUTH RIVER

South River

INTRODUCTION

The South River from Vesuvius to the Maury River was one of the most beautiful streams in Virginia before Hurricane Camille. It was nestled in a secluded valley that attracted few tourists, even though it was convenient to Lexington and I-81, and it was protected from the more adverse weather by mountains to the east and hills to the west. It was known for its trout fishing, the unpolluted water, its fertile farmland, and its scenic mills. Then came the hurricane, followed by the river channelizing. It will be many years before things look natural again.

Section 1. Vesuvius (Rte 56) to Route 608 Bridge

Gradient	Difficulty	Distance	Time	Width	Scenery	Map
44	1-2	5	2	30-50	Good	73

Section 2. Route 608 Bridge to Cornwall (Rte 716)

Gradient	Difficulty	Distance	Time	Width	Scenery	Map
31	1-2	7	2.5	50-70	Fair	73

Section 3. Cornwall (Rte 716) to Maury River (Rte 608)

Gradient	Difficulty	Distance	Time	Width	Scenery	Map
31	1-2	5	2	60-80	Fair	73

Trip Description: The flood waters from Hurricane Camille virtually destroyed the South River valley, turning a beautiful stream into a valley wide cobble bar. There was not a well-defined stream bed in most parts after the flood; the river was merely a series of trickles among the rocks. When the state restored the South River to its approximate river bed, however, the construction firms turned it into a 16-mile long gravel bar. The gradient of 31 to 44 feet per mile is still there. You can see the gradient; it is like looking downhill all of the time. When you compare the 41 feet/mile gradient of the South River with other rivers flowing in a natural state over Class 2-3 rapids, it is hard to believe the difference. But the same thing happened to Wolf Creek between South Gap and Rocky Gap and the Tye River below Route 29.

At present, the South River is a steady Class 1-2 gravel bar for 16 miles, with no ledges, no rock gardens, no chutes, no intricate turns, no pools. The river is a fairly uniform width in most stretches, gradually widening as it picks up water. It has been constructed so that the water is a uniform depth from start to finish, so that the dangerous big rocks are on the banks and that there is a guarantee of repetition. Only in the last mile above Route 632 bridge can the stream's natural characteristics be seen, as the rocks/ledges were too tough to be graded over. The firms that restore rivers for the state must specialize in highway construction or railway construction.

Route 608 crosses the South River many times, and the river is alongside the road at many points. So it is easy to vary the length of the trips on this river. There is a very good takeout on the left bank below Route 632. Be sure to stop before the last bridge (Route 608) just above the Maury River; it may be too low to pass under.

Hazards: Low-water bridge at Maury River.

Water Conditions: Canoeable in winter and spring normally or during the early summer following an extended wet spell or very heavy rain.

GAUGE

A reading of 3.8' on the USGS Buena Vista gauge should be zero for the upper sections; 3.2' on the lower sections.

OTHER INFORMATION

The old mills in Steeles Tavern and Vesuvius, the waterfalls on Marl Run between Steeles Tavern and Vesuvius, the three principal tributaries in the upper reaches (St. Mary's River, Big Mary Creek, and Little Mary Creek), the Blue Ridge Parkway, the falls on the right bank (about two miles above Route 632), the old iron furnace at South River, and the remains of old mines, all give the South River a character of its own. During trout season, it has more spots for stopping alongside the river and fishing from both scenic and convenient cobble bars or sand bars than any stream in Virginia. These same fishing spots are ideal camping spots for the canoeist who wants to sleep to the music of rushing water. The Cyrus McCormick Farm Museum is just east of Vesuvius and Steeles Tavern; it is worth a visit to the home and workshop of the man who revolutionized agriculture. Crabtree Falls is just 10 miles east of Vesuvius alongside Route 56; the water falls almost 2,000 feet into the South Fork of the Tye River.

There are four rather scenic or interesting spots near the crossroads of South River. First, there is the remains of an old iron furnace on the south side of the road junction at South River; this iron furnace was used to smelt ore from the nearby mines; the iron was then transported by batteau on the North River and James River (later the canals) to Richmond where there was a major iron industry. Few people know that Richmond has coal seams nearby that were mined in the 1700's and 1800's, but the coal mines were a definite asset to the foundries and mills.

There are the locks of the South River dam and canal just upstream of the point where the South River enters the Maury River; the dam is only riffles now, but, during the summer, one can wade across the Maury to inspect the lock which is still in fair condition. Just west of South River, alongside the road, Marl Creek (the second one) drops over a small waterfall into a little, deep pool; it is a tremendous spot to stop and jump in for a cool dip on a hot day. Just upstream from South River, a small stream drops into the river over an impressive rock formation; this is Cypress Falls. In high water, it is a cascade to delight the heart; in low water, the gnarled, weathered rock formation is just beautiful. Durng the summer, it is easy to wade across to the falls, and sit under the small streams or in the small pools.

Irish Creek

INTRODUCTION

Irish Creek is the classic example of the white-water stream that drains an upland valley through a mountain pass. The canoeing trip begins at the Irish Creek Mission picnic grounds, just below the point where a major tributary enters the creek. It ends 7.5 miles later at a highway bridge just above its confluence with the South River at Cornwall, having dropped from an elevation of 1620 feet to 1015 feet. It is an absolute terror for the entire distance.

Section 1. Irish Creek Mission (Rte 603/605) to South River (Rte 608)

Gradient	Difficulty	Distance	Time	Width	Scenery	Map
80	2-4$_5$	7.5	1.5	20-30	Excellent	74

Trip Description: It is impossible to describe this terror of a stream in complete detail, so a general summary of the more memorable features is appropriate. At the putin, the stream is about 20 feet wide and flows swiftly over gravel and rocks. Within 600 yards, it has dashed over very strong Class 2 rapids without a pool or eddy and has entered a rats' nest of rocks (Class 3) that requires fast reactions and good judgment. Then about 800 yards downstream, there is a ledge, then a short pool, and a rock garden of VW size rocks, followed by two three-foot ledges that dump into a horrible rock garden. Everything looks white and frothy.

About a mile below the putin, there is a rapid with two three-foot ledges in quick succession, another rapid with a 20' drop in 50 yards through broken ledges and a complex rock garden, and a third rapid with a 3' ledge and a 4' ledge just below. Then it becomes a strong, steady Class 2 to the cemetery at 1.25 miles. The putin below the ledge at the cemetery is the recommended place for starting on this stream. Below the cemetery, after 800 yards of steady rock garden rapids (Class 2) there is a small island with heavy drops on both sides through narrow passages between desk-size rocks requiring precise, quick turns. Then it funnels to the right close to the road, over an entry ledge into a rock garden.

About 1.7 miles from the putin, there is a very complex rapid in which a sloping rock on the left funnels the water to a drop on the right. Then there are comparatively quiet rock gardens with big waves, hard turns, narrow passages, and no pools, eddies, before reaching the highway/bridge; this is the third bridge upstream. Look at the bridge at this point, about 2 miles below the putin; if the rapids here look too tough, do not start upstream, these are easy rapids.

From the first bridge crossing down to the next bridge crossing, there is continuous action, but not comparable to the action above. About three hundred yards below this second bridge when the creek returns to the road, there is a Class 5 rapid that has a complex entry followed by a 4' ledge, a 3' ledge, and a 4' ledge, all in the space of 50 feet followed by a nasty rock garden; each of these ledges has a strong hydraulic from bank to bank. While fighting to line up the bow for the second and third ledges, the stern is being drawn back under the ledges. Yuck!

From the Class 5 rapid to mile 2.9, there are stone levees on the bank and continuous white-water in the stream, a steady Class 2-3. At mile 2.9, the terrain opens into a small valley and there is a private bridge; from this point down to mile 4.8, the river is more tricky, complex, fast and tough. It has one section with over a mile of solid rock bottom in which the water moves even faster and the waves become bigger. The rapids are mostly small, continuous ledges with hydraulics that span almost all of the stream and Class 2 or 3 rock gardens with every chute complicated at the entry or exit by a rock placed by some demon.

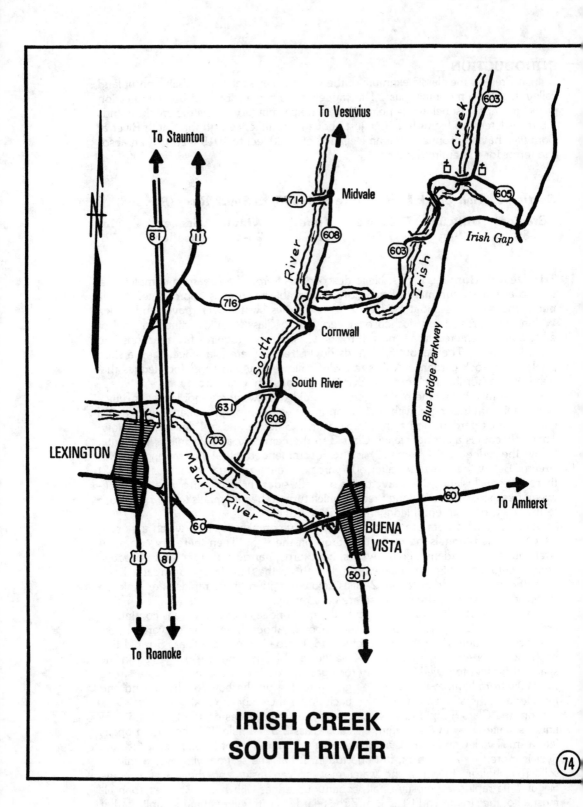

**IRISH CREEK
SOUTH RIVER**

At mile 5.8, the stream crosses under the road again. Look at the ledges and rock gardens here; if this Class 3 section is too complex, too difficult, do not try the upper section. Just below this bridge, the stream enters the South River Valley and its gradient drops to about 30 fpm. The rapids are relatively easy cobble bars to the takeout. Just look out for that footbridge built of large steel I beams; it could dent your boat and spoil your day to underestimate this hazard.

There is no chance that a canoeist or kayaker will be able to relate this trip description to the river while paddling Irish Creek. The description is to give the paddler an idea what is in store for him -- steady Class 2-3-4 rapids for six miles. Many ledges will not be recognizable when there is enough water to run this trip and the rock gardens will be one continuous series of white nightmares. So use the description for a general appreciation and not for detailed planning.

If the paddler has time for watching the scenery, the rock cliffs are most impressive. There are some very interesting levees along the creek bank formed by millions of cobble stones held together by a wire mesh. There are a lot of spots to camp alongside a beautiful trout stream. One word of caution, the nearest hospitals are in Buena Vista and Lexington.

Hazards: Plenty of major rapids. One tree blocking the stream. Steel foot bridge.

Water Conditions: Canoeable only in winter and spring following a prolonged wet period or very heavy rain.

GAUGE

A reading of 6.0' on the USGS Buena Vista guage is zero for canoeing on this section. There is a RC gauge on Route 608 bridge across Irish Creek near Cornwall.

OTHER INFORMATION

There is one thing that one will always remember about the valley through which Irish Creek flows. It is the use of stones and cobbles to build large levees along the stream to protect the road from erosion by the creek. These levees are constructed using a very heavy wire mesh to form the walls of the levees and then filling them with millions of stones. When the wire forms are filled, a wire mesh is put on top of the levee, holding the sides together and making for a most remarkable structure. Some of these levees are four feet high, four feet wide, and one hundred feet long. Imagine how many rocks, stones, and cobbles were handled in this task. The only other stream known to have such structures is Jennings Creek, near Arcadia.

The road that leads from the South River into the Irish Creek valley splits near Irish Mission Church. Both of these roads lead to the Blue Ridge Parkway, one to Irish Gap, on to Tye River Gap. Both routes are scenic and worth the drive. If one likes camping in a rather private area with good scenery and a natural stream, the road along Irish Creek has many such spots that are used regularly by fishermen.

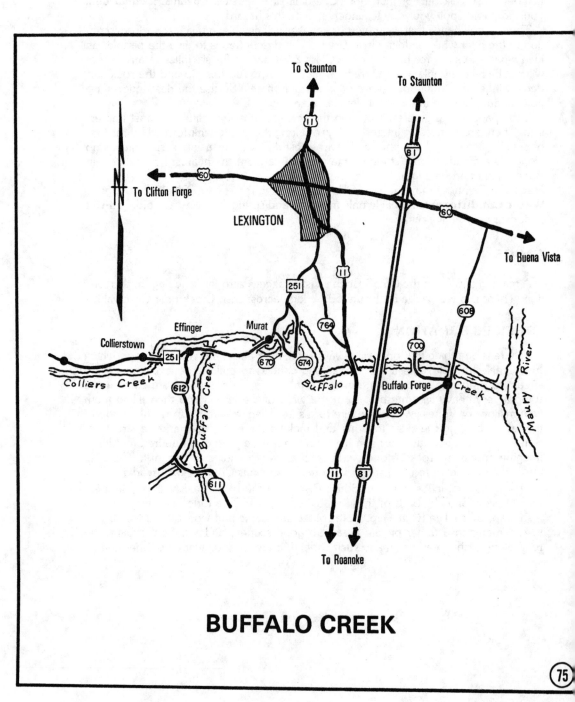

BUFFALO CREEK

Buffalo Creek

INTRODUCTION

Buffalo Creek is one of the prettiest streams in Rockbridge County and it offers a diversity of rapids, scenery, and history. The first three miles and the final three miles are the best and it would be super if they comprised one long set of rapids. The middle stretch is not bad, however, as there are many gravel bar riffles, small passages with quick turns, and occasional ledges up to 2' in drop. It is well worth the time and energy to canoe this stream.

Section 1. Collierstown (Rte 251) to Buffalo Forge (Rte 700)

Gradient	Difficulty	Distance	Time	Width	Scenery	Map
25	2-3	12.5	4	50-60	Very Good	75

Trip Description: The trip normally starts at the confluence of Colliers Creek and Buffalo Creek at the Route 251 bridge over Buffalo Creek. In high water, the trip can begin above Collierstown on Colliers Creek for three additional miles of good white-water (Class 2) or it can begin on Buffalo Creek near the confluence of its North Branch and South Branch for two miles of good white-water (Class 2). On the upper Buffalo trip, beware of the electric fence *and* barbed wire fence under the Route 251 bridge where it joins Colliers Creek. If the trip begins upstream of the normal putin, the trip can be ended at the second low-water bridge (Route 674 bridge) for a shorter trip. This will include Mill Rapid, but will miss a lot of good steady rapids below Route 11, particularly those that can be seen from I-81. The normal takeout is at an underwater bridge near the end of Route 700, below Buffalo Forge.

The rapids on this stream are generally of the ledge type and require a lot of intricate maneuvering. Only a couple of the rapids, Murat Ledge and Mill Rapid, present a risk at all water levels. Murat Ledge is a four foot drop (Class 3) about 1 mile downstream from the putin; it can be seen from Route 251 bridge at Murat. Mill Rapid is the remains of a dam built on a major ledge; it has narrow chutes, big drops, and steel spikes in the rocks. The rapids below I-81 bridge could become Class 4 in high water, as there must be at least thirty closely-spaced ledges in quick succession; some ledges are at least 2' high. At one spot, about ½ mile below I-81 bridge, the river funnels to the right against a massive vertical cliff; although it really looks ominous, it is only a small rapid with good wave motion.

Buffalo Creek should be canoed only if there is at least 4" of water at the putin, as it gets wide at a couple of spots and the water gets mighty thin, principally at a couple of gravel bars and the ledges just below I-81 bridge. It is a constant width stream, surprisingly so, and 4" at the start will mean 4" of water for about 97% of the trip, but it also means 2" for about 3% of the trip. And 600 yards without water is 600 yards without pleasure.

While canoeing on Buffalo Creek on a fine, early summer day, the lead canoe hit a single-strand electric fence and broke a wire. A herd of cows who were all afraid of the electric fence immediately began to stampede to get out of the field in which they were fenced. Only the prompt action of a country boy canoeist who raced the cows to the fence prevented the situation of postponing a canoe trip for a roundup. The fence was not energized, as the farmers frequently turn the electricity off after the cattle have been shocked a number of times; the cows did not know it was off, but they heard the wire go and freedom beckoned. On the same trip, the lead canoe popped around a bend and over a ledge to find an empty chaise lounge and spot a sunbather suddenly turned streaker. In spite of all efforts on the part of the canoeist, the woman sunbather would not accept his apologies at close range. The two-foot ledge is now named Streaker Ledge.

Hazards: Three low-water bridges. Electric wire fence.

Water Conditions: Canoeable in winter and spring normally or during the early summer following an extended wet spell or very heavy rain.

GAUGE

None.

HISTORY

The takeout area, Buffalo Forge, is quite old and has a history of its own. It was the upper terminus of the Maury Navigation Company at one time and had docks, warehouses, boat yards, and an iron foundry -- a prosperous community. When the Maury canal system moved upstream, finally to Lexington, the fortunes of the town declined, even though it still had one major industry -- the construction of barges and boats for the James River and Kanawha Canal. This industry died when the canal was paved over for a railroad bed, and now there are few signs of the busy commercial center of the early 1800's.

When the first explorers entered the Shenandoah Valley, there were herds of wild buffalo. Now there are many rivers and towns in Virginia that are named for these herds or as a result of these herds. The Cowpasture River, the Calfpasture River, the Little Calfpasture River, the Bullpasture River, the Buffalo River, Buffalo Creek, Buffalo Forge, Buffalo Station, and Buffalo Ford were named for these herds.

Other towns, crossroads, or areas were named in a similar manner, but for other reasons, all quite logical, and these names can be a major asset to the canoeist that does not have maps or intimate knowledge of a certain area. There are towns or villages named after the early iron industries (such as Clifton Forge, Columbia Furnace); after the early mills and industries (such as Star Tannery, Millville, Jordan Mines, Rock Mills); after the fords, ferries, bridges, and other river crossings (such as Carters Bridge, Speers Ferry, Kellys Ford, Canoe House Landing); after geographical features (such as Coleman Falls, Big Stone Gap, Max Meadows, Taylors Valley, Keen Mountain, Mountain Lake); after river features (such as Big Island, Willis Wharf); after the streams that are nearby (such as Swords Creek, Piney River); after the churches and forts in the area (such as Fort Blackmore, Carmel Church); and after the nearby springs in the vicinity (such as Warm Springs, Cedar Springs). Quite logical and most informative.

Pedlar River

INTRODUCTION

The Pedlar River is the first canoeable stream that enters the James River east of the Blue Ridge. It drops from the Lynchburg Reservoir at a horrendous (non-canoeable) gradient into a very narrow valley, meanders through that valley to Route 130, and then drops into the James River at Holcomb Rock. The Pedlar drains such a very small area that it is very difficult to find it with water; but when it has water, it is a must for the white-water canoeist.

Section 1. Pleasantview (Rte 610) to James River

Gradient	Difficulty	Distance	Time	Width	Scenery	Map
15	2-3₄	9	3	15-30	Very Good	76

Trip Description: The trip normally starts near Pleasantview when there is enough water; at this point, the Pedlar is a very small stream, barely 15 feet wide. From Pleasantview to Pedlar Mills, just above Route 130, it is a fast Class 2 run over small ledges and through small rock gardens. The water is clean and clear; the bottom is rock, sand, and gravel; the banks are fairly low; the current is fairly fast. A number of small streams enter on the right side from Big Piney Mountain, so the water volume increases steadily. The fact that it is so narrow and that it has high hills on both banks makes one feel twinges of claustophobia.

Below Route 130, the Pedlar River really begins its descent to the James River and the rapids become stronger, more difficult, and closer together. There are three rapids that are more easily remembered, but there are many more goods ones that still offer a real challenge. The first of the memorable ones is a "C" turn through a boulder choked rapid with a drop of at least 5'; similar to the Moorefield River. The second is a rock garden with large boulders and a sharp turn; the total drop is about 4' to 5'; in low water, rocks await the paddler at the bottom, in high water a lot of turbulence and cross currents. The last big rapid (Class 4) occurs just after an island; it has a big drop of 5' to 6' with two ledges requiring a lot of turns in tight quarters while fighting cross currents and turbulence. Scout this one.

The takeout is the last bridge (Route 650) on the Pedlar River, about 200 yards above the James River. About 400 yards below the point where the Pedlar enters the James is one of the many dams on the James River, Holcomb Rock Dam.

Hazards: Fences and trees across the stream. One major rapid about 7 miles downstream.

Water Conditions: Canoeable only in winter and spring following a prolonged wet period or very heavy rain.

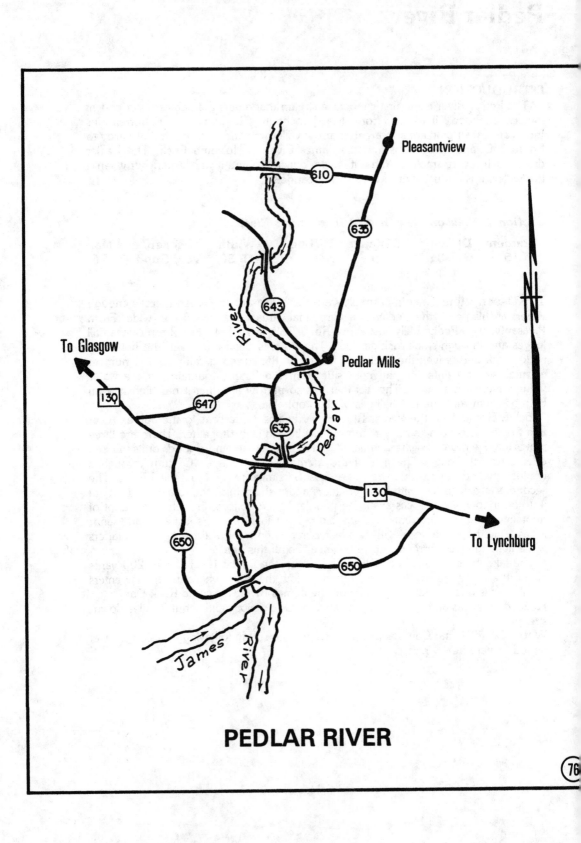

PEDLAR RIVER

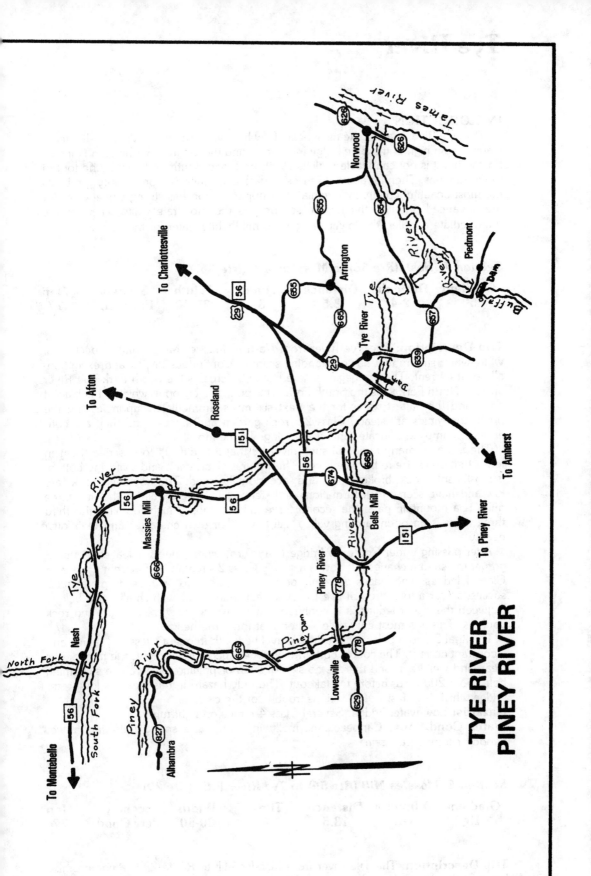

TYE RIVER
PINEY RIVER

Tye River

INTRODUCTION

The Tye River may be the most beautiful white-water stream in Virginia. Its head-waters begin high in the Blue Ridge Mountains and the George Washington National Forest, but it is not canoeable until its North Fork and South Fork join at the foot of the mountains. Then for about 34 miles, it dashes through Nelson County, probably the most beautiful county in Virginia. The upper section has strong white-water for the advanced paddler, the middle section has the moderate white-water for the intermediate paddler, the lower section has mild white-water for the novice.

Section 1. Nash (Rte 56) to Massies Mill (Rte 56)

Gradient	Difficulty	Distance	Time	Width	Scenery	Map
50	2-4	8.5	3	25-40	Excellent	77

Trip Description: The Tye River from Nash to Massies Mill is truly a spectacular white-water stream that has outstanding scenery, continuous rapids, and exceptionally swift current. The trip begins where Route 56 crosses the North Fork Tye River and the North Fork joins the South Fork. This putin is a big pool, which is the biggest eddy and the flattest water for the next six miles. Immediately upon leaving the putin, the rapids are steady Class 2-3 rock garden and ledges. And they are continuous, complex, intricate, and challenging. Tremendous!

There are so many rapids of such diversity that it is difficult to describe them in terms that do justice to the Tye River. The water is clear, cold, and swift; the bottom is mostly solid rock, broken rock, and, occasionally, sand. The tree-lined banks are low and have scenic rock formations and steep cliffs. The terrain in the first three miles is a mountain pass; the second three miles is mostly high foothills; the third three miles is an open farming valley. All have their own character and their own beauty.

After passing under Route 56 bridge near Tyro, where the river leaves its upper gorge, the stream changes. It now is a steady Class 2 stream with frequent Class 3 or Class 4 ledges. The ledges generally occur in steps of two or three drops in quick succession for a total drop of five to seven feet (minimum) with small pools below. Between the bigger ledges, it is continuous white-water over small ledges and rock gardens. This is a most enjoyable section that thrills the heart.

The final 2.5 to 3 miles is basically a gravel bed with frequent Class 1-2 rapids and a constant current. The cobble bottom would be a geologists delight, the farmland is clean and well kept, and there is no sign of trash or pollution. There is a swimming hole about 200 yards before the takeout. The only hazard in this area is a low water bridge which is in fast water; serious trouble for the careless.

Hazards: Low-water bridge. Several Class 4 rapids on right turns.

Water Conditions: Canoeable normally in winter and spring following a wet period or a moderate rain.

Section 2. Massies Mill (Rte 56) to Tye River P.O. (Rte 29)

Gradient	Difficulty	Distance	Time	Width	Scenery	Map
15	1-2	13.5	4	30-50	Very Good	77

Trip Description: The Tye River from Massies Mill to Route 29 is a compromise between the demanding white-water of the upper section and the mild gravel bars of the lower section. It has a fast current flowing over a sand and gravel bottom; the rapids are mostly gravel bars and small ledges, with a few rock garden rapids. The valley is moderately wide and has many well-tended farms, truly a beautiful valley. The river is crossed by many bridges, there are many access points, and the area is remote in some sections.

There were many mills and fords on this section; many creeks flow into the river, and the Piney River joins it near the end. The water is clear, cool, and unpolluted. The people in this area are pleasant. Everything needed for a good trip. Just be sure to takeout upstream of the 6-foot dam about 200 yards below Route 29 bridge.

Hazards: Barbed wire fences across the stream. Six-foot dam just below takeout.

Water Conditions: Canoeable in winter and spring normally or during the early summer following an extended wet spell or very heavy rain.

Section 3. Tye River P.O. (Rte 29) to James River (Rte 626)

Gradient	Difficulty	Distance	Time	Width	Scenery	Map
11	1-23	11.5	4	40-60	Good	77

Trip Description: The Tye River, from Route 29 to Norwood, is a pleasant, relaxing trip with miles and miles of gravel bar rapids/riffles. Before Hurricane Camille devestated Nelson County, it had strong rock garden rapids Class 2-3, much like the Kellys Ford rapids on the Rappahannock River. Then, after channelization to restore the river to its old bed, it was an eleven-mile-long gravel bar. All rocks bigger than a basketball have been removed from the river in some sections.

The water is cool, clear, and unpolluted; it becomes a bit discolored where the Buffalo River enters on the right. The bottom is sand and gravel, the banks are 4' to 6' high, the valley is not inhabited very much, and the terrain is rolling foothills. There are two bridge crossings between Route 29 and Norwood, and they are very close to the putin, so the paddler is committed to a long trip.

The normal takeout is alongside Route 655 where Rucker Run enters the Tye River; this is about 1.5 miles above Norwood. The last practical takeout is the bridge (Route 626) at Norwood, about 300 yards above the James River. A trip to the James River means about four additional miles of paddling to Wingina (all flatwater).

Hazards: None.

Water Conditions: Canoeable in winter, spring, and early summer, except following periods of little precipitation. Canoeable after a heavy rain in the summer and fall.

GAUGE

A reading of 3.5' on the USGS Culpeper gauge of 4.5' on the USGS Cootes Store Gauge is zero for canoeing on section 1. For section 2 and 3, deduct 6" and 1' respectively. There is an RC gauge on Rte 29 bridge.

OTHER INFORMATION

About two miles upstream from Nash, Crabtree Falls drops into the South Fork Tye River. This tiny falls is comprised of a series of cascades of 50' to 100', for a total drop of about 2000' from the top of a mountain. This is a truly spectacular sight and is well worth a trip to see it; it can be seen on the left of Route 56, dropping off Pinnacle Ridge.

The Appalachian Trail crosses the Tye River about midway between Nash and Massies Mill; there is a swinging footbridge across the Tye river for the trail. Just south of the Tye River, the Appalachian Trail climbs up the Priest, a mountain of 4056 feet. The names of the towns in this area have a musical ring, including Montebello, Vesuvius, Roseland, Tyro, Coleen, Lanes Ford, Piedmont, Buffalo Ridge, and Tye River Gap.

Piney River

INTRODUCTION

The Piney River is a very beautiful mountain stream that offers a wide diversity of white-water challenges to the intermediate and advanced paddlers. The gorge section, between Alhambra and Woodson is for the advanced paddlers only; the section between Woodson and Piney River is for intermediate paddlers; the section between the town of Piney River and the Tye River can be paddled by beginners. It is, throughout, a jewel of a stream, typical of the Nelson-Amherst county streams.

Section 1. Alhambra to Woodson (Rte 666)

Gradient	Difficulty	Distance	Time	Width	Scenery	Map
150'	2-4₅	4	2	25-35	Excellent	77

Trip Description: The gorge section of the Piney River drops at a horrendous 150 feet/mile for about three miles, through rapids of the highest degree of complexity. It is hard to describe the rapids other than to identify two similar Class 4-5 rapids; they are entered on the left through a maze of a rock garden, they require the canoeist to work to the right to line up for a 4' to 5' drop, to maneuver hard to the left to avoid the big rocks at the center and right below the chute, and to be ready for the Class 3 rapid immediately below. Other rapids include boulder fields, broken ledges, ledges, and rock gardens; all rapids are fairly long and continuous and there are only a few pools for one to regain his composure. One canoeist chased his waterproof packs for over two miles because there were no eddies to capture the packs.

The trip can begin at the confluence of the North Fork and the South Fork of the Piney River, although the usual starting point is just below an island. It is a very small stream at this point and the water is cold and clear. The current is very fast, the bottom is rock or rock and sand, the banks are lined with evergreens, the road is close on the right, and the left bank is mostly a high rock bluff/cliff. It is truly a beautiful stream and a magnificent gorge.

Hazards: Strong Class 4-5 rapids. Low-water bridge.

Water Conditions: Canoeable only in winter and spring following a prolonged wet period of very heavy rain.

Section 2. Woodson (Rte 666) to Piney River (Rte 151)

Gradient	Difficulty	Distance	Time	Width	Scenery	Map
55	2-3	7	2	30-40	Good	77

Trip Description: The section from Woodson to Lowesville is a good Class 2-3 run that begins with three strong (Class 3) rapids just below the pool at the Route 666 bridge putin; they are not to be regarded lightly. Then there are steady rapids to the next bridge with few eddies. From this bridge to Lowesville is fast current, steady Class 1-2 rapids, and an unrunnable dam (portage on right, stopping well upstream). The trip ends with an honest Class 3 rapid at Lowesville that has a very strong hydraulic on the right side; this hydraulic can easily draw the unwary or weak paddler to a spectacular wipeout.

Below Lowesville the Piney River tends to widen and the rapids are more of the gravel bar type for the first mile. At the quarry, however, the river is narrow with a strong Class 3 rapid that can swamp open boats in high water. Then there are two nice rapids (Class 2-3), just before the town of Piney River. This section is definitely worth running, even if one has already run the gorge and has high expectations. It flows through a beautiful valley, the current is very fast, the water is clear and cold, the bottom is sand and gravel. There is very little litter, the houses are well-tended, and the fields are cultivated. Only the quarry, about 2 miles below Lowesville, detracts from the trip.

Hazards: Four-foot dam.

Water Conditions: Canoeable normally in winter and spring following a wet period or a moderate rain.

Section 3. Piney River (Rte 151) to Tye River

Gradient	Difficulty	Distance	Time	Width	Scenery	Map
18	1-2	7*	2.5	40-60	Good	77

*plus 1.5 miles on the Tye River

Trip Description: Below the town of Piney River, the river changes its nature and becomes a classic Piedmont river. It has a good current, many riffles, gravel bars, and, occasionally, Class 2 rapids of the ledge type. The stream flows between high (6' to 8') clay banks, the water is becoming a bit yellowish, and the bottom has more clayey-sand. The trip can be ended in the vicinity of Bells Mill for a 4.5 mile trip or it can continue to the Tye River; it is 2.5 miles from Bells Mill to the Tye River and 1.5 miles to Route 29 from the Tye-Piney confluence. The takeout is just *above* the six-foot dam 100 yards below Route 29 bridge over the Tye River.

The town of Piney River is located in an area of open-pit non-metallic (aplite, kyanite, etc.) mining. A number of mines are still operating, but a number of larger ones have closed. Just downstream from Route 151 bridge, there is an abandoned complex of buildings and equipment that must have been a major operation. In that section, there is a pipe across the river that is a hazard in very low water.

Hazards: Pipe at water level in low water.

Water Conditions: Canoeable in winter and spring normally or during the early summer following an extended wet spell or very heavy rain.

GAUGE

There is a RC gauge on the bridge at Lowesville for sections 2 and 3.

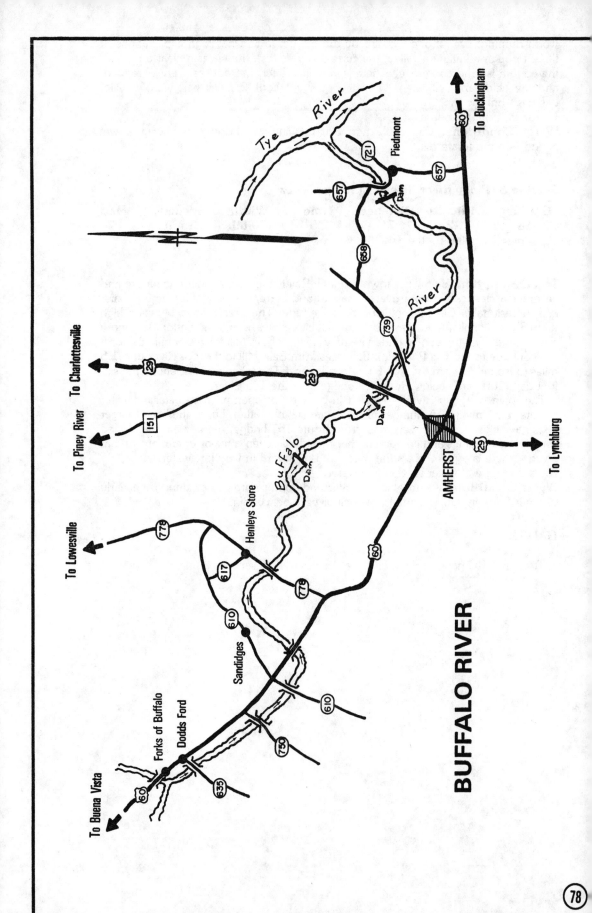

BUFFALO RIVER

Buffalo River

INTRODUCTION

The Buffalo River is one of the prettier streams in the Blue Ridge foothills, flowing out of the George Washington National Forest into the Tye River. It passes through two of the most beautiful counties in Virginia, Amherst and Nelson, so the scenery is mostly unspoiled woodlands and well-tended farmlands. It is crossed by many bridges and is close to roads at many points, so it is an easy stream to reach. The Buffalo River is not a great white-water stream; it is just a beautiful small stream flowing through the foothills over a sand and gravel bottom with occasional rapids and frequent riffles.

Section 1. Forks of Buffalo (Rte 60) to Henleys Store (Rte 778)

Gradient	Difficulty	Distance	Time	Width	Scenery	Map
35	2	9	3.5	15-25	Good	78

Trip Description: From Forks of Buffalo to Henley's Store, the Buffalo River is a fast mountain stream with clean, clear water rushing over a bed of sand and gravel. It parallels Route 60 for about five miles, passing under four bridges enroute to Henley's Store (there is no store there any longer), one of which is a low water bridge. The rapids are only Class 2 or less, in spite of the gradient, and are of the gravel bar type for the most part. The little valley through which it flows is really pretty, particularly when passing between a series of small mountains. This stream has an almost uniform width of 20-25 feet throughout even though it picks up water from small tributaries. The banks are fairly low, so it is easy to see the scenery, which varies from small mountains, to high hills, to rolling terrain.
Hazards: Low-water bridge. Fences across the stream.
Water Conditions: Canoeable normally in winter and spring following a wet period or a moderate rain.

Section 2. Henleys Store (Rte 778) to Amherst (Rte 29).

Gradient	Difficulty	Distance	Time	Width	Scenery	Map
10	1-2	10	4	20-30	Good	78

Trip Description: From Henley Store to Route 29 near Amherst, the Buffalo River meanders quite a bit, passing between small mountains and through flat valleys. It has a moderate current, the water is clear and unpolluted, the bottom is sand and gravel, the banks are fairly low, and the scenery is good. The rapids are Class 1-2 gravel bars for the most part, with an occasional rock garden. The banks are fairly high and are tree-lined for most of the trip. There is a 2' dam about 6½ miles downstream; it might be runnable, but only after scouting and a show of reverence. About three miles below this dam, about ½ mile above Route 29, there is an 8' dam that must be portaged. The takeout can be at Route 29 bridge or the road alongside near the bridge.
Hazards: Two dams, one 2-foot, one 8-foot.
Water Conditions: Canoeable in winter and spring normally or during the early summer following an extended wet spell or very heavy rain.

Section 3. Amherst (Rte 29) to Tye River

Gradient	Difficulty	Distance	Time	Width	Scenery	Map
11*	1-2₃	13**	4	25-40	Good	78

*2 miles at 20 feet/mile   **plus 5.5 miles on the Tye River.

Trip Description: From Route 29 to the Tye River, the Buffalo River has two natures. For the first 11 miles, it has a gradient of only 5 feet/mile. The current is slow, there is only one rapid of note, and there is a 10' dam to back up water for two miles. The best rapid on this section is just below the railroad bridge (Class 2, maybe). At Piedmont, just below the dam, the Buffalo River is a white-water stream, dropping at a respectable gradient (40 feet/mile) with an increased volume of water. It is a steady rock garden for two miles, Class 2 for the most part. There is no take-out on the Tye River until the Rucker Run bridge on the left, about 5½ miles downstream, is reached.

The river in this section flows over a sandy bottom, the water is still clear, and the scenery is good. The area is wooded and fairly remote for the most part and there are no bridges for a long distance. The dam at Piedmont (there is no town there) has been completely silted in and the water above it is shallow. The drop over the dam is still damn high, however. On the Tye, the rapids are gravel bars and remains of small ledges, so the action is still good.

Hazards: Eighteen-foot dam 11 miles downstream.

Water Conditions: Canoeable in winter, spring, and early summer, except following an extended wet spell or very heavy rain.

GAUGE

There is an RC gauge on the bridge at Piedmont.

OTHER INFORMATION

The high dam near the bridge at Piedmont was part of a mining (non-metallic) operation at one time. There is a quarry mine site on the right (south) bank and there are the ruins of an old mill on the right side of the dam. It appears that there was a turbine installed in the structure on the right side, similar to the old mill at the Coleman Falls dam on the James River. The route from the mill to the quarry area is fairly obvious, as it was a quite large operation at one time. It is easy to reach this dam and it is well worth the hike to see this site.

Rockfish River

INTRODUCTION

The Rockfish River is the most northern river in Nelson county, beginning in the Blue Ridge Mountains and ending in the James River. It is a stream that flows through a narrow valley, surrounded on both banks by mountains and high hills. It has mild rapids, good scenery, and many access points. All in all, a relaxing and enjoyable stream.

Section 1. Martins Store (Rte 6) to Woods Mill (Rte 29)

Gradient	Difficulty	Distance	Time	Width	Scenery	Map
14	1-2	6	2	30-40	Very Good	79

Trip Description: This trip normally begins at the Route 6 bridge across the North Fork, about 400 yards upstream from the point where the Rockfish River is formed by the South Fork and the North Fork. When there is sufficient water, the trip can begin on the South Fork Rockfish River at Nellysford (Route 634); this adds three miles to the trip. The takeout is at Route 29, an easy access point.

The South Fork of the Rockfish River is so narrow in spots that a steer standing ankle deep in this river, blocked the entire stream. The only passage for a 15' Grumann was under the belly between the fore and aft legs until the steer took flight in the nick of time. That is how tight this stream is in the upper reaches. The trip has a fair gradient, there are a number of very tight turns, the rapids are mostly cobble bars, and the scenery is mostly farmland. By the time it reaches its confluence with the North Fork, it is almost 20' wide. The Rockfish, which begins where the two forks join just below the Route 6 bridge over the North Fork, is a fine trip. It is not far from Route 6, but the bluffs on the right (south) bank make it a secluded, scenic trip.

The Rockfish River has a fast current flowing over a bottom of sand and gravel. The water is cool, clear, and unpolluted; the terrain varies from high bluffs to open flat farmland. The rapids are mostly gravel bars and occasional rock gardens.
Hazards: None.
Water Conditions: Canoeable normally in winter and spring following a wet period or a moderate rain.

Section 2. Woods Mill (Rte 29) to Rockfish (Rte 639)

Gradient	Difficulty	Distance	Time	Width	Scenery	Map
9	12	9	4	30-40	Fair	79

Trip Description: The Wood's Mill to Rockfish trip is a pleasant trip that always fails to meet the expectation of the white-water canoeist. There are frequent rock bluffs that appear to signal ledges, but none appear. There are sections where rock garden and gravel bar rapids should exist, but there are none. The river was channelized after Hurricane Camille had turned the entire valley into a river bed. This channelization means a uniform gradient with no rapids. The trip is best remembered for its gravel bar riffles, clay colored water over a sand bottom, a very steady gradient, and a fairly uniform width.

This is a good stream for beginning canoeists, as it has roads nearby and frequent bridge crossings. There is a dam below the first bridge downstream; this is the Long-

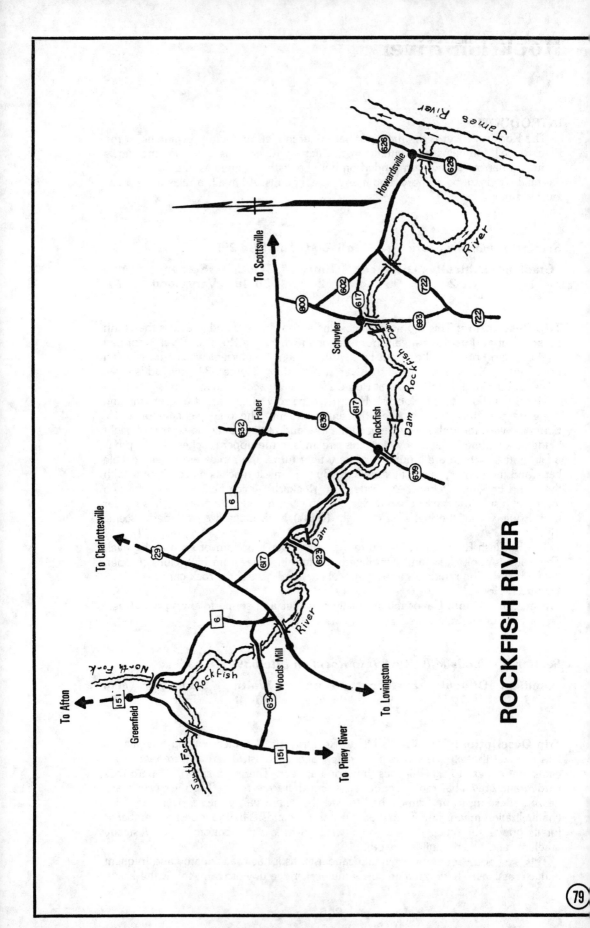

ROCKFISH RIVER

horne Mill dam, a five foot sheer drop. The dam is anchored on a sloping rock face on the right, with a drop on the left that might be runnable. This beautiful mill was destroyed by the hurricane in 1969, and parts of the machinery are just below the chute on the left side. Careful. The takeout is at Route 639, just above the backwater of the next dam.

Hazards: Six-foot dam just below Stage Bridge, about 4 miles downstream.

Water Conditions: Canoeable in winter and spring normally or during the early summer following an extended wet spell or very heavy rain.

Section 3. Rockfish (Rte 639) to Schuyler (Rte 593)

Gradient	Difficulty	Distance	Time	Width	Scenery	Map
6	A	3.5	2	30-50	Fair	79

Trip Description: The section from Rockfish to Schuyler is not really a canoeing section, as it has two dams with a lot of backwater. The first dam is about 1 mile downstream from Rockfish, the second is a high dam at Schuyler, just above Route 593. The Schuyler dam is at least a twenty foot drop with a five foot breakout on the right side; don't get swept into this gap -- the concrete footing at the bottom will probably kill you and dent your boat severely.

This section is mostly flat water through the Piedmont area of Nelson County. The water is fairly yellow in color, but still unpolluted; there is no current in this section.

Hazards: Six-foot dam and twenty-foot dam.

Water Conditions: Canoeable in winter, spring, and early summer, except following periods of little precipitation. Canoeable after a heavy rain in the summer and fall.

Section 4. Schuyler (Rte 593) to James River

Gradient	Difficulty	Distance	Time	Width	Scenery	Map
6	1-2	10	4	35-50	Fair	79

Trip Description: The section from Schuyler to Howardsville is a pleasant trip in many respects. The flat sections and the riffles have scenic backgrounds, and the four good rapids are evenly spaced so that things do not become dull. The last (and best) rapid comes unexpectedly on a right turn less than a mile from the takeout. The steep, high (480 ft.) right bank muffles the roar of the rapid until you are rounding the bend and are in the rapid itself. After the previous flat-water, it seems to be all of the white-water in the world. The takeout is where the bridge crosses the James River.

The water is definitely clayey in color, the clay banks are high. The bottom is clayey sand, and the valley is fairly narrow. The current is only moderate, the rapids/riffles are gravel bars and rock gardens, and there are few signs of litter on the banks. The takeout is where the bridge crosses the James River at Howardsville; the Virginia Game Commission landing makes it very easy.

Hazards: None.

Water Conditions: Canoeable in winter, spring, and early summer, except following periods of little precipitation. Canoeable after a heavy rain in the summer and fall.

GAUGE

A reading of 4.5' on the USGS Cootes Store gauge should be zero for canoeing on section 1; a reading of 4.0' should be zero for canoeing on the lower sections. There is an RC gauge on Rte 29 bridge at Woods Mill.

North Fork Rockfish River

INTRODUCTION

The North Fork Rockfish River begins at Rockfish Gap, where I-64 and Route 250 cross the Blue Ridge Mountains. It flows past the town of Afton, to Onan, and then to join the South Fork near Greenfield. It is a tiny stream throughout its short time and it is a white-water delight.

Section 1. Onan (Rte 151) to Martins Store (Rte 6)

Gradient	Difficulty	Distance	Time	Width	Scenery	Map
24	2	5	1.5	10-25	Good	79

Trip Description: The North Fork Rockfish River is identified as Goodwins Creek where it crosses under Route 151; technically, the creek joins the North Fork just above Route 609. But it is at Route 151 that there is water to start. The trip ends only too quickly at Route 6, about 400 yards from the point where the South Fork enters.

The North Fork is a very tiny stream that drops from the Blue Ridge foothills into the Rockfish River Valley. It has clear and unpolluted water flowing over a bed of sand and gravel. The rapids are small ledges, small rock gardens, and gravel bars. There are barbed/woven wire fences, underwater bridges, and trees across the stream. The hairpin turns make the canoeist wish for a canoe that was hinged.

Hazards: Fences and trees across streams.

Water Conditions: Canoeable only in winter and spring following a prolonged wet period or very heavy rain.

GAUGE

A reading of 4.5' on the USGS Cootes Store gauge is probably zero for canoeing on this stream.

Hardware River

INTRODUCTION

The Hardware River is a small winding stream that flows through the Virginia Piedmont area and merges with the James River. It is almost midway between the Rivanna River and the Rockfish River, and has many of the characteristics of these two streams. There are many bridges crossing the Hardware River, there are roads in close proximity to the river, and there is a Virginia Game Commission landing near the James River. So the length of the trip can be varied by putins and takeouts at a number of different points. It is a pleasant river, but it does not have much white-water.

Section 1. Route 20 to Temperance Wayside (Rte 6)

Gradient	Difficulty	Distance	Time	Width	Scenery	Map
8	1	14.5	5.5	20-30	Good	80

Trip Description: From Route 20 to Route 6, the Hardware River is a very small stream that meanders through a historic section of Virginia. In places, the stream is only about 20 feet wide; in narrow chutes or passages, it is much less. It flows over a sand and gravel bottom, the clay banks are not too high, the current is slow to moderate, and the scenery is good. Near the mid-point, there is a beautiful old mill beside a 4' dam. This is one of the prettiest spots on any stream in Virginia. The riffles are of the gravel bar type and there may be trees blocking the stream.
Hazards: Four-foot dam at mid-point. Trees blocking the stream.
Water Conditions: Canoeable in winter and spring normally or during the early summer following an extended wet spell or very heavy rain.

Section 2. Temperance Wayside (Rte 6) to James River

Gradient	Difficulty	Distance	Time	Width	Scenery	Map
6	1-2	12*	5	30-40	Good	80

Plus 2 miles on the James River to Bremo Bluff

Trip Description: From Route 6 to the James River, the Hardware River moves along much faster than the upper section. It is still a small stream, 40' to 50' wide at the widest parts. It is fairly flat in most parts, but the current is fairly good; there will be a couple of trees across the stream. It has at least three Class 2 rapids before joining the James River and then there are good Class 2 rapids on the James River enroute to Bremo Bluff. The three rapids are as follows: gravel bar with a discernible drop, 2' drop on a left turn, 2' ledge with a number of chutes, all Class 2 or less. There is a convenient takeout bridge on the Hardware River at a Virginia Game Commission landing just before reaching the James River; this bridge may be too low, so when passing under the RR bridge, be alert. Also, stop and admire the viaduct where the James River and Kanawha canal passed over the Hardware; the keystone is dated 1832.
Hazards: None.
Water Conditions: Canoeable in winter and spring normally or during the early summer following an extended wet spell or very heavy rain.

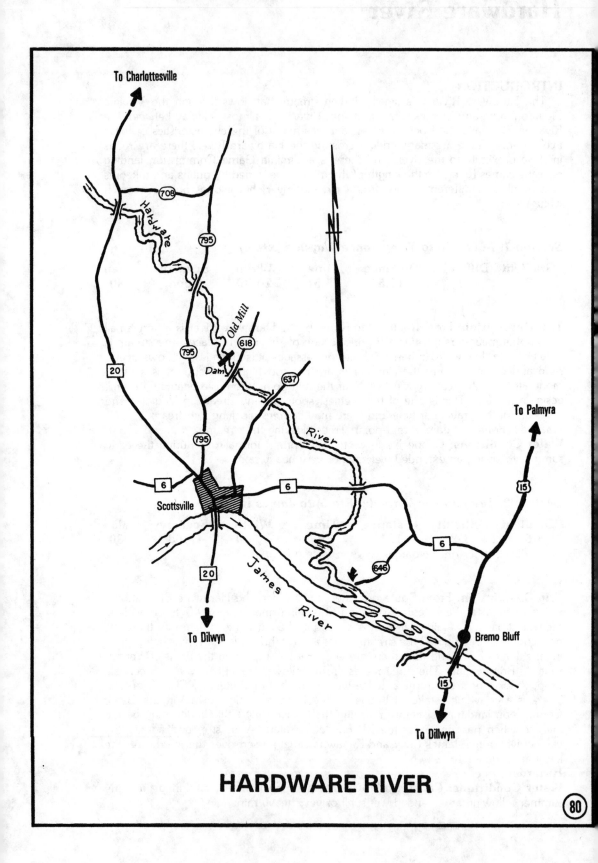

To Charlottesville

708

Hardware

795

Old Mill

795

618

Dam

637

20

795

River

To Palmyra

15

6

Scottsville

6

20

646

6

To Dilwyn

James

River

Bremo Bluff

15

To Dillwyn

HARDWARE RIVER

80

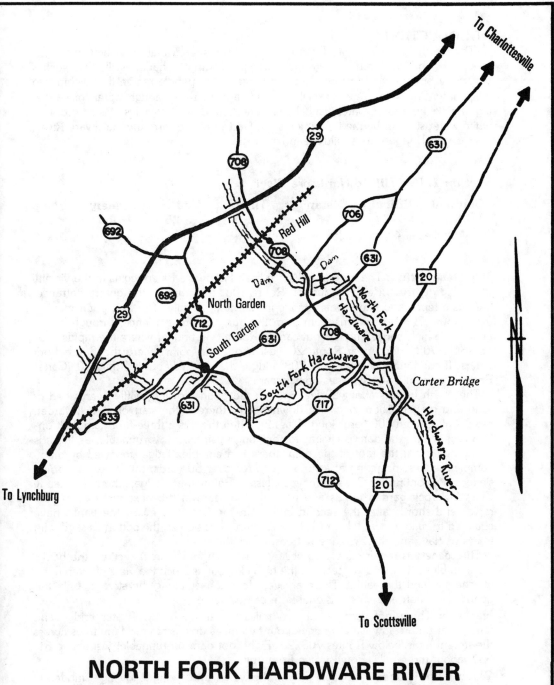

NORTH FORK HARDWARE RIVER
SOUTH FORK HARDWARE RIVER

81

North Fork Hardware River

INTRODUCTION

The North Fork Hardware River is a very small stream that flows between small mountains and low foothills in a remote area just south of Charlottesville. It is such a very small stream where Route 29 crosses it that few people realize that within two miles downstream, there are excellent rapids and there is enough water for canoeing. It picks up a lot of water just below Route 29 and, for two miles, it is a terror of a white-water stream; by the time it joins the North Fork to form the Hardware River, near Carter Bridge, it is a mild meandering stream.

Section 1. Red Hill to Hardware River

Gradient	Difficulty	Distance	Time	Width	Scenery	Map
28*	2-34	6	2	15-25	Good	81

*3 miles at 47 feet/mile

Trip Description: The trip on the North Fork Hardware River begins in the vicinity of the big quarry at Red Hill, just off Route 708. If starting at the quarry entrance, there is a fence and a low water bridge in the next ½ mile. The best putin may be from Route 708, just downstream from the quarry, across a fence, through briars, and over a high bank. The takeout can be Route 631 bridge, where the rapids end, or Route 708 bridge near Route 20, just above the point where the South Fork enters. If continuing below Route 708 bridge, the next takeout is Route 20 (Carter Bridge), one mile and six trees downstream.

The North Fork is about 20 feet wide at the putin, flowing swiftly over a bed of sand and gravel. About one mile downstream, there is the start of a rock garden rapid that is about 800 yards long (Class 2). Then there is a three-foot dam built onto a rock ledge; the dam is U-shaped, pointing upstream; it is runnable, as there is no hydraulic. At the foot of the dam, there is a complex ledge, followed by many complex ledges, dropping at a furious rate for over 50 yards; this array of sloping sledges is a continuous Class 4, maybe Class 5. Below these ledges, there are steady Class 2-3 rock garden rapids and an eight-foot dam in the next three miles; the rapids end shortly after the second bridge. In the final two miles, the banks have changed from low to very high (8'-10'), the current is slower, the bottom is sand with traces of clay, and there are many trees across the stream.

The scenery is rather difficult to observe. In the upper (gorge) section, the banks are high bluffs; in the lower section, the high clay banks block the view of everything but the sky and the banks. There are very few houses along the stream; only the quarry operation and an occasional farm can be seen.

Hazards: Three-foot dam about two miles downstream. Low-water bridge and fence near put-in; low-water bridge about two miles downstream. Many trees across the stream near/below Routes 708/20. Eight foot dam (unrunnable) just above Rte 631, about three miles downstream from putin.

Water Conditions: Canoeable only in the winter and spring following a moderate wet period.

GAUGE

There is a RC gauge at Route 708 bridge near Route 20.

South Fork Hardware River

INTRODUCTION

The South Fork Hardware River is one of the smallest canoeing streams in Virginia, but it has the biggest rapid of any stream in Virginia. While passing through a small gorge between Fan Mountain and Ammonett Mountain, just east of Route 29, it drops over a monster of a rapid and then dashes through steady rapids that are complex and unforgiving; it drops over forty feet in a distance of four hundred yards (or less) in one section. It joins the North Fork Hardware River to form the Hardware River near Carter Bridge, about fifteen miles south of Charlottesville.

Section 1. South Garden (Rte 631) to Hardware River

Gradient	Difficulty	Distance	Time	Width	Scenery	Map
19˚	2-3-45	7.5	3	20-30	Very Good	81

Plus 1.5 miles at 60 feet mile

Trip Description: The trip on the South Fork Hardware River normally begins at South Garden, Route 631 bridge. There is a nice Class 2 ledge just upstream of the bridge, and there is a nice Class 2 ledge just below the bridge. Then there is the biggest canoeable rapid in Virginia, the absolute biggest, about 100 feet below the putin bridge. Monstrous, but beautiful.

There is no doubt that the Falls of the South Fork Hardware River is a Class 5 rapid in low water (higher in high water) and that it is one of the most beautiful spots along any river in Virginia. It is comprised of sloping ledges (similar to the Chauga River in South Carolina), narrow chutes, and complex rock gardens. The major part of the Falls is comprised of four drops of about four feet each; the first is a narrow chute on the right, then a sloping rock chute on the right, a sloping rock chute on the left, and an abrupt drop in the center. There is a pool of five feet between the first and second drops, ten feet between the second and the third drops (where one has to make a sharp left turn, cross the river, and make a sharp right turn), and virtually no pool whatsoever between the third and fourth drops. There is a pool of about thirty feet below these drops in which to recover and reorganize before the river drops through a narrow, complex chute with a total drop of at least four feet. All of this in the first hundred yards from the putin.

Then there is a pool of quiet water for about 50 feet before the start of complex rock garden rapids (Class 2-3, at least). Below this set of rapids, the South Fork settles down to a steady Class 2-3 stream for about one more mile; these rapids are comprised of rock gardens and ledges in equal proportion. The rapids end at the first bridge downstream, Route 712, which is 1.5 miles from the putin and ninety feet lower in elevation. Below Route 712, there are a few Class 1 riffles and fast current to its juncture with the North Fork.

This is a very small stream from start to finish. Its width is only about 20 to 25 feet. The banks are low in the upper part, but are about 10 to 12 feet high near the takeout. The scenery in the section near South Garden is largely high rock bluffs; below Route 712, low banks and farmland; below Route 717, high clay banks and the sky. The water is cool, clear and light green in color.

The trip can be started at Route 633, about 1.5 miles above South Garden, but there is little to commend this putin. The last takeout should be Route 717 bridge; to continue to the Hardware means a lot of passing over/under/around trees down across the stream and negotiating a number of fences. If continuing to the Hardware, the takeout is Route 20 bridge, about ¾ miles below the point where the South Fork joins the North Fork.

Hazards: One major (Class 5) rapid that is almost a waterfall. Many trees and/or fences across the stream in the lower parts.
Water Conditions: Canoeable only in the winter and spring following a moderate wet spell.

GAUGE

There is an RC gauge of unproven accuracy on Route 631 bridge at South Garden.

OTHER INFORMATION

If canoeing in this area, the ideal white-water day would be a short trip on the North Fork as a warmup. Then a lunch break. Then a short trip on the South Fork for a capital day. This is recommended only for those canoeists that want to test themselves, to prove something to themselves, to show off their abilities to certain onlookers, or to find an excuse for having to buy a new boat.

The South Fork Hardware River and the North Fork Hardware River were the last two streams selected for this book. The author had passed these streams numerous times on Route 29 where they are too small to float a stick and near Route 20 where they are small, flat, and blocked with trees. A casual conversation with a group of Coastal Canoeists was the first indication that these streams were, in fact, canoeable and had major rapids. A scouting trip confirmed the fact that these small rivers must be included in any book on the white water rivers of Virginia.

When the topographic, watershed, and highway maps of the area south of Charlottesville were reviewed in detail, it was found that the two streams did have sufficient watershed to maintain an adequate stream flow for canoeing, that there were a number of small streams feeding into these rivers just before the rapids began, and that these rivers were dropping through passes between two low mountains. The map reconnaisance confirmed the scouting report.

It is very difficult to judge a stream solely from a topographic map, even though these maps are in detail and do indicate distance and gradient. It is also very difficult to judge a stream solely from the points where bridges cross the stream. When both of these methods are combined, it is possible to get a reasonably good feeling about the stream. However, scouting or paddling the stream are the only two methods for determining the types and difficulties of the rapids and the hazards that will be encountered. So it was with the North Fork Hardware River and the South Fork Hardware River, and this book is better for having them.

Rivanna River

INTRODUCTION

The Rivanna River is the largest of the Piedmont rivers that flow into the James River from the north. It begins about six miles northeast of Charlottesville and flows southward for about 42 miles to Columbia, where it joins the mighty James River. It is truly the classic example of the Virginia Piedmont river. It is not a white-water stream, however.

Section 1. Confluence NF/SF to Shadwell (Rte 729)

Gradient	Difficulty	Distance	Time	Width	Scenery	Map
5	1	9.0*	3.5	50-90	Fair	82

*Plus distance on North Fork or South Fork

Trip Description: A trip on the upper section of the Rivanna River must begin on either the South Fork Rivanna at Route 29 or on the North Fork Rivanna at Route 649. The trip on the South Fork from Route 29 to the Rivanna River is about 3.5 miles; the trip on the North Fork is slightly more than 2 miles before it joins the Rivanna River. The distance from the confluence of the North Fork and South Fork to Shadwell (Rte 729) is about 9 miles. The Rivanna has three small ledges above the 250 bridge at Charlottesville, hardly enough to compensate for the 1.5 mile backwater from the dam. Portage the 8' dam on the left.

The river flows through a country side of rolling hills and horse farms; the water is usually yellow (clayey) in color, the current is only moderate, the bottom is sand and clay. There is very little in the way of construction in the area, and there is very little litter. It is surprisingly remote considering its proximity to Charlottesville, although it is obviously in a city at Route 250 bridge. There are warehouses, old mills, and abandoned factories along the bank near the takeout.

Hazards: Eight-foot dam at takeout.

Water Conditions: Canoeable in winter, spring, and early summer, except following periods of little precipitation. Canoeable after a heavy rain in the summer and fall.

Section 2. Shadwell (Rte 729) to Palmyra (Rte 15)

Gradient	Difficulty	Distance	Time	Width	Scenery	Map
3.5	A	16.5	7	60-90	Fair	82

Trip Description: From Shadwell to Palmyra, where there is a Virginia Game Commission Landing, the Rivanna River is a pleasant trip even though it is all flat-water. There are a few gravel bars, a lot of sand bars, a few riffles, and a moderate current -- but no rapids. The banks are fairly high, so it is difficult to see much of the terrain, but the river flows through a beautiful farming area. Many of the riffles are the result of old mill dams and old wing dams, but it takes a skilled eye to detect them. The takeout is very convenient and presents no problem.

This is a pleasant summer float trip that has few difficulties, has no hazards, and has a lot of spots to stop and relax. It can be divided into shorter trips, if so desired, or can be extended into a longer trip. The factors that detract the most from the trip are the color of the water and the high clay banks -- which are typical of the meandering Piedmont rivers.

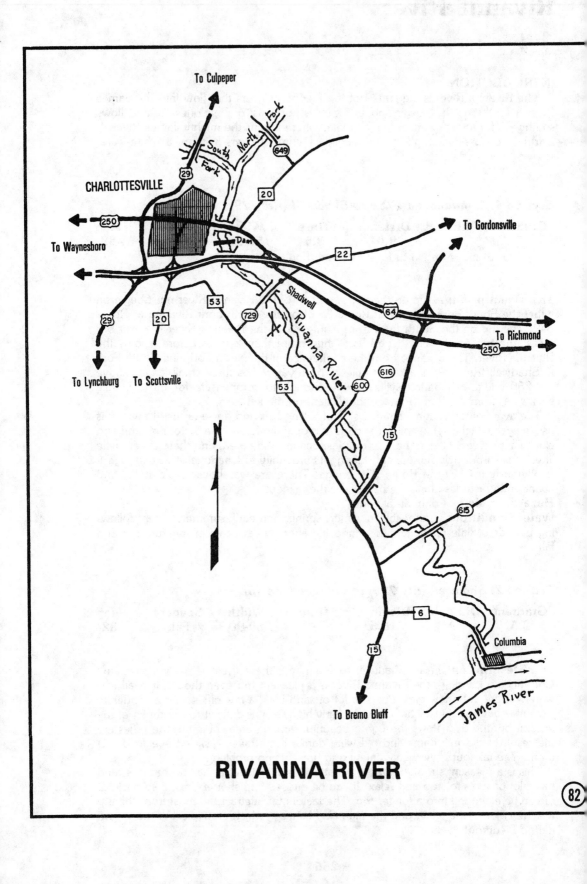

To Culpeper

North Fork

South Fork

849

CHARLOTTESVILLE

29

20

To Waynesboro

250

Dam

To Gordonsville

22

64

To Richmond

250

29

20

53

729

Shadwell

Rivanna River

To Lynchburg   To Scottsville

53

600

616

615

15

N

6

Columbia

15

To Bremo Bluff

James River

RIVANNA RIVER

Hazards: None.
Water Conditions: Canoeable in winter, spring, and early summer, except following periods of little precipitation. Canoeable after a heavy rain in the summer and fall.

Section 3. Palmyra (Rte 15) to James River (Columbia)

Gradient	Difficulty	Distance	Time	Width	Scenery	Map
2	A	16	6.5	70-90	Fair	82

Trip Description: From Palmyra to Columbia, the river is even flatter than the two other sections upstream. The current is very slow, the bottom is sandy, the riffles are less frequent, and the scenery is still a bit difficult to see. This is a beginners trip or a float-fishing trip that can be paddled at any time during the summer. No difficulties, but the ruins of old mill dams and wing dams can be detected in low water.

The terrain along the river is comprised of rolling hills, dotted with large estates and very large farms. It is difficult to see a lot of the terrain, however, because of the high clay banks. Any wind will be bad news on this section, as the river winds about in many directions. Only an occasional gravel bar riffle breaks the monotony. It is good that the trip can be broken up into shorter trips. Takeout at the VGC landing at Columbia.

Hazards: None.
Water Conditions: Canoeable most of the year except following a long dry spell. Canoeable after a moderate rain in the summer.

GAUGE

None, as this river is canoeable in all seasons except following a long, severe drought.

HISTORY

In 1763 Thomas Jefferson organized the first effort to improve navigation on the Rivanna River. In 1795, Jefferson said that navigation by canoes and batteaux was possible for 22 miles from the James River upstream. By 1810, sluices and wing dams were constructed to improve low water navigation; wooden locks had replaced these sluices by the 1839's. Locks, dams, and bypass canals were built at Lewis Ferry (Moores Ford), Moores Creek (Merriwether Bridge), Shadwell Mills, Milton's Ford, Stump Island, and Buck Island (Campbell's Mill).

The first construction work was undertaken by the Rivanna Navigation Company, under a state charter. The RNC cleared trees, deepened sluices, and rebuilt wing dams at 27 falls/shoals/fords. Several mill dams were required by state law to have locks. In 1818, there were seven wooden locks, and in 1830, construction was begun on 14 dams and 19 locks between Route 250 at Charlottesville and the James River. Work continued into the 1850's, and records indicate that the canal was still in use in 1871. By 1880, however, the railroad finished its useful life of the canal.

There was enough traffic on the Rivanna by 1789 that the first state tobacco station was installed, Henderson Warehouse, at "The Shallows". This first station was named Milton; it died when the canal reached Charlottesville. Another tobacco inspection station, Rivanna Warehouse, was established at the mouth of the Rivanna, near the town of Columbia.

North Fork Rivanna River

INTRODUCTION

The North Fork of the Rivanna River is a small white-water stream that has its headwaters in the Blue Ridge Mountains near Swift Run Gap. It does not drain a very large area, so it does not hold water for a very long time; it is a very narrow stream throughout, particularly in the upper reaches. It is crossed by a lot of bridges, so it is easy to vary the length of the trip.

Section 1. Nortonsville (Rte 810) to Route 29

Gradient	Difficulty	Distance	Time	Width	Scenery	Map
24	2-3	12	4	15-25	Good	83

Trip Description: The road complex at Nortonsville is rather confusing, as Route 810 crosses the Lynch River at least two, and maybe three, times. The best advice is to start at the uppermost bridge where there is still water. The takeout can be at Advance Mills where there is a 10' dam, or at Route 606 Bridge, two miles further downstream, or at Route 29.

The North Fork Rivanna is a white-water canoeing stream in its upper reaches, but it is best remembered for the number of trees across the stream. The rapids are mostly of the ledge type near Nortonsville, changing to gravel bars, small ledges and rock gardens as it approaches Advance Mills. Below Advance Mills, it is a gravel bar type of stream with only a few riffles or appearances of ledges. The water is clear and cool, there is a fast current, the banks are low, the barbed/woven wire fences are numerous, and the area is very remote.

The canoeist spends about as much time in the water holding the boat as he spends in the boat paddling the boat -- trees, trees, and more trees block the stream in the upper section to the point that one could lose all vestiges of a Christian upbringing with little trouble. Definitely not a stream for decked boats unless accompanied by open boats in the lead.

Hazards: Ten foot dam at Advance Mills (10 miles downstream). Two foot dam ½ mile above Route 29. Many, many trees and fences across the stream.

Water Conditions: Canoeable only in winter and spring following a prolonged wet period or very heavy rain.

Section 2. Route 29 to Rivanna River

Gradient	Difficulty	Distance	Time	Width	Scenery	Map
5.5	1	10.5*	4	30-40	Fair	82, 83

*Plus 4 miles on Rivanna River

Trip Description: Below Route 29, the North Fork Rivanna River is a mild, pleasant Piedmont stream flowing over a sand and gravel bottom. The clay banks are high, the current is slow, the water is turning yellow in color, and the banks are tree-lined. The terrain is largely rolling hills but trees block the view from the river. Before joining the Rivanna, there are remains of old wing dams constructed in the late 1700's to improve navigation. There are a number of rock garden riffles that are the remains of old mill dams, but most of the Class 1 riffles are gravel bars.

The recommended takeout is Route 649 bridge, about two miles above the Rivanna River. If continuing below Route 649, the next takeout is slightly more then four miles downstream on the Rivanna River to Charlottesville.

258

Hazards: Wire fences across the stream.
Water Conditions: Canoeable normally in winter and spring following a wet period or a moderate rain.

GAUGE

A reading of 3.5' on the USGS Culpeper gauge should be zero for canoeing on Section 1. Six inches less for Section 2.

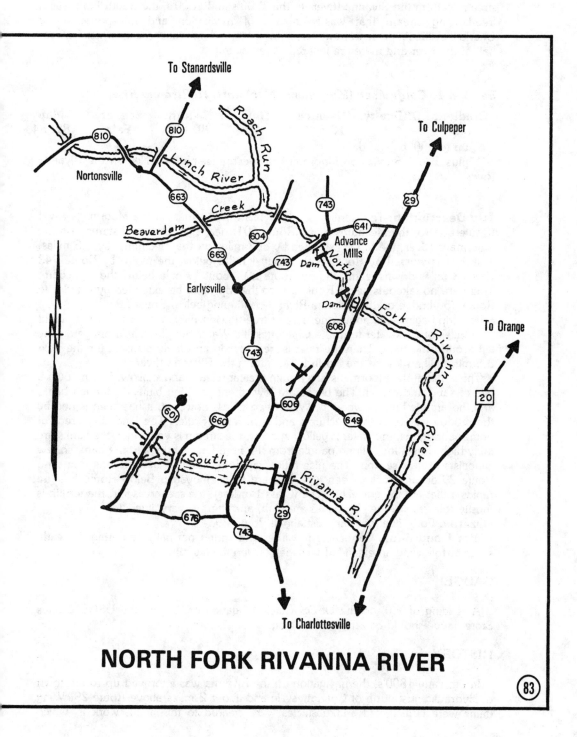

NORTH FORK RIVANNA RIVER

South Fork Rivanna River

INTRODUCTION

The South Fork Rivanna River is formed by the Mechums River and the Moormans River; it, in turn, joins the North Fork Rivanna River about 14 miles downstream to form the Rivanna River. In the 1700's and 1800's, the South Fork was a free-flowing stream that was a means of navigation and transportation for Charlottesville. At present, however, it has a major dam that backs up water for over half of the river and there are few rapids remaining.

Section 1. Confluence (Moormans/Mechums) to Rivanna River

Gradient	Difficulty	Distance	Time	Width	Scenery	Map
7.5	A,1	13.5**	7	30-60*	Fair	82, 84

*up to 300' behind dam

**plus 1 to 1.5 miles on Moormans or Mechums, plus 4 miles on the Rivanna River.

Trip Description: The starting point for this trip is either on the Moormans River (Route 601) or the Mechums River (Route 601) near Free Union. If starting on the Moormans River, the trip is extended by one mile; on the Mechums, by 1.5 miles. The river is crossed by Route 660, about 4 miles below the putin, by Route 743 about 8 miles downstream, and by Route 29, about ½ mile below the high dam. There are no takeouts below Route 29, so the trip must be extended by 4 miles to Route 250 bridge on the Rivanna River if continuing below Route 29.

The trip begins with about one mile of free-flowing river; then it turns into about nine miles of backwater from the Charlottesville Water Supply dam. Portage on the left around the dam. Then the river is free-flowing and fairly pleasant for the next 3.5 miles. Then it joins the North Fork to form the Rivanna River.

The water at the Moormans River putin is clear, clean, and shallow, flowing over a bed of sand and gravel. The banks are low, there are high bluffs on the left bank, and the area is heavily wooded. Within two miles, however, it has been joined by the muddy waters of the Mechums and is now backwater. The land is cleared for homes and farms, the water is yellow in color, the stream is very deep, the banks are fairly high. It is a long, tiring paddle from the Free Union bridge to the dam, so few canoeists try this section. The nice riffles/rapids (Class 1-2) between the dam and Route 29 are the rock garden type and are very enjoyable. Below Route 29, the rapids/riffles are the gravel bar type (Class 1 or less), the scenery is fair, the terrain is mostly rolling hills, the clay banks are high, and there is very little litter.

Hazards: Forty-five foot dam just above Route 29.

Water Conditions: Canoeable in winter and spring normally or during the early summer following an extended wet spell or very heavy rain.

GAUGE

A reading of 2.0' on the USGS Culpeper gauge or 3.5' on the USGS Cootes Store gauge should be zero for canoeing.

HISTORY

In the early 1800's, the navigation on the Rivanna was improved up to the town of Hydraulic, just north of Charlottesville and about 2 miles above Route 29. Wing dams were constructed and obstacles were cleared to this point, work in which

Thomas Jefferson played a role. The high dam has inundated the site of Hydraulic; only the name, Hydraulic Road, remains to remind one that Hydraulic was the "head of navigation" at one time.

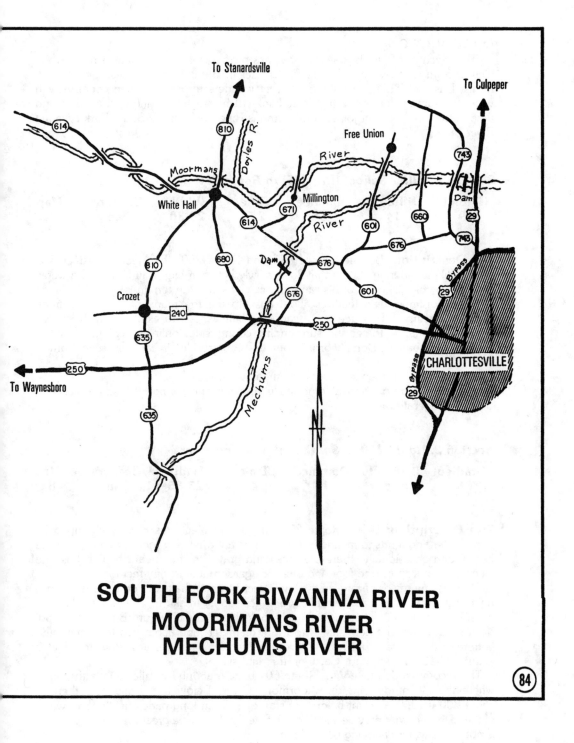

SOUTH FORK RIVANNA RIVER
MOORMANS RIVER
MECHUMS RIVER

84

Mechums River

INTRODUCTION

The Mechums River is a stream that has promise of a white-water stream when viewed from virtually every bridge that crosses it. But it only promises; it never performs. It is itself only, a small stream that wanders through farming country, with water the same color as the high clay banks. It begins by flowing to the North and then to the east where it joins the Moormons River to form the South Fork Rivanna River.

Section 1. Miller School (Rte 635) to Route 250

Gradient	Difficulty	Distance	Time	Width	Scenery	Map
9	12	6	2.5	20-30	Fair	84

Trip Description: Between Route 635 and Route 250, the Mechums River is a very small meandering stream that flows slowly between high clay banks. The water is yellow in color, the bottom is sand and clayey sand, the terrain is open farmland. The most distinguishing features about this trip are the many places where trees block the stream and the feeling of canoeing between six to eight foot high levees. There is no chance to see the surrounding countryside, only the stream, the sky, and the clay banks. Don't worry about the countryside, it can't be seen from a canoe.
Hazards: Trees and fences across the stream.
Water Conditions: Canoeable normally in winter and spring following a wet period or a moderate rain.

Section 2. Route 250 to South Fork Rivanna River

Gradient	Difficulty	Distance	Time	Width	Scenery	Map
8	12	10	4	25-35	Fair	84

Trip Description: Below Route 250 bridge, the Mechums River picks up a bit more water and tends to meander more. There are a few big rock formations on the banks, and occasionally, there are rocks and gravel in the stream bed. It has one ledge with a drop of one foot and one rock garden at least fifty feet long.

There is one major hazard on the lower section about half-way down, a dam on a right turn with no notice; this dam is a water supply intake for Charlottesville. The left side is a sheer 8' drop, the right side looks like it could be run. But less than 50' downstream from the right side is a 3 foot diameter pipe about two feet above the bottom of the chute -- not two feet from the water; clearance at zero water level is about 10"-12". A real trap. Carry on the right side.

The recommended takeout is Route 601 bridge, about 1.5 miles above the point where the Mechums joins the Moormon's River. Below the confluence, there is about 800 yards of current before the start of a damn long paddle in the backwater of the high dam that may be seen from Route 29. It may be great for fishermen but it is not white-water canoeing below Free Union.
Hazards: Eight-foot dam about five miles downstream. Several trees blocking the stream.
Water Conditions: Canoeable in winter and spring normally or during the early summer following an extended wet spell or very heavy rain.

262

Moormans River

INTRODUCTION

The Moormans River is a genuine white-water stream from its headwaters to its junction with the Mechums River, where the South Fork Rivanna River begins. It is very small in its upper reaches, but since it is fed by many small streams, it becomes a modest-size small river by the time it reaches Free Union. It is crossed by many bridges, it has no dams, and it is not usually blocked by trees; so it is a delightful river for the intermediate white-water canoeist.

Section 1. Charlottesville Reservoir to White Hall (Rte 810)

Gradient	Difficulty	Distance	Time	Width	Scenery	Map
62	2-3	5.5	1.5	15-25	Very Good	84

Trip Description: The trip from Charlottesville Reservoir to White Hall begins alongside Route 614 west of White Hall, well above the third bridge. Continue upstream until there is no water; the best putin is an obvious choice. Then prepare for an exciting Class 3 downstream dash through immovable slalom gates (trees), over flexible obstacles (bushes), and under country guillotines (wire fences); then you are ready for the rock gardens, quick turns, low hanging trees, small ledges, and narrow passages. Sheer delight, except for one moment of sheer (but unwarranted) terror. If you make the trip, you will recognize that spot; make an eddy turn and set up below that point to see the expressions on the faces of the following canoeists.

The upper part of the Moormans River is best for open boaters who can and will jump out and hold their canoes. Decked boaters will find it hard to stop and hold themselves, so open boaters should help the decked boaters. This is no place to be swept into trees or fences that wait for the hesitant, the unskilled, or the benumbed. But don't let these hazards be the reason for not running this beautiful, fast, and challenging stream that will be remembered for a lifetime.

Below the middle bridge on Route 614, west of White Hall, the stream changes its nature and becomes a delightful Class 2 run. But look out for the cattle gate at Route 810 bridge, the takeout. It would be ridiculous to escape harm and/or humiliation on the challenging sections and then be wiped out at the takeout.

Hazards: Barbed/woven wire fences. Trees blocking and standing in the streambed. Cattle gate at takeout bridge.

Water Conditions: Canoeable only in winter and spring following a prolonged wet period or very heavy rain.

Section 2. White Hall (Rte 810) to Free Union (Rte 601)

Gradient	Difficulty	Distance	Time	Width	Scenery	Map
24	23	8	3	25-40	Very Good	84

Trip Description: Below White Hall, the Moorman's is much bigger, more predictable, and more reserved. But it is still a stream that cannot be taken lightly, for it has rock garden rapids, ledges, and cobble bars that will present steady challenges to the intermediate paddler. The first rapid below Route 810 bridge is a nice long Class 2 rapid, an indication of things to come. Below the mid-point bridge at Millington (Route 671), the Moormans' becomes a pleasant run over gravel bars, small rock gardens, and occasional small ledges. The underwater bridge about 3 miles below

Millington will necessitate a short carry; watch for the barbed wire fence at this bridge. Then watch for the barbed wire fence that parallels a set of ledges sloping downstream from right to left.

The lower portion of this trip has a number of rock bluffs along the bank, towering over deep spots in the river. Swimming holes of the highest order. Deep water and high spots to jump/dive from. In warm weather, add an hour to the trip for swim calls. In addition to the swimming holes, the lower part has the best scenery; or maybe one just has the time to enjoy the scenery.

There are a number of old mill sites along the stream and the location of colonial roads that led to the mills can be detected by the observant. The ledge at the Millington Bridge was part of the dam for that mill; other mill sites can be identified by recognizing that some of the rock garden rapids are the remains of old mill dams that have been strewn about by the force of the stream.

The takeout at Route 601 is the last point for avoiding the backwater from the high dam on the South Fork Rivanna River; this dam can be seen from Route 29. The backwater starts less than two miles below Route 601 and it is at least four miles of backwater to the next bridge. Then it is three miles of flat water to the dam. It is not worth the effort to canoe the last 400 to 600 yards of the Moormans to where the Mechums joins and the South Fork Rivanna River begins.

Hazards: Barbed wire fences. Underwater bridge.

Water Conditions: Canoeable in winter and spring normally or during the early summer following an extended wet spell or very heavy rain.

GAUGE

A reading of 4.0' on the USGS Culpeper gauge should be zero for canoeing on Section 1; 3.0' for Section 2. There is an RC gauge on Route 810 bridge for the lower section; deduct 8" from this gauge to determine zero for the upper section.

Slate River

INTRODUCTION

The Slate River is one of the two major Piedmont streams flowing into the James River from the South. In its upper stretches, above Diana Mills, it is a rather flat meandering stream; below Diana Mills, there is some good white-water. This small stream was developed into a slack water canal with a series of dams in the colonial days, serving Buckingham county above Buckingham (on Route 60). It joins the James River just above Bremo Bluff, spewing yellow water into a river that has almost become clear. In very wet weather, trips can begin as high upstream as Buckingham (Route 60).

Section 1. Buckingham (Rte 60) to Rte 20

Gradient	Difficulty	Distance	Time	Width	Scenery	Map
4.5	A,1	12	5	20-30	Good	85

Section 2. Rte 20 to Diana Mills (Rte 671)

Gradient	Difficulty	Distance	Time	Width	Scenery	Map
4	A,1	10.5	4	25-35	Good	85

Trip Description: From Buckingham to Route 20 and from Route 20 to Diana Mills, the Slate River is a slow moving, meandering, small stream, about 20' to 30' wide. There are very few rapids in these sections, as the gradient is a very slight 4' per mile. There are riffles at the location of old dams, but there are no ledges or big rock gardens. The clay banks are not very high, the banks are wooded in most stretches, and there is a lot of farmland along both banks. The current is barely moderate, but the water is not polluted. There is no dam at Diana Mills at the present time, but there are trees blocking the stream at a few points.

The Slate River flows through the heart of Buckingham County, flowing to the north by a rather devious route. There are high hills to the east and to the west, but it flows through a rather wide valley. It is so hard to find water at Route 60, that most trips on the upper Slate River must begin after it is joined by a small river and two small creeks about three miles downstream. At Slate River Mills, which is about 5.5 miles downstream from Route 60, there is much more water.

Hazards: Trees blocking the stream.

Water Conditions: Canoeable normally in winter and spring following a wet period or a moderate rain.

Section 3. Diana Mills (Rte 671) to James River

Gradient	Dificulty	Distance	Time	Width	Scenery	Map
8	1-2	9.5	3.5	30-50	Good	85

Trip Description: From Diana Mills to the James River, the Slate River is a quite different stream. Its gradient would lead the paddler to expect very little white-water, but there are two very good rapids in this section. Below the mid-point bridge and gauging station, there is the remains of an old mill; the ruins of the mill dam itself is a good Class 2 rapid. Then there is a very long, steady Class 2 rock garden rapid that

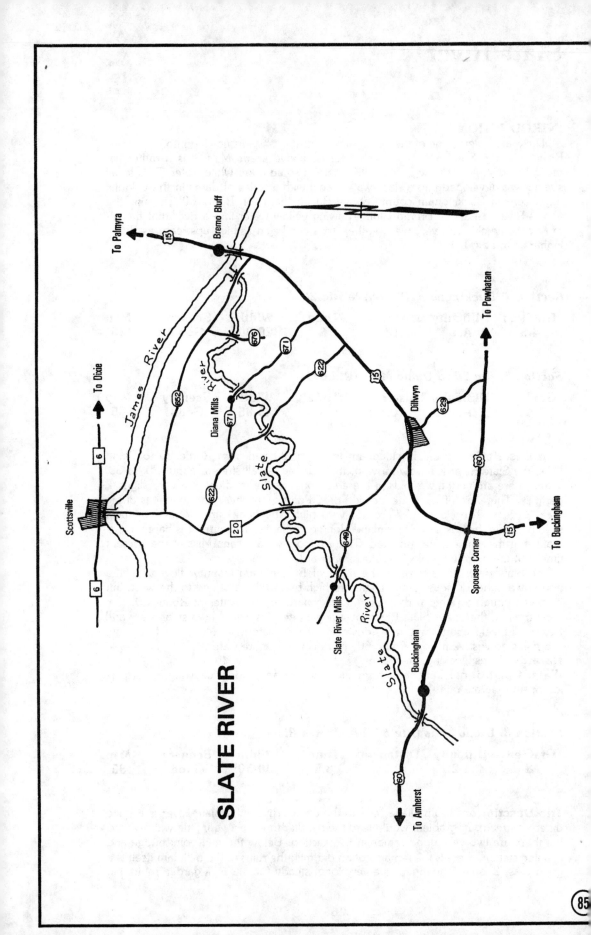

SLATE RIVER

requires a lot of maneuvering for over 100 yards; good action, good white-water. In this stretch the river widens to about 60' to 70' in places, but it is narrower than that in most sections. The current is fairly good, the water is unpolluted, the area seems surprisingly remote. The takeout can be Route 652 just before the James River or Route 15 bridge on the James River. It is about two miles from Route 652 bridge to Route 15 bridge at Bremo Bluff.

Hazards: None.

Water Conditions: Canoeable in winter and spring normally or during the early summer following an extended wet spell or very heavy rain.

HISTORY

The first mention of navigation on the Slate River was in 1788, when the Virginia Assembly appointed commissioners to examine the feasibility of making the river navigable. In 1794, actual work began with the clearing of obstructions from Buckingham Courthouse to the James River. This initial project was doomed from the onset, however, as there was no provision to construct locks bypassing existing mill dams. When the mill owners refused to cooperate, river traffic was limited to the pools between successive dams and was required to portage the cargo and, maybe, the boats.

In 1823, the Slate River Company began work on the river, using the low dams and falling gates that were used on the nearby Willis River. From Buckingham Courthouse to the James River, a total of 15 locks and dams were constructed and it was ready for operations, provided the five mill owners cooperated. When they didn't, the Slate River Company gave up its "slaves and other property" and dissolved in 1835. It then fell into neglect, and only a few signs remain of this effort.

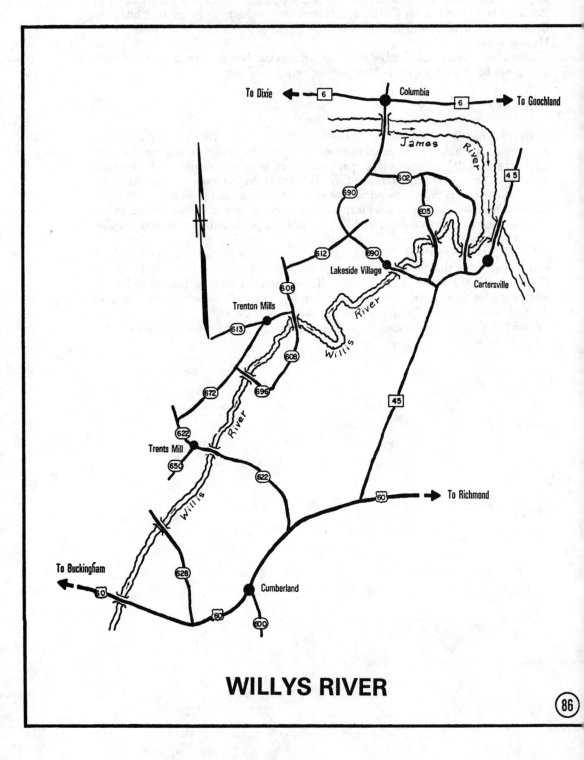

WILLYS RIVER

86

Willis River

INTRODUCTION

The Willis River is one of the major tributaries of the James River from the south. It flows alongside the Cumberland State Park area in Cumberland County, joining the James River upstream of Cartersville. It is crossed by many bridges, many mills were located on it in early days, and a canal was started on the Willys in the 1800's. A number of its tributaries are dammed for private lakes and for a state forest/camp-ground lake. It has been voted as one of the five flattest small rivers in Virginia by a panel of bitter paddlers.

Section 1. Ca Ira (Rte 60) to Trents Mill (Rte 622)

Gradient	Difficulty	Distance	Time	Width	Scenery	Map
2	A,1	10	5	20-30	Fair	86

Section 2. Trents Mill (Rte 622) to Trenton Mill (Rte 608)

Gradient	Difficulty	Distance	Time	Width	Scenery	Map
4	A,1	9	4	20-30	Fair	86

Section 3. Trenton Mill (Rte 600) to Lakeside Village (Rte 690)

Gradient	Difficulty	Distance	Time	Width	Scenery	Map
2	A	9.5	4.5	25-30	Fair	86

Section 4. Lakeside Village (Rte 690) to James River

Gradient	Difficulty	Distance	Time	Width	Scenery	Map
2	A	6	3	30-40	Fair	86

Trip Description: The Willis River from Route 60 to Trents Mill, from Trents Mill to Route 608, from Route 608 to Lakeside Village, and from Lakeside Village to the James River can be described in one word, "flat". This stream has less gradient, less current, fewer riffles, and longer flat stretches than almost any other stream in Virginia. If flat water paddling builds character, the Willis will produce a better America.

The Willis River flows alongside the Cumberland State Park and through farmland for the most part and it is a typical Piedmont river. Clay banks, yellow water when it rains, wooded banks, sand and gravel bottom, and quite slow. It would seem that a stream that does not meander would have more white-water, but all riffles are the result of old mill dams that have washed out and the old flash locks associated with the Willis canal system. The river never seems to wash out trees that block the passages, or maybe new trees just replace the old ones.

It is still possible to canoe on the Willis River above Route 60; it is very small, but still canoeable. It is much like the section below Route 60, only flatter. Further, there is an 8' dam above Route 60 that backs up the Willis for a very long way; the putin for that section is near the confluence of the Little Willis River and the Willis River. The section above Route 60 is a genuine Piedmont swamp that is both eerie and beautiful, but there must be at least 45 trees across the passages. There is virtually no current, and there are very long, very flat stretches. But beautiful -- keep saying that.

The recommended takeout for the section below Lakeside Village is Route 602, about ½ mile above the James River; if continuing beyond this point, a trip of about two miles on the James River to Cartersville is required.

Hazards: Trees too numerous to count blocking the river. Occasional fences across the stream.

Water Conditions: Canoeable in winter and spring normally or during the early summer following an extended wet spell or very heavy rain.

HISTORY

The first organized efforts to make the Willis River navigable began before the Revolutionary War, in 1774, but it was 1787 before an act was passed to improve the Willis for navigation by "boats, batteaus, and canoes", capable of carrying four hogshead of tobacco. The act required all mills with dams across the Willis to construct locks or the dam would be removed. By about 1797, navigation was open up to Ca Ira (Deanes Mill and Deanes Tobacco Warehouse). By 1798, or shortly thereafter, it was extended up to Curdsville, about 40 miles from the James River.

The canal used flash locks in the upper reaches to provide sufficient depth (1.5' to 2') for navigation by batteaus. The batteaus were about 60 feet long, 8 feet wide, and were of shallow draft. They were propelled by men with poles. The flash locks, or water gates were basically constructed of jetties extending from each shore towards each other, leaving a sluice that was closed by a gate mounted on horizontal hinges. The gate was dropped, the water flushed through, and the boats shot down or were pulled up.

Navigation continued until the 1890's on the Willis River with batteaus carrying lumber, cattle, flour, and grain to the railroad that replaced the James River and Kanawha Canal. When canoeing this stream, it is hard to recognize the sites of the flash locks, but the locks around the mill dams are fairly easily recognized.

The Willis River and the Slate River are similar in many respects; they are Piedmont rivers, they flow to the northeast, they are fairly flat in most stretches, they join the James River from the south, and they flow through quite similar areas. They have a lot of small tributaries that may be canoeable for very short distances, but there are trees across these streams, their clay banks are quite high, and the stream bed meanders a lot. The area through which those rivers flow does not have particularly attractive scenery; it is red clay farming land with many houses that indicate a marginal existence — in North Carolina, they would be called tenant houses.

Appomattox River

INTRODUCTION

The Appomattox River can be divided into four general sections: the upper reaches where it is a small stream; the backwater from the Chesdin dam; the white-water section from Chesdin Dam to Petersburg; and the flat water/tidewater section below Petersburg. The first section is a small, wandering stream through farm country; Lake Chesdin is a long flat stretch for motorboats; the Appomattox falls/line rapids make a super canoeing trip, and the tidewater area is for the motorboaters.

Section 1. Farmville (Rte 15) to Chesdin Dam

Gradient	Difficulty	Distance	Time	Width	Scenery	Map
3	A-1	107*	*	20-50	Good	87

*See Table Below

Trip Description: From Route 15 above Farmville to Route 602, a distance of about 79 miles, the Appomattox is a small wandering stream. It is crossed by seven bridges in the stretch, breaking the stream into eight sections. The average gradient is less than 3 feet/mile on all sections, and in some areas, the Appomattox actually flows through a swamp. Below Route 360, the river drops only 10' while travelling 12 miles to the Lake Chesdin backwater. The stream has other disenchanting features; there are trees across the river in the upper parts, the current is quite slow, and there are old low mill dams (or remains of old mill dams) at most of the bridge crossings. Its best features in this stretch are its remoteness from civilization in most parts, the clear water flowing over a sandy bottom, the improbability of meeting motorboaters, and the building of character and strength through hard work. In many spots, there are signs of old wing dams, built in the late 1700's/early 1800's to improve navigation between Farmville and Petersburg.

From Route 602 to Chesdin Dam, there is a swamp area for the first seven miles, with the river dropping about one foot/mile. In the backwater of the dam, Lake Chesdin, it drops zero feet in 22 miles. It is rather difficult to describe the backwater to a dam, but when you have seen one, you have seen them all. They are flat, they have motorboats and fishermen, they require a portage, and they require a lot of paddling.

The following table can be used to plan 45 different down-river trips (or 45 upriver trips if you have strange urges).

Table 7
Appomattox River Section Guide

Section		Distance	Time
Farmville (Rte 15)	to Farmville (Rte 45)	9.5	4.5
Farmville (Rte 45)	to Stony Point Mills (Rte 620)	21.5	10.0
Stony Point Mills (Rte 620)	to Tobaccoville (Rte 621)	4.5	2.5
Tobaccoville (Rte 621)	to Morven (Rte 681)	5.0	2.5
Morven (Rte 681)	to Giles Mill (Rte 609)	12.5	6.0
Giles Mill (Rte 609)	to Gerito (Rte 604)	8.5	4.0
Gerito (Rte 604)	to Amelia (Rte 360)	11.0	5.0
Amelia (Rte 360)	to Devils Bridge (Rte 602)	5.5	2.5
Devils Bridge (Rte 602)	to Chesdin Dam	29.0	15.0

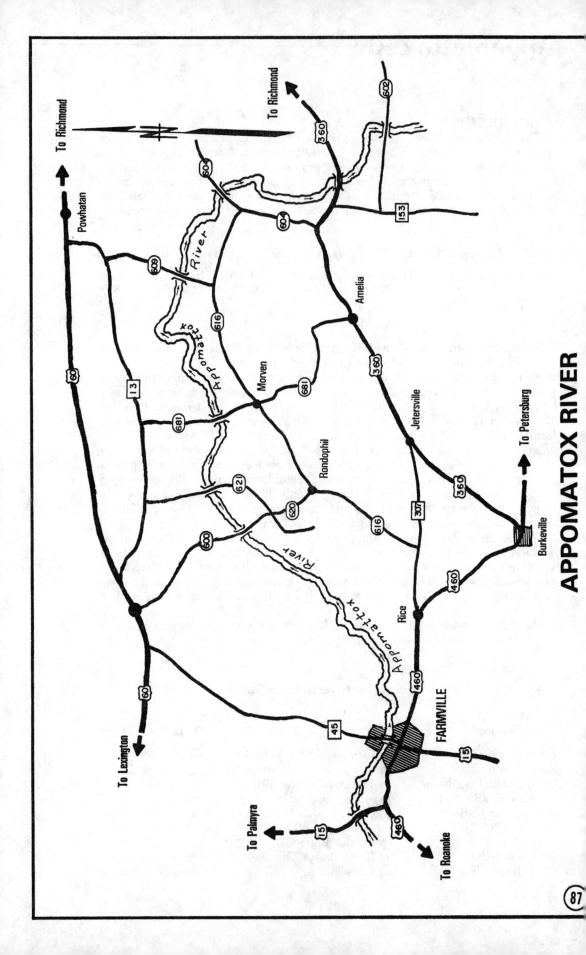

APPOMATOX RIVER

This river has been canoed by Boy Scout troops in past years from Farmville to Petersburg. They all agreed that the rumors of Class 2 rapids on the upper 70 + miles are just rumors. The stream has a slow current on all sections above Chesdin Dam, the clay banks are fairly high above Route 602, and the bottom is sand and clayey sand. The banks are heavily wooded on most sections and there are few houses (and no towns) along the river. All sections look pretty much alike above Route 602.

Hazards: Thirty-five foot dam at takeout (Chesdin). Trees and fences across the stream.

Water Conditions: Canoeable in winter and spring normally or during the early summer following an extended wet spell or very heavy rain.

Section 2. Chesdin Dam to Petersburg (Rte 36)

Gradient	Difficulty	Distance	Time	Width	Scenery	Map
13	2-3	6.5	2.5	50-80	Fair	88

Trip Description: From Chesdin Dam to Route 36 bridge in Petersburg, the Appomattox River is one of the best white-water trips in Virginia. It offers the intermediate canoeist a wide choice in rapids, scenery, and obstacles. It has ledges, rock gardens, islands, narrow passages, broken dams, and strong rapids. For most of the trip, the paddler is unaware of the build-up areas; only at the Matoaca Bridge and the takeout bridge is there much sign of people, except for a power substation and a little junk near the end of the trip. Its beauty and its diversity outweigh these aspects, however, and this trip is becoming one of the most popular trips in Virginia

The trip begins with a one mile (plus) flat water section to a seven-foot dam; portage on the left or let down at the fishladder in the left-center. Below the dam, there are two Class 2 rapids in quick succession, followed by riffles and another Class 2. There is a bypass to the left through an old canal, with a strong Class 3 rapid where the canal bank is broken out. Then there are wide stretches with a lot of riffles, wide stretches with hundreds of small islands, remains of an old dam with a bypass to the right, and challenging rock gardens. Then within sight of the power station smoke stack, there are two good rapids.

There is an eight-foot dam about 400 yards above Route 36 with a canal bypass to the right. The dam is broken out on the right side, for a four foot drop (Class 3) followed by a tough rock garden (Class 3). Enter the bypass canal and prepare for a quick left turn. Below the Broken Dam Rapid, there is a quiet section of 100 yards, followed by a strong Class 3 rapid; take this rapid close to the left -- very close. Then there are light riffles to the takeout bridge. Just below the last big rapid, there is an impressive rapid on the left bank, where a bypass canal to an old power station has broken through its banks. This is a difficult and exciting rapid (Class 4) with a total drop of ten feet in thirty feet. Portage up to this drop, you brave in heart.

Hazards: Seven-foot dam 1.25 miles below putin.

Water Conditions: Canoeable in winter, spring, and early summer, except following periods of little precipitation. Canoeable after a heavy rain in the summer and fall.

GAUGE

Three inches across the Chesdin Dam is zero for canoeing on Section 2. There is an RC gauge on Route 36 bridge.

HISTORY

There was a major dam near Matoaca for a mill in the early 1900's; picture postcards showed an 8' dam on a beautiful river; few signs exist of this dam and this mill.

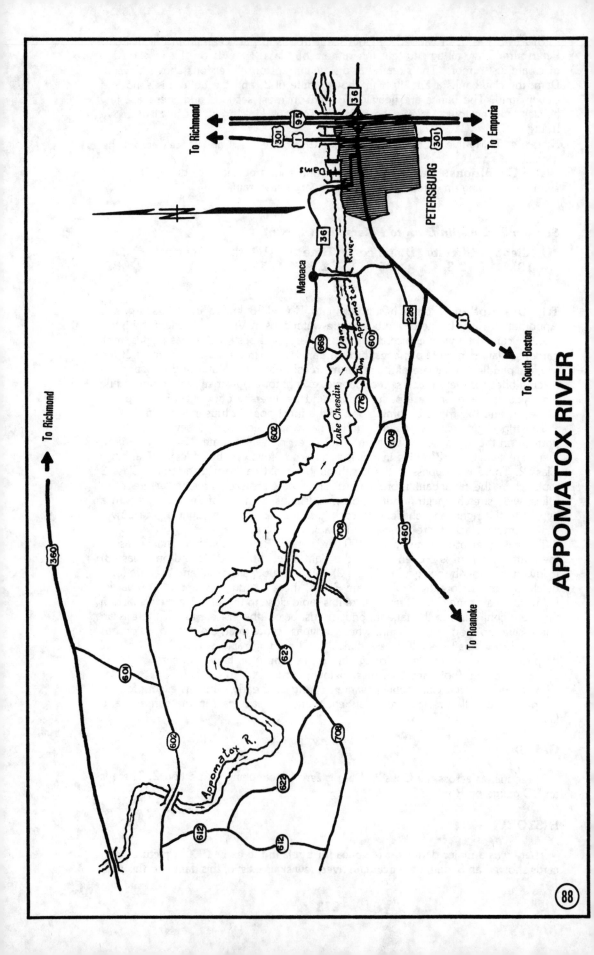

APPOMATOX RIVER

88

There was a power station on the left bank at the takeout bridge, its canal and the ruined building are still there. The dams on the river were part of a major canal system that bypassed the rapids from tidewater to above the Lake Chesdin Dam. There is a canal along the right bank for much of this trip.

Below Route 36, about 300 yards below the takeout on the right bank, there is a four foot dam that is a major hazard. In medium to high water, the hydraulic is a real "keeper". Below this dam, there is another dam, and then there is flatwater/tide-water. Avoid this section between Route 36 and the James River. It really isn't paddling, its painful, its hard work, its unattractive, and its risky.

Petersburg was one of the early colonial cities in Virginia. Like Richmond, it was built at the end of navigation, where the Appomattox River drops from the Piedmont to the Coastal Plains. It was the home of one of the Indian tribes in the Powhatan Confederacy. In the Civil War, it was the scene of a major siege in which the Union/Confederate forces fought trench warfare, a sign of things to come in WW I. The Gatling Gun was introduced, siege guns were employed, tunnels under the trenches were dug by miner/soldiers, Negro troops fought effectively for the Union, and the Confederates withdrew to Appomattox, enroute to Danville.

It was at Appomattox Courthouse that General Robert E. Lee surrendered the Army of Northern Virginia to General U.S. Grant and the Grand Army of the Poto-mac. Other Confederate forces surrendered to other Union forces later, but the surrender of Lee's forces was the final blow to the C.S.A. Lee chose not to disband his combat units and fight on as a guerilla force, prolonging the agony; Grant, in turn, treated the Confederate forces with respect and granted moderate terms for the surrender. The actions of these two leaders did much to unite our nation again.

When the Appomatox River is high (above four feet), there are a special set of hazards on the section near Route 36; a large whirlpool forms right below Route 36 bridge; it cannot be seen when looking at the river from a car. This whirlpool is formed by the complex rock structure and deep water at the bridge, and it has brought grief, pain, and fright to a few canoeists. One canoeist swamped in this whirlpool and, when he washed out of the whirlpool, he was swept over 400 yards downstream to the dam. He was trapped beneath the dam by the hydraulic; only by taking off his life jacket and swimming deep did he escape sure death. This canoeist knew about the dam and tried to swim ashore after swamping, but the swift current was too much. This prematurely grey haired paddler is lucky to be alive today.

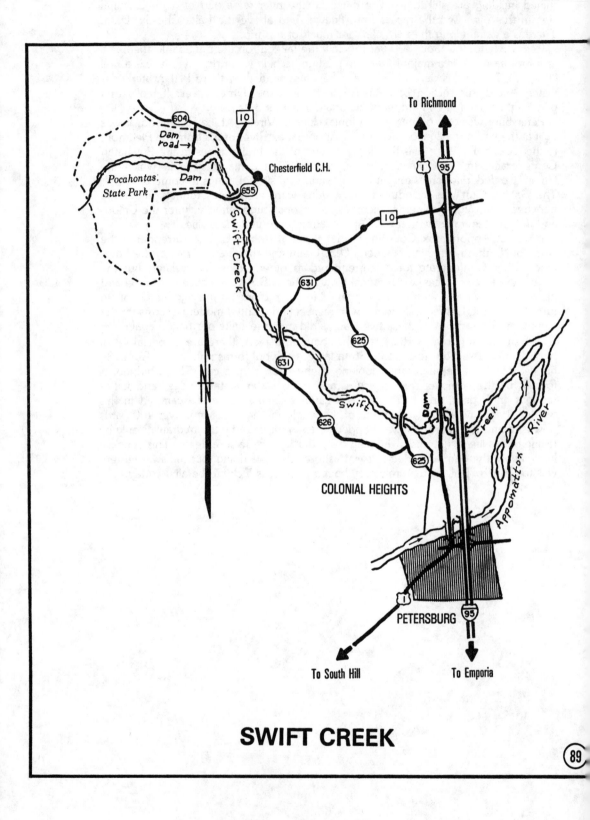

SWIFT CREEK

Swift Creek

INTRODUCTION

Swift Creek is a very small stream that flows through the Pocahontas State Park and into the Appomattox River. It is located about midway between Richmond and Petersburg in its upper reaches, flowing through a suburban/urban area. It must have been named after someone named Swift, for it was not named after the speed of its current. If there were fallsline rapids on this stream, they must be under the lake in the state park.

Section 1. Chesterfield Courthouse (Rte 655) to Rte 625 Bridge

Gradient	Difficulty	Distance	Time	Width	Scenery	Map
3	A-2	12.5	5	25-35	Fair	89

Trip Description: The Swift Creek trip begins below a dam and ends in backwater of a dam and drops only 40' over a 12.5 mile length, 50 feet over a 14.5 stretch. The area is fairly remote, there are trees along the bank, and the banks are fairly low. There is one Class 2 rapid about 3 miles below Route 655 at the ruins of an old mill and mill dam; otherwise it is quite flat. There are at least fifteen trees blocking the stream, presenting a real obstacle course. The bottom is muddy, the banks are clay, and the current is very slow.

The putin can be extended two miles upstream to Route 604, just below the dam, but the gradient is only 5 feet/mile. The takeout at Route 625 is not great and the adjacent landowners are ill-tempered; try a spot one-half mile downstream on the right at an apartment complex.

Hazards: Many slippery/muddy trees across the stream.

Water Conditions: Canoeable in winter and spring normally or during the early summer following an extended wet spell or very heavy rain.

277

Chicohominy River

INTRODUCTION

The Chicohominy River is a coastal plains river that begins just north of Richmond and flows into the James River southeast of Richmond. It is a flat-water stream from beginning to end, with the final stretches being tidewater. There is not a single rock in the stream in its lower reaches.

Section 1. Mechanicsville (Rte 360) to Bottoms Bridge (Rte 60)

Gradient	Difficulty	Distance	Time	Width	Scenery	Map
1	A	14	7.5	15-30	Good	90

Trip Description: The Chicohominy River is a very small stream that runs through forests and swamps in this section. The section from Route 360 to Creighton Bridge, the upper part, is not a particularly pretty section. It is cluttered with debris and trash and passage over the fallen trees is very tough. After about one and a half miles, the scenery and passage improve.

The last part of Route 360 to Creighton Bridge (Route 615) and from Creighton Bridge to Grapevine Bridge (Route 156) is a very rewarding trip. The scenery is that of a small stream enclosed by a forest made up primarily of hardwood trees. Although there are a few barbed wire fences on the adjacent land and a couple of "No Fishing" signs, there are no boat landings, paths, etc. which would hint the nearness of an urban community. Many fallen trees require the maximum of man-euvering, however; in high water, most obstructions can be bypassed and a few "lifted over" without much difficulty. These obstructions actually add a little zest to the trip as well as being insurance against fishermen, picnickers, and boaters (including other canoeists). The initial banks of solid ground soon give way to a semi-swamp area with occasional patches of solid ground and a few cypress trees.

Swampland takes over from Grapevine Bridge to Bottoms Bridge and cypress trees replace the various hardwoods. The river which was 15 to 30 feet wide spreads out. This portion of the trip is most interesting. With the water level high, following the stream's channel is difficult. Obstructions are numerous but, in high water, there is usually some path bypassing a potential "lift" area. This is real "Florida type" swampland. (With plenty of snakes in the summer, according to the Bottoms Bridge service station owner.) One should allow about eight hours to make this trip. The best time to go in this section probably is April. Low water would reveal the channel but going would be difficult.

The river is crossed by two bridges (Route 615 and Route 156) so the trip can be divided into shorter trips.

Hazards: Many trees across the stream.

Water Conditions: Canoeable in winter and spring normally or during the early summer following an extended wet spell or very heavy rain.

Section 2. Bottoms Bridge (Rte 60) to Providence Forge (Rte 155)

Gradient	Difficulty	Distance	Time	Width	Scenery	Map
1	A	13.5	7	30-150	Good	90

Trip Description: From Bottoms Bridge to Providence Forge, the Chicohominy River winds through the coastal plains and swamps. It winds across the peninsula

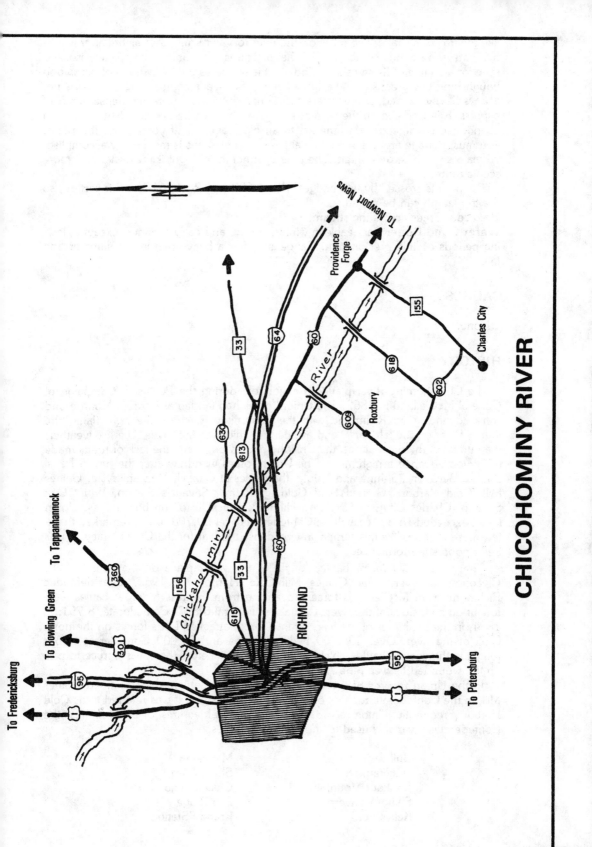

CHICOHOMINY RIVER

like the trail of a snake, two miles on the river for every mile of straight-line travel. It has horseshoe bends combined with hairpin turns. The area is completely isolated save for a couple of fishing shacks. Sunlight is scarce as a thick canopy of hardwood boughs and evergreens create a tunnel along the river's course. The channel is not always clearly defined, as the waters occasionally extend far back into dense stands of cypress. Keep an eye on the current and follow it. Two miles below Route 618, an abandoned canal leads off to the left to an old gravel pit. If you choose this route, you must portage around a roadbed at the gravel pit. This is most easily accomplished via a small lake on the left. The river channel to the right is the easier and more scenic route.

The river is crossed by two bridges (Route 609 and Route 618) in this section, so the trip length can be varied.

Hazards: Trees across the stream.

Water Conditions: Canoeable in winter, spring, and early summer, except following periods of little precipitation. Canoeable after a heavy rain in the summer and fall.

GAUGES

None.

HISTORY

The Chicohominy River played a major role during the Peninsula Campaign of General McClelland in 1862. The Union forces had landed at Fortress Monroe and were advancing on Richmond with the Pamunkey River on the right flank, the James River on the left flank, and astride the Chicohominy River. The hot weather, the humidity, the mosquitoes, the Chicohominy swamp, and the lack of roads made the union advance a nightmare. The Union forces withdrew after the Seven Days' Battles. Between 25 June and 1 July, the battles at Oakhill, Mechanicsville, Gaines Mill (Cold Harbor), Garnetts and Goldings Farms, Savage's Station, White Oak Swamp (Charles City), and Malvern Hill took a terrible toll on both forces. Union losses exceeded 15,800 casualties; Confederates over 20,700. It was remarked that a few more victories like this campaign would lose the war for the Confederacy. It was Lee's poorest performance.

There were two major battles fought at the same place on the banks of the Chicohominy river, near Gaines Mill/Cold Harbor. In 1962, Lee defended Richmond from McClellands forces advancing from Fortress Monroe; battles were fought on both sides of the river. Casualties; Federal 6,837; Confederate, 8,751. In 1864, in the final days of the war, Grant's forces attacked Lee's forces on the north bank of the river. Over 108,000 Federal troops and 59,000 Confederate troops fought in this second battle, which lasted for six days before there was a truce to pick up the wounded between the lines.

In the Union records of the Great Rebellion, this battlefield was named Gaines Mill; in the Confederate records of the War for Secession, it was referred to as Cold Harbor. Frequently, Union records used geographical features for battle names; the Confederates invariably used town names. Examples:

Bull Run		Manassaa
Antietam		Sharpsburg
Lookout Mountain	vs	Chicamauga
Elkhorn Tavern		Pea Ridge
Kellys Ford		Brandy Station

Chapter 7

Virginia Canal Systems

THE JAMES RIVER AND KANAWHA CANAL.

The James River Company was organized in 1785, with George Washington as honorary President. By 1789 two canals were in operation in Richmond, one 200 yards long with three stone locks at Westham (Dead Man's Hill), and a 3½ mile canal from the present Byrd Park Pumphouse to a basin in the city. By 1801 the James had been improved for batteau navigation by wing dams and sluices for 220 miles to Buchanan.

In 1820 the navigation became a State enterprise, and the canal was enlarged and extended to Maiden's Adventure, 30 miles from Richmond. By 1829 the Blue Ridge Canal, 7 miles long, around falls in the mountains, was complete, as well as the Kanawha Turnpike (now U.S. 60) from Covington to Huntington, 208 miles long; and 60 miles of river improvements for flats, horseboats and steamboats on the Kanawha River from Charleston to the Ohio. Thus the Company's works connected the Atlantic seaboard with the Mississippi valley.

In 1835 the company was again reorganized, and became the James River and Kanawha Company. Stockholders included R. E. Lee and John Marshall. By 1840 the canal had been enlarged again for horse-drawn boats and extended to Lynchburg, 146 miles above Richmond, involving 52 locks, each with a lamp post. A flight of five stone locks and a ship lock, the Tidewater Connection, was completed in 1854 to connect the Richmond basin with tidewater. By 1851 a lock-and-dam system with 11 dams and 32 locks had extended the canal 50 more miles westward to its final terminus at Buchanan. In 1858 the company bought the North River Navigation, then under construction, and completed it to Lexington, 20 miles from the James, by 1862. A 4½ mile connection was made with the works of the Rivanna Navigation Company in 1851, and bridges at New Canton, Hardwickesville (Wingina), and Bent Creek, and a river lock at Cartersville, were constructed to serve customers on the opposite side of the James from the canal. A westward extension of the canal from Buchanan was begun in 1853, but lack of funds caused its abandonment in 1856.

The continuation of the canal over the Allegheny Mountains to the Kanawha River was greatly debated until its demise. Although badly hurt by the War of Northern Aggression and by floods, the company was building the Buchanan and Clifton Forge Railway to connect the canal with the C&O Railway, when it decided to sell the canal to the Richmond and Allegheny Railroad Company, which built its line (now the C&O James River Line) on the towpath in 1881. Today the only long stretch of the canal with water is a 9-mile stretch at Richmond, which the city plans to restore. Of the 101 locks, about 38 are still in good condition, as well as 8 aqueducts and a number of dams. Many of these can be seen on the annual fall excursion of the Old Dominion Chapter of the National Railway Historical Society. There was an impressive flight of five locks in downtown Richmond, but three were destroyed by the Downtown Expressway; happily the other two were made into a park (now on the Richmond tourist route) by Reynolds Metals, with a display area and Virginia's first canal library.

Battery Creek Lock, under the Blue Ridge Parkway, has been fully restored by the National Park Service. Over 200 stone-arch culverts, large enough to walk through, are still used by the railway.

THE RIVANNA NAVIGATION.

The first organized effort to improve the Rivanna River for navigation was begun by Thomas Jefferson in 1763, over two hundred years ago. His 1795 pamphlet, "Notes on Virginia", mentions the fact that the Rivanna was then navigable for batteaux from just below Charlottesville (near Monticello) to Columbia, on the James River, Virginia's major route to the coastal markets. This early work consisted primarily of clearing fallen trees from the channel, cutting sluices through rapids, and building long rock-pile dams to direct water into the sluices.

In 1805 the Rivanna Navigation Company was organized to take over and improve the works. By the 1830's the navigation had been extended above Charlottesville and there were about 18 wooden locks, one stone lock, and some 13 dams on the Rivanna. However, the works were still for batteaux, which were poled up and down stream, and there was no towpath. By 1840, however, the batteau navigation on the James had been superseded by the James River and Kanawha Canal. This spurred a similar development of the Rivanna. By 1854 the Rivanna Navigation Company had completed a lock, dam and canal system for canal boats as far up as the Albemarle County line, 20 miles from the James. These works included 20½ miles of towpath, 9 fine stone locks, two large stone walk-through culverts, and seven miles of canal. The JR&K Company helped by building the lower 4½ miles of the navigation as their "Rivanna Connexion". Further extension of the new works to Charlottesville was thwarted by the arrival there of the Virginia Central Railway in 1850. Much of the Rivanna Navigation remained in use until 1908, and is today Virginia's best preserved navigation, almost undefiled by modern man.

THE NORTH RIVER NAVIGATION.

By 1801, the James River Company had cleared the North (now Maury) River for batteaux from Lexington to the James, a distance of 20 miles, but the head of navigation became Cedar Grove, 10 miles upstream toward Goshen Pass. After the James River and Kanawha Canal had been completed as far as the Maury, the North River Navigation Company, organized in 1841, began construction of a lock-and-dam system for canal boats from the James to Lexington. In 1858 the still unfinished works were bought by the JR&K Company, which opened the line to traffic in 1860 and completed it in 1862. The works included 9 stone dams, one crib dam, 9 stone guard locks, 14 stone lift locks, 2 stone guard gates, 5 small aqueducts, 20 miles of towpath, 10 miles of canal, 10 change bridges, 12 farm and road bridges, 4 ferries, and 12 lockhouses.

Navigation ceased in the 1880's. Except for the JR&K Canal, no navigation in Virginia has as many well-preserved canal structures as the North River Navigation. Of the 25 locks, 16 are still in excellent condition, 6 have been mined for stone, and 3 have disappeared; 3 of the dams are still practically intact. A number of the locks and dams are readily accessible by road, and are very good future picnic sites. Three of the dams are intact, or readily made so, for water recreation, including the dam below Lexington. Ben Salem lock has been made a wayside park on Route 60.

THE WILLIS'S RIVER NAVIGATION.

This was a navigation for batteaux carrying tobacco hogsheads and other agricultural products from Ca Ira near Cumberland Courthouse, to the James, 30 miles by water, constructed in 1775-1797 and later said to have been extended 10 more miles to Curdsville, in Buckingham County. Its locks were not of the usual box type, but were flash locks, single gates which held back a pool of water and were suddenly lowered to provide a flood of water for navigation. It was rebuilt about 1820, and perhaps in the 1850's when the JR&K Company built a river lock at Cartersville to draw trade from the Willis into the canal. Boats were still being poled up the lower reaches of the Willis in the 1890's. There are still a few signs of the flash locks, expecially between Curdsville and Ca Ira. The Willis flows through Cumberland State Forest and is a quiet fisherman's stream.

THE SLATE RIVER NAVIGATION.

Several attempts, in 1794, 1819, and in 1852, were made to construct this batteau navigation from Buckingham Courthouse to the James, a distance of 30 miles, but a through route was never possible because of the opposition of mill owners who would not allow locks in their mill dams. The earlier locks were probably flash locks, as on the Willis's River; works of the 1819 period included 15 of these. Several locks of unspecified type were built in the 1850's. Some of these had wooden lock walls filled with loose stone; now the wood is gone, leaving long piles of stone. The river has not yet been thoroughly searched for navigation remains. It is a quiet fisherman's stream.

THE TUCKAHOE CREEK NAVIGATION.

The Tuckahoe Creek Navigation Company, organized in 1827, had by 1828 completed a navigation system for batteaux carrying coal from the Tuckahoe coal pits to the James River Canal at Tuckahoe Aqueduct, 12 miles above Richmond. The navigation was about 6½ miles long, including 1¾ miles of canal and the rest slackwater and sluice. The works included 2 dams, 3 wooden locks, 2 lockhouses, about 3 miles of towpath, and a feeder ditch over a mile long, with 2 wooden flumes, to provide water supply from the James River Canal. In 1840 the navigation was replaced by the Tuckahoe and James River Railroad. The canal towpath and the tramway bed are still in good condition and would make good hiking trails; the abutments of Tuckahoe Aqueduct are still intact. Tuckahoe Creek basin is a fascinating mixture of swamps, wooded flood plain and remnants of navigation, railways, and coal mining. Every effort should be made to make this area a nature preserve.

THE RAPPANANNOCK NAVIGATION.

The Rappahannock Company was organized in 1816 to construct a batteau navigation from Carter's Run, near U.S. 211, to Fredericksburg, a distance of 50 miles, and on the Rapidan, a major tributary. By 1834 the navigation was almost complete to Deep Run, 10 miles above Fredericksburg, and much work had been done on the canal around Kelly's Ford, all this involving some 20 wooden locks, at least 7 dams, about 10 miles of canals, and a basin in Fredericksburg. The system was entirely rebuilt in 1846-1849, successfully reaching Carter's Run, involving 55 wooden locks, 25 stone locks, 15 miles of canals and 20 dams. By 1855 the navigation had declined and was maintained by farmers using it.

Today all of the wooden locks are gone above ground, but most of the best-built part of the navigation, containing most of the stone locks and a good deal of massive earthworks, is in quite good condition. The lower 20 miles of the navigation, below the Stafford County line, would have been inundated by the controversial Salem

Church Dam. Although there was no continuous towpath since the works were for batteaux, several nearly connected canals provide an excellent 5-mile hiking trail from near Doswell Chapel to opposite Deep Run Creek. There are said to be locks on the Rapidan, although the Company records do not mention any work on this tributary

THE HAZEL RIVER NAVIGATION.

When the Rappahannock Navigation was complete, the Hazel River Navigation Company was organized, in 1850, to make 20 miles of that tributary navigable, as far as Castle Mountain near Estes. By 1854 the work was complete except for some dredging, but the Rappahannock Navigation was already in decline and the Hazel was apparently little used. There were 8 dams and locks; at least one lock was stone, the rest of wood.

THE UPPER APPOMATTOX NAVIGATION.

The Appomattox was possibly cleared for batteau navigation sometime after 1745, when an act was passed to the effect. The Upper Apponmattox Company, incorporated in 1795, built by 1816 the 5½ mile Upper Appomattox Canal from the river into Petersburg, and constructed numerous wing-dams from Farmville down to Petersburg, a distance of 100 miles. Works on the canal included four well-built stone locks connected in staircase fashion, a stone-arch aqueduct, several stone culverts and a basin in Petersburg. The several mills along the river had locks in their dams; two of these were stone. The navigation was rebuilt in the 1830's as a lock-and-dam system, still for poled batteaux, which involved 3½ more miles of canal and 13 more wooden locks. Navigation on parts of the navigation continued into the 1890's.

Today, 3 miles of the Upper Appomattox Canal still holds water, although it was enlarged in modern times to feed a now defunct generating plant. The aqueduct fell down in Civil War times, but the locks were apparently unchanged since 1816 until VEPCO destroyed the upper lock, The Appomattox River Water Authority ran a pipeline through another lock, and the lower lock was allowed to cave in by using it as a drain. One mile of watered canal was recently filled in by Petersburg. Over 10 miles of the navigation works, including the best canal works and the only other surviving stone lock, has been inundated by Lake Chesdin. However, the still watered canal and the towpaths of mill canals closer to Petersburg should still offer excellent hiking trails connecting the city with the lake, along the section proposed as a state scenic river.

THE DEEP CREEK NAVIGATION.

The Deep Creek Navigation Company was organized in 1825 to provide a flash-lock type of navigation from Nottoway County to the Appomattox, a distance of some 20 miles. Signs of the canal around Holcomb's Mill near the Appomattox can still be seen, but it is not known how far the navigation was completed, how long it was in operation, and what other remains there are of it.

THE LOWER APPOMATTOX NAVIGATION.

The Lower Appomattox Company was organized in 1802 to construct a 7 foot deep channel for ships navigating the meandering river below Petersburg. In 1827 the river was directed into the new channel, which included 1200 yards of excavated canal with jetties "as on the Rhine". The navigation was a success and is still used today, having obvious recreational potential.

THE DRAGON SWAMP NAVIGATION.

The Dragon Swamp Navigation Company was organized by 1839 to make a navigable channel into the swamp at the head of the Piankitank River, to provide access to the timber. By 1840 the channel had been cleared for 20 miles, to New Dragon Bridge, for lighters of 22 inches draft. Traffic ceased within a couple of years. Today the swamp is perfect for preservation as a natural area.

THE SHENANDOAH NAVIGATION.

The Shenandoah was first improved by George Washington's Potowmack Company, which by 1808 had cleared the river bed for about 133 miles via the South Fork to Port Republic, and had overcome the falls near the Potomac with 5 locks and a mile of canals, thereby extending a similar treatment of the Potomac. The New Shanandoah Company, organized in 1815, renewed the works to Port Republic by 1823 and opened up about 13 miles of the North Fork to Strasburg after 1835. The last boats from Rileyville on the South Fork descended in 1889. Signs of the wooden locks and chutes, where waterlogged, are still to be found. Most of the present dams are probably at nineteenth-century sites.

THE PATOWMACK NAVIGATION.

The Patowmack Company was organized in 1785 with George Washington as its first president, to make navigable the Potomac River and its branches. Work on the Virginia side of the river consisted of a sluice around Seneca Falls, and a canal at Great Falls. The latter was the most difficult part of the navigation works and included a mile of canal and five stone locks (two blasted out of solid rock, a tremendous accomplishment in those days), built between 1786 and 1802. This was one of the earliest canals in the U.S. It was abandoned in 1830 when the C&O Canal replaced it. The falls and well-preserved canal works now make a splendid park in the hands of the National Park Service, which has erected a Visitor's Center. Directly across the falls, but not directly accessible, is Great Falls Tavern on the Maryland side, a museum for the C&O Canal, also provided by the Park Service.

THE ALEXANDRIA CANAL

The Alexandria Canal Company, chartered in 1830, built a 7-mile extension of the Chesapeake and Ohio Canal to draw coal boats from Georgetown, D.C. to the wharves at Alexandria. The canal crossed the Potomac on an aqueduct with 8 piers and a wooden trough, and followed the Virginia shore over 6 culverts and a small aqueduct, and entered the Potomac through a flight of 4 locks in Alexandria. The canal was completed in 1843 and abandoned by 1888; all but one pier of the aqueduct, saved by the Arlington Historical Society, were blown up by the C of E in 1962, and the rest of the works were destroyed by parkways. The lock on the Potomac in Alexandria is buried but may become a park.

THE GOOSE CREEK AND LITTLE RIVER NAVIGATION.

The Goose Creek and Little River Navigation Company was organized in 1832 to construct a canal-boat navigation from the Potomac for 20 miles up Goose Creek, with a 5-mile branch up Little River, a tributary, to Aldie. President of the Company was George Carter of Oatlands. The project was aided by the C&O Canal Company which conducted a survey of the navigation and built a river lock from its canal to accommodate boats from Goose Creek. Work began on Goose Creek in 1849 and stopped in 1854 because of railway competition, after the work had been completed for 12 miles up to Ball's Mill, involving 9 stone locks, 4 canals with stone guard gates, and 4 dams. Today 4 of the locks are submerged by a new dam, 2 are in good condition and 3 of the guard gates are in very good condition. The gem of the navigation is the double lock (Clapham's) which is in perfect shape, as is its one-mile canal. The Goose Creek Scenic River includes the section with the old locks and canals

THE WASHINGTON DITCH.

The Washington Ditch was built by "A Company of Adventurers for Draining the Great Dismal Swamp" which included George Washington, in the 1760's. This was a cut from the western shore of the swamp to Lake Drummond at its center, a distance of 5 miles, to provide access to the swamp timber. This is probably the oldest still useable canal in the U.S.

THE JERICHO CANAL.

The Jericho Canal is a 10-mile cut through Dismal Swamp from Shingle Creek, a tributary of Nansemond River, near Suffolk, to Lake Drummond. This cut was made about 1810 and was considerably used for carrying shingles and other swamp products to a landing on Shingle Creek, and was a favorite route for tourists. All but the outer couple of miles of the cut is still intact. The Jericho Canal, together with the Washington Ditch and the score of cuts made since that time, should be used for connected tours into the swamp, whose delicate ecology should be preserved instead of being destroyed by timbering and draining. It appeared destined to become a housing development, "unfit for Respiration" (Wm. Byrd), until recently when the Dismal Swamp was declared a National Wildlife Refuge.

THE DISMAL SWAMP CANAL.

The Dismal Swamp Canal was designed to connect Chesapeake Bay with Albemarle South in North Carolina, by a 22-mile cut through the swamp, thus giving access to the swamp timber as well as furnishing a through route. Work began in 1793, and the canal was open to vessels larger than flatboats by 1814. At first there were seven wooden locks but by 1829 the canal had been rebuilt using 4 stone locks (two of them double staircase locks); and a 3¼ mile feeder with a stone lock had been constructed from Lake Drummond. Gilmerton Cut, a northern extension of the canal, was completed by 1843, 2½ miles long with a stone lock. Turner's cut, a 3½ mile southern extension, was completed in 1856. These extensions replaced difficult creek channels. Although a road paralleled the canal, there were none on the rivers it connected, so through vessels had to be towed or be self-propelled. In later years some of the lock chambers were lengthened, and in 1896 the whole canal was rebuilt; the four stone locks were removed and replaced by two 40 to 250 foot timber ones, at Deep Creek and at South Mills. The Gilmerton level was bypassed and abandoned, leaving the 24 by 100 foot stone lock undisturbed. The lock at Lake Drummond was also rebuilt by timber. In 1929 the canal was taken over by the U.S. Corps of Engineers, which again rebuilt the two locks of steel and concrete, 52 by 300 feet in the chamber, and replaced the lock at the lake by a spillway in 1936. Today the canal still retains its small canal atmosphere and is used by small craft plying the Intracoastal Waterway. The Gilmerton Lock is in excellent condition, although derelict. Public pressure rather than C of E economics has kept the canal open. It is now the major water route into the Dismal Swamp National Wildlife Refuge.

THE NORTH WEST CANAL.

This canal, constructed by the Dismal Swamp Company, began as a waste ditch in 1820, and was rebuilt in 1828-1830 into a canal with 3 wooden locks and 7 miles long, from Wallaceton on the Dismal Swamp Canal to the North West River, which flows into Currituck Sound. Its primary function was to give access to the swamp timber. It was abandoned in the 1860's. The route can stil be traced but the only lock remains are those of the outlet lock, partially submerged in North West River. Although only the waterlogged wood remains, this is the best preserved wooden lock in Virginia.

THE ALBEMARLE AND CHESAPEAKE CANAL.

This canal was surveyed as early as 1774 as the shortest inland water connection between Chesapeake Bay and Albemarle Sound. Work began in 1855 under the A & C Canal Company, which made a 3½ mile cut with a large tide lock at Great Bridge, Va.; and a 5½ mile cut between Currituck and Albemarle Sounds in North Carolina. The works were open in 1959. The tide lock was of stone, 40 by 220 feet in the chamber, with two double pairs of gates to provide lift in either direction, depending upon the tide. In 1912 the canal was taken over by the C of E, which removed the lock and enlarged the canal. The resulting currents and inflow of salt water into Currituck sound required the building of the present concrete and steel lock, 75 by 600 feet, in 1932. From the beginning this canal was designed for through commercial traffic rather than timbering, and is still very much in use.

THE KEMPSVILLE CANAL.

The Kempsville Canal Company was organized in 1840 and again in 1851 to construct a canal between the Eastern Branch of the Elizabeth River, near Kempsville, to Lynnhaven Bay, a distance of 4 miles, with several locks. By 1860, two miles had been completed and the third had been partially excavated. The Civil War interrupted the work, and little was done thereafter. The canal route can still be traced, but part of it has become a series of ponds. Cuts in the Elizabeth River are still used for boat access toward Kempsville.

THE ROANOKE NAVIGATION.

Bills permitting the organization of the Roanoke Navigation Company were passed by both Virginia and North Carolina in 1783, with the help of Patrick Henry, but it was not until 1812 that North Carolina chartered such a company, and Virginia in 1815, forming a single interstate organization. Construction began in 1819 on the Roanoke Canal, around the falls at Weldon, N.C., 9 miles long with deep cuts and high embankments, 4 stone locks, an aqueduct, 4 large culverts, and a basin at Weldon. This was completed in 1823. A sluice navigation for batteaux was completed from Salem (near Roanoke, Va.) to Weldon, 244 miles; from Leaksville, N.C. on the Dan River to its junction with the Roanoke, 82 miles; and on the Banister River from Meadville to the Dan, 25 miles. This required a stone lock above Weldon and a wood and stone lock just above the N.C. line; both of these are probably inundated. There were also four wooden locks with basins at Danville. The lower Roanoke below Weldon to Albemarle Sound was made navigable for steamboats, a distance of 100 miles. Four wooden locks were constructed between the Weldon basin and the river in 1828-1834, but they lasted only a year and were never rebuilt. Today most of the sluice navigation is under one or another of the lakes on the Roanoke; the Roanoke Rapids Dam has covered the upper couple of miles of the Roanoke Canal, but the rest is easily followed. Of the four stone locks on the canal, two are in fairly good condition, one has been partially broken by a railway, and the third is missing. The aqueduct, over Chockaott Creek at Weldon, is in perfect condition and is a real gem worth recognition, it should be carefully preserved. Roanoke canal through Weldon is now on the National Register of historic places. The proposed scenic river section between Long Island and Brookneal was one of the worst places for boats on the river. Canoeists still go down the sluices built to aid navigation in 1827.

THE SMITH'S RIVER NAVIGATION.

The Smith's River Navigation Company was organized by 1850, by which time it had made that river navigable for batteaux from the Blue Falls, now under Philpott Lake at Fairy Stone State Park, to the Dan River, a distance of 50 miles. However, the anticipated trade was not realized, for only two boats seem to have ever made the trip. Perhaps there are still signs of sluices and wing dams.

Lexington Dam. Head of navigation. Seven feet high

Reid Dam, Lock. Fourteen feet high. Mill on left bank. Still in very good condition.

South River Dam, Lock. Lock on right bank. Only riffles remain at dam site.

Ben Salem Dam, Lock. Only a few riffles left from dam. Lock beside Rte 60 in good condition. Canal path still apparent

Moomaws Dam, Lock, Canal. High dam still in use. Converted to power dam. Twelve feet high. Two mile canal on left bank.

Zimmermans Dam, Lock. No sign of dam and locks. A few riffles

Anger's Dam, Lock, Canal. Lock and canal on right. Canal was ½ mile long. No sign of dam

Savernakes Dam, Guard Lock. Canal on left bank. No sign of dam at present.

Gooseneck Dam, Lock, Canal. High 14' dam converted to power dam. Dam now broken out on right side - nice rapid.

Devil's Step Dam, Lock. No sign of dam. Lock covered by R.R.

Spillers Dam, Lock, Canal. Also called Buffalo Creek Dam. Five mile canal on left bank now covered by R.R. Dam removed for its stones.

Blue Ridge (Mountain) Dam on James River. Lock on right.

Lexington

Buena Vista

Maury River

Glasgow

James River

11

60

663

501

130

North (Maury) River Canal System

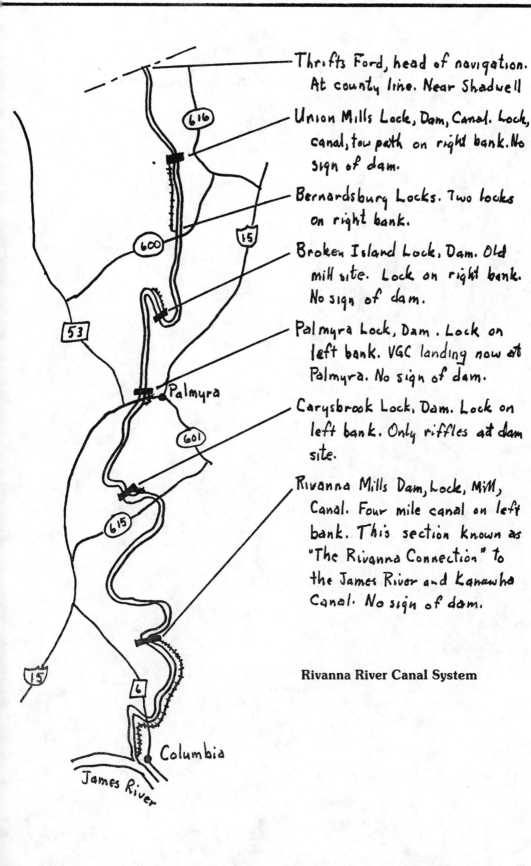

Thrifts Ford, head of navigation. At county line. Near Shadwell

Union Mills Lock, Dam, Canal. Lock, canal, tow path on right bank. No sign of dam.

Bernardsburg Locks. Two locks on right bank.

Broken Island Lock, Dam. Old mill site. Lock on right bank. No sign of dam.

Palmyra Lock, Dam. Lock on left bank. VGC landing now at Palmyra. No sign of dam.

Carysbrook Lock, Dam. Lock on left bank. Only riffles at dam site.

Rivanna Mills Dam, Lock, Mill, Canal. Four mile canal on left bank. This section known as "The Rivanna Connection" to the James River and Kanawha Canal. No sign of dam.

Rivanna River Canal System